Created by Spike Chunsoft Manga by Kyousuke Suga

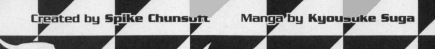

Danganronpa 2
ULTIMATE LUCK AND HOPE AND DESPAIR

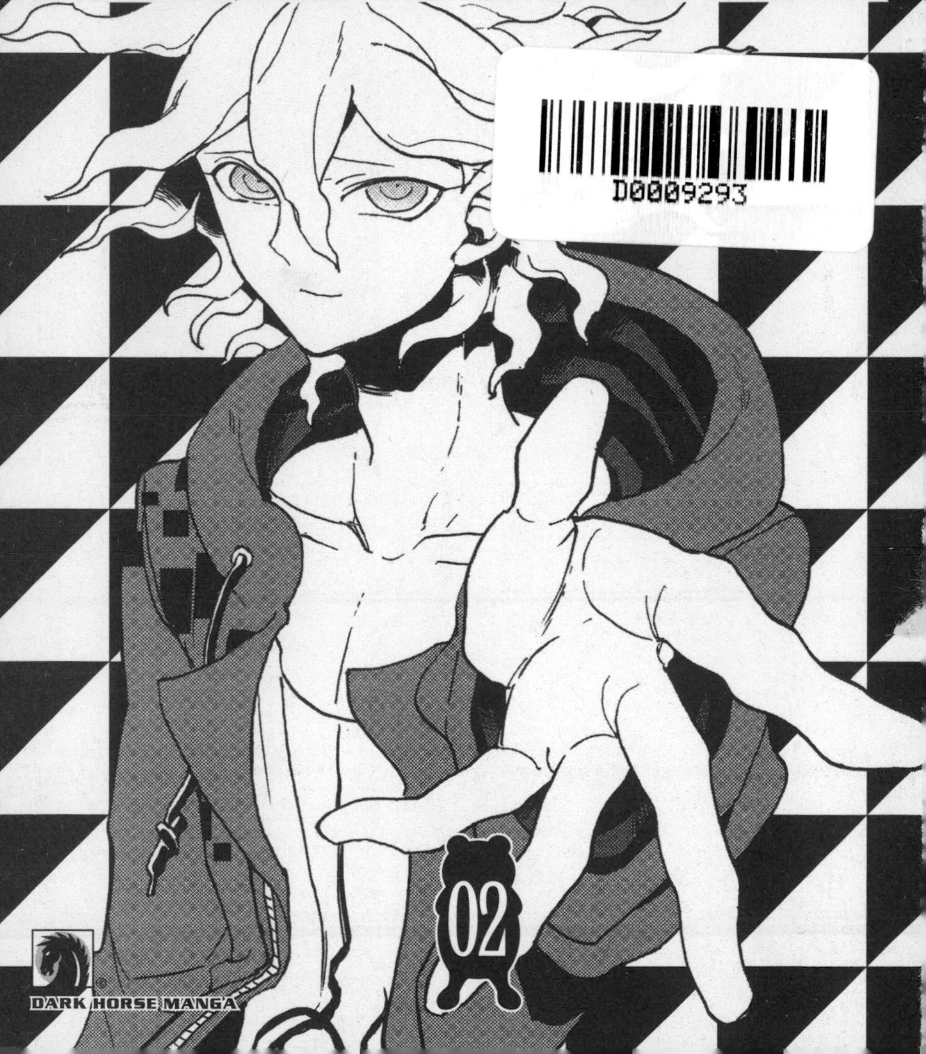
02

DARK HORSE MANGA

Translation by **Jackie McClure**
Lettering and touchup by **John Clark**
Edited by **Carl Gustav Horn**

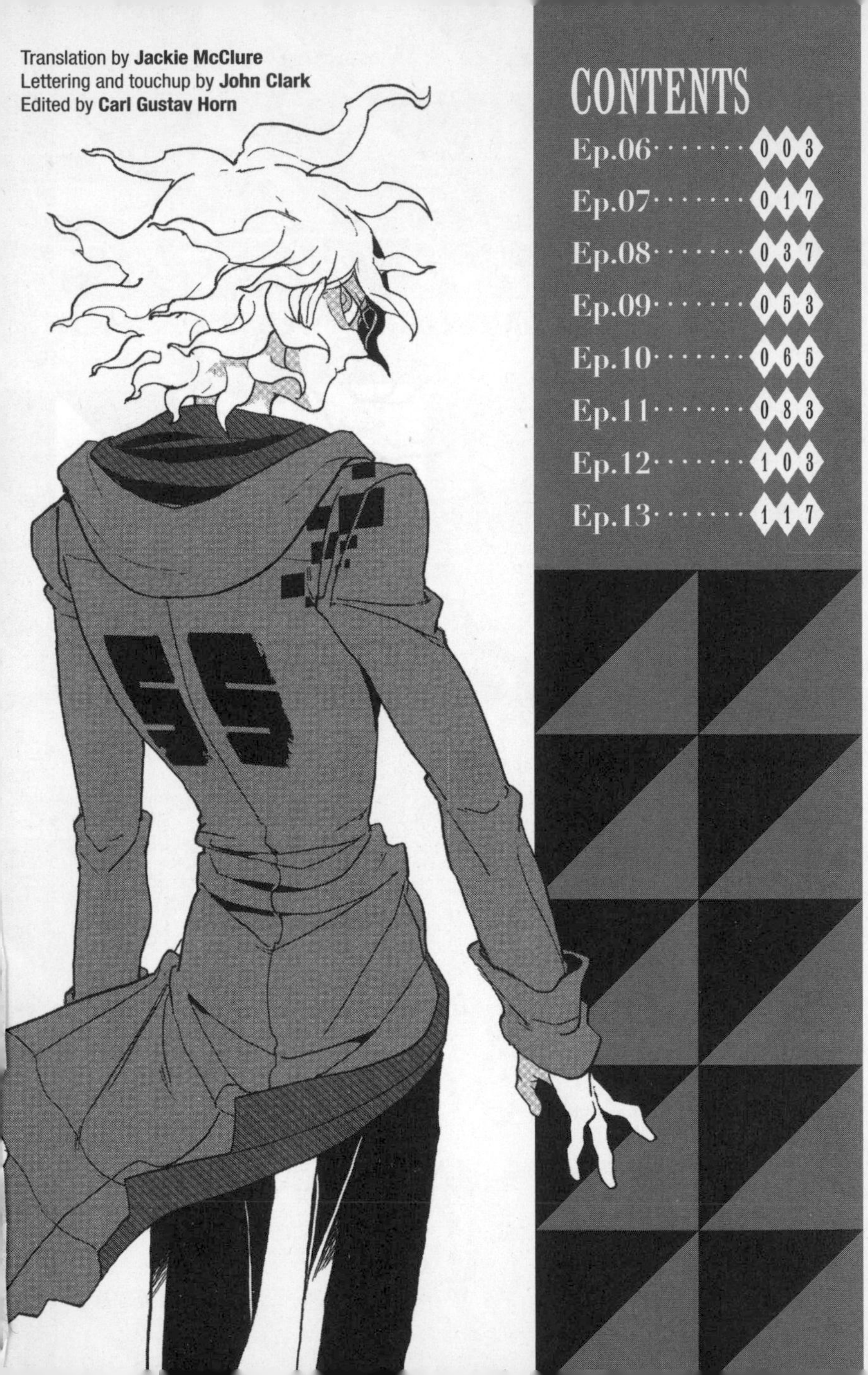

CONTENTS

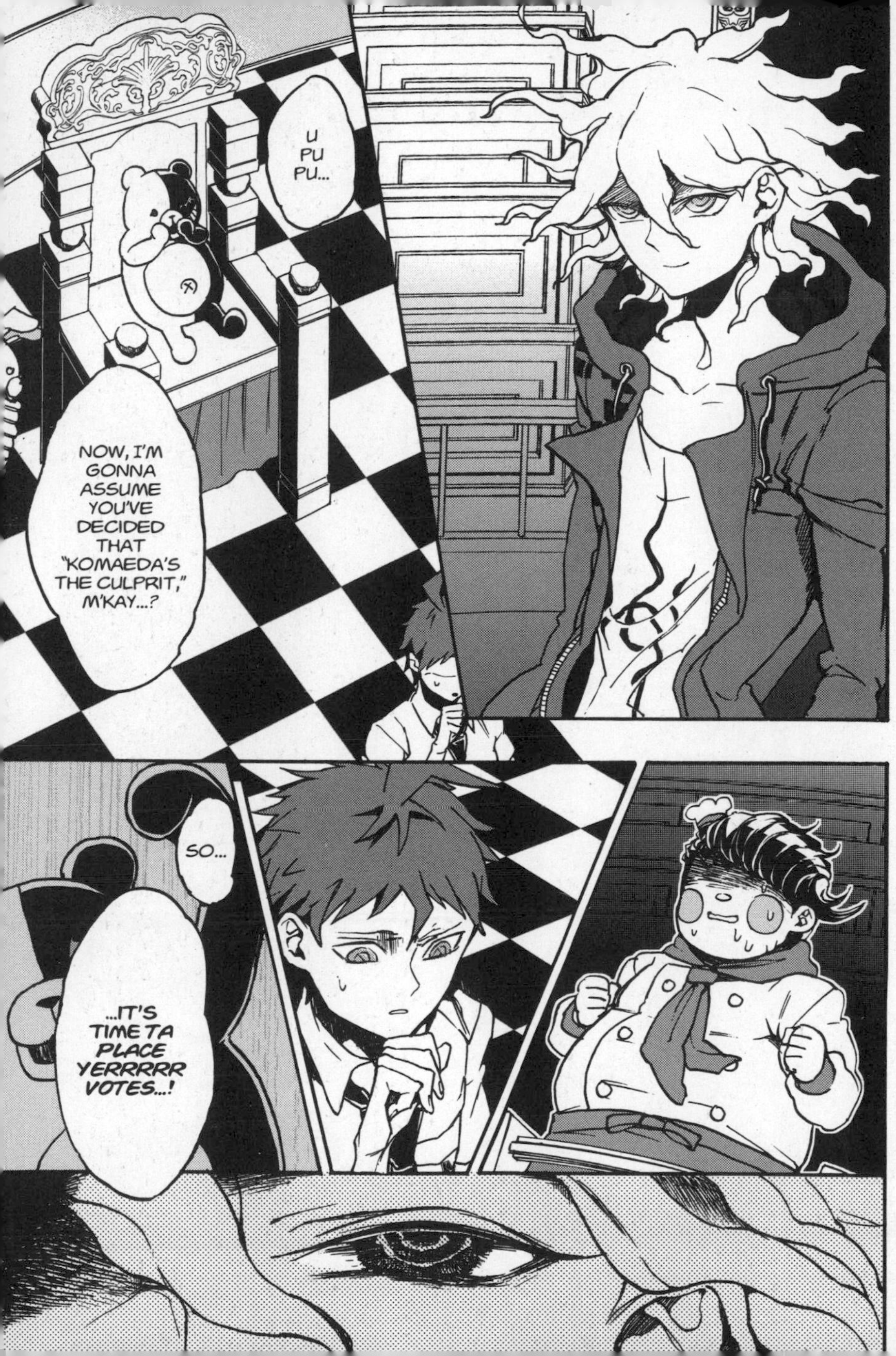
U PU PU...
NOW, I'M GONNA ASSUME YOU'VE DECIDED THAT "KOMAEDA'S THE CULPRIT," M'KAY...?
SO...
...IT'S TIME TA *PLACE YERRRRR VOTES*...!

Ep.06

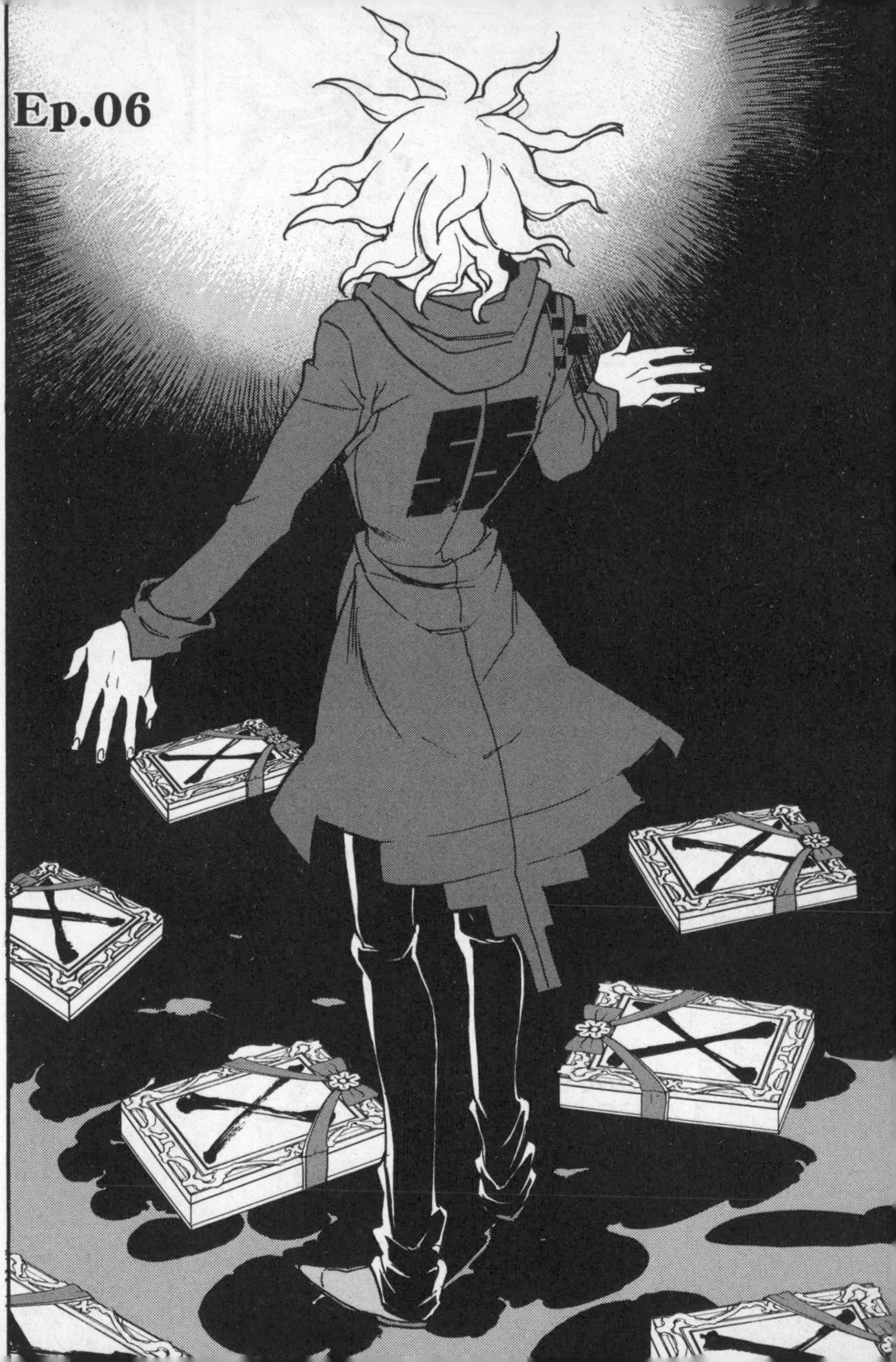

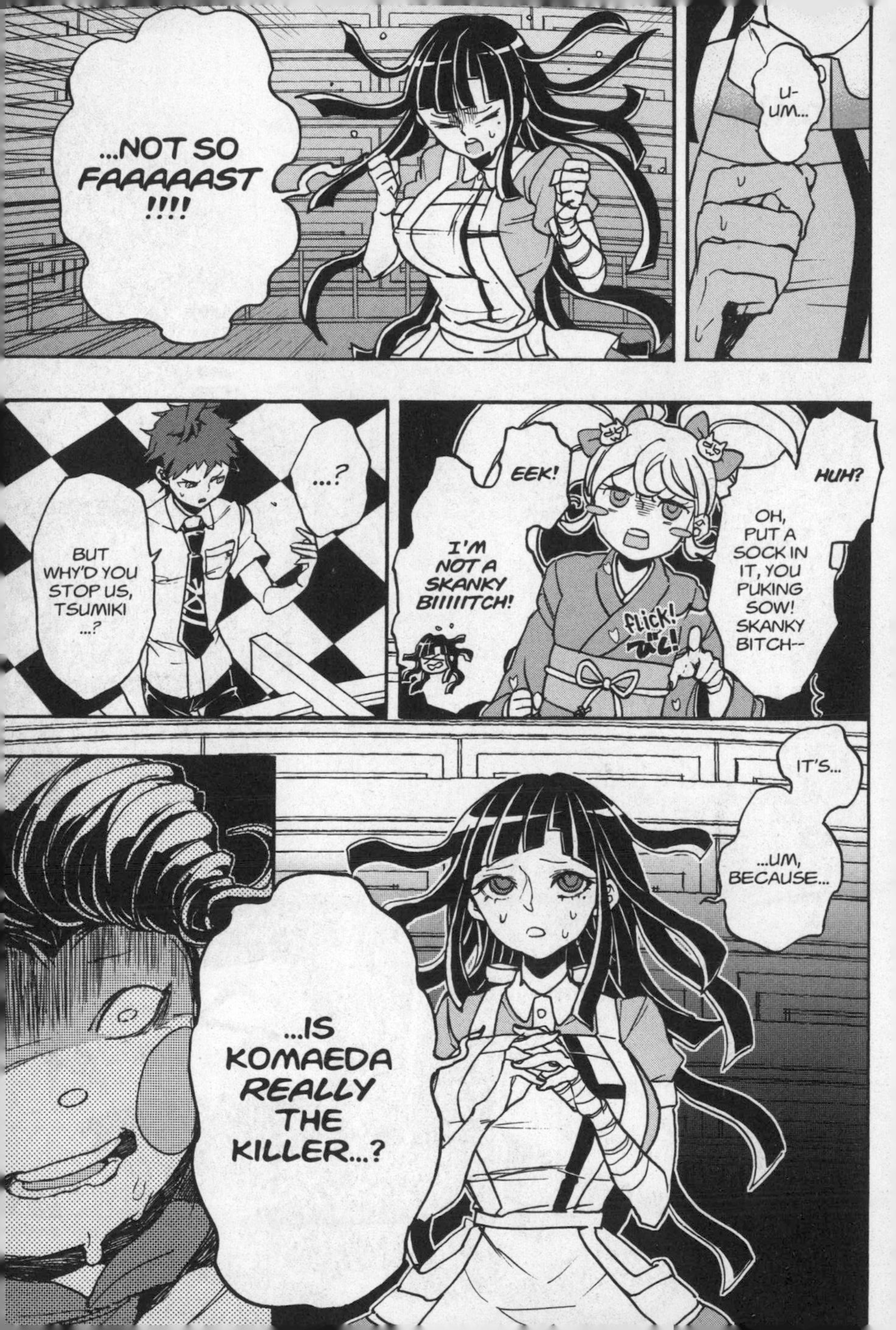
U-
UM...
...NOT SO FAAAAAAST !!!!
HUH?
OH, PUT A SOCK IN IT, YOU PUKING SOW! SKANKY BITCH--
flick!
EEK!
I'M NOT A SKANKY BIIIIITCH!
...?
BUT WHY'D YOU STOP US, TSUMIKI ...?
IT'S...
...UM, BECAUSE...
...IS KOMAEDA REALLY THE KILLER...?

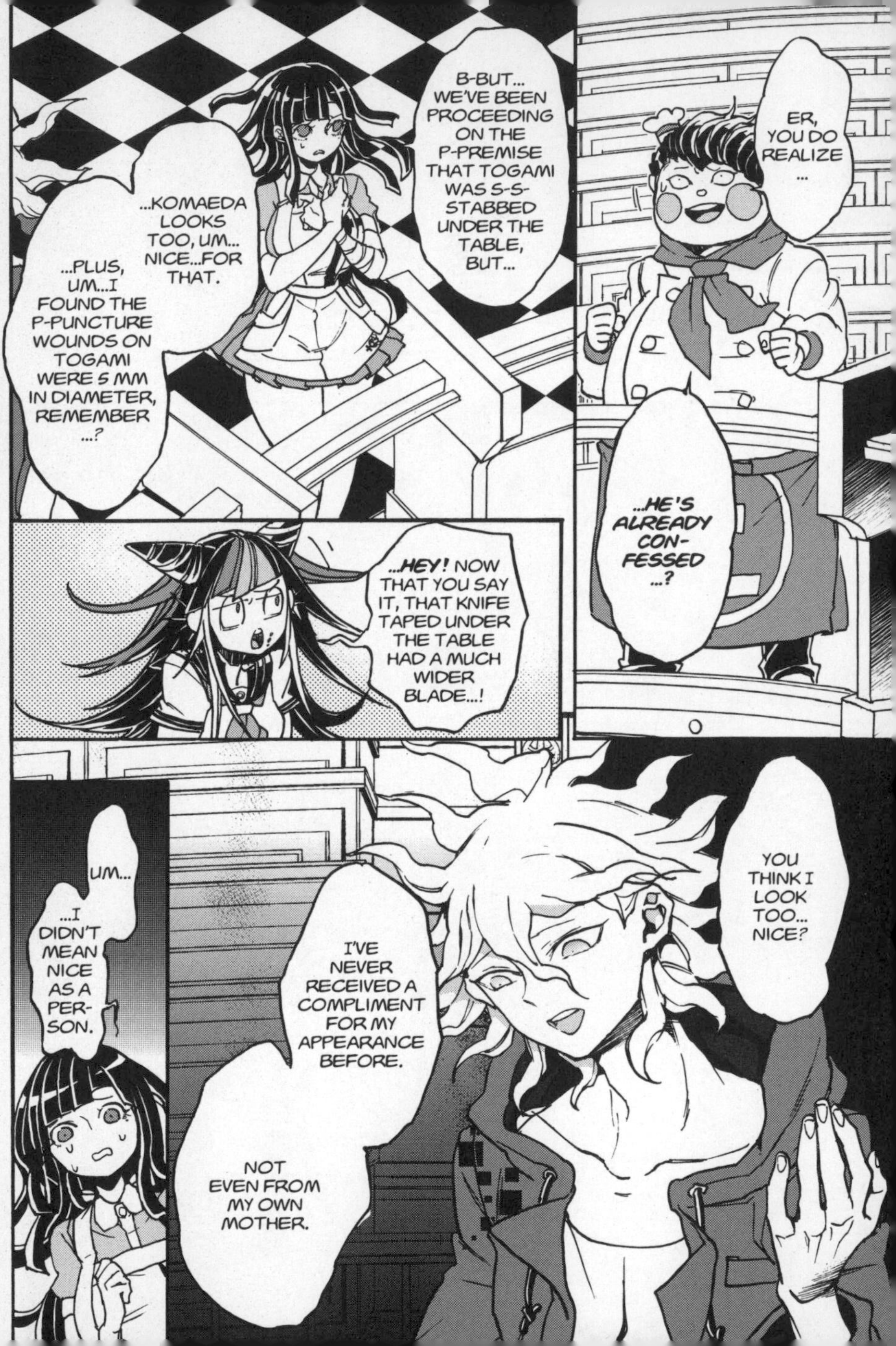
ER, YOU DO REALIZE ...
...HE'S ALREADY CON-FESSED ...?
B-BUT... WE'VE BEEN PROCEEDING ON THE P-PREMISE THAT TOGAMI WAS S-S-STABBED UNDER THE TABLE, BUT...
...KOMAEDA LOOKS TOO, UM... NICE...FOR THAT.
...PLUS, UM...I FOUND THE P-PUNCTURE WOUNDS ON TOGAMI WERE 5 MM IN DIAMETER, REMEMBER ...?
...HEY! NOW THAT YOU SAY IT, THAT KNIFE TAPED UNDER THE TABLE HAD A MUCH WIDER BLADE...!
YOU THINK I LOOK TOO... NICE?
I'VE NEVER RECEIVED A COMPLIMENT FOR MY APPEARANCE BEFORE.
NOT EVEN FROM MY OWN MOTHER.
UM...
...I DIDN'T MEAN NICE AS A PERSON.

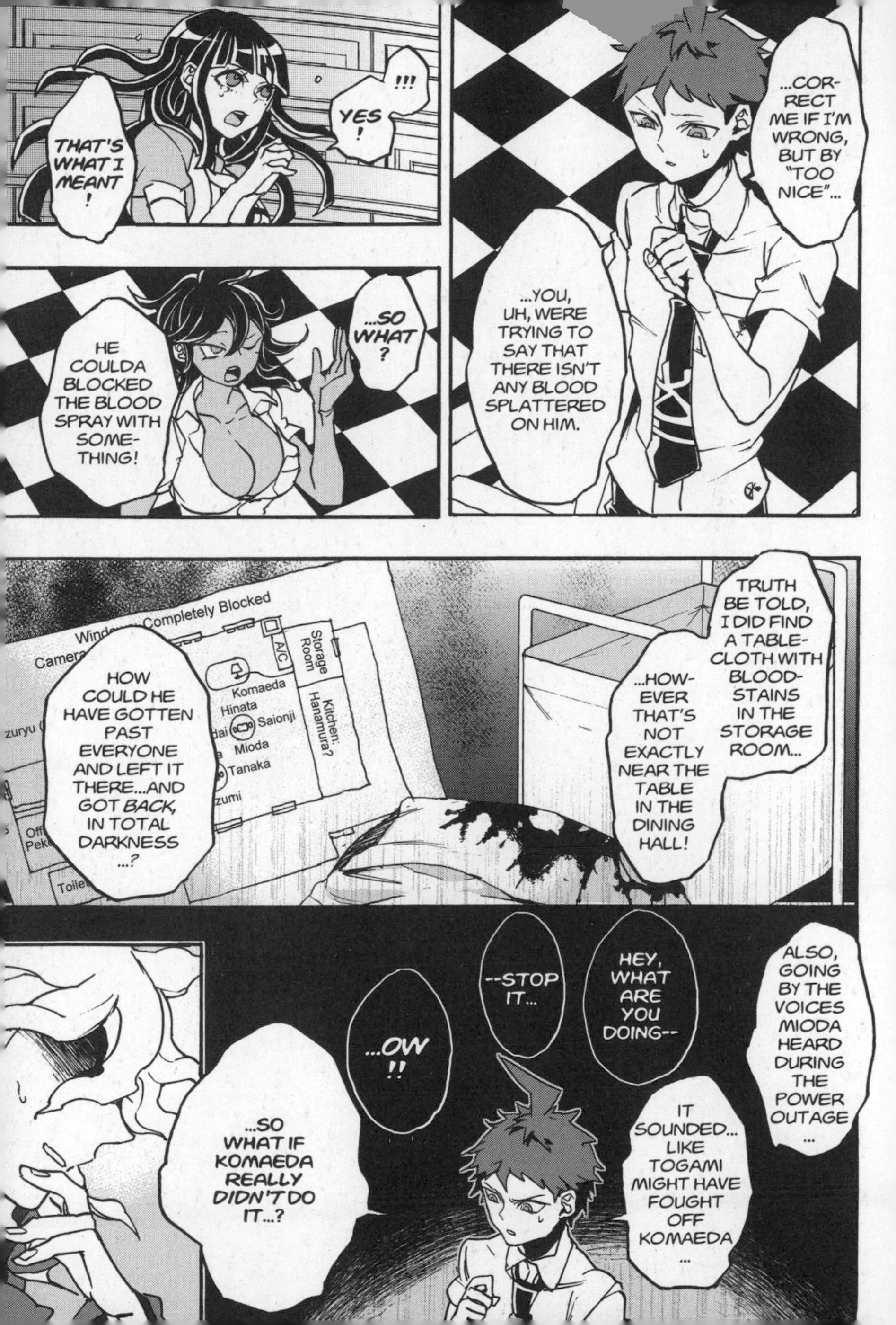
...CORRECT ME IF I'M WRONG, BUT BY "TOO NICE"...
...YOU, UH, WERE TRYING TO SAY THAT THERE ISN'T ANY BLOOD SPLATTERED ON HIM.
!!!
YES!
THAT'S WHAT I MEANT!
...SO WHAT?
HE COULDA BLOCKED THE BLOOD SPRAY WITH SOMETHING!
TRUTH BE TOLD, I DID FIND A TABLECLOTH WITH BLOODSTAINS IN THE STORAGE ROOM...
...HOWEVER THAT'S NOT EXACTLY NEAR THE TABLE IN THE DINING HALL!
Completely Blocked
Storage Room
A/C
Kitchen: Hanamura?
Komaeda
Hinata
Saionji
Mioda
Tanaka
HOW COULD HE HAVE GOTTEN PAST EVERYONE AND LEFT IT THERE...AND GOT *BACK*, IN TOTAL DARKNESS...?
ALSO, GOING BY THE VOICES MIODA HEARD DURING THE POWER OUTAGE...
IT SOUNDED... LIKE TOGAMI MIGHT HAVE FOUGHT OFF KOMAEDA...
HEY, WHAT ARE YOU DOING--
--STOP IT...
...OW!!
...SO WHAT IF KOMAEDA REALLY DIDN'T DO IT...?

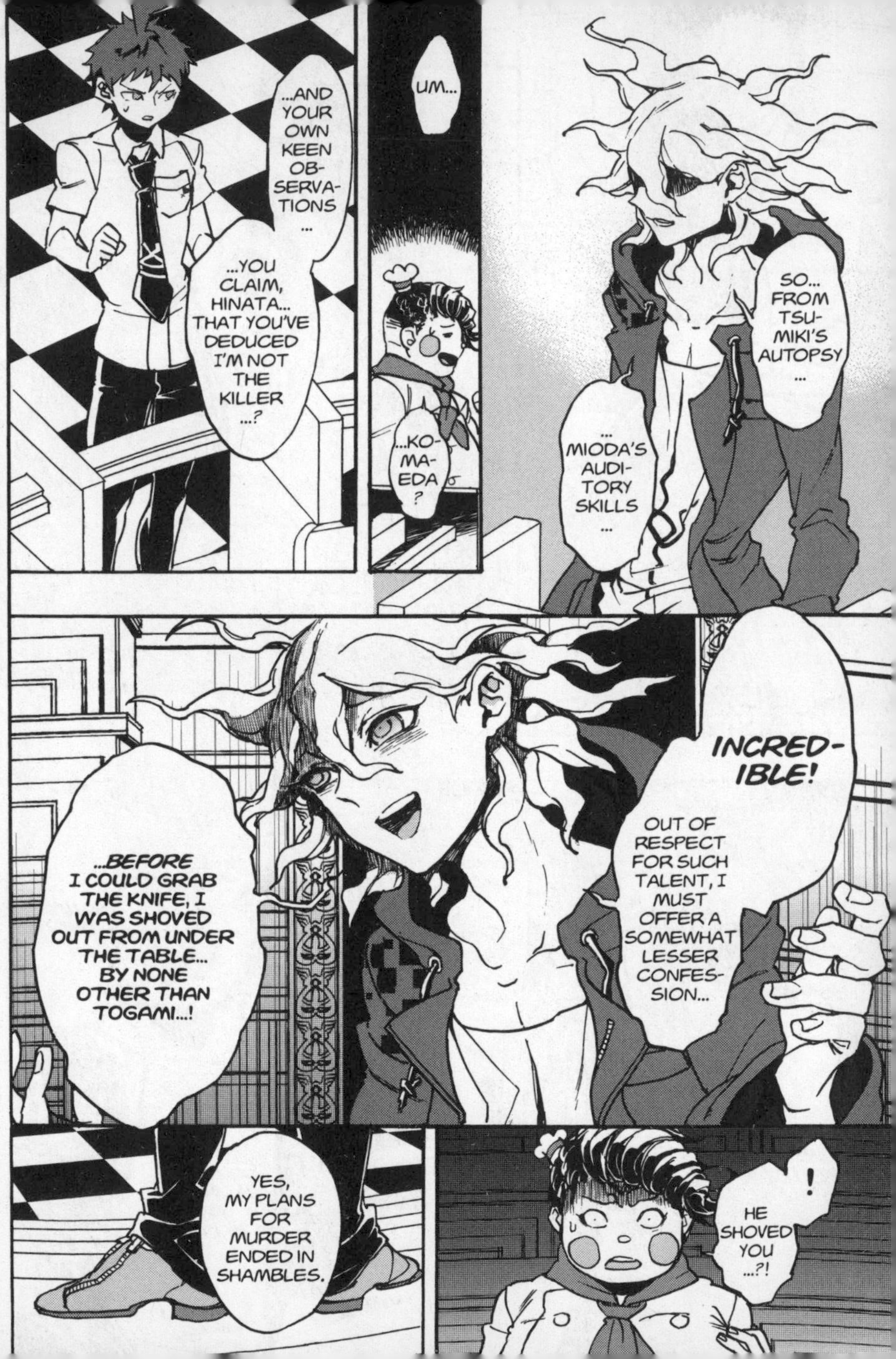
SO... FROM TSU-MIKI'S AUTOPSY...
...MIODA'S AUDI-TORY SKILLS...
UM...
...KO-MA-EDA?
...AND YOUR OWN KEEN OB-SERVA-TIONS...
...YOU CLAIM, HINATA... THAT YOU'VE DEDUCED I'M NOT THE KILLER...?
INCRED-IBLE!
OUT OF RESPECT FOR SUCH TALENT, I MUST OFFER A SOMEWHAT LESSER CONFES-SION...
...BEFORE I COULD GRAB THE KNIFE, I WAS SHOVED OUT FROM UNDER THE TABLE... BY NONE OTHER THAN TOGAMI...!
!
HE SHOVED YOU...?!
YES, MY PLANS FOR MURDER ENDED IN SHAMBLES.

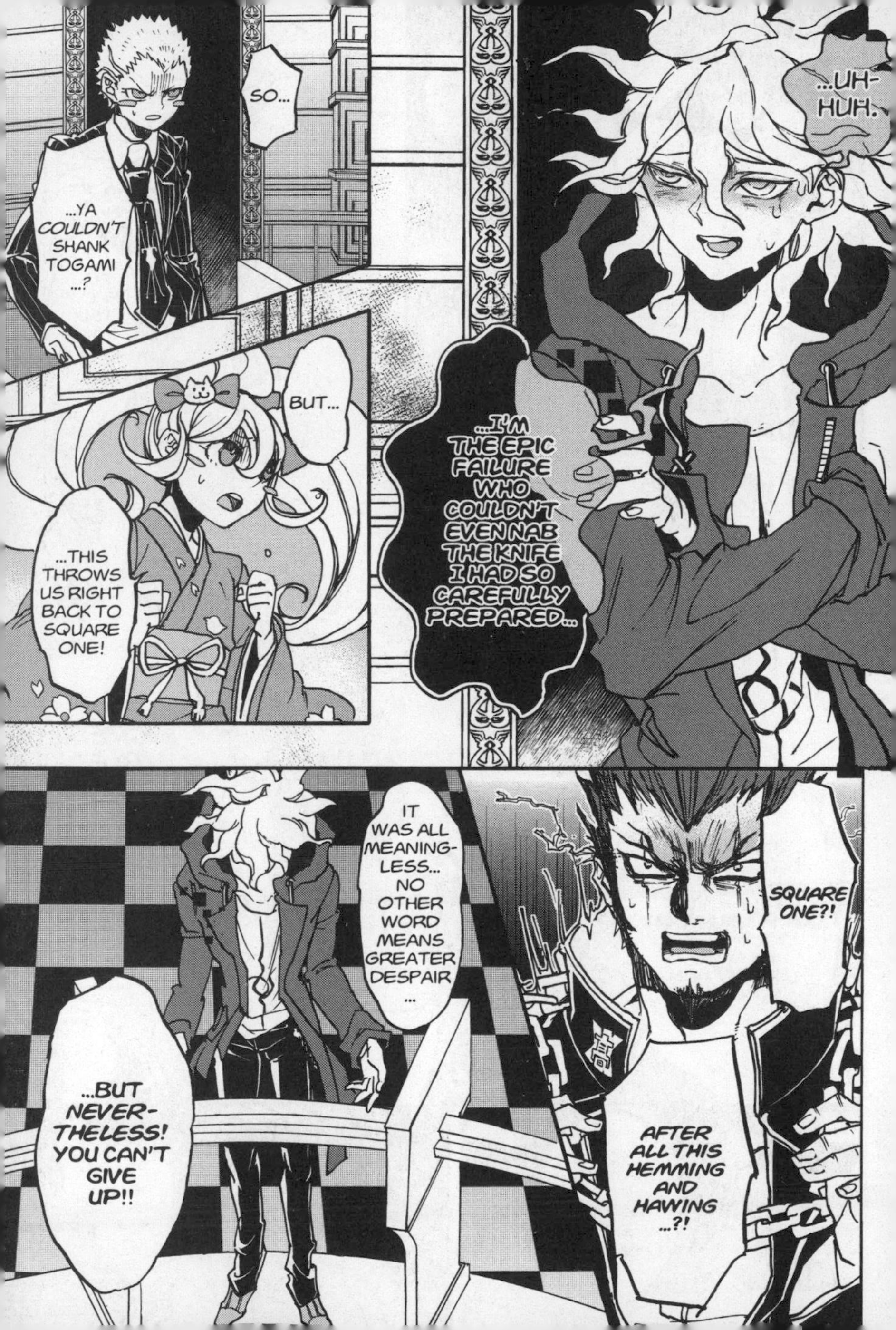
...UH-HUH.
...I'M THE EPIC FAILURE WHO COULDN'T EVEN NAB THE KNIFE I HAD SO CAREFULLY PREPARED...
SO...
...YA COULDN'T SHANK TOGAMI ...?
BUT...
...THIS THROWS US RIGHT BACK TO SQUARE ONE!
SQUARE ONE?!
AFTER ALL THIS HEMMING AND HAWING ...?!
IT WAS ALL MEANINGLESS... NO OTHER WORD MEANS GREATER DESPAIR ...
...BUT NEVERTHELESS! YOU CAN'T GIVE UP!!

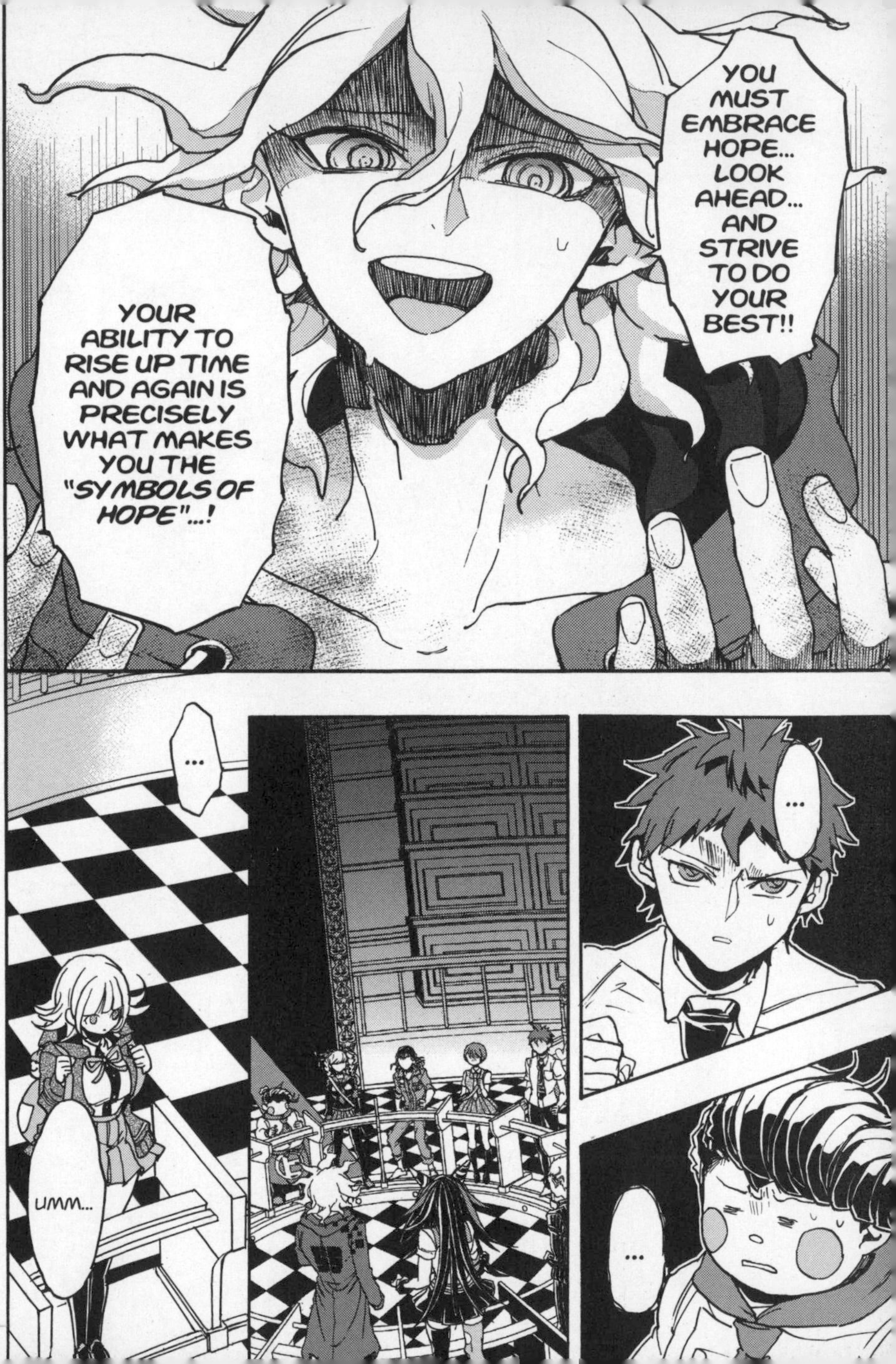

YOU MUST EMBRACE HOPE... LOOK AHEAD... AND STRIVE TO DO YOUR BEST!!
YOUR ABILITY TO RISE UP TIME AND AGAIN IS PRECISELY WHAT MAKES YOU THE "SYMBOLS OF HOPE"...!
...
...
...
UMM...

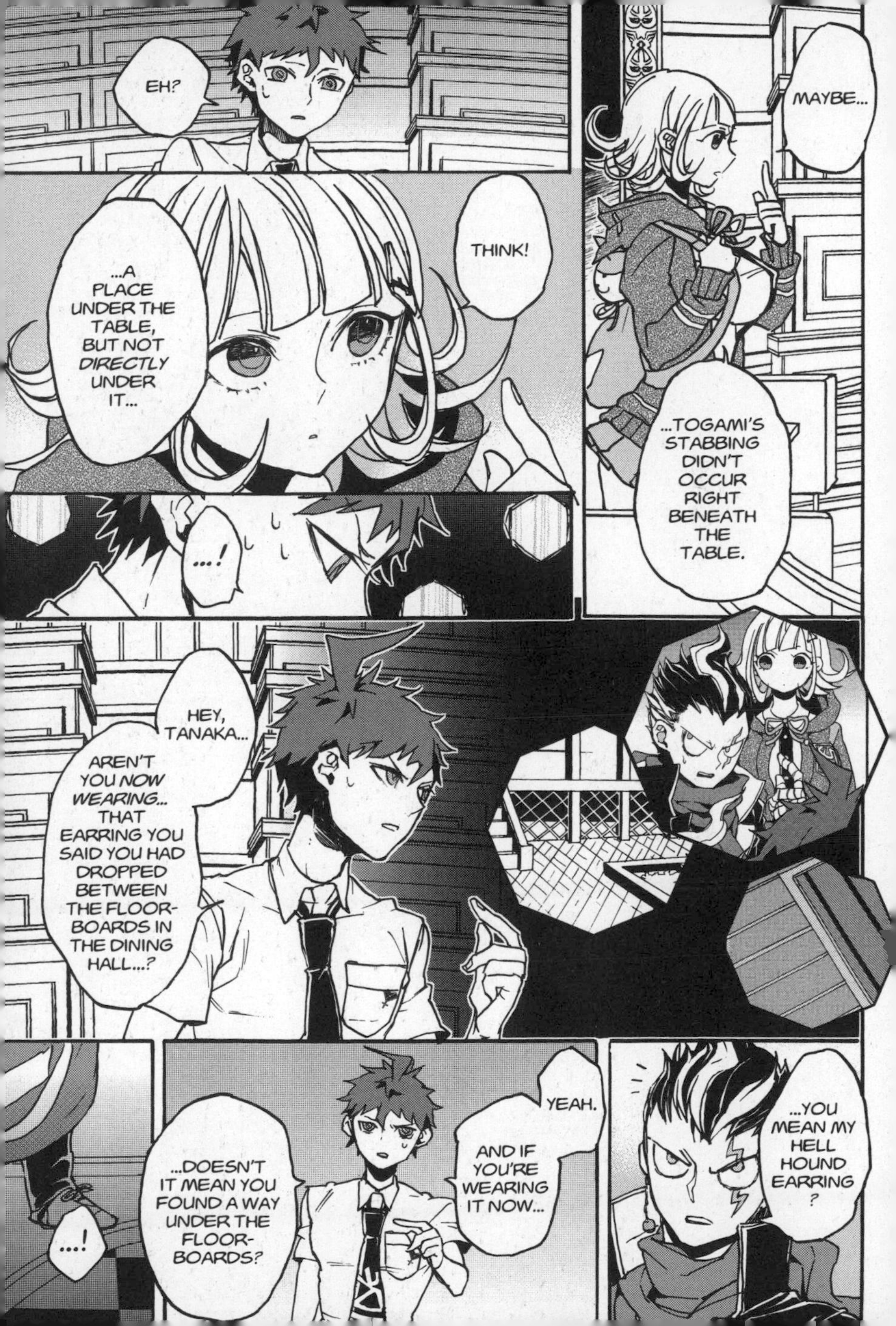
MAYBE...
...TOGAMI'S STABBING DIDN'T OCCUR RIGHT BENEATH THE TABLE.
EH?
THINK!
...A PLACE UNDER THE TABLE, BUT NOT *DIRECTLY* UNDER IT...
...!
HEY, TANAKA...
AREN'T YOU *NOW WEARING*... THAT EARRING YOU SAID YOU HAD DROPPED BETWEEN THE FLOORBOARDS IN THE DINING HALL...?
...YOU MEAN MY HELL HOUND EARRING?
YEAH.
AND IF YOU'RE WEARING IT NOW...
...DOESN'T IT MEAN YOU FOUND A WAY UNDER THE FLOORBOARDS?
...!

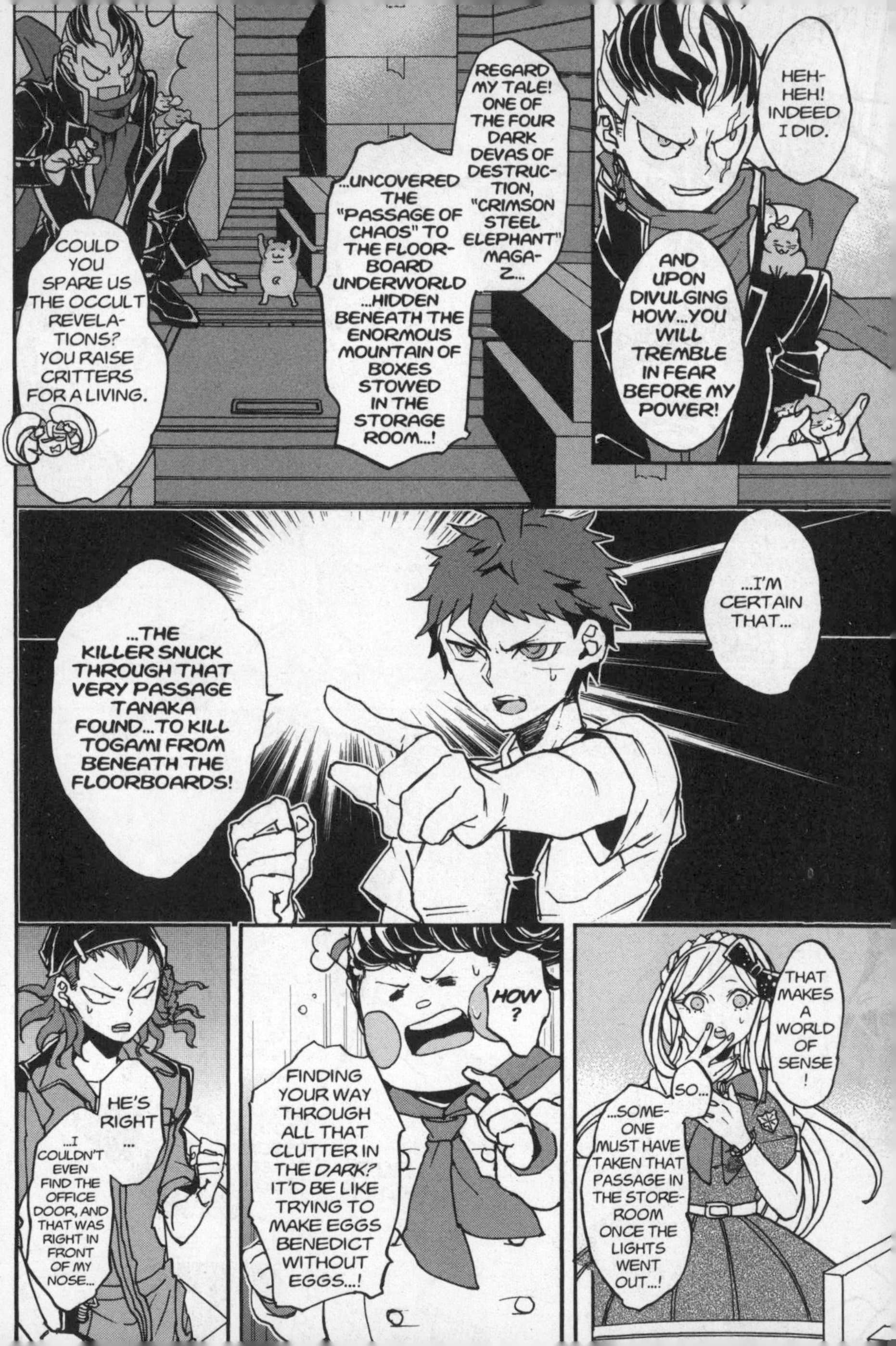
HEH-HEH! INDEED I DID.
AND UPON DIVULGING HOW...YOU WILL TREMBLE IN FEAR BEFORE MY POWER!
REGARD MY TALE! ONE OF THE FOUR DARK DEVAS OF DESTRUCTION, "CRIMSON STEEL ELEPHANT" MAGA-Z...
...UNCOVERED THE "PASSAGE OF CHAOS" TO THE FLOOR-BOARD UNDERWORLD ...HIDDEN BENEATH THE ENORMOUS MOUNTAIN OF BOXES STOWED IN THE STORAGE ROOM...!
COULD YOU SPARE US THE OCCULT REVELA-TIONS? YOU RAISE CRITTERS FOR A LIVING.
...I'M CERTAIN THAT...
...THE KILLER SNUCK THROUGH THAT VERY PASSAGE TANAKA FOUND...TO KILL TOGAMI FROM BENEATH THE FLOORBOARDS!
THAT MAKES A WORLD OF SENSE!
SO...
...SOME-ONE MUST HAVE TAKEN THAT PASSAGE IN THE STORE-ROOM ONCE THE LIGHTS WENT OUT...!
HOW?
FINDING YOUR WAY THROUGH ALL THAT CLUTTER IN THE DARK? IT'D BE LIKE TRYING TO MAKE EGGS BENEDICT WITHOUT EGGS...!
HE'S RIGHT...
...I COULDN'T EVEN FIND THE OFFICE DOOR, AND THAT WAS RIGHT IN FRONT OF MY NOSE...

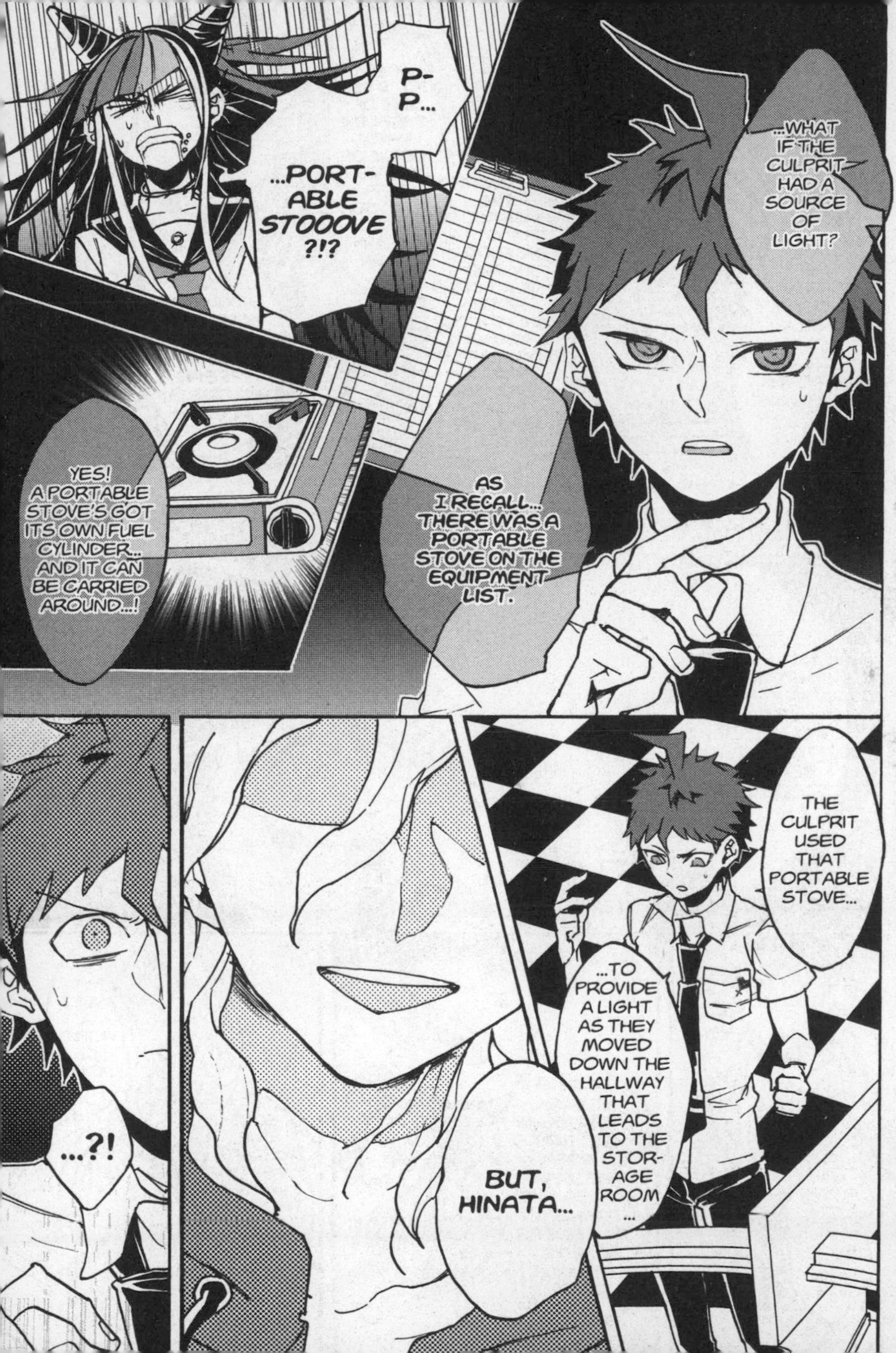
...WHAT IF THE CULPRIT HAD A SOURCE OF LIGHT?
AS I RECALL... THERE WAS A PORTABLE STOVE ON THE EQUIPMENT LIST.
P-P...
...PORT-ABLE STOOOVE ?!?
YES! A PORTABLE STOVE'S GOT ITS OWN FUEL CYLINDER... AND IT CAN BE CARRIED AROUND...!
THE CULPRIT USED THAT PORTABLE STOVE...
...TO PROVIDE A LIGHT AS THEY MOVED DOWN THE HALLWAY THAT LEADS TO THE STOR-AGE ROOM...
BUT, HINATA...
...?!

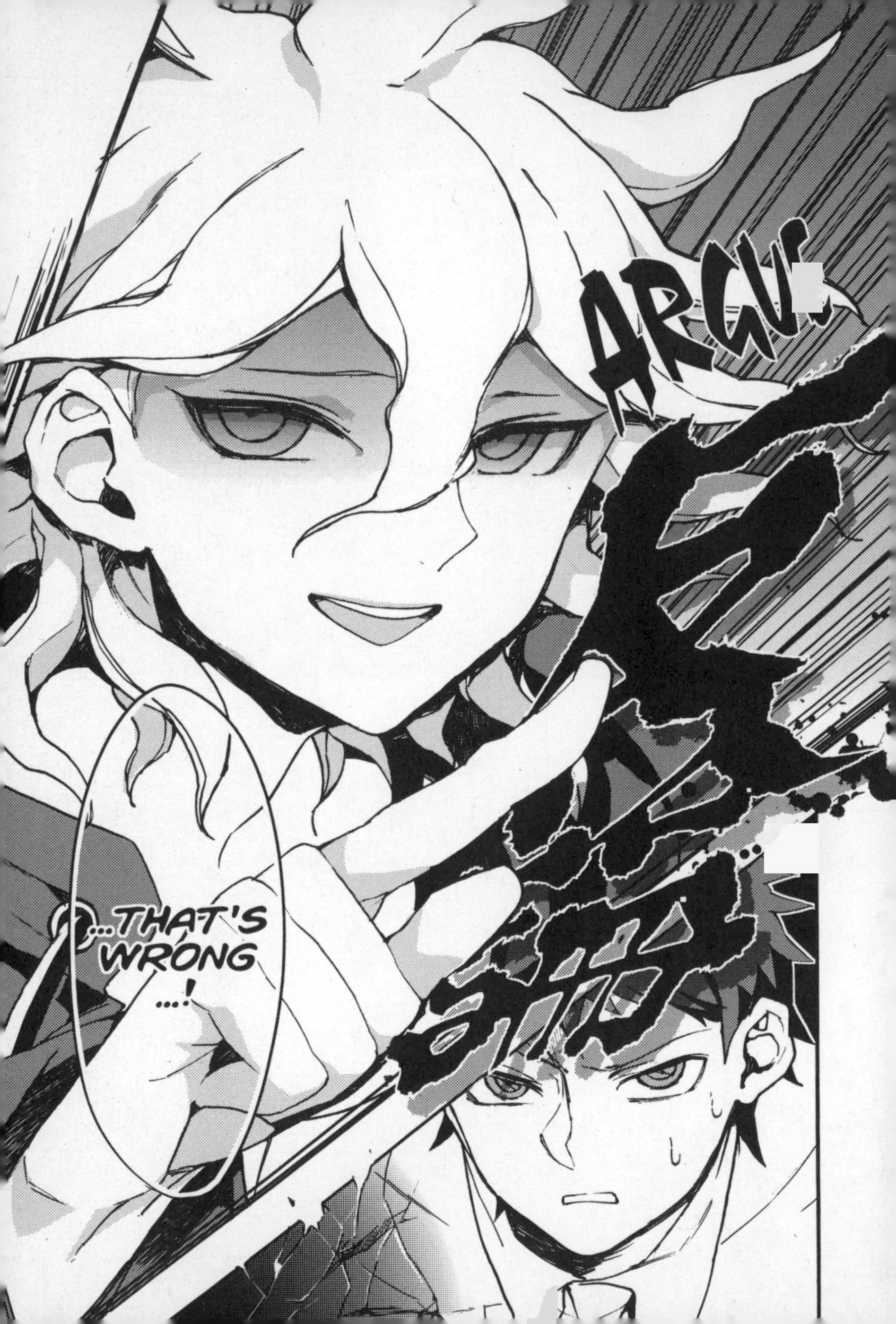
ARGU
...THAT'S WRONG ...!

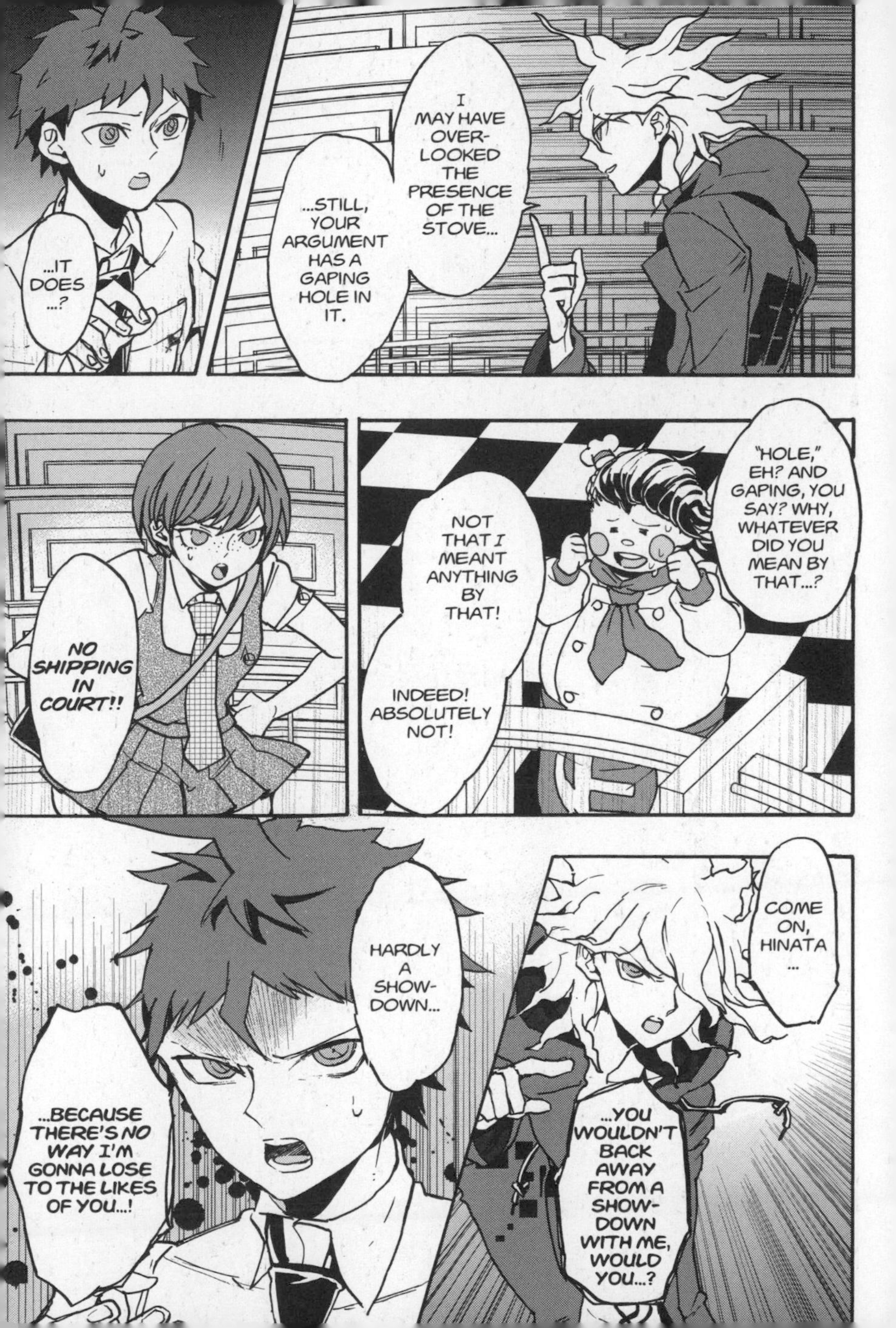
I MAY HAVE OVER-LOOKED THE PRESENCE OF THE STOVE...
...STILL, YOUR ARGUMENT HAS A GAPING HOLE IN IT.
...IT DOES ...?
"HOLE," EH? AND GAPING, YOU SAY? WHY, WHATEVER DID YOU MEAN BY THAT...?
NOT THAT *I* MEANT ANYTHING BY THAT!
INDEED! ABSOLUTELY NOT!
NO SHIPPING IN COURT!!
COME ON, HINATA ...
...YOU WOULDN'T BACK AWAY FROM A SHOW-DOWN WITH ME, WOULD YOU...?
HARDLY A SHOW-DOWN...
...BECAUSE THERE'S NO WAY I'M GONNA LOSE TO THE LIKES OF YOU...!

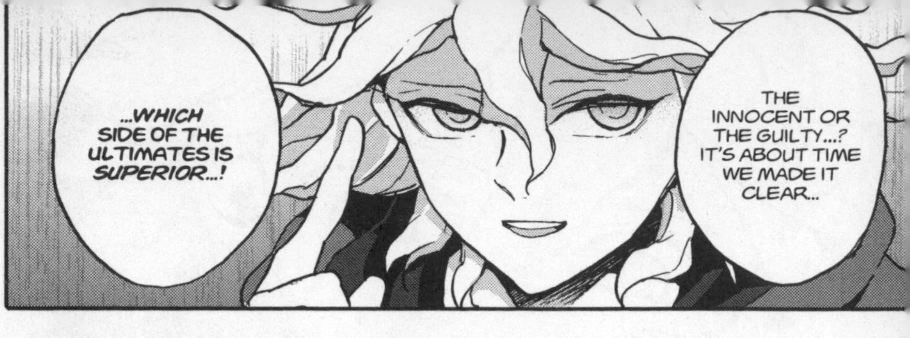
THE INNOCENT OR THE GUILTY...? IT'S ABOUT TIME WE MADE IT CLEAR...
...WHICH SIDE OF THE ULTIMATES IS *SUPERIOR*...!

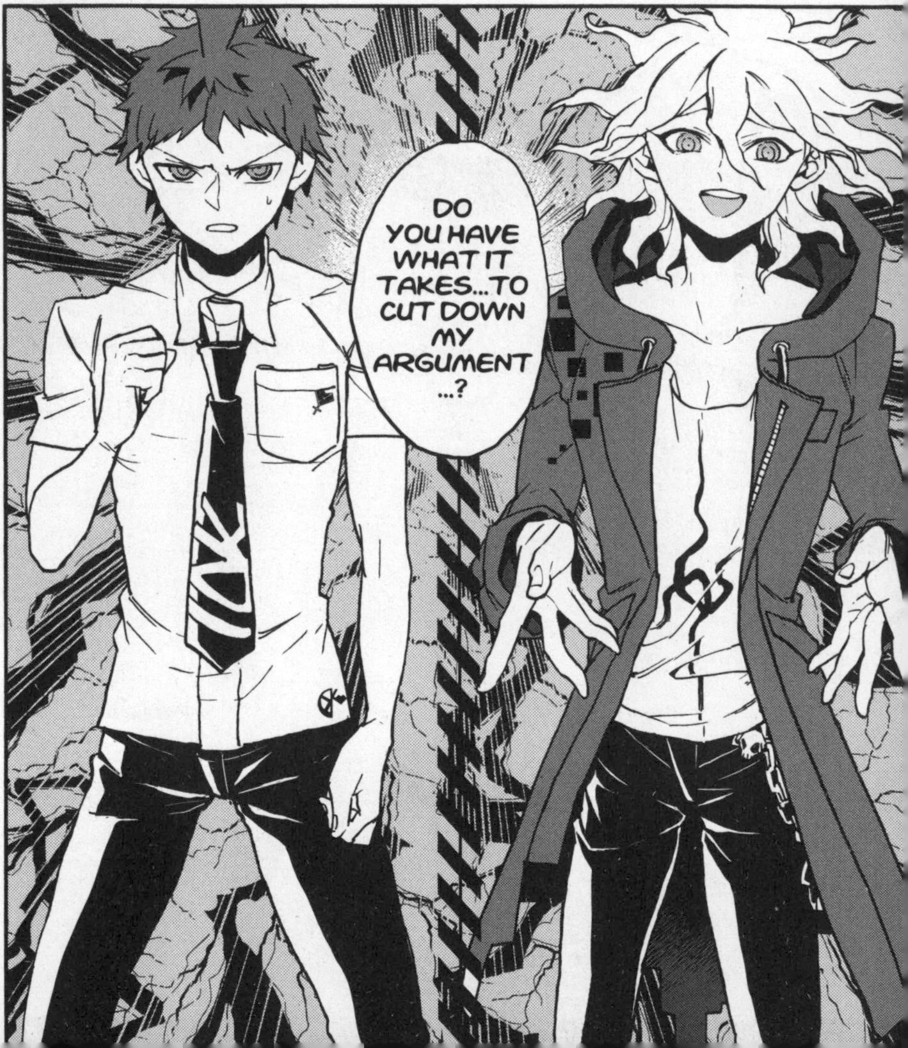
DO YOU HAVE WHAT IT TAKES...TO CUT DOWN MY ARGUMENT ...?

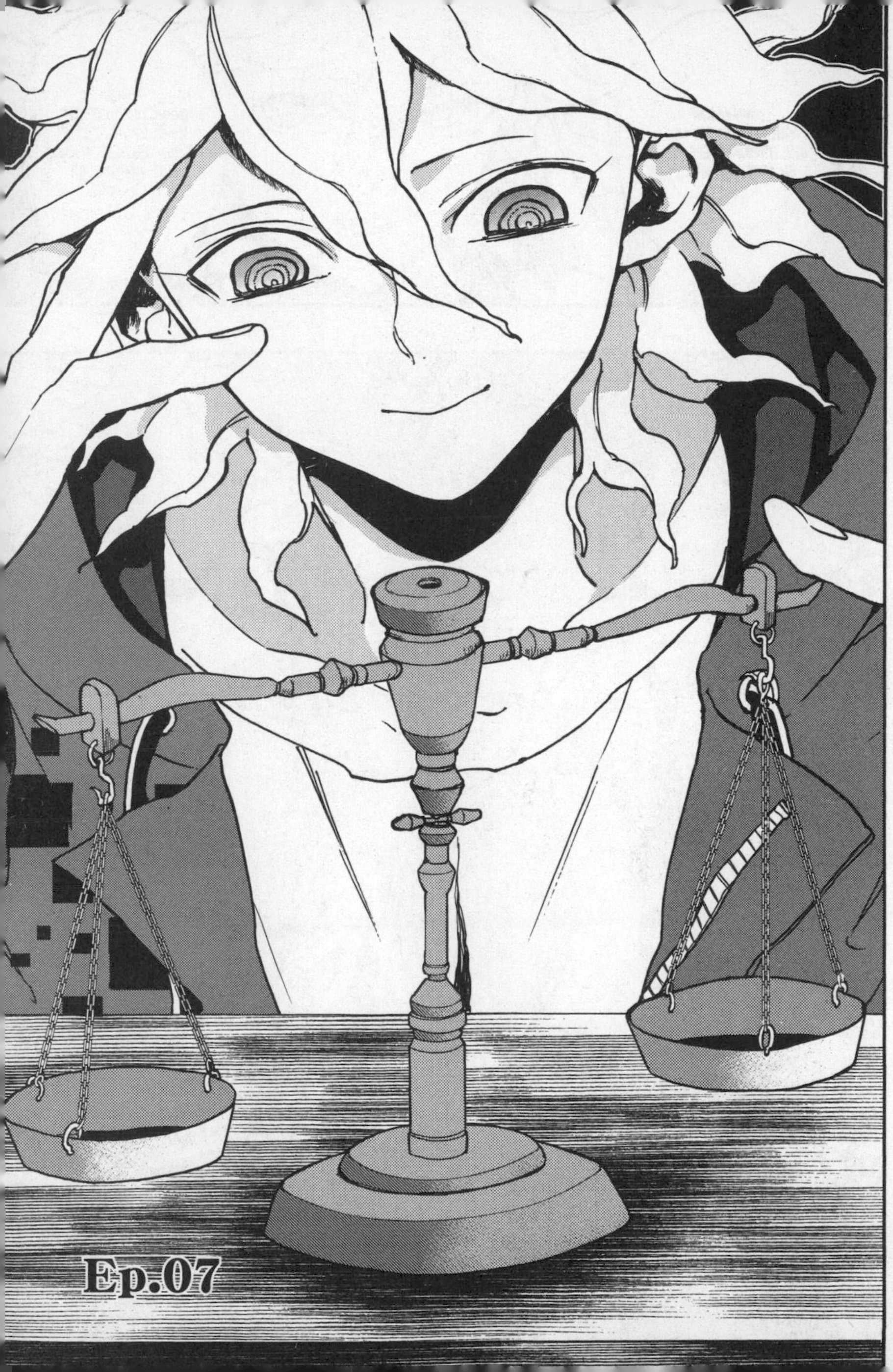
Ep.07

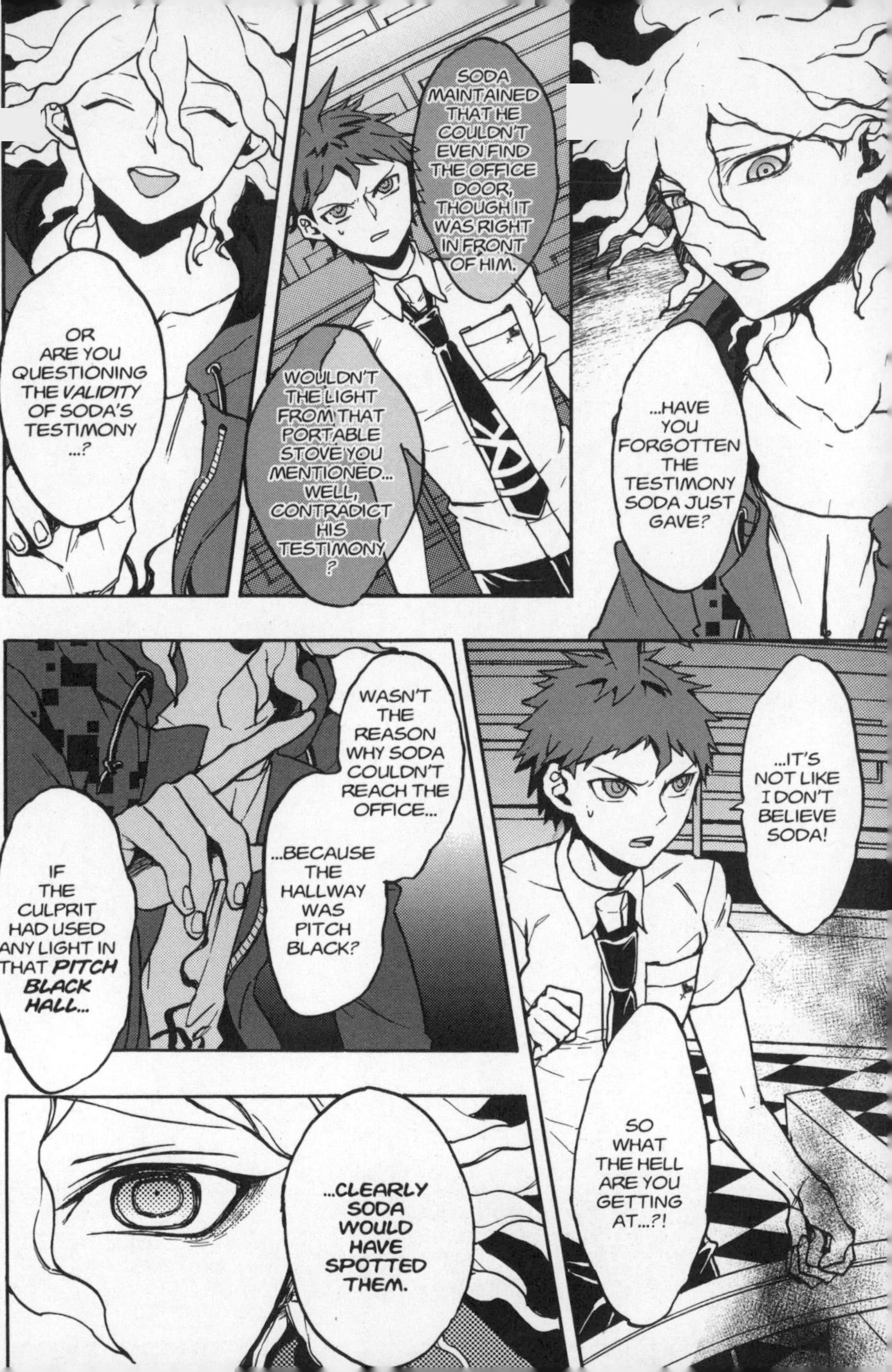
...HAVE YOU FORGOTTEN THE TESTIMONY SODA JUST GAVE?
SODA MAINTAINED THAT HE COULDN'T EVEN FIND THE OFFICE DOOR, THOUGH IT WAS RIGHT IN FRONT OF HIM.
WOULDN'T THE LIGHT FROM THAT PORTABLE STOVE YOU MENTIONED... WELL, CONTRADICT HIS TESTIMONY?
OR ARE YOU QUESTIONING THE *VALIDITY* OF SODA'S TESTIMONY...?
...IT'S NOT LIKE I DON'T BELIEVE SODA!
SO WHAT THE HELL ARE YOU GETTING AT...?!
WASN'T THE REASON WHY SODA COULDN'T REACH THE OFFICE...
...BECAUSE THE HALLWAY WAS PITCH BLACK?
IF THE CULPRIT HAD USED ANY LIGHT IN THAT ***PITCH BLACK HALL...***
...CLEARLY SODA WOULD HAVE SPOTTED THEM.

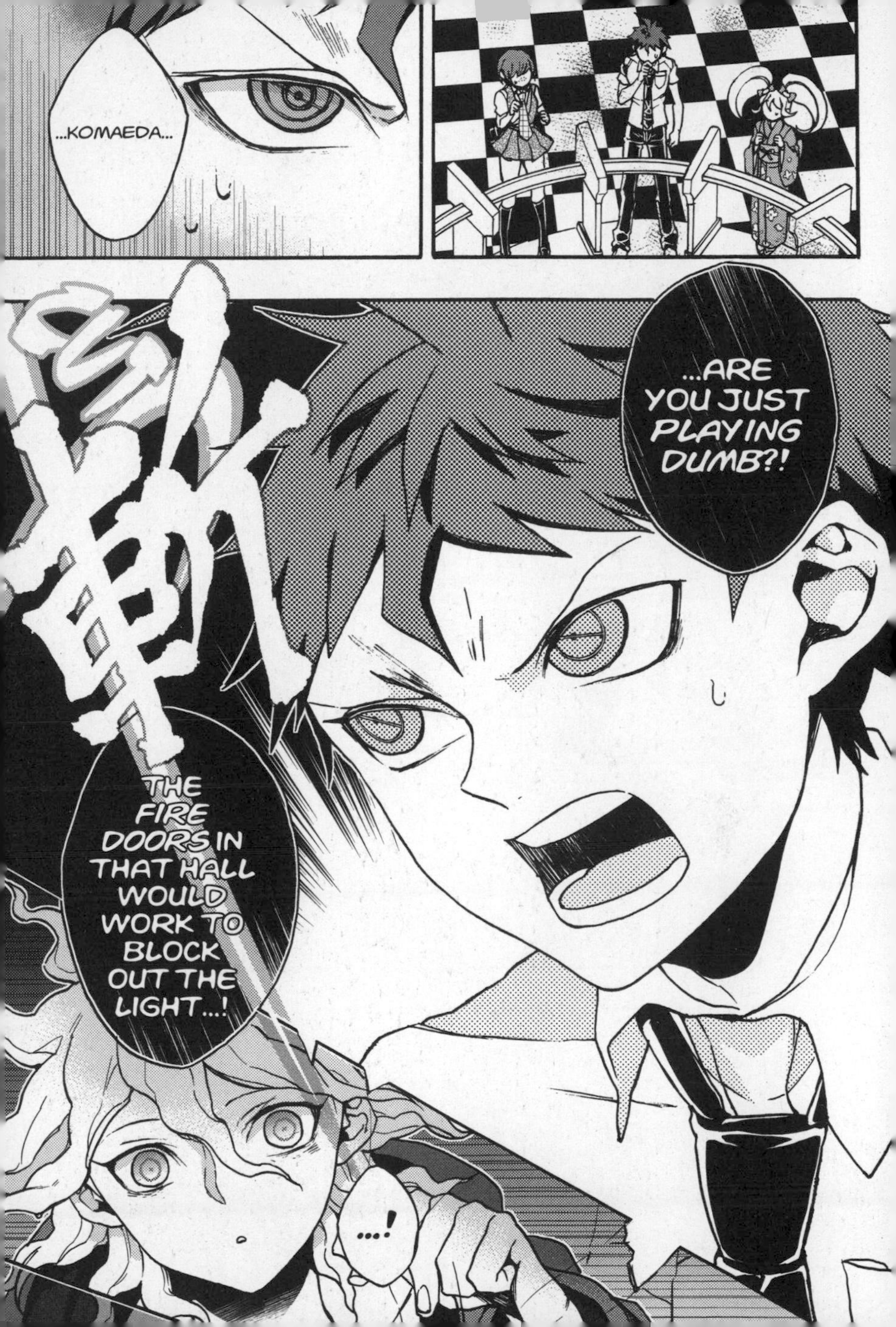
...KOMAEDA...
...ARE YOU JUST PLAYING DUMB?!
THE FIRE DOORS IN THAT HALL WOULD WORK TO BLOCK OUT THE LIGHT...!
...!

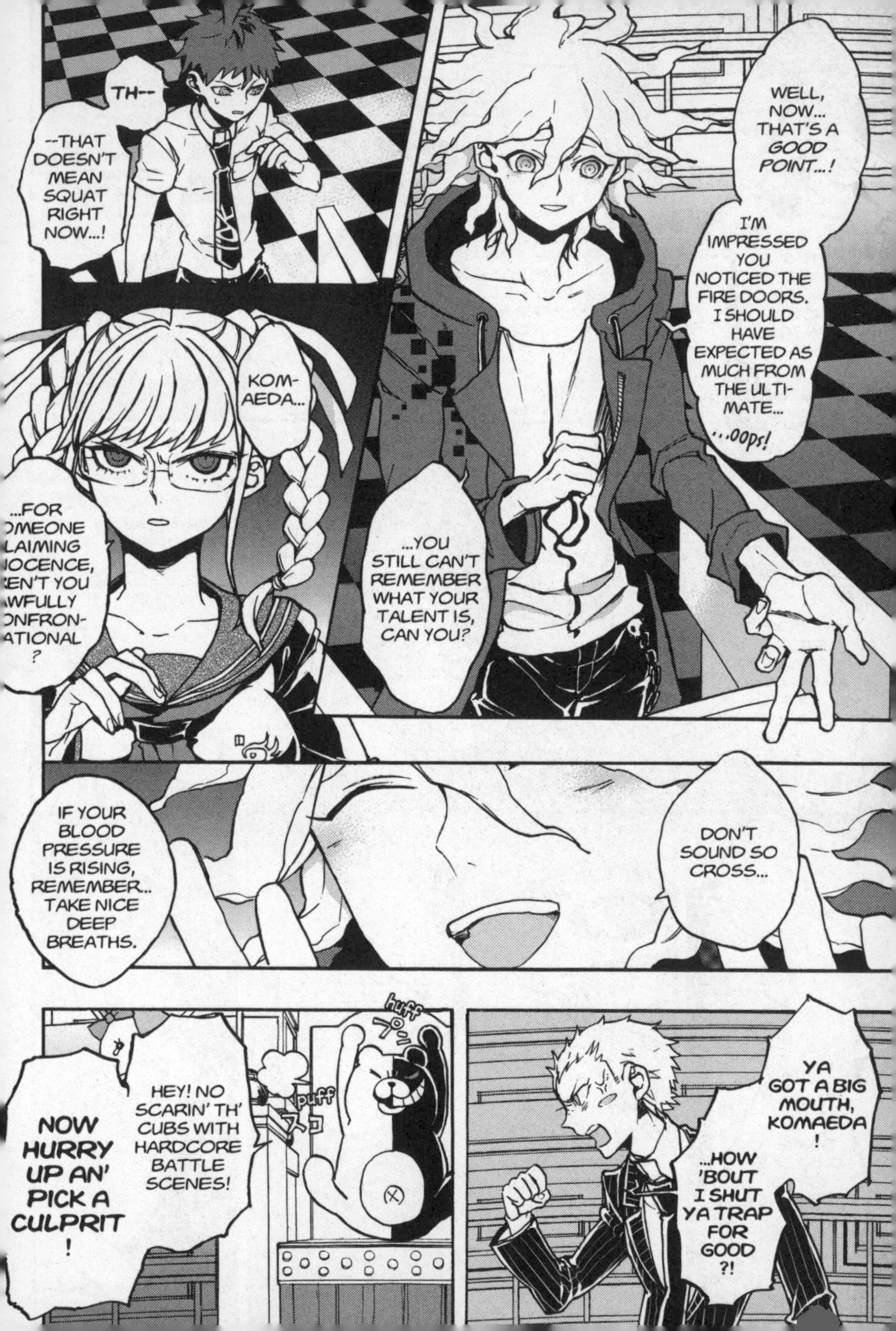
WELL, NOW... THAT'S A GOOD POINT...!
I'M IMPRESSED YOU NOTICED THE FIRE DOORS. I SHOULD HAVE EXPECTED AS MUCH FROM THE ULTI-MATE... ...oops!
...YOU STILL CAN'T REMEMBER WHAT YOUR TALENT IS, CAN YOU?
TH--
--THAT DOESN'T MEAN SQUAT RIGHT NOW...!
KOM-AEDA...
...FOR OMEONE LAIMING NOCENCE, REN'T YOU WFULLY ONFRON-ATIONAL ?
DON'T SOUND SO CROSS...
IF YOUR BLOOD PRESSURE IS RISING, REMEMBER... TAKE NICE DEEP BREATHS.
YA GOT A BIG MOUTH, KOMAEDA !
...HOW 'BOUT I SHUT YA TRAP FOR GOOD ?!
huff
puff
HEY! NO SCARIN' TH' CUBS WITH HARDCORE BATTLE SCENES!
NOW HURRY UP AN' PICK A CULPRIT !

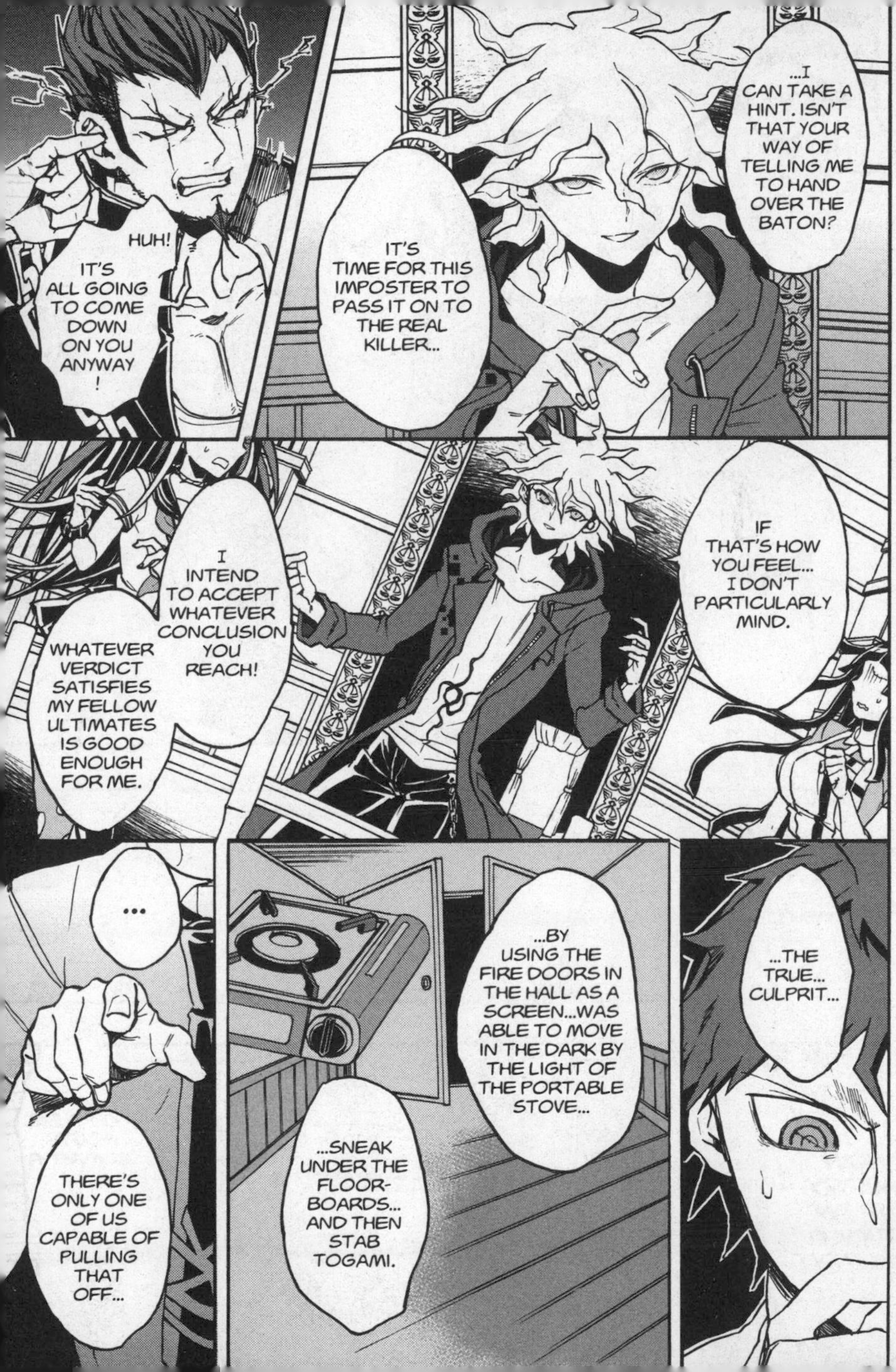
...I CAN TAKE A HINT. ISN'T THAT YOUR WAY OF TELLING ME TO HAND OVER THE BATON?
IT'S TIME FOR THIS IMPOSTER TO PASS IT ON TO THE REAL KILLER...
HUH!
IT'S ALL GOING TO COME DOWN ON YOU ANYWAY!
IF THAT'S HOW YOU FEEL... I DON'T PARTICULARLY MIND.
I INTEND TO ACCEPT WHATEVER CONCLUSION YOU REACH!
WHATEVER VERDICT SATISFIES MY FELLOW ULTIMATES IS GOOD ENOUGH FOR ME.
...THE TRUE... CULPRIT...
...BY USING THE FIRE DOORS IN THE HALL AS A SCREEN...WAS ABLE TO MOVE IN THE DARK BY THE LIGHT OF THE PORTABLE STOVE...
...SNEAK UNDER THE FLOOR-BOARDS... AND THEN STAB TOGAMI.
...
THERE'S ONLY ONE OF US CAPABLE OF PULLING THAT OFF...

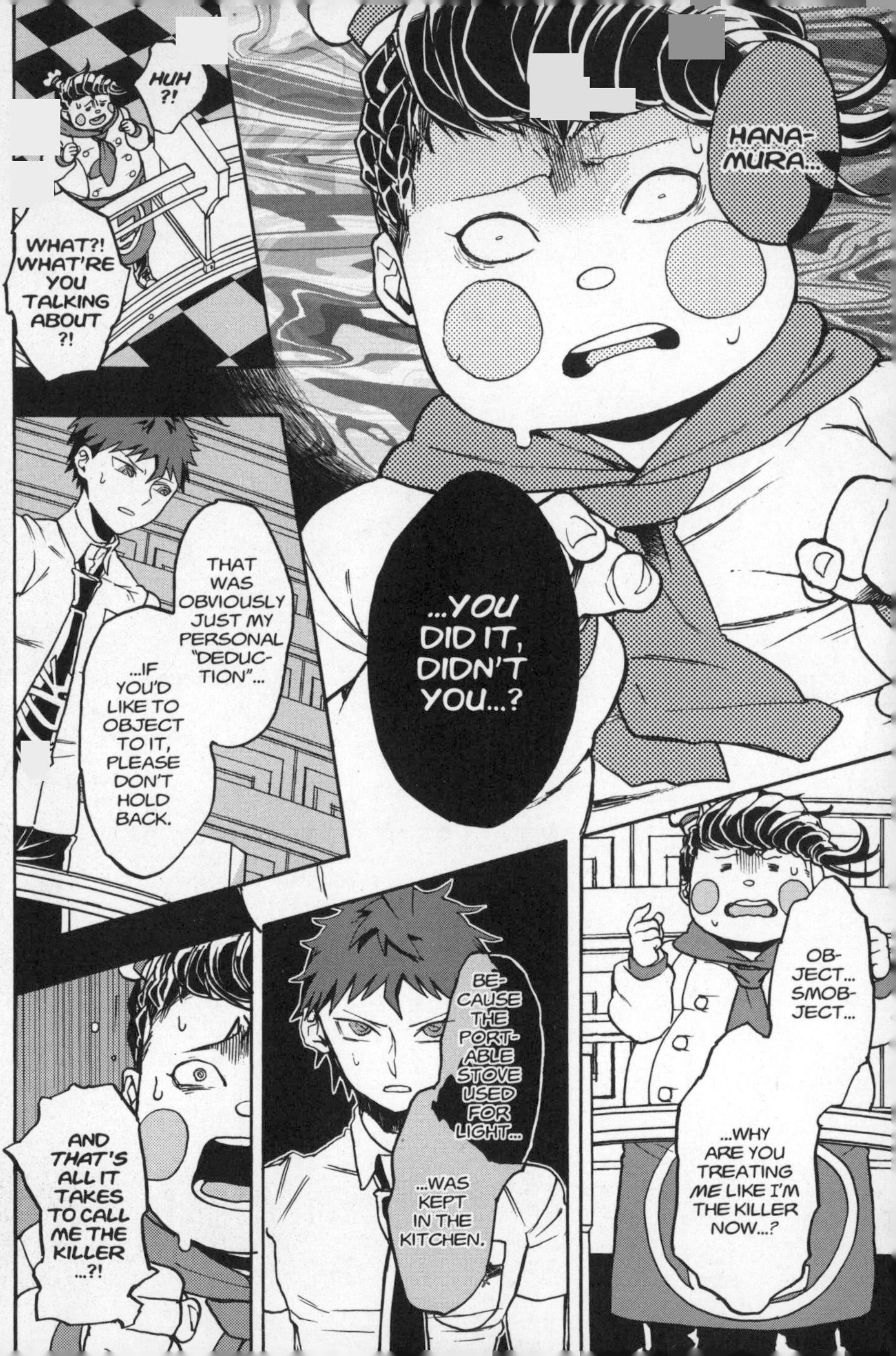
HANA-MURA...
...YOU DID IT, DIDN'T YOU...?
HUH?!
WHAT?! WHAT'RE YOU TALKING ABOUT?!
THAT WAS OBVIOUSLY JUST MY PERSONAL "DEDUC-TION"...
...IF YOU'D LIKE TO OBJECT TO IT, PLEASE DON'T HOLD BACK.
OB-JECT... SMOB-JECT...
...WHY ARE YOU TREATING ME LIKE I'M THE KILLER NOW...?
BE-CAUSE THE PORT-ABLE STOVE USED FOR LIGHT...
...WAS KEPT IN THE KITCHEN.
AND THAT'S ALL IT TAKES TO CALL ME THE KILLER...?!

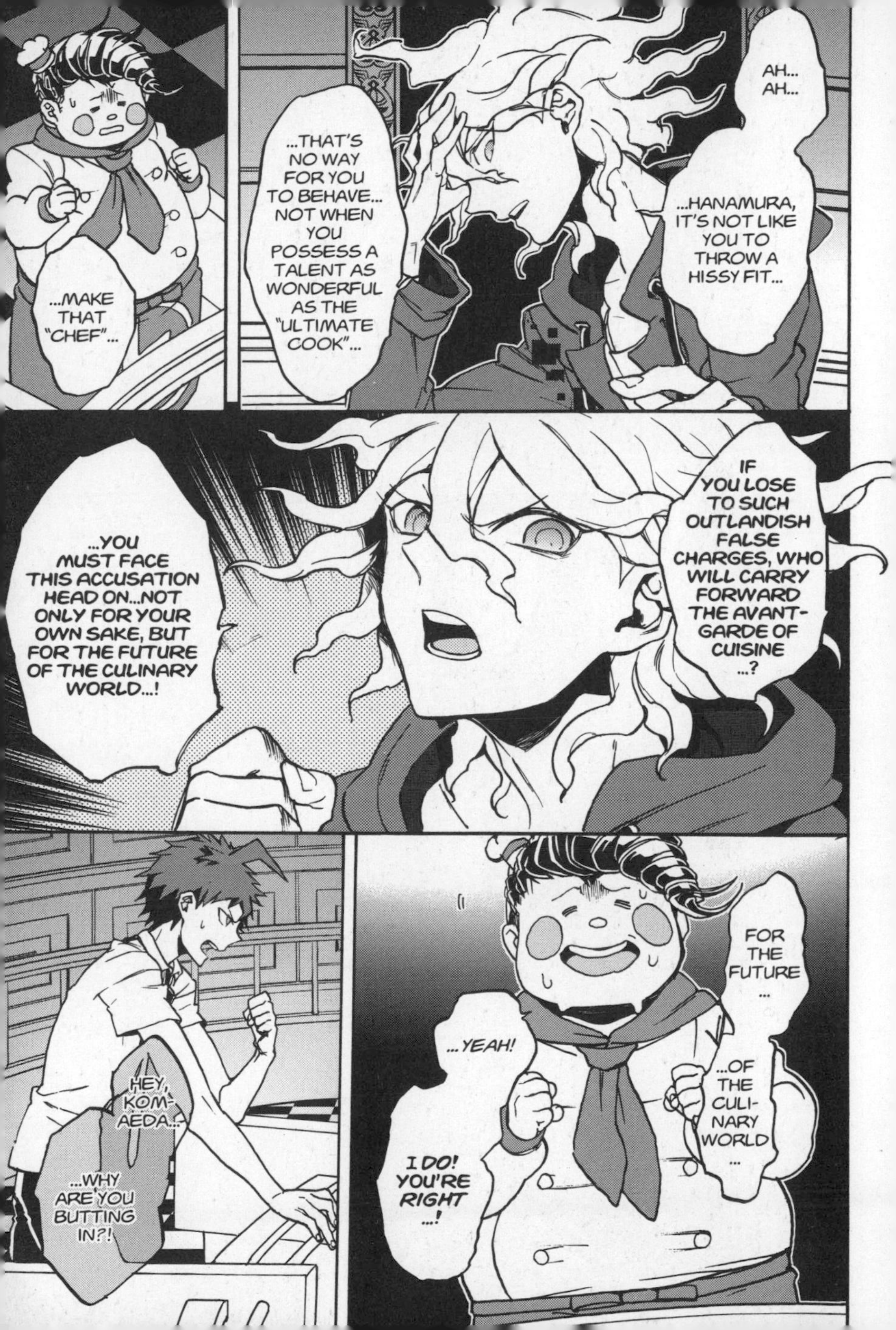
AH... AH...
...HANAMURA, IT'S NOT LIKE YOU TO THROW A HISSY FIT...
...THAT'S NO WAY FOR YOU TO BEHAVE... NOT WHEN YOU POSSESS A TALENT AS WONDERFUL AS THE "ULTIMATE COOK"...
...MAKE THAT "CHEF"...
IF YOU LOSE TO SUCH OUTLANDISH FALSE CHARGES, WHO WILL CARRY FORWARD THE AVANT-GARDE OF CUISINE ...?
...YOU MUST FACE THIS ACCUSATION HEAD ON...NOT ONLY FOR YOUR OWN SAKE, BUT FOR THE FUTURE OF THE CULINARY WORLD...!
FOR THE FUTURE ...
...OF THE CULI-NARY WORLD ...
...YEAH!
I DO! YOU'RE RIGHT ...!
HEY, KOM-AEDA...
...WHY ARE YOU BUTTING IN?!

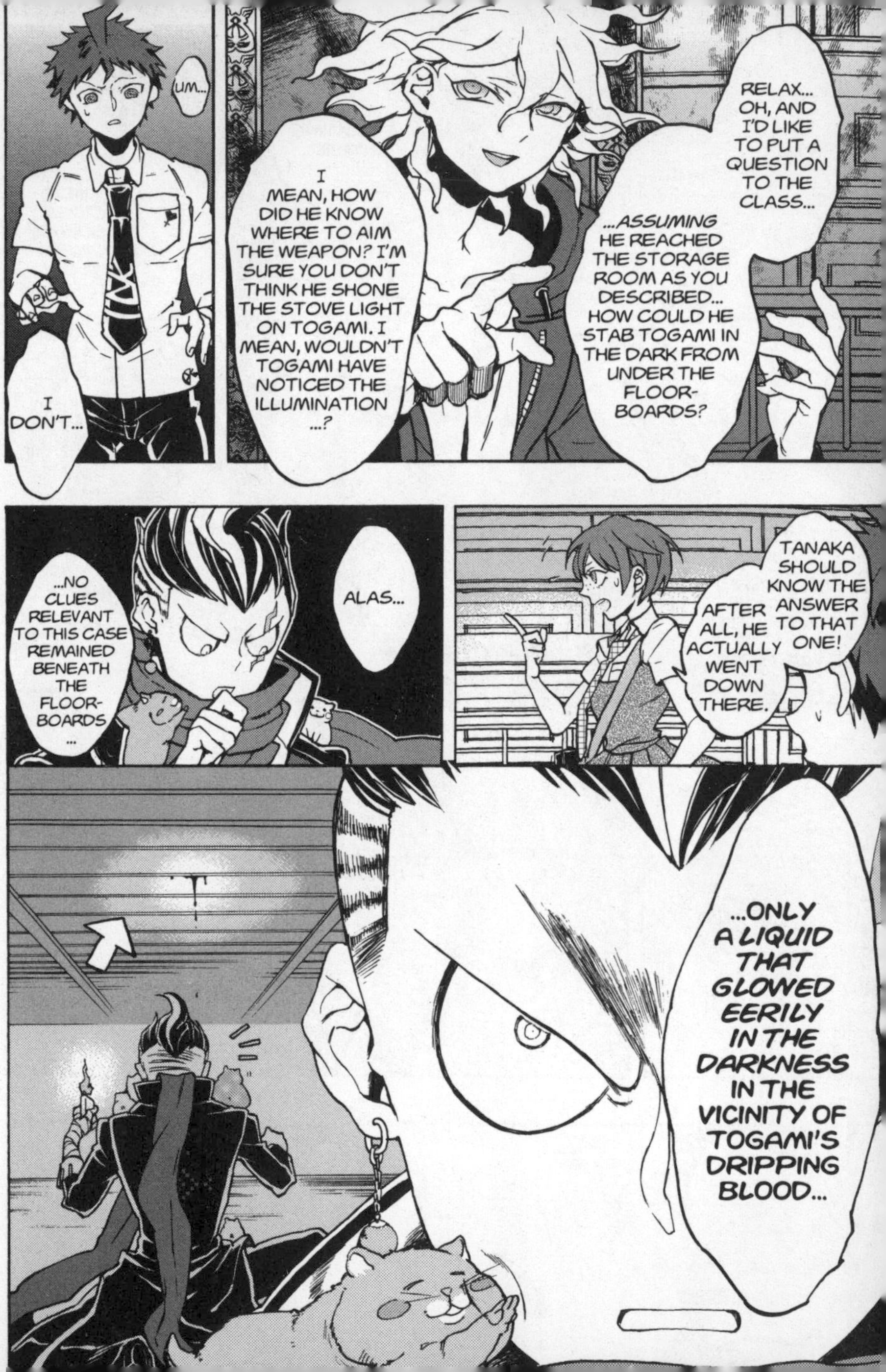
RELAX... OH, AND I'D LIKE TO PUT A QUESTION TO THE CLASS...
...ASSUMING HE REACHED THE STORAGE ROOM AS YOU DESCRIBED... HOW COULD HE STAB TOGAMI IN THE DARK FROM UNDER THE FLOOR-BOARDS?
I MEAN, HOW DID HE KNOW WHERE TO AIM THE WEAPON? I'M SURE YOU DON'T THINK HE SHONE THE STOVE LIGHT ON TOGAMI. I MEAN, WOULDN'T TOGAMI HAVE NOTICED THE ILLUMINATION ...?
UM...
I DON'T...
TANAKA SHOULD KNOW THE ANSWER TO THAT ONE!
AFTER ALL, HE ACTUALLY WENT DOWN THERE.
ALAS...
...NO CLUES RELEVANT TO THIS CASE REMAINED BENEATH THE FLOOR-BOARDS ...
...ONLY A LIQUID THAT GLOWED EERILY IN THE DARKNESS IN THE VICINITY OF TOGAMI'S DRIPPING BLOOD...

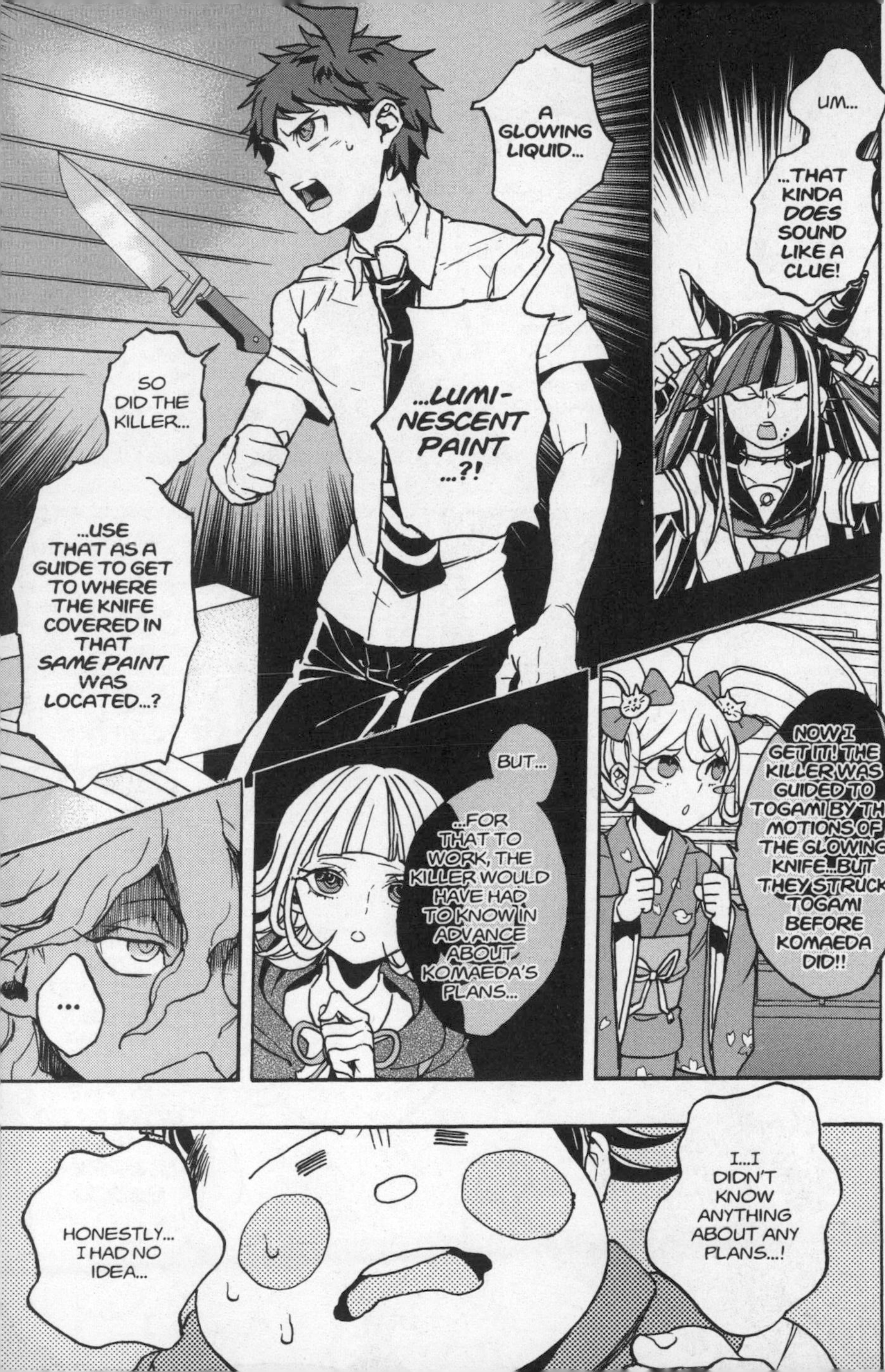
UM...
...THAT KINDA DOES SOUND LIKE A CLUE!
A GLOWING LIQUID...
...LUMI-NESCENT PAINT ...?!
SO DID THE KILLER...
...USE THAT AS A GUIDE TO GET TO WHERE THE KNIFE COVERED IN THAT SAME PAINT WAS LOCATED...?
NOW I GET IT! THE KILLER WAS GUIDED TO TOGAMI BY THE MOTIONS OF THE GLOWING KNIFE...BUT THEY STRUCK TOGAMI BEFORE KOMAEDA DID!!
BUT...
...FOR THAT TO WORK, THE KILLER WOULD HAVE HAD TO KNOW IN ADVANCE ABOUT KOMAEDA'S PLANS...
...
I...I DIDN'T KNOW ANYTHING ABOUT ANY PLANS...!
HONESTLY... I HAD NO IDEA...

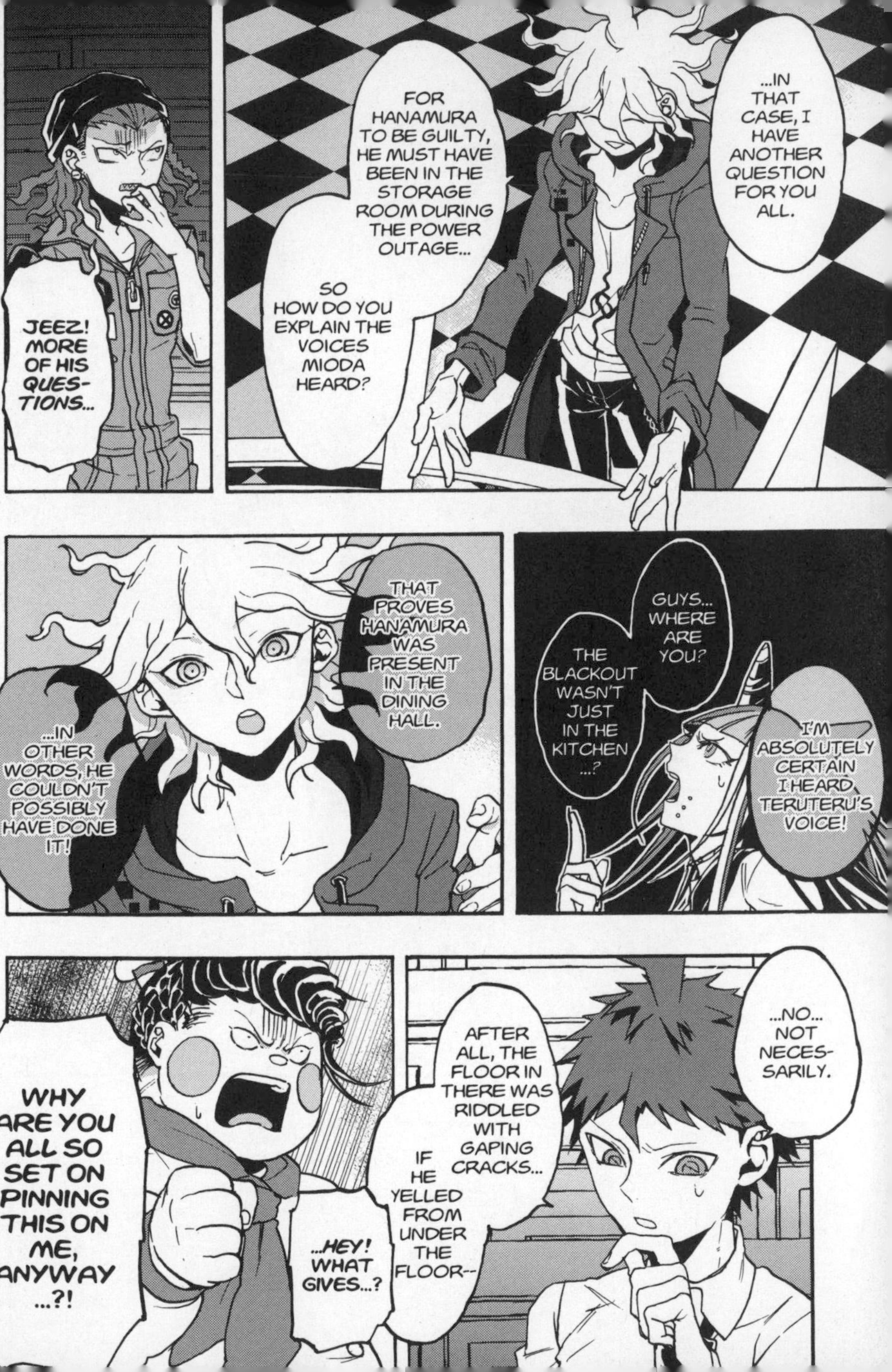
...IN THAT CASE, I HAVE ANOTHER QUESTION FOR YOU ALL.
FOR HANAMURA TO BE GUILTY, HE MUST HAVE BEEN IN THE STORAGE ROOM DURING THE POWER OUTAGE...
SO HOW DO YOU EXPLAIN THE VOICES MIODA HEARD?
JEEZ! MORE OF HIS QUES-TIONS...
GUYS... WHERE ARE YOU?
THE BLACKOUT WASN'T JUST IN THE KITCHEN ...?
I'M ABSOLUTELY CERTAIN I HEARD TERUTERU'S VOICE!
THAT PROVES HANAMURA WAS PRESENT IN THE DINING HALL.
...IN OTHER WORDS, HE COULDN'T POSSIBLY HAVE DONE IT!
...NO... NOT NECES-SARILY.
AFTER ALL, THE FLOOR IN THERE WAS RIDDLED WITH GAPING CRACKS...
IF HE YELLED FROM UNDER THE FLOOR--
...HEY! WHAT GIVES...?
WHY ARE YOU ALL SO SET ON PINNING THIS ON ME, ANYWAY ...?!

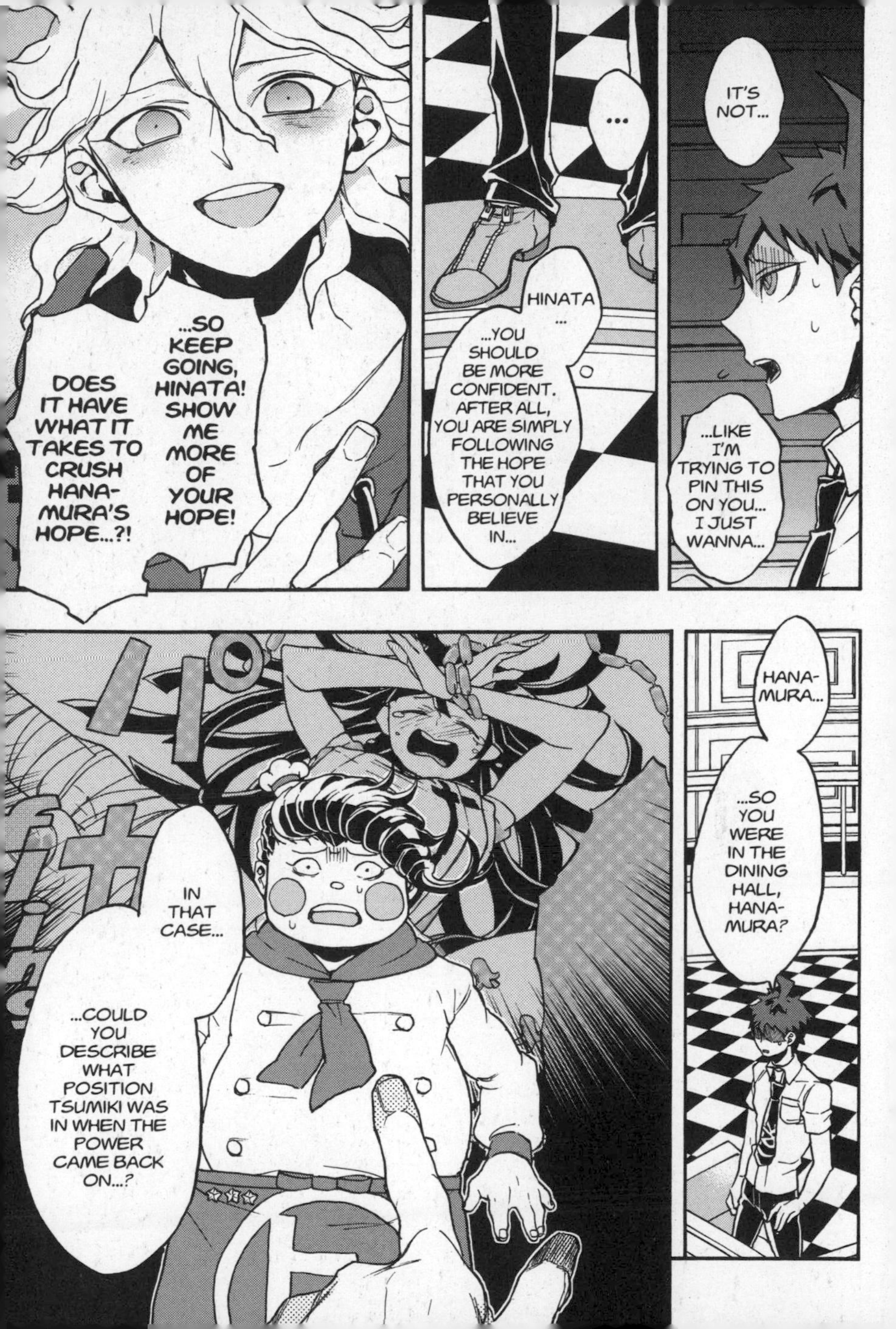
IT'S NOT...
...LIKE I'M TRYING TO PIN THIS ON YOU... I JUST WANNA...
...
HINATA...
...YOU SHOULD BE MORE CONFIDENT. AFTER ALL, YOU ARE SIMPLY FOLLOWING THE HOPE THAT YOU PERSONALLY BELIEVE IN...
...SO KEEP GOING, HINATA! SHOW ME MORE OF YOUR HOPE!
DOES IT HAVE WHAT IT TAKES TO CRUSH HANA-MURA'S HOPE...?!
HANA-MURA...
...SO YOU WERE IN THE DINING HALL, HANA-MURA?
IN THAT CASE...
...COULD YOU DESCRIBE WHAT POSITION TSUMIKI WAS IN WHEN THE POWER CAME BACK ON...?

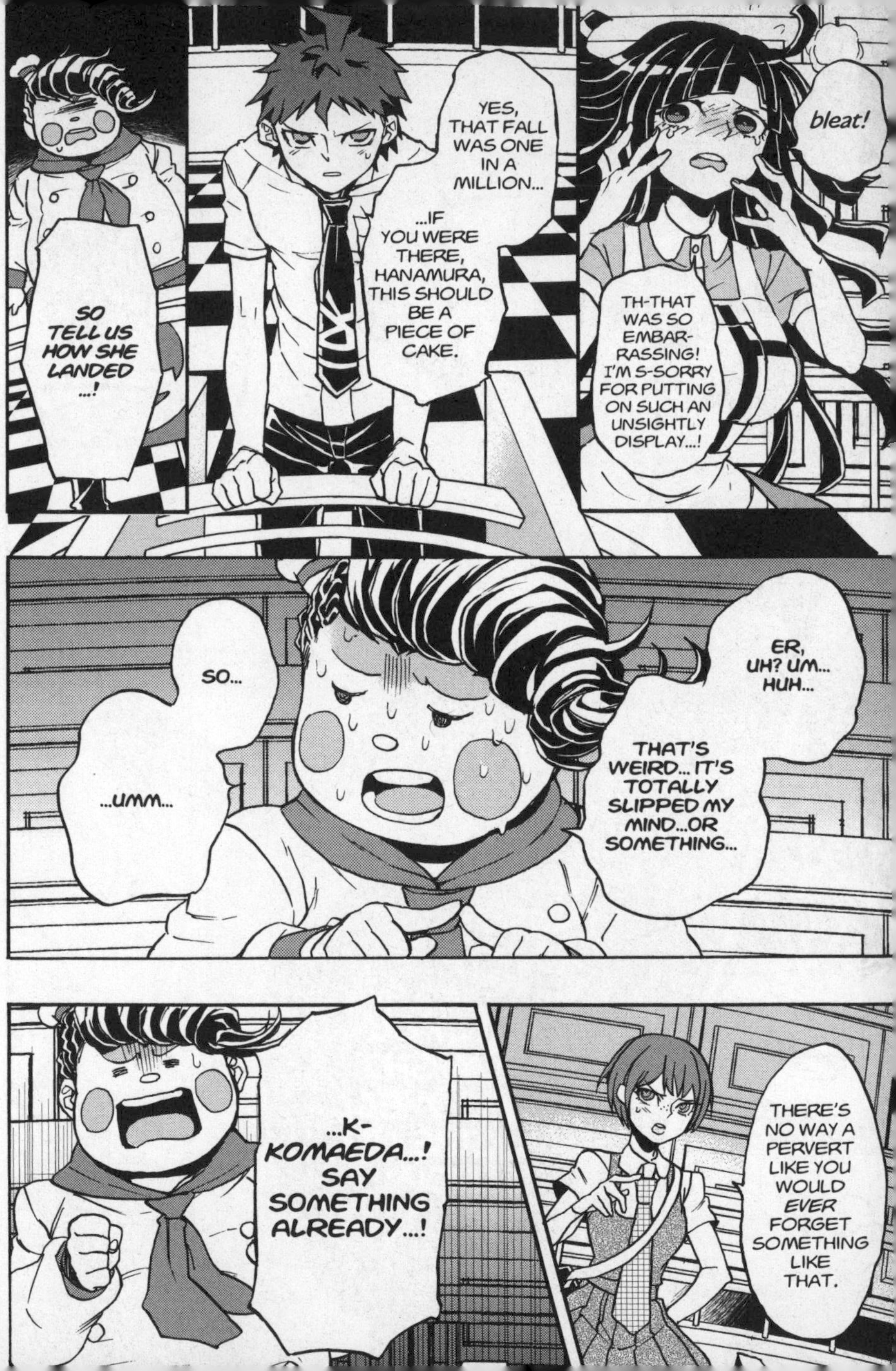
bleat!
TH-THAT WAS SO EMBARRASSING! I'M S-SORRY FOR PUTTING ON SUCH AN UNSIGHTLY DISPLAY...!
YES, THAT FALL WAS ONE IN A MILLION...
...IF YOU WERE THERE, HANAMURA, THIS SHOULD BE A PIECE OF CAKE.
SO TELL US HOW SHE LANDED ...!
ER, UH? UM... HUH...
THAT'S WEIRD... IT'S TOTALLY SLIPPED MY MIND...OR SOMETHING...
SO...
...UMM...
THERE'S NO WAY A PERVERT LIKE YOU WOULD *EVER* FORGET SOMETHING LIKE THAT.
...K-KOMAEDA...! SAY SOMETHING ALREADY...!

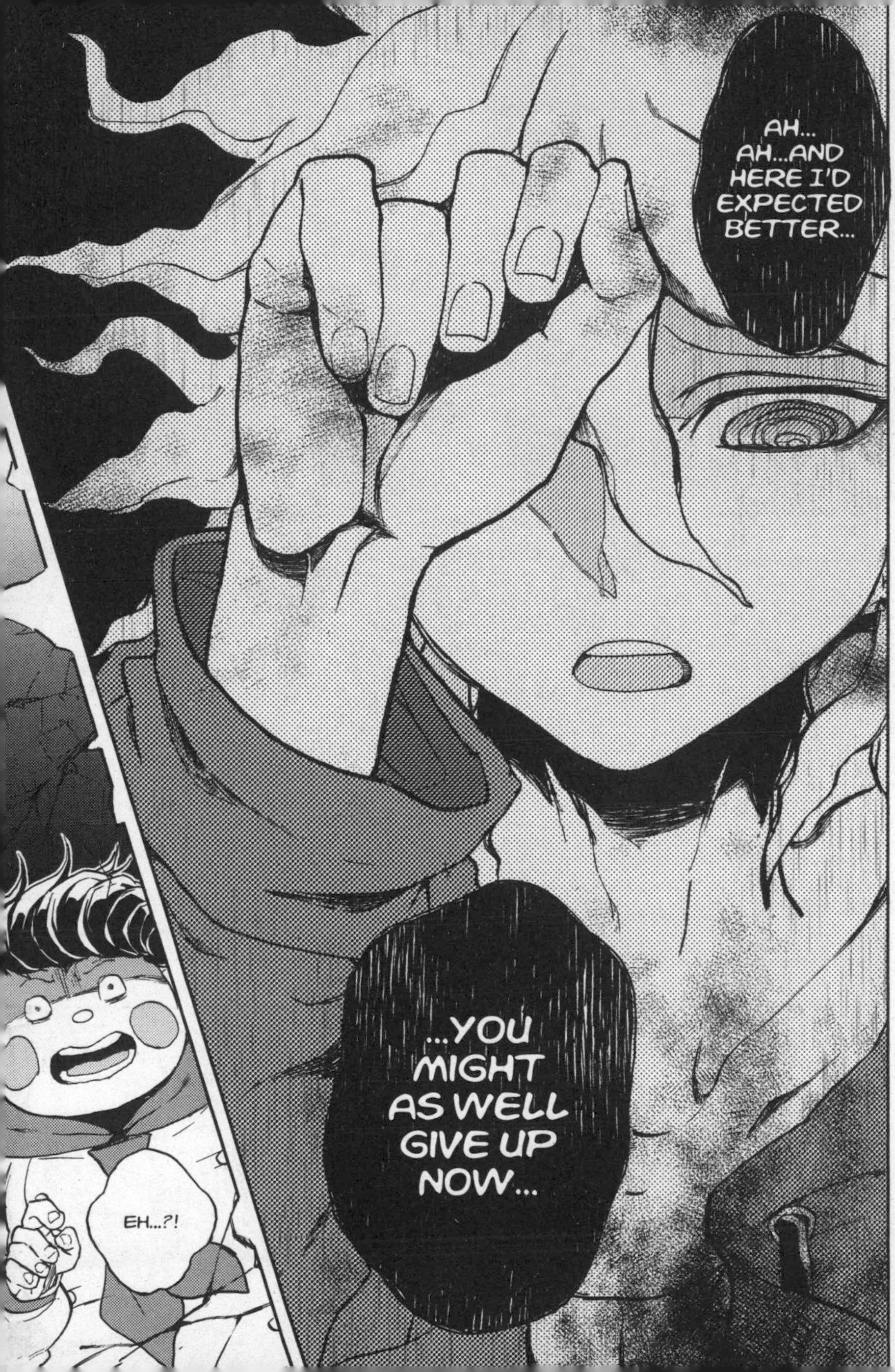
AH... AH...AND HERE I'D EXPECTED BETTER...
...YOU MIGHT AS WELL GIVE UP NOW...
EH...?!

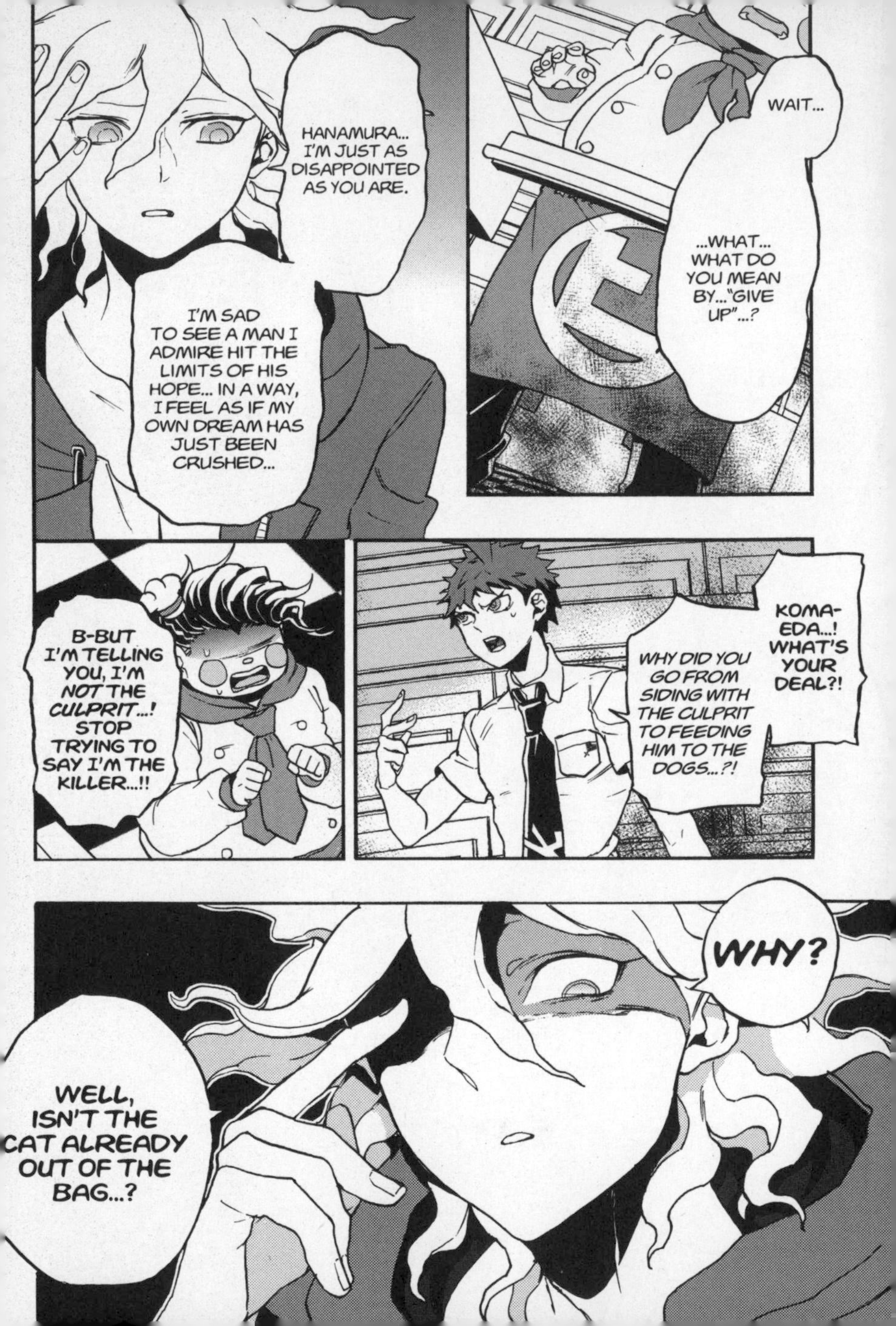
WAIT...
...WHAT... WHAT DO YOU MEAN BY..."GIVE UP"...?
HANAMURA... I'M JUST AS DISAPPOINTED AS YOU ARE.
I'M SAD TO SEE A MAN I ADMIRE HIT THE LIMITS OF HIS HOPE... IN A WAY, I FEEL AS IF MY OWN DREAM HAS JUST BEEN CRUSHED...
KOMA-EDA...! WHAT'S YOUR DEAL?!
WHY DID YOU GO FROM SIDING WITH THE CULPRIT TO FEEDING HIM TO THE DOGS...?!
B-BUT I'M TELLING YOU, I'M NOT THE CULPRIT...! STOP TRYING TO SAY I'M THE KILLER...!!
WHY?
WELL, ISN'T THE CAT ALREADY OUT OF THE BAG...?

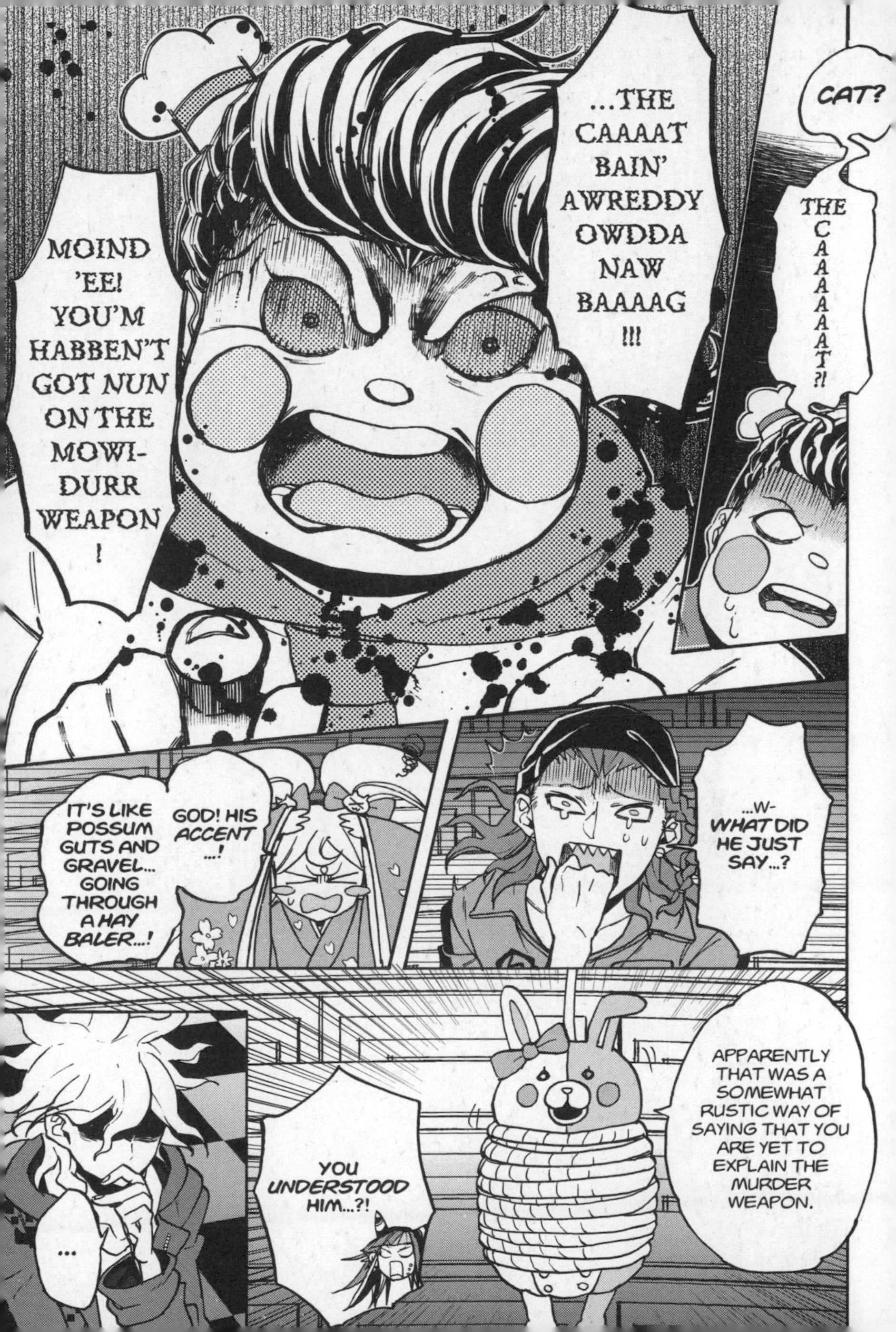
CAT?
THE CAAAAAAT?!
...THE CAAAAT BAIN' AWREDDY OWDDA NAW BAAAAG!!!
MOIND 'EE! YOU'M HABBEN'T GOT NUN ON THE MOWI-DURR WEAPON!
...W- WHAT DID HE JUST SAY...?
GOD! HIS ACCENT...!
IT'S LIKE POSSUM GUTS AND GRAVEL... GOING THROUGH A HAY BALER...!
APPARENTLY THAT WAS A SOMEWHAT RUSTIC WAY OF SAYING THAT YOU ARE YET TO EXPLAIN THE MURDER WEAPON.
YOU UNDERSTOOD HIM...?!
...

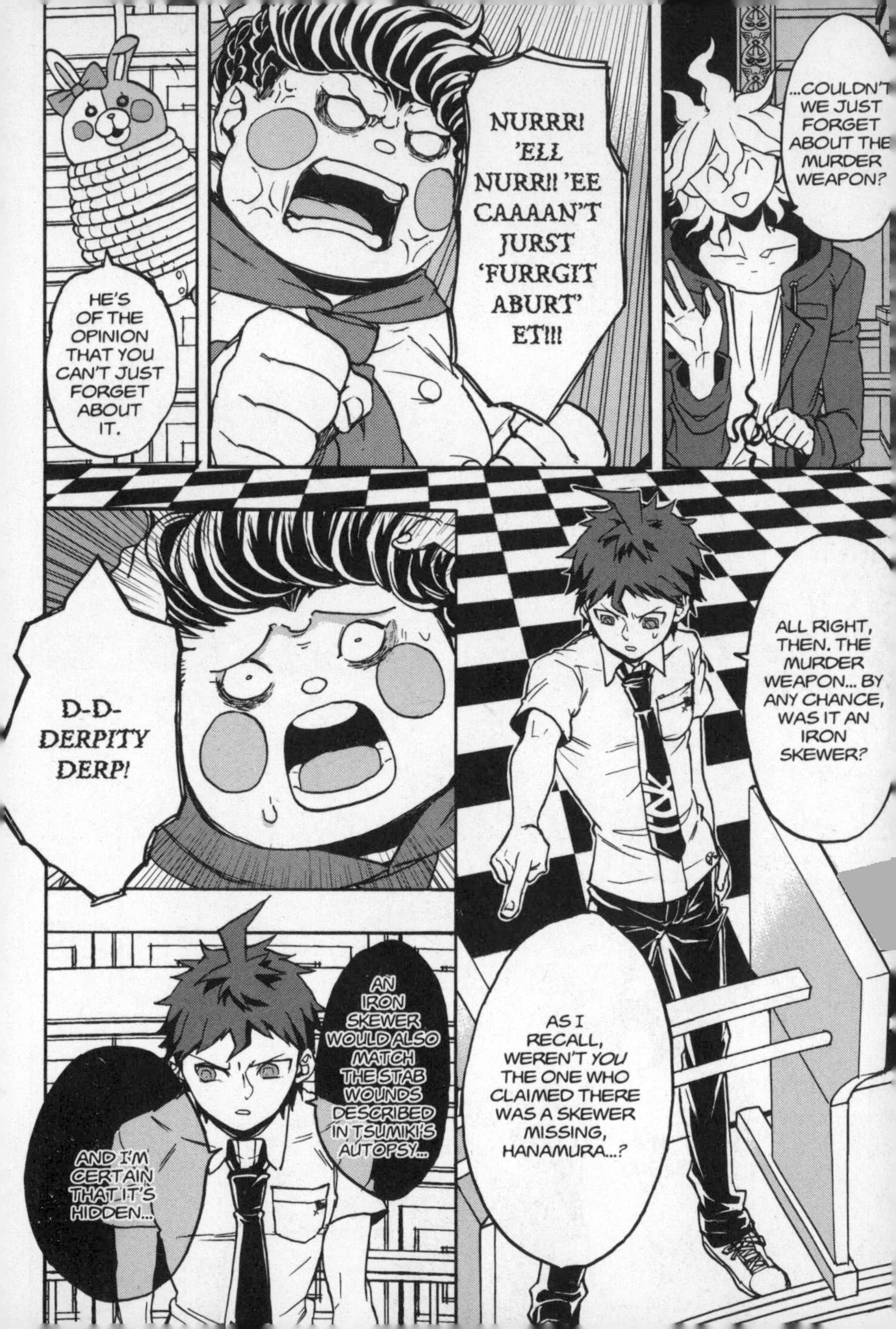
...COULDN'T WE JUST FORGET ABOUT THE MURDER WEAPON?
NURRR! 'ELL NURR!! 'EE CAAAAN'T JURST 'FURRGIT ABURT' ET!!!
HE'S OF THE OPINION THAT YOU CAN'T JUST FORGET ABOUT IT.
ALL RIGHT, THEN. THE MURDER WEAPON... BY ANY CHANCE, WAS IT AN IRON SKEWER?
AS I RECALL, WEREN'T *YOU* THE ONE WHO CLAIMED THERE WAS A SKEWER MISSING, HANAMURA...?
D-D-DERPITY DERP!
AN IRON SKEWER WOULD ALSO MATCH THE STAB WOUNDS DESCRIBED IN TSUMIKI'S AUTOPSY...
AND I'M CERTAIN THAT IT'S HIDDEN...

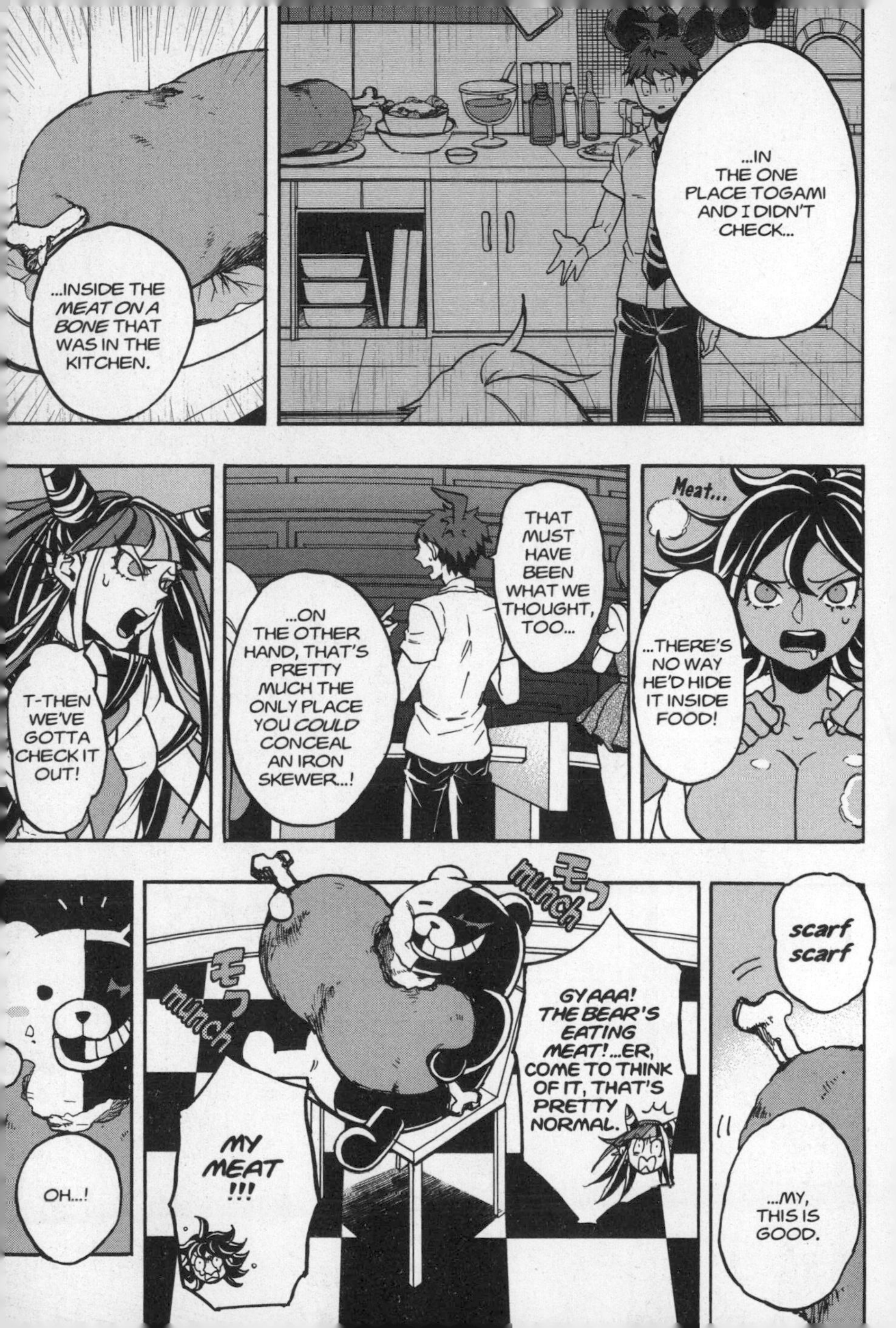
...IN THE ONE PLACE TOGAMI AND I DIDN'T CHECK...
...INSIDE THE MEAT ON A BONE THAT WAS IN THE KITCHEN.
Meat...
...THERE'S NO WAY HE'D HIDE IT INSIDE FOOD!
THAT MUST HAVE BEEN WHAT WE THOUGHT, TOO...
...ON THE OTHER HAND, THAT'S PRETTY MUCH THE ONLY PLACE YOU COULD CONCEAL AN IRON SKEWER...!
T-THEN WE'VE GOTTA CHECK IT OUT!
scarf scarf
...MY, THIS IS GOOD.
munch
munch
GYAAA! THE BEAR'S EATING MEAT! ...ER, COME TO THINK OF IT, THAT'S PRETTY NORMAL.
MY MEAT!!!
OH...!

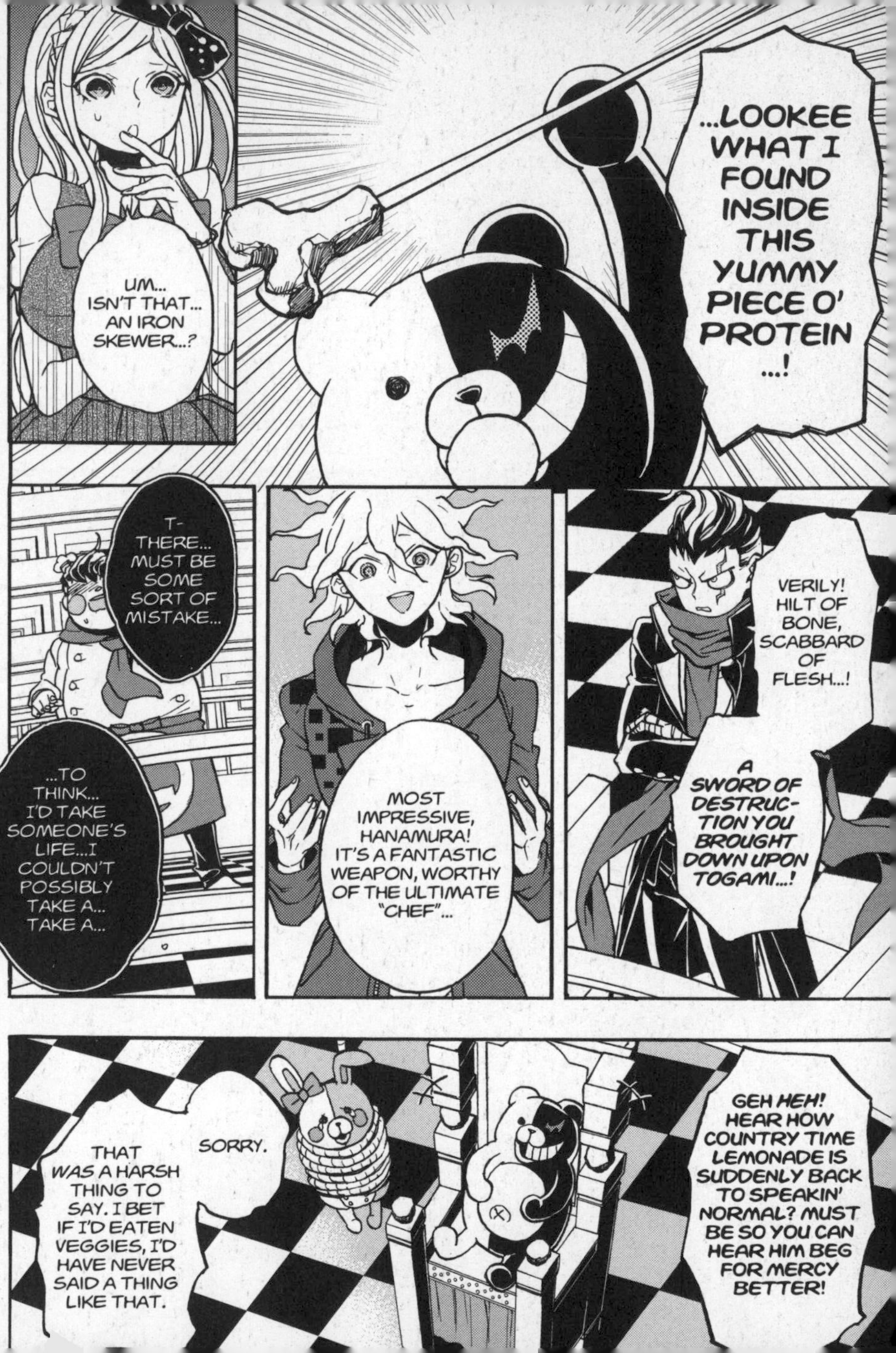
...LOOKEE WHAT I FOUND INSIDE THIS YUMMY PIECE O' PROTEIN ...!
UM... ISN'T THAT... AN IRON SKEWER...?
VERILY! HILT OF BONE, SCABBARD OF FLESH...!
A SWORD OF DESTRUC-TION YOU BROUGHT DOWN UPON TOGAMI...!
MOST IMPRESSIVE, HANAMURA! IT'S A FANTASTIC WEAPON, WORTHY OF THE ULTIMATE "CHEF"...
T-THERE... MUST BE SOME SORT OF MISTAKE...
...TO THINK... I'D TAKE SOMEONE'S LIFE...I COULDN'T POSSIBLY TAKE A... TAKE A...
GEH HEH! HEAR HOW COUNTRY TIME LEMONADE IS SUDDENLY BACK TO SPEAKIN' NORMAL? MUST BE SO YOU CAN HEAR HIM BEG FOR MERCY BETTER!
SORRY.
THAT WAS A HARSH THING TO SAY. I BET IF I'D EATEN VEGGIES, I'D HAVE NEVER SAID A THING LIKE THAT.

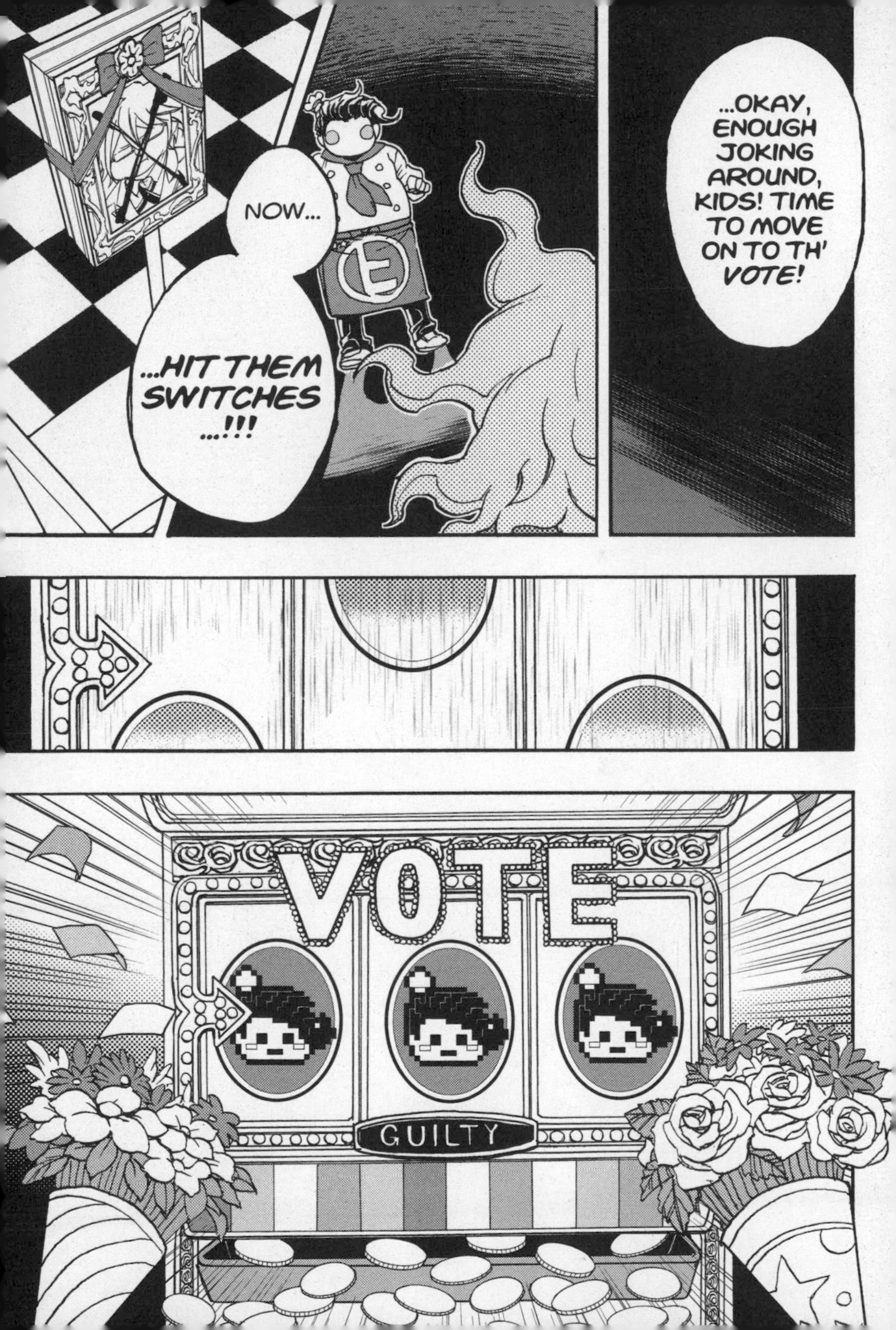
...OKAY, ENOUGH JOKING AROUND, KIDS! TIME TO MOVE ON TO TH' VOTE!
NOW...
...HIT THEM SWITCHES ...!!!
VOTE
GUILTY

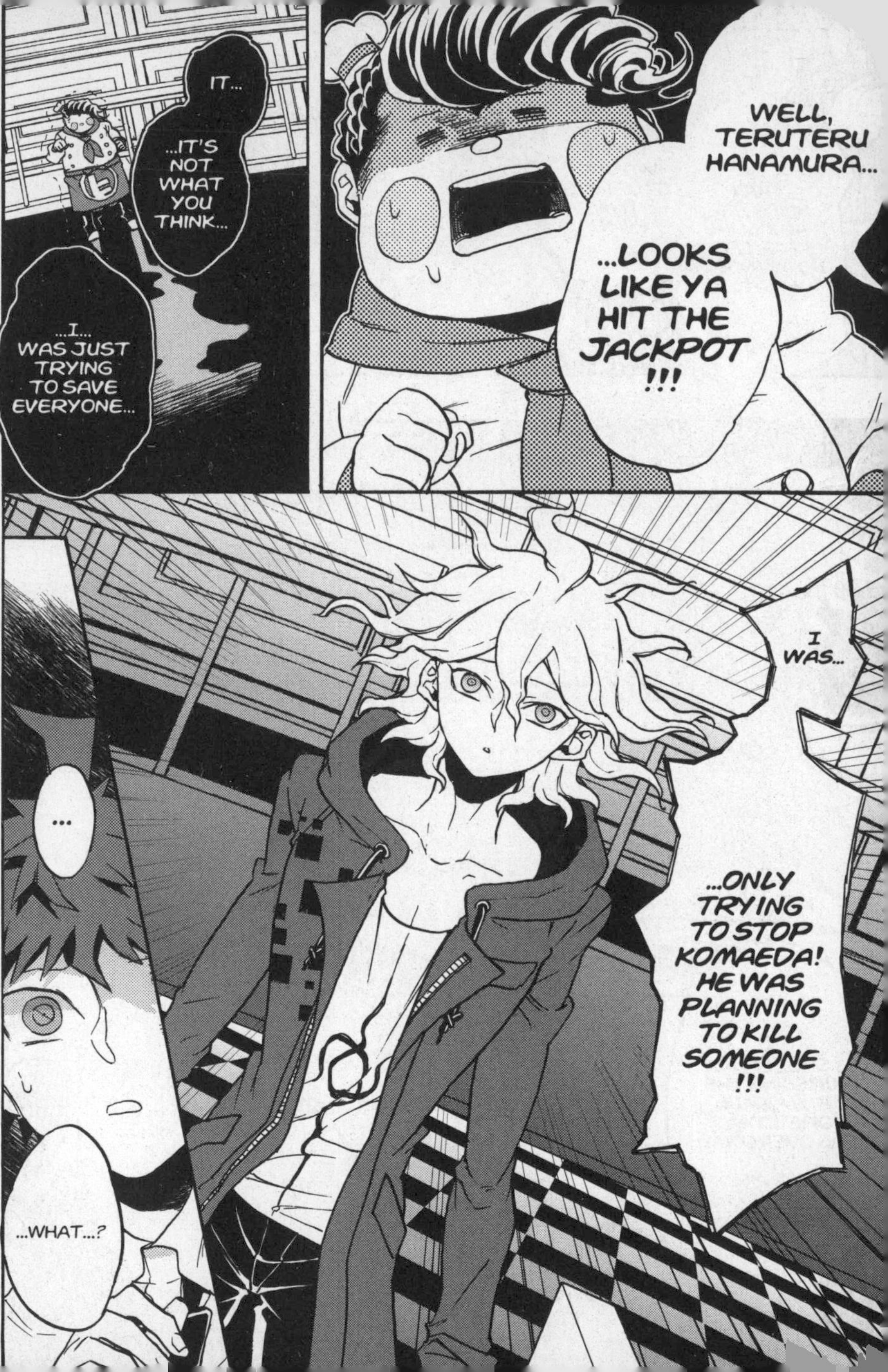
WELL, TERUTERU HANAMURA...
...LOOKS LIKE YA HIT THE JACKPOT !!!
IT...
...IT'S NOT WHAT YOU THINK...
...I... WAS JUST TRYING TO SAVE EVERYONE...
I WAS...
...ONLY TRYING TO STOP KOMAEDA! HE WAS PLANNING TO KILL SOMEONE !!!
...
...WHAT...?

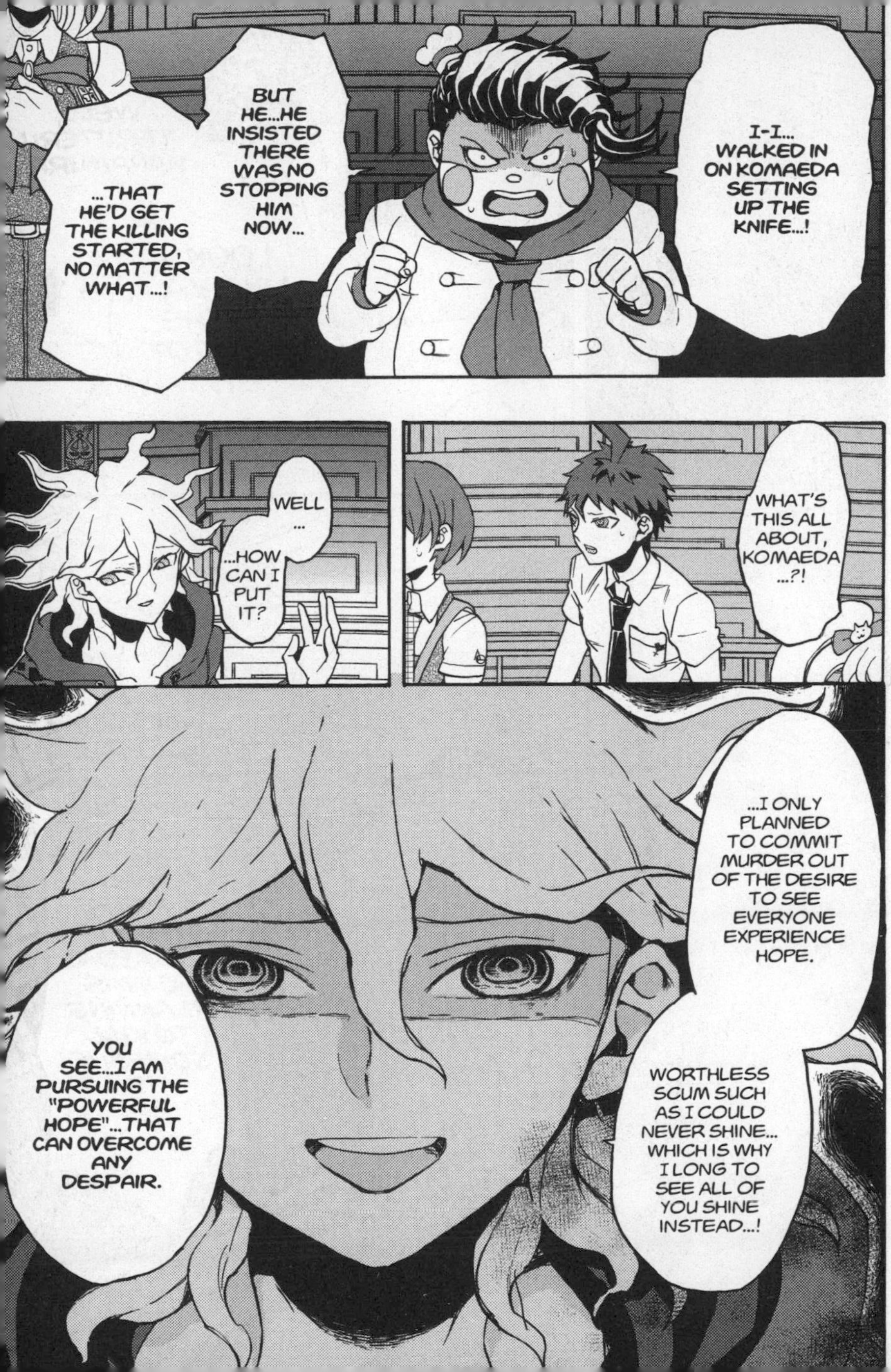
I-I... WALKED IN ON KOMAEDA SETTING UP THE KNIFE...!
BUT HE...HE INSISTED THERE WAS NO STOPPING HIM NOW...
...THAT HE'D GET THE KILLING STARTED, NO MATTER WHAT...!
WHAT'S THIS ALL ABOUT, KOMAEDA...?!
WELL...
...HOW CAN I PUT IT?
...I ONLY PLANNED TO COMMIT MURDER OUT OF THE DESIRE TO SEE EVERYONE EXPERIENCE HOPE.
WORTHLESS SCUM SUCH AS I COULD NEVER SHINE... WHICH IS WHY I LONG TO SEE ALL OF YOU SHINE INSTEAD...!
YOU SEE...I AM PURSUING THE "POWERFUL HOPE"...THAT CAN OVERCOME ANY DESPAIR.

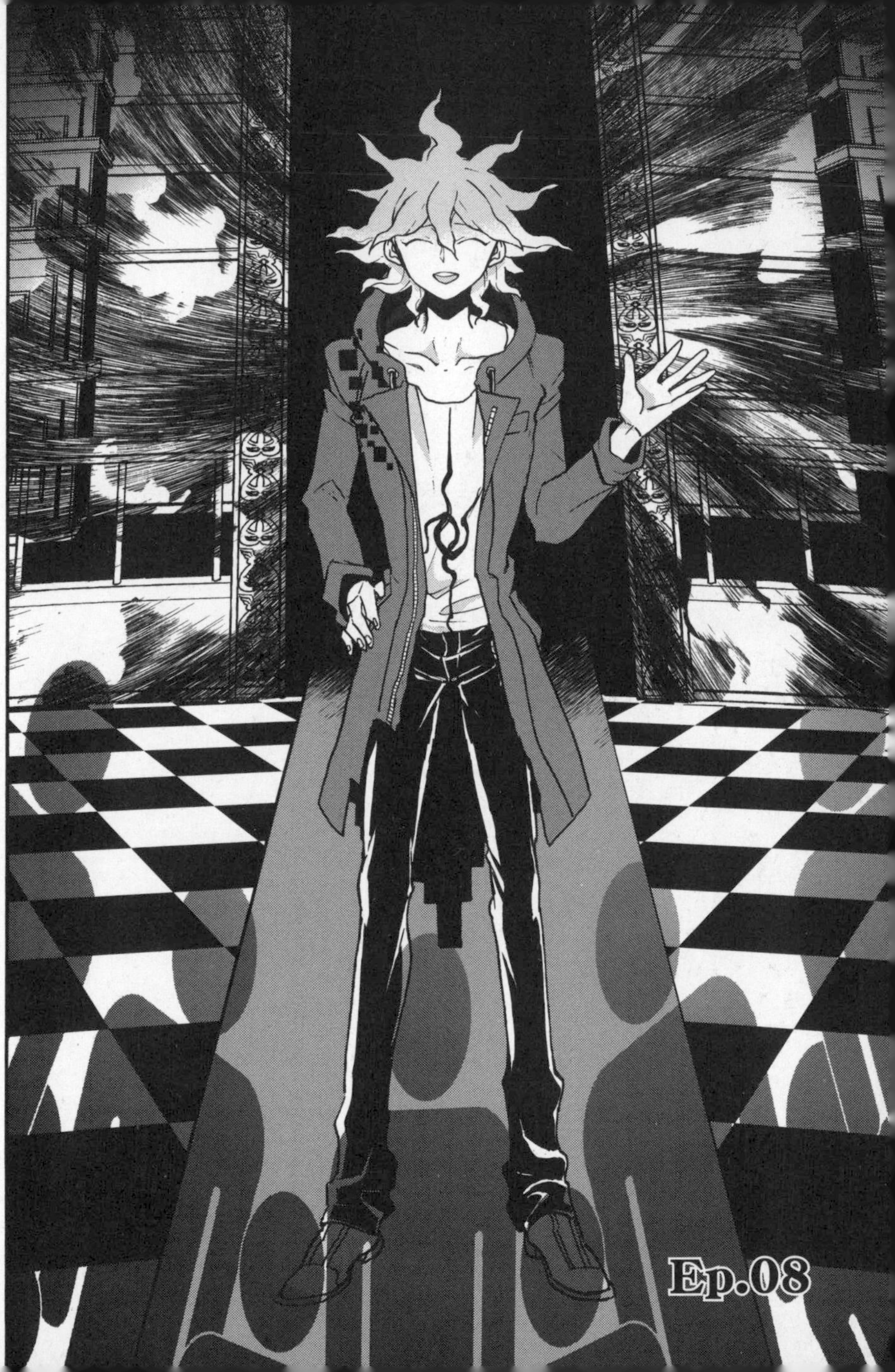
Ep.08

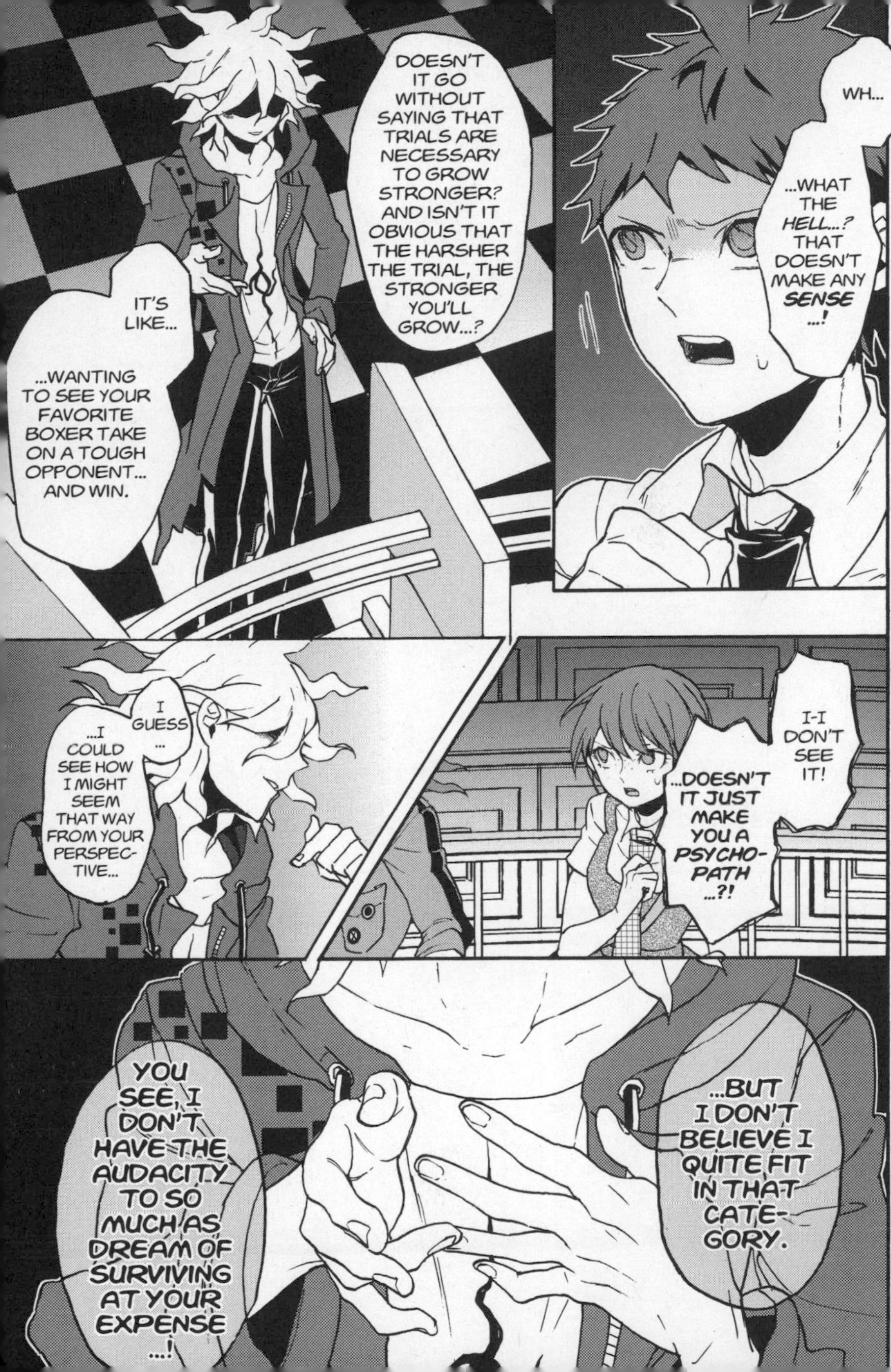
WH...
...WHAT THE HELL...? THAT DOESN'T MAKE ANY SENSE ...!
DOESN'T IT GO WITHOUT SAYING THAT TRIALS ARE NECESSARY TO GROW STRONGER? AND ISN'T IT OBVIOUS THAT THE HARSHER THE TRIAL, THE STRONGER YOU'LL GROW...?
IT'S LIKE...
...WANTING TO SEE YOUR FAVORITE BOXER TAKE ON A TOUGH OPPONENT... AND WIN.
I-I DON'T SEE IT!
...DOESN'T IT JUST MAKE YOU A PSYCHOPATH ...?!
I GUESS ...
...I COULD SEE HOW I MIGHT SEEM THAT WAY FROM YOUR PERSPECTIVE...
...BUT I DON'T BELIEVE I QUITE FIT IN THAT CATEGORY.
YOU SEE, I DON'T HAVE THE AUDACITY TO SO MUCH AS DREAM OF SURVIVING AT YOUR EXPENSE ...!

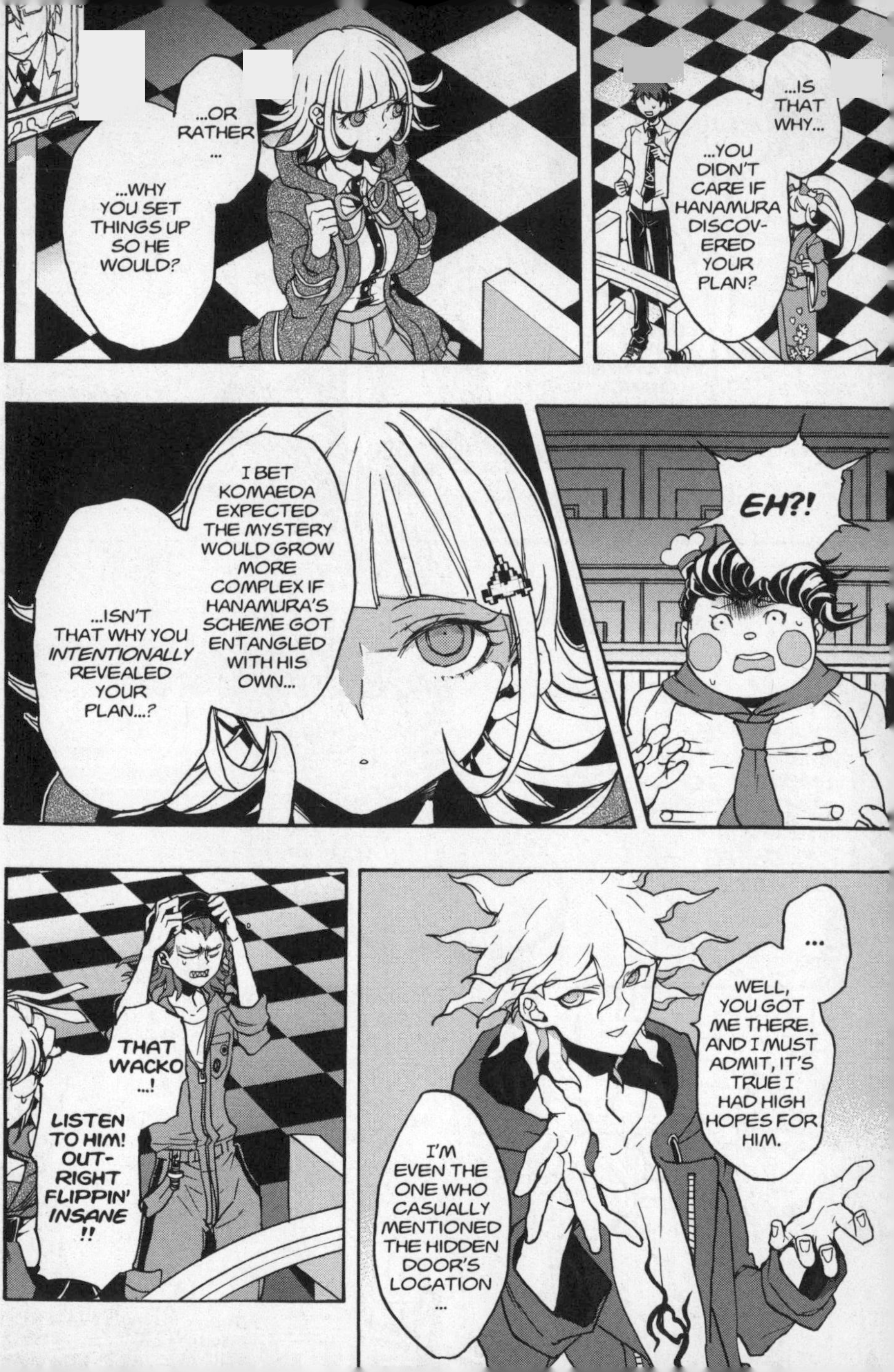
...IS THAT WHY...
...YOU DIDN'T CARE IF HANAMURA DISCOV-ERED YOUR PLAN?
...OR RATHER ...
...WHY YOU SET THINGS UP SO HE WOULD?
EH?!
I BET KOMAEDA EXPECTED THE MYSTERY WOULD GROW MORE COMPLEX IF HANAMURA'S SCHEME GOT ENTANGLED WITH HIS OWN...
...ISN'T THAT WHY YOU *INTENTIONALLY* REVEALED YOUR PLAN...?
...
WELL, YOU GOT ME THERE. AND I MUST ADMIT, IT'S TRUE I HAD HIGH HOPES FOR HIM.
I'M EVEN THE ONE WHO CASUALLY MENTIONED THE HIDDEN DOOR'S LOCATION ...
THAT WACKO ...!
LISTEN TO HIM! OUT-RIGHT FLIPPIN' INSANE !!

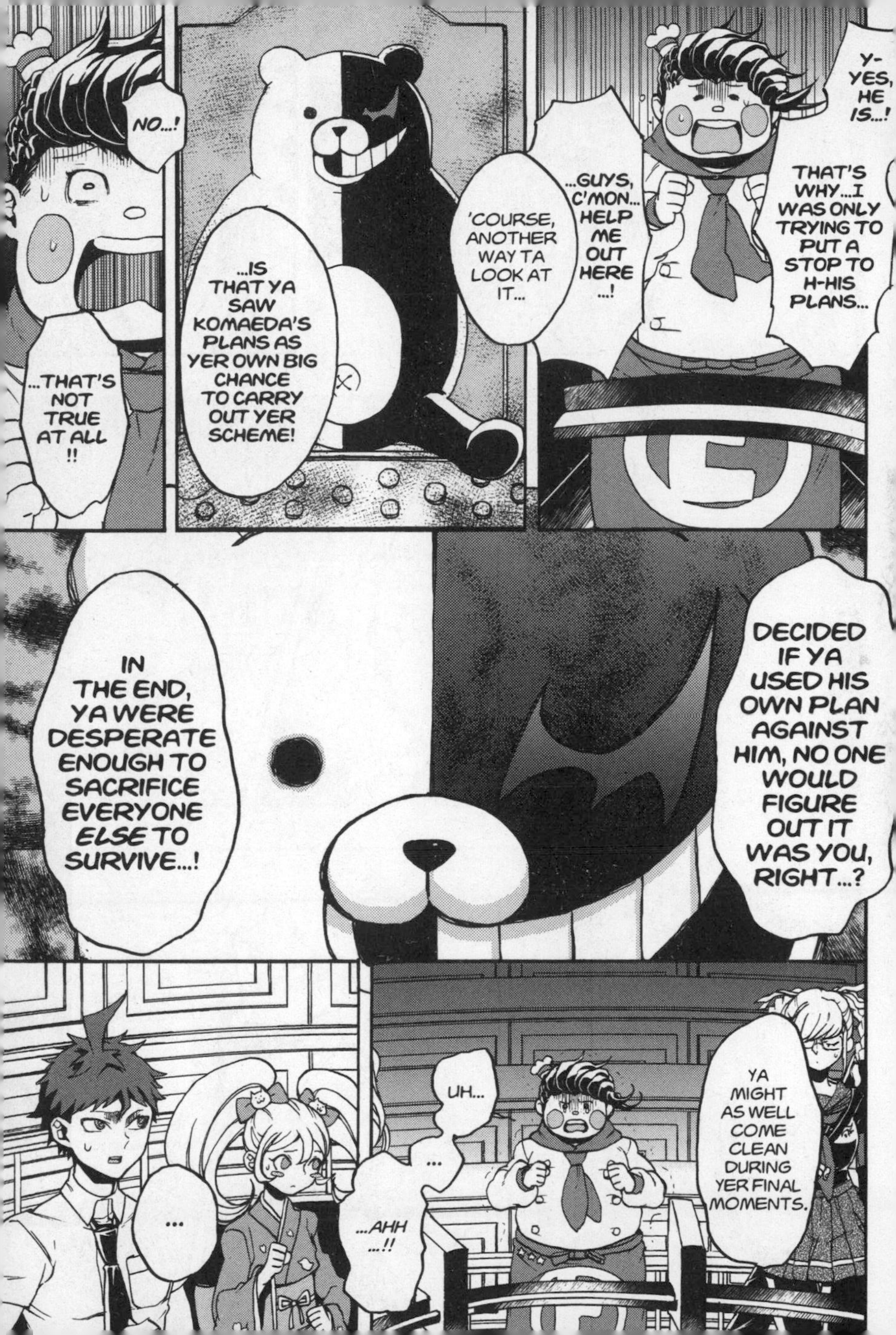
Y-YES, HE IS...!
THAT'S WHY...I WAS ONLY TRYING TO PUT A STOP TO H-HIS PLANS...
...GUYS, C'MON... HELP ME OUT HERE...!
'COURSE, ANOTHER WAY TA LOOK AT IT...
...IS THAT YA SAW KOMAEDA'S PLANS AS YER OWN BIG CHANCE TO CARRY OUT YER SCHEME!
NO...!
...THAT'S NOT TRUE AT ALL!!
DECIDED IF YA USED HIS OWN PLAN AGAINST HIM, NO ONE WOULD FIGURE OUT IT WAS YOU, RIGHT...?
IN THE END, YA WERE DESPERATE ENOUGH TO SACRIFICE EVERYONE *ELSE* TO SURVIVE...!
YA MIGHT AS WELL COME CLEAN DURING YER FINAL MOMENTS.
UH...
...
...AHH...!!
...

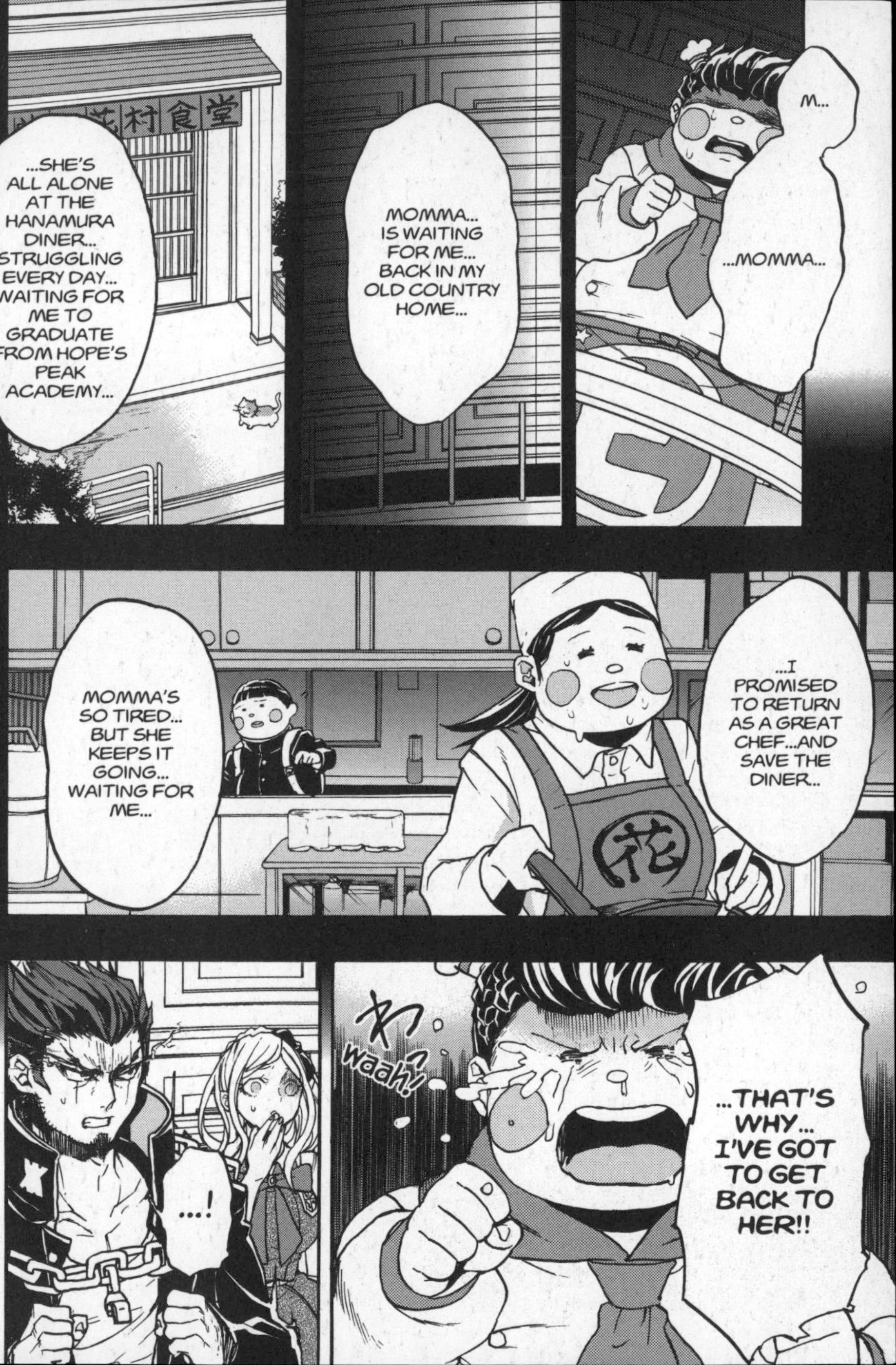
M...
...MOMMA...
MOMMA... IS WAITING FOR ME... BACK IN MY OLD COUNTRY HOME...
花村食堂
...SHE'S ALL ALONE AT THE HANAMURA DINER... STRUGGLING EVERY DAY... WAITING FOR ME TO GRADUATE FROM HOPE'S PEAK ACADEMY...
...I PROMISED TO RETURN AS A GREAT CHEF...AND SAVE THE DINER...
MOMMA'S SO TIRED... BUT SHE KEEPS IT GOING... WAITING FOR ME...
...THAT'S WHY... I'VE GOT TO GET BACK TO HER!!
Waah!
...!

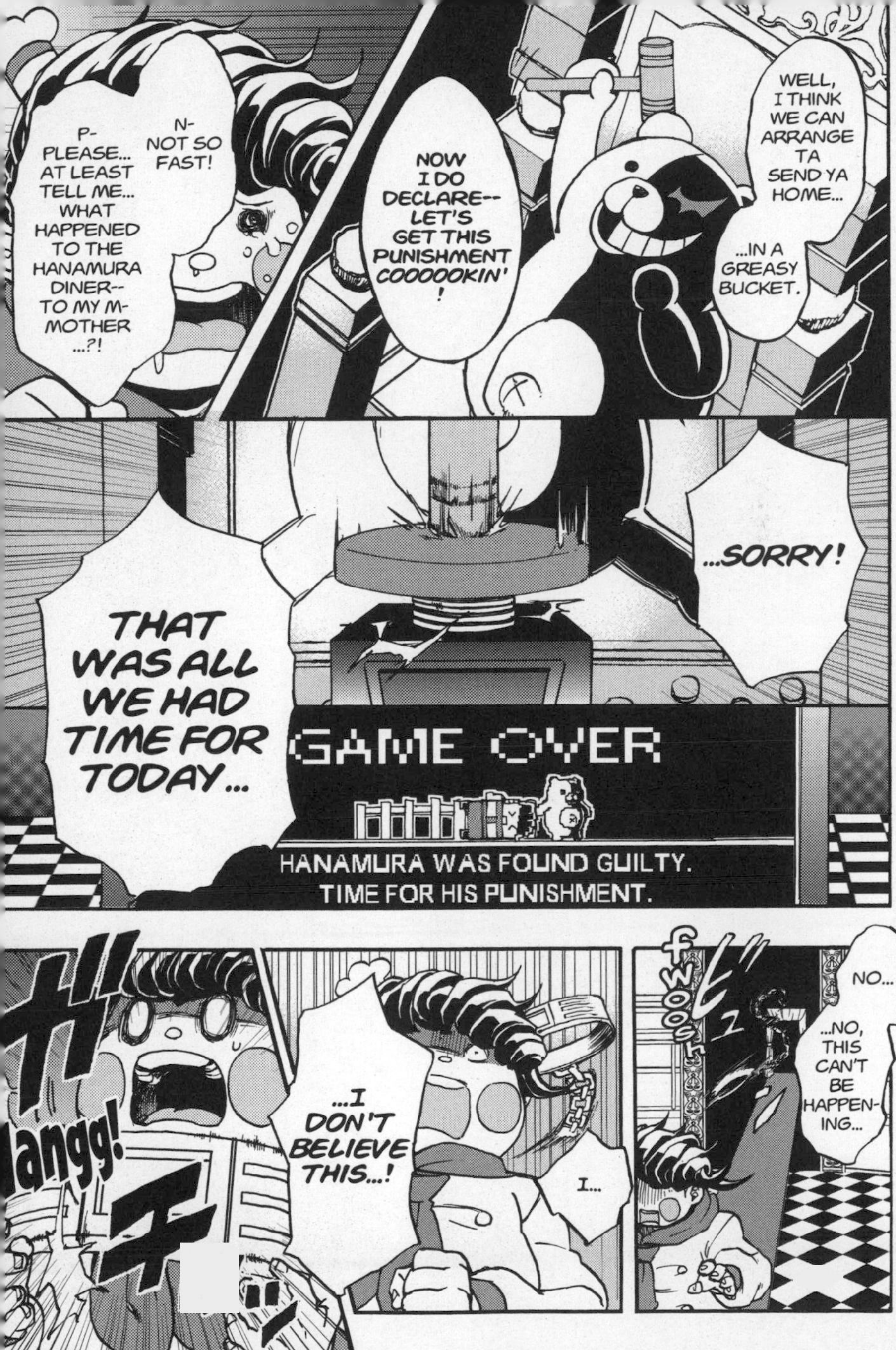
WELL, I THINK WE CAN ARRANGE TA SEND YA HOME...
...IN A GREASY BUCKET.
NOW I DO DECLARE-- LET'S GET THIS PUNISHMENT COOOOOKIN' !
N- NOT SO FAST!
P- PLEASE... AT LEAST TELL ME... WHAT HAPPENED TO THE HANAMURA DINER-- TO MY M- MOTHER ...?!
...SORRY!
THAT WAS ALL WE HAD TIME FOR TODAY...
GAME OVER
HANAMURA WAS FOUND GUILTY.
TIME FOR HIS PUNISHMENT.
fwoosh
NO...
...NO, THIS CAN'T BE HAPPENING...
I...
...I DON'T BELIEVE THIS...!
angg!

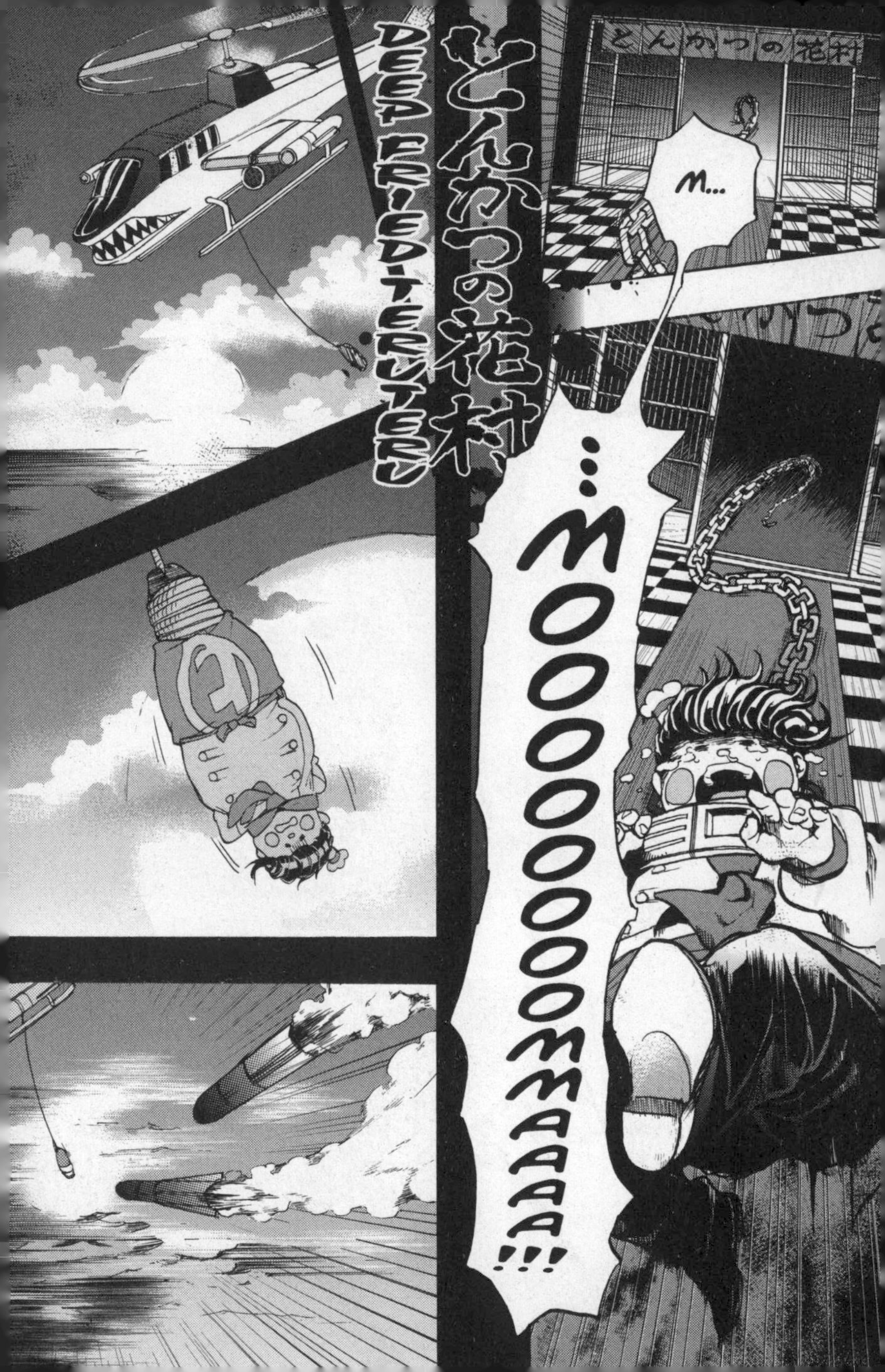
とんかつの花村
M...
...MOOOOOOOOOMMAAAA!!!
とんかつの花村
DEEP FRIED-TERUTERU

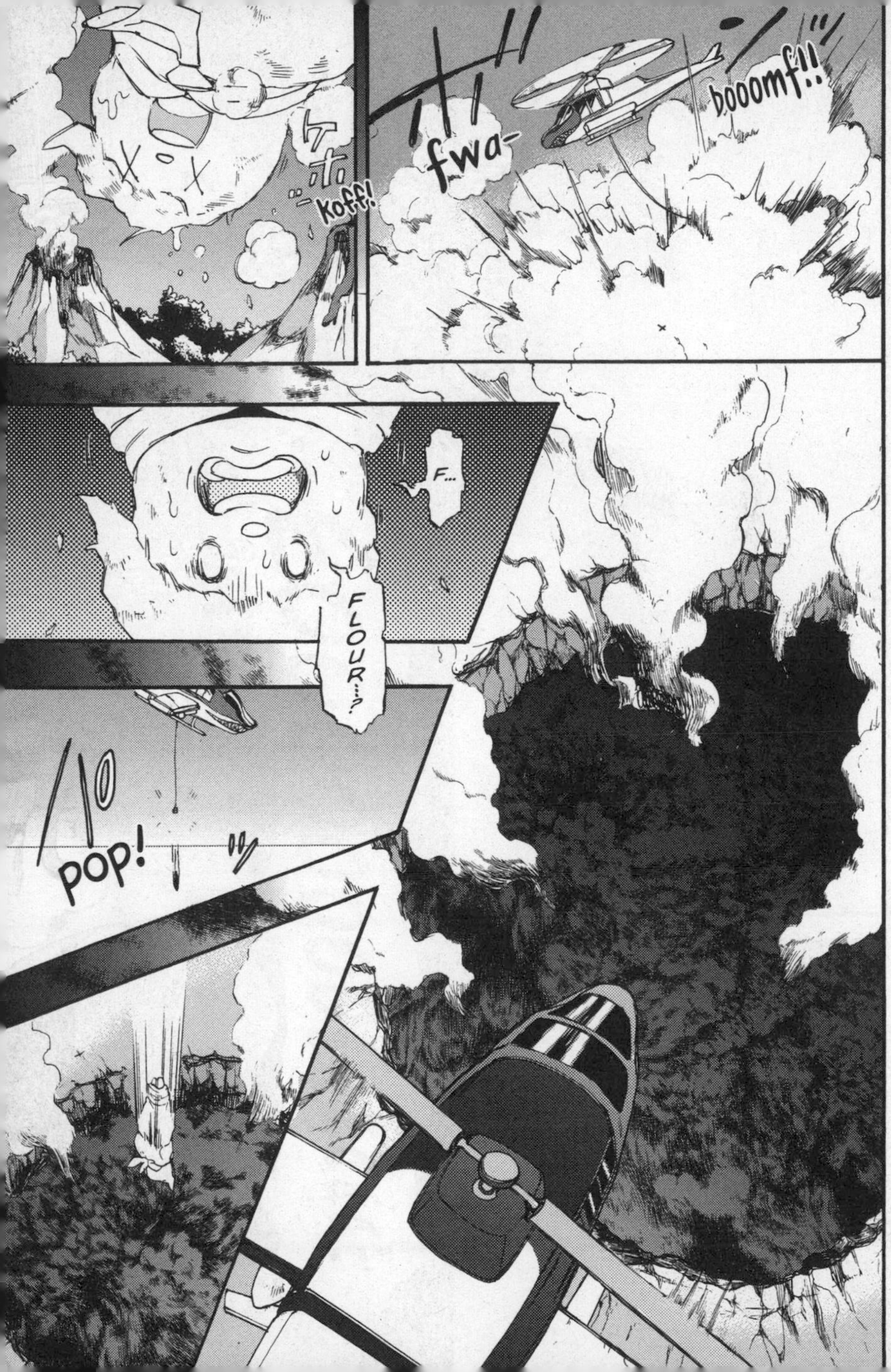
booomf!!
fwa-
ケホ
koff!
F...
FLOUR...?
POP!

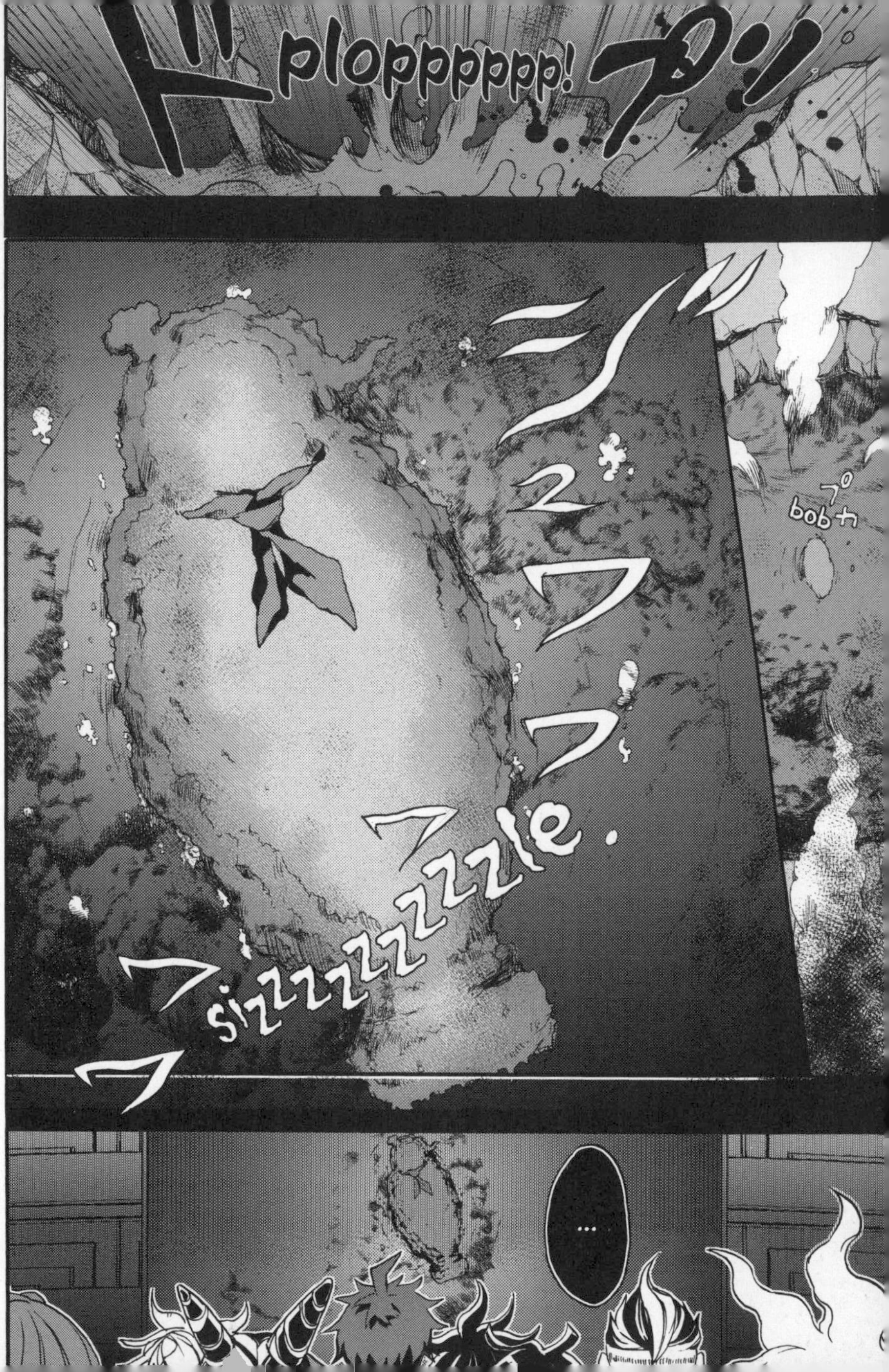
ドッ plopppppp! プッ!!
ジュワワワワ
sizzzzzzzzzzzle.
プカ bob
...

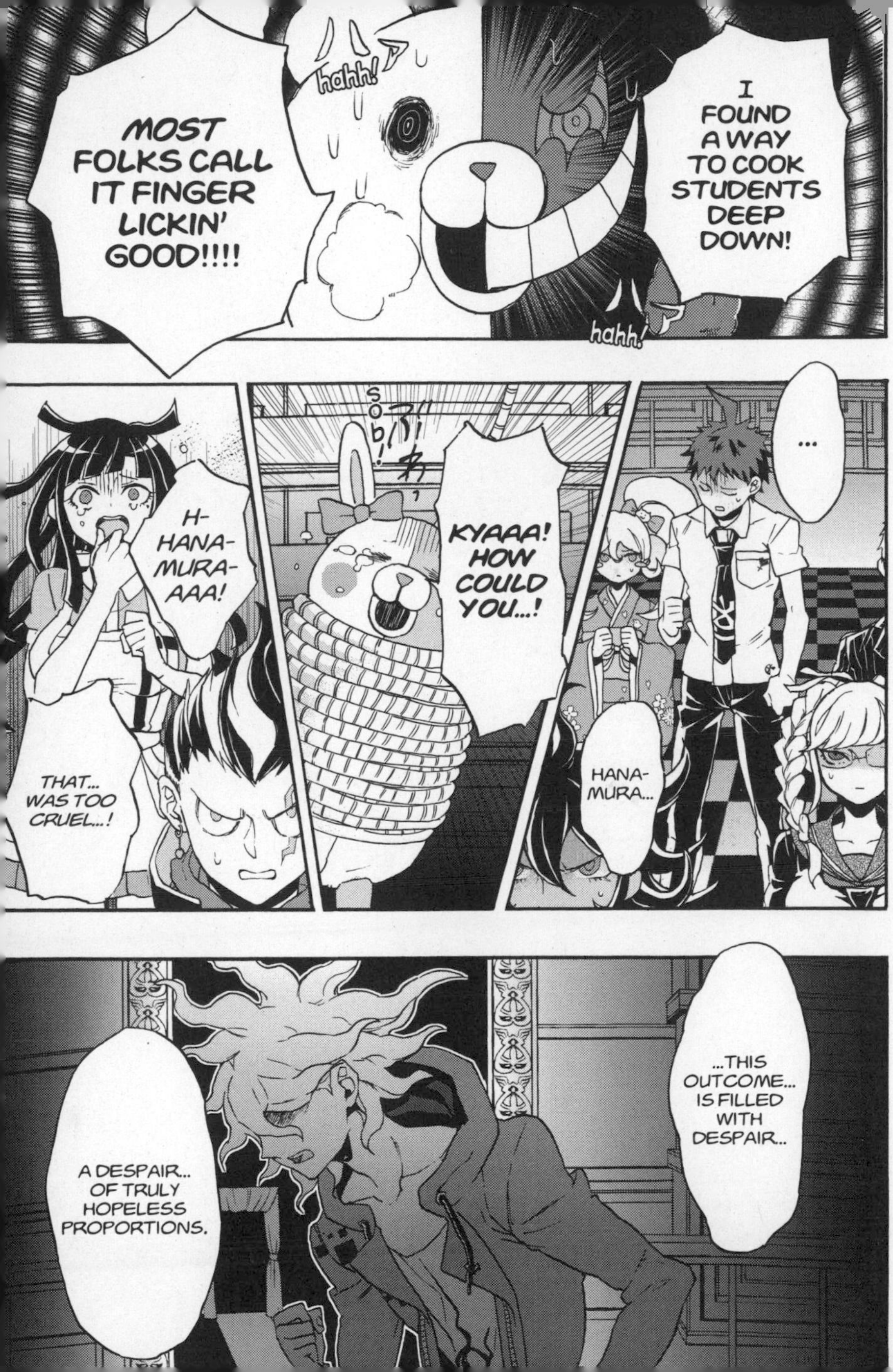
I FOUND A WAY TO COOK STUDENTS DEEP DOWN!
hahh!
MOST FOLKS CALL IT FINGER LICKIN' GOOD!!!!
hahh!
...
HANA-MURA...
sob
KYAAA! HOW COULD YOU...!
H-HANA-MURA-AAA!
THAT... WAS TOO CRUEL...!
...THIS OUTCOME... IS FILLED WITH DESPAIR...
A DESPAIR... OF TRULY HOPELESS PROPORTIONS.

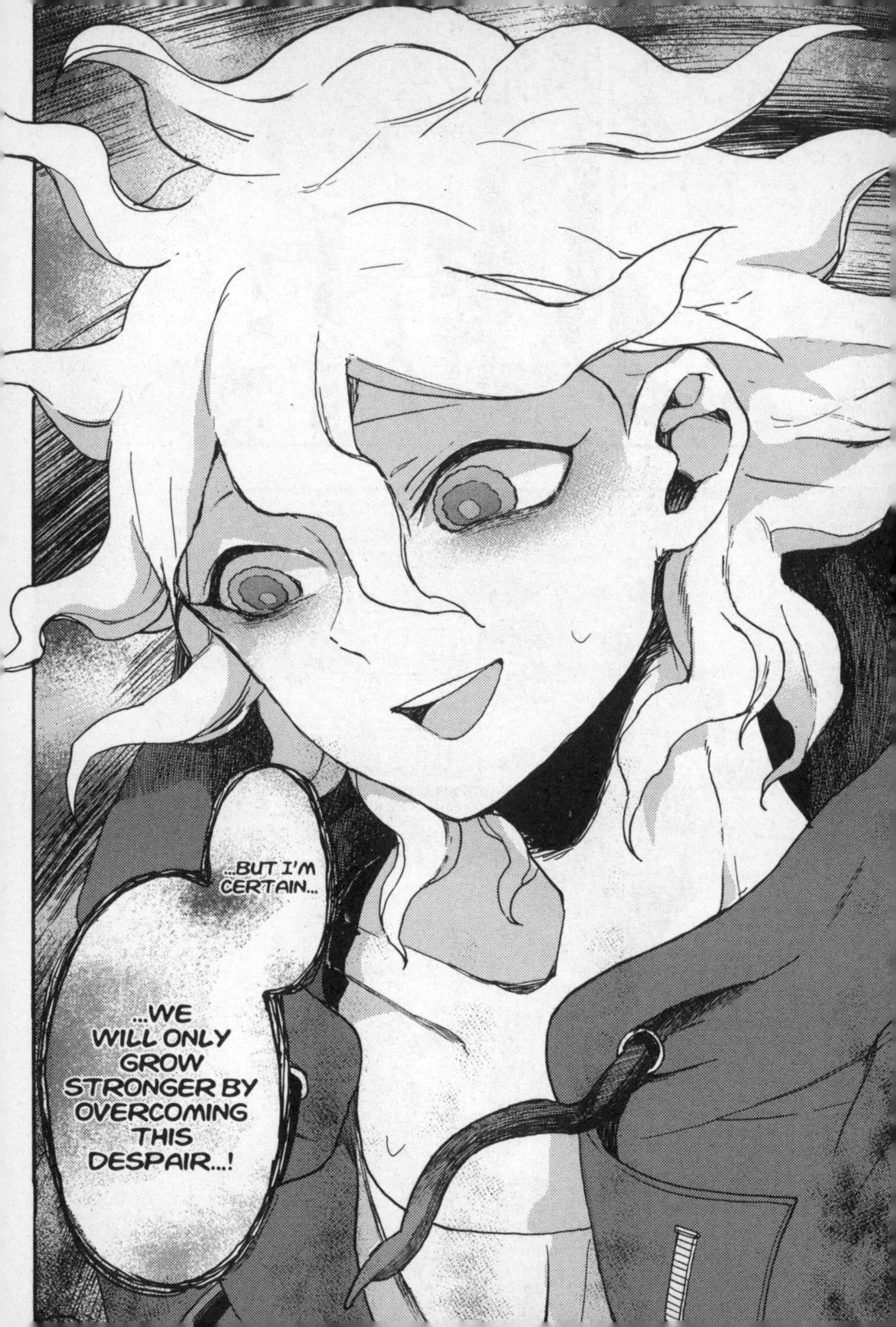
...BUT I'M CERTAIN...
...WE WILL ONLY GROW STRONGER BY OVERCOMING THIS DESPAIR...!

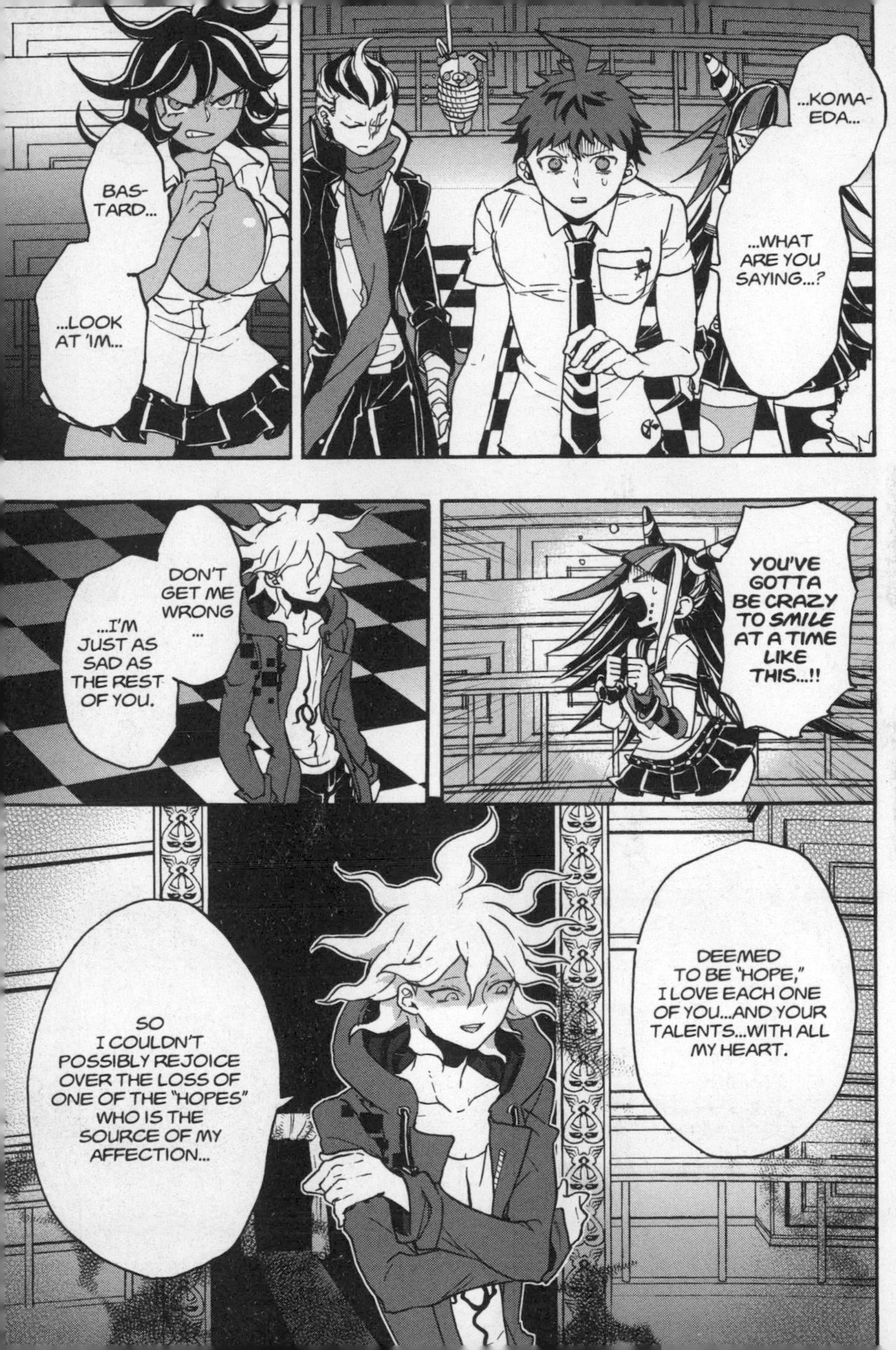
...KOMA-EDA...
...WHAT ARE YOU SAYING...?
BAS-TARD...
...LOOK AT 'IM...
YOU'VE GOTTA BE CRAZY TO SMILE AT A TIME LIKE THIS...!!
DON'T GET ME WRONG ...
...I'M JUST AS SAD AS THE REST OF YOU.
DEEMED TO BE "HOPE," I LOVE EACH ONE OF YOU...AND YOUR TALENTS...WITH ALL MY HEART.
SO I COULDN'T POSSIBLY REJOICE OVER THE LOSS OF ONE OF THE "HOPES" WHO IS THE SOURCE OF MY AFFECTION...

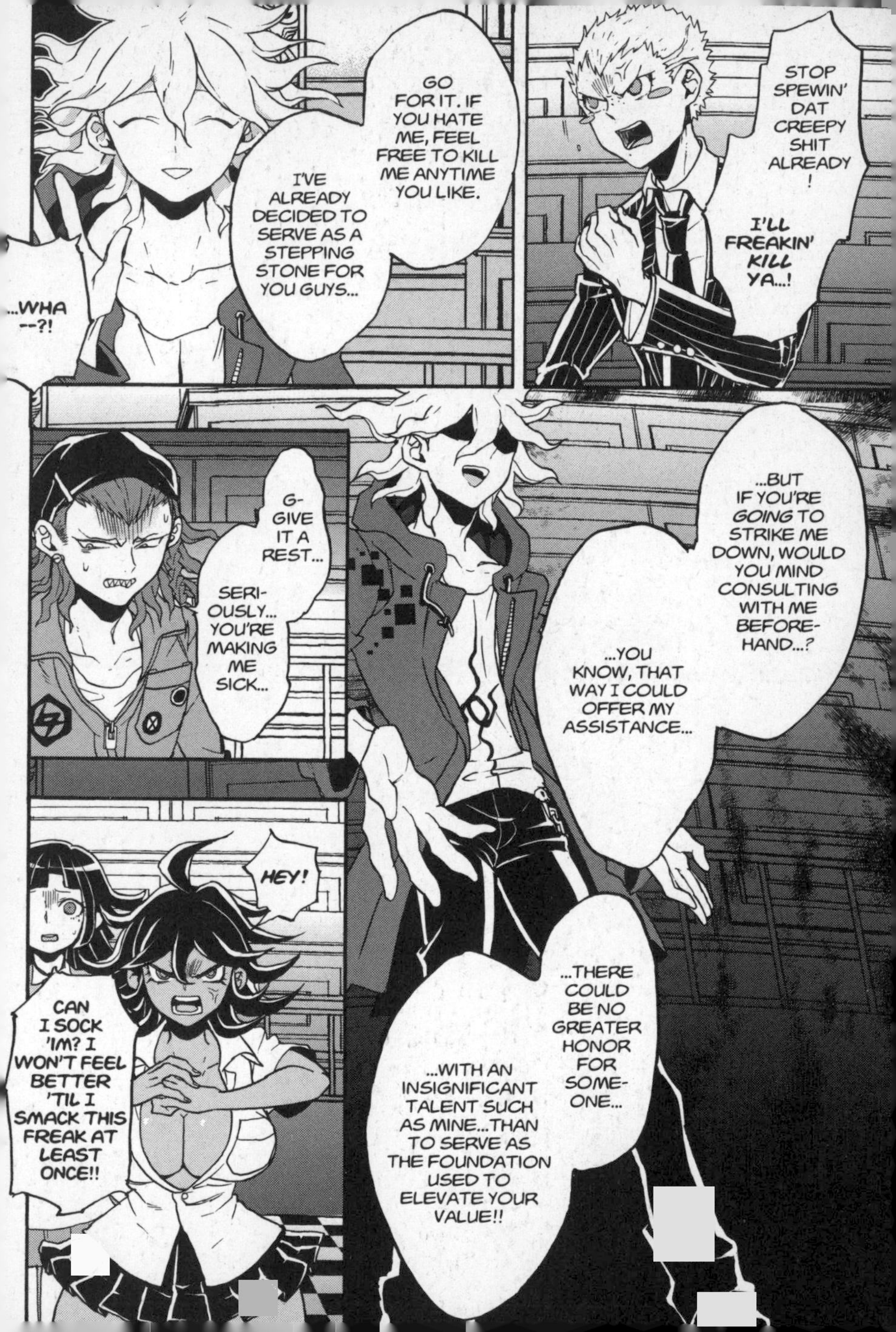
STOP SPEWIN' DAT CREEPY SHIT ALREADY!
I'LL FREAKIN' KILL YA...!
GO FOR IT. IF YOU HATE ME, FEEL FREE TO KILL ME ANYTIME YOU LIKE.
I'VE ALREADY DECIDED TO SERVE AS A STEPPING STONE FOR YOU GUYS...
...WHA--?!
...BUT IF YOU'RE *GOING* TO STRIKE ME DOWN, WOULD YOU MIND CONSULTING WITH ME BEFOREHAND...?
...YOU KNOW, THAT WAY I COULD OFFER MY ASSISTANCE...
...THERE COULD BE NO GREATER HONOR FOR SOMEONE...
...WITH AN INSIGNIFICANT TALENT SUCH AS MINE...THAN TO SERVE AS THE FOUNDATION USED TO ELEVATE YOUR VALUE!!
G-GIVE IT A REST...
SERIOUSLY... YOU'RE MAKING ME SICK...
HEY!
CAN I SOCK 'IM? I WON'T FEEL BETTER 'TIL I SMACK THIS FREAK AT LEAST ONCE!!

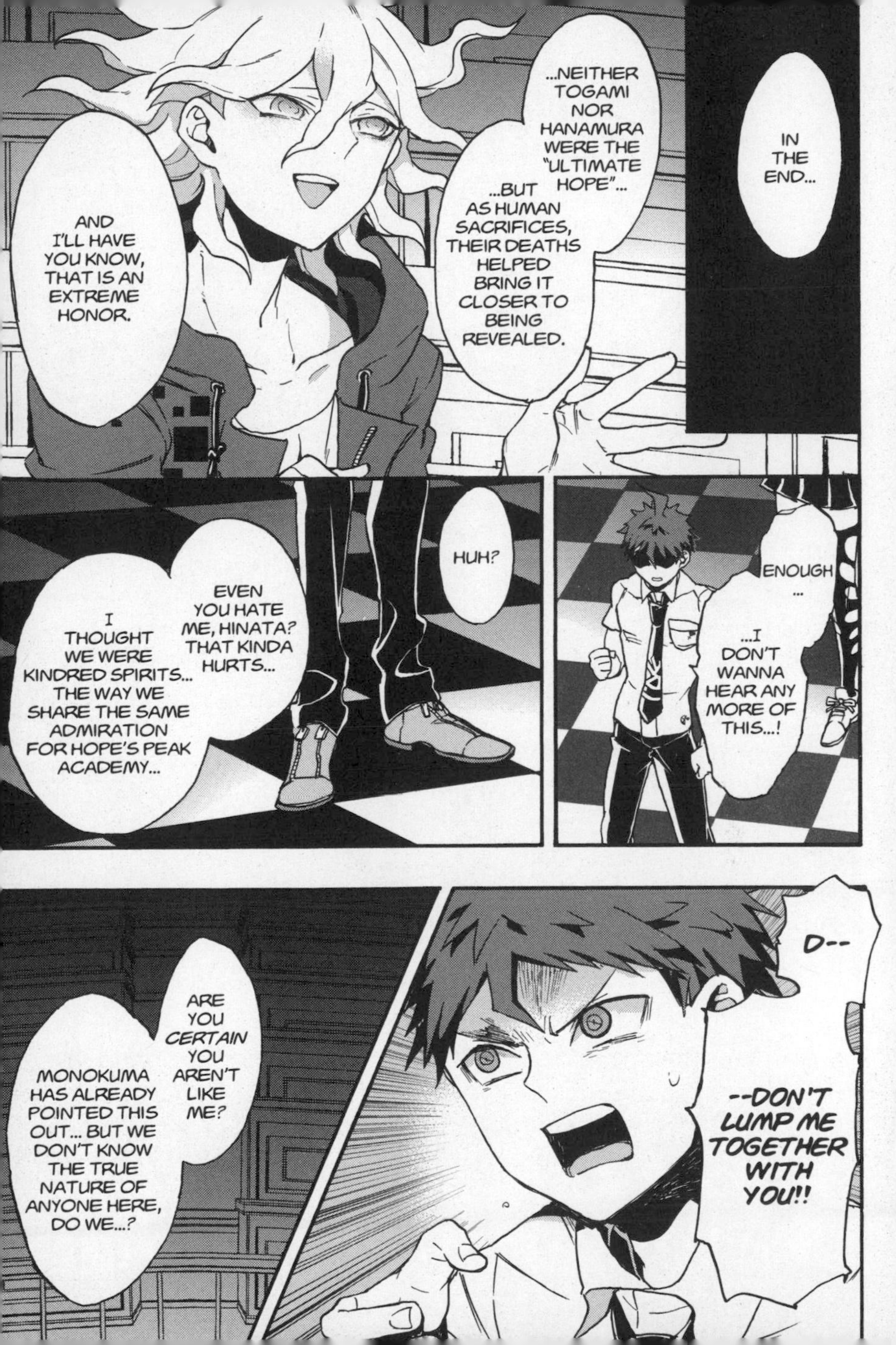
IN THE END...
...NEITHER TOGAMI NOR HANAMURA WERE THE "ULTIMATE HOPE"...
...BUT AS HUMAN SACRIFICES, THEIR DEATHS HELPED BRING IT CLOSER TO BEING REVEALED.
AND I'LL HAVE YOU KNOW, THAT IS AN EXTREME HONOR.
ENOUGH...
...I DON'T WANNA HEAR ANY MORE OF THIS...!
HUH?
EVEN YOU HATE ME, HINATA? THAT KINDA HURTS...
I THOUGHT WE WERE KINDRED SPIRITS... THE WAY WE SHARE THE SAME ADMIRATION FOR HOPE'S PEAK ACADEMY...
D--
--DON'T LUMP ME TOGETHER WITH YOU!!
ARE YOU CERTAIN YOU AREN'T LIKE ME?
MONOKUMA HAS ALREADY POINTED THIS OUT... BUT WE DON'T KNOW THE TRUE NATURE OF ANYONE HERE, DO WE...?

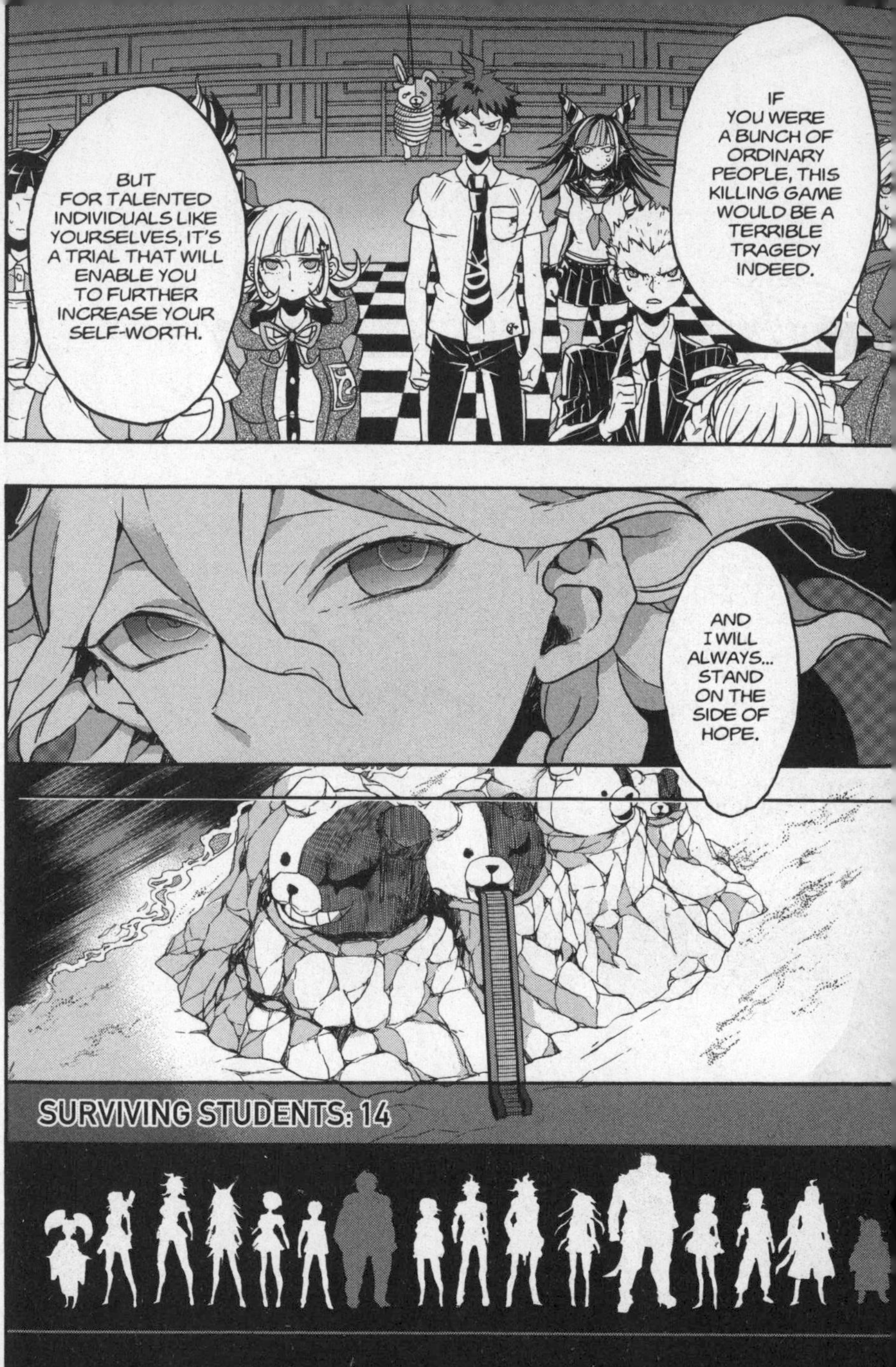
IF YOU WERE A BUNCH OF ORDINARY PEOPLE, THIS KILLING GAME WOULD BE A TERRIBLE TRAGEDY INDEED.
BUT FOR TALENTED INDIVIDUALS LIKE YOURSELVES, IT'S A TRIAL THAT WILL ENABLE YOU TO FURTHER INCREASE YOUR SELF-WORTH.
AND I WILL ALWAYS... STAND ON THE SIDE OF HOPE.
SURVIVING STUDENTS: 14

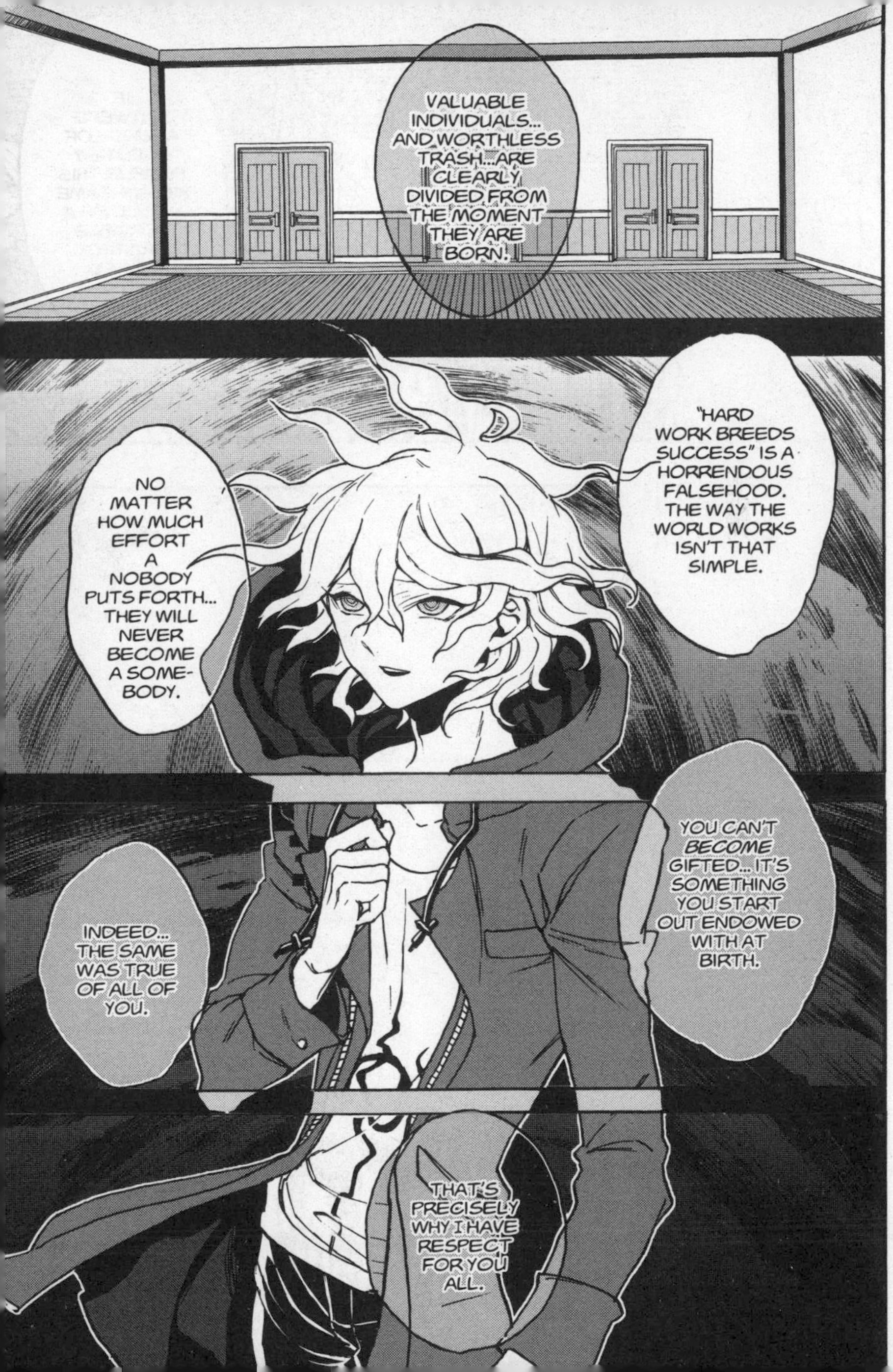
VALUABLE INDIVIDUALS... AND WORTHLESS TRASH...ARE CLEARLY DIVIDED FROM THE MOMENT THEY ARE BORN.
"HARD WORK BREEDS SUCCESS" IS A HORRENDOUS FALSEHOOD. THE WAY THE WORLD WORKS ISN'T THAT SIMPLE.
NO MATTER HOW MUCH EFFORT A NOBODY PUTS FORTH... THEY WILL NEVER BECOME A SOME-BODY.
YOU CAN'T *BECOME* GIFTED... IT'S SOMETHING YOU START OUT ENDOWED WITH AT BIRTH.
INDEED... THE SAME WAS TRUE OF ALL OF YOU.
THAT'S PRECISELY WHY I HAVE RESPECT FOR YOU ALL.

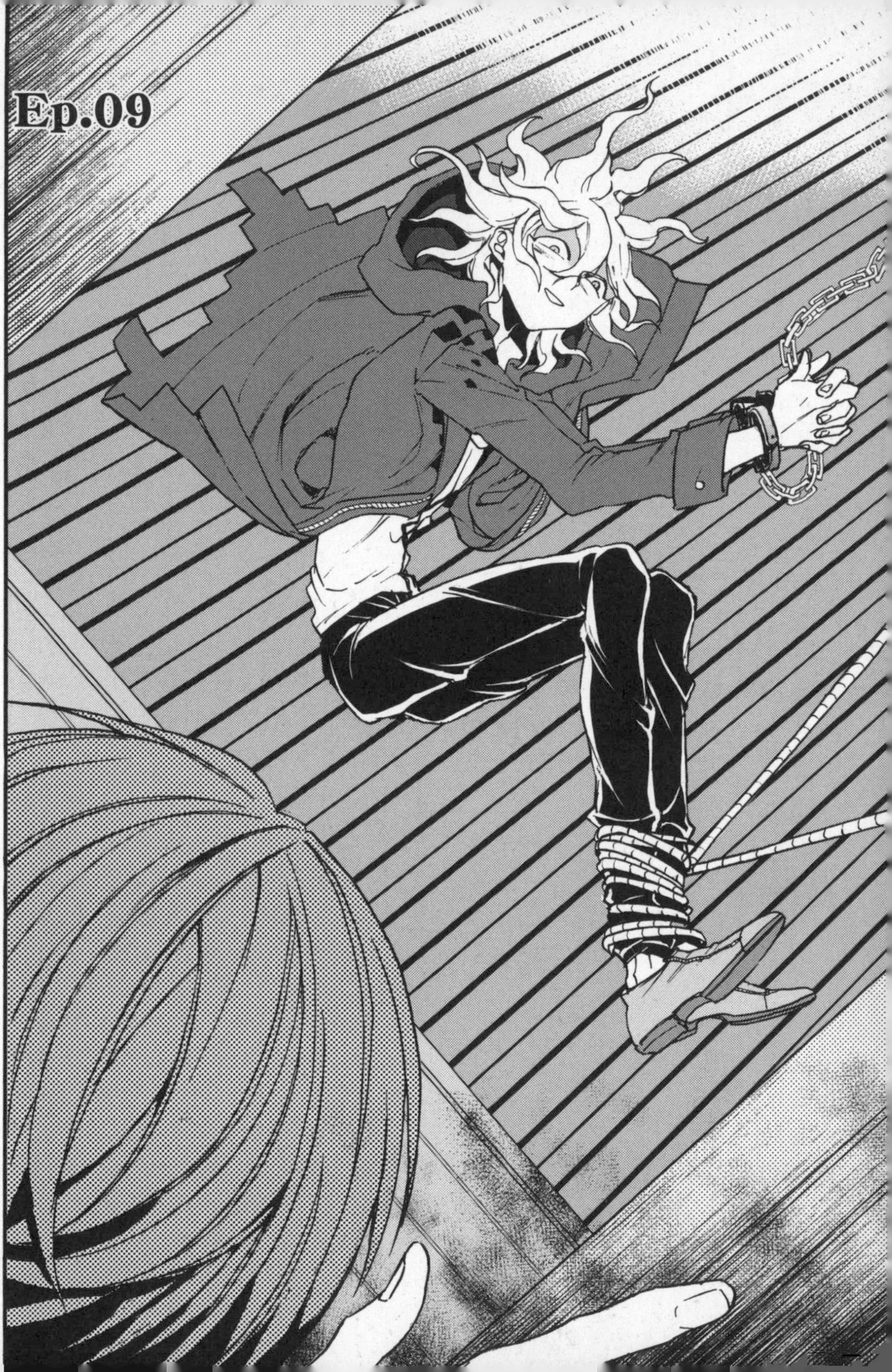
Ep.09

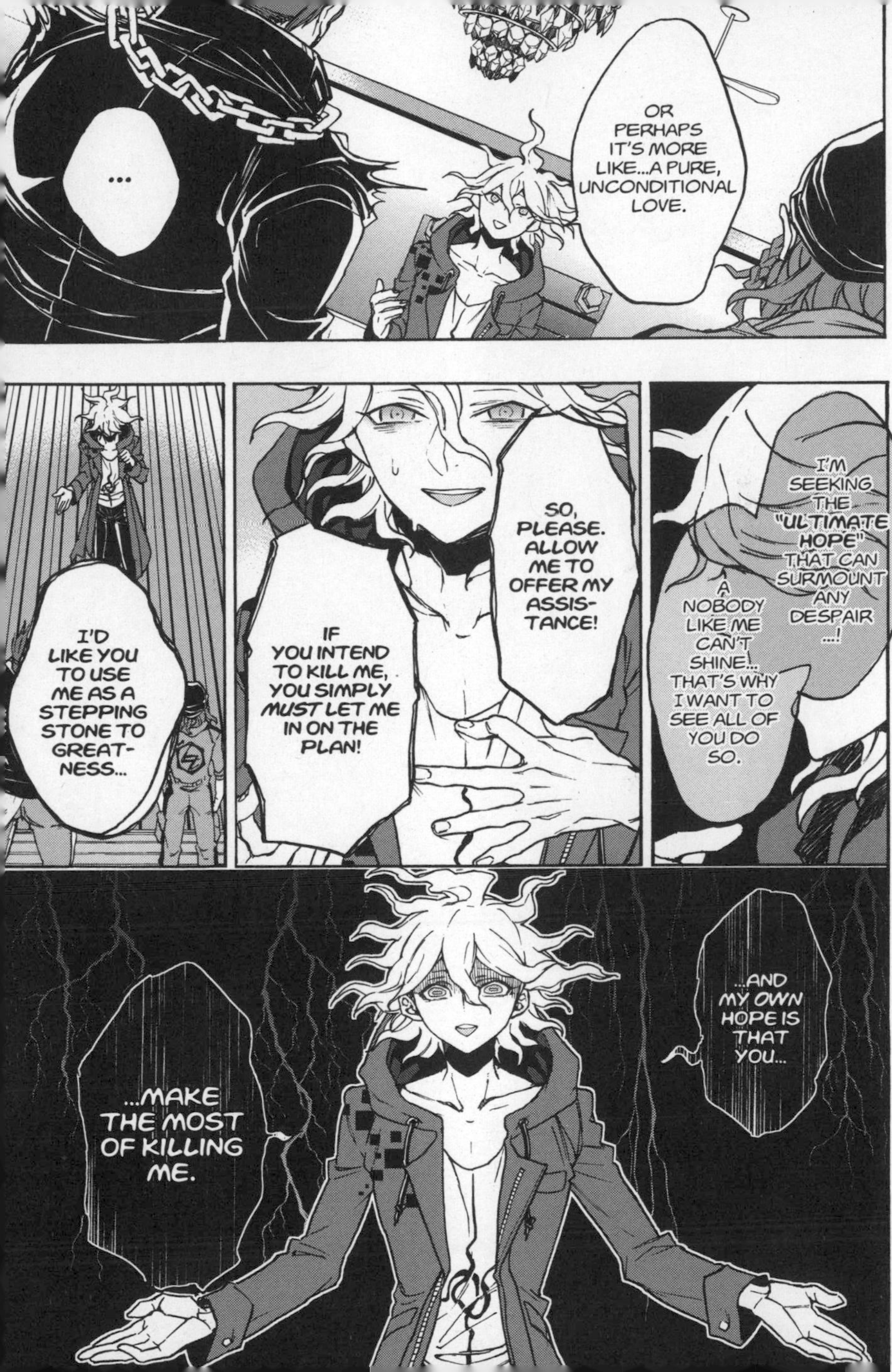
OR PERHAPS IT'S MORE LIKE...A PURE, UNCONDITIONAL LOVE.
...
I'M SEEKING THE "ULTIMATE HOPE" THAT CAN SURMOUNT ANY DESPAIR...!
A NOBODY LIKE ME CAN'T SHINE... THAT'S WHY I WANT TO SEE ALL OF YOU DO SO.
SO, PLEASE. ALLOW ME TO OFFER MY ASSISTANCE!
IF YOU INTEND TO KILL ME, YOU SIMPLY *MUST* LET ME IN ON THE PLAN!
I'D LIKE YOU TO USE ME AS A STEPPING STONE TO GREATNESS...
...AND MY OWN HOPE IS THAT YOU...
...MAKE THE MOST OF KILLING ME.

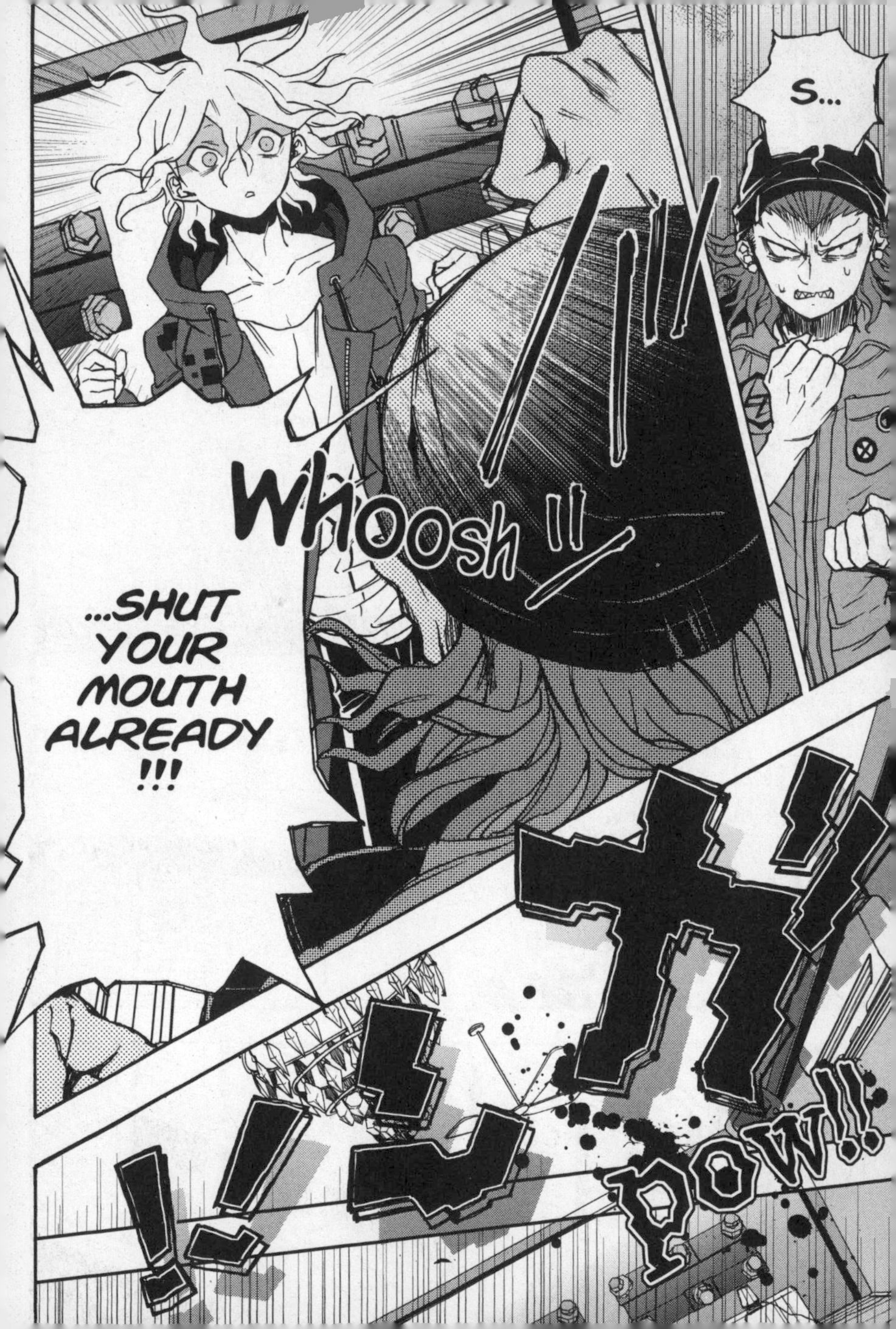
S...
WHOOSH !!
...SHUT YOUR MOUTH ALREADY !!!
POW!!

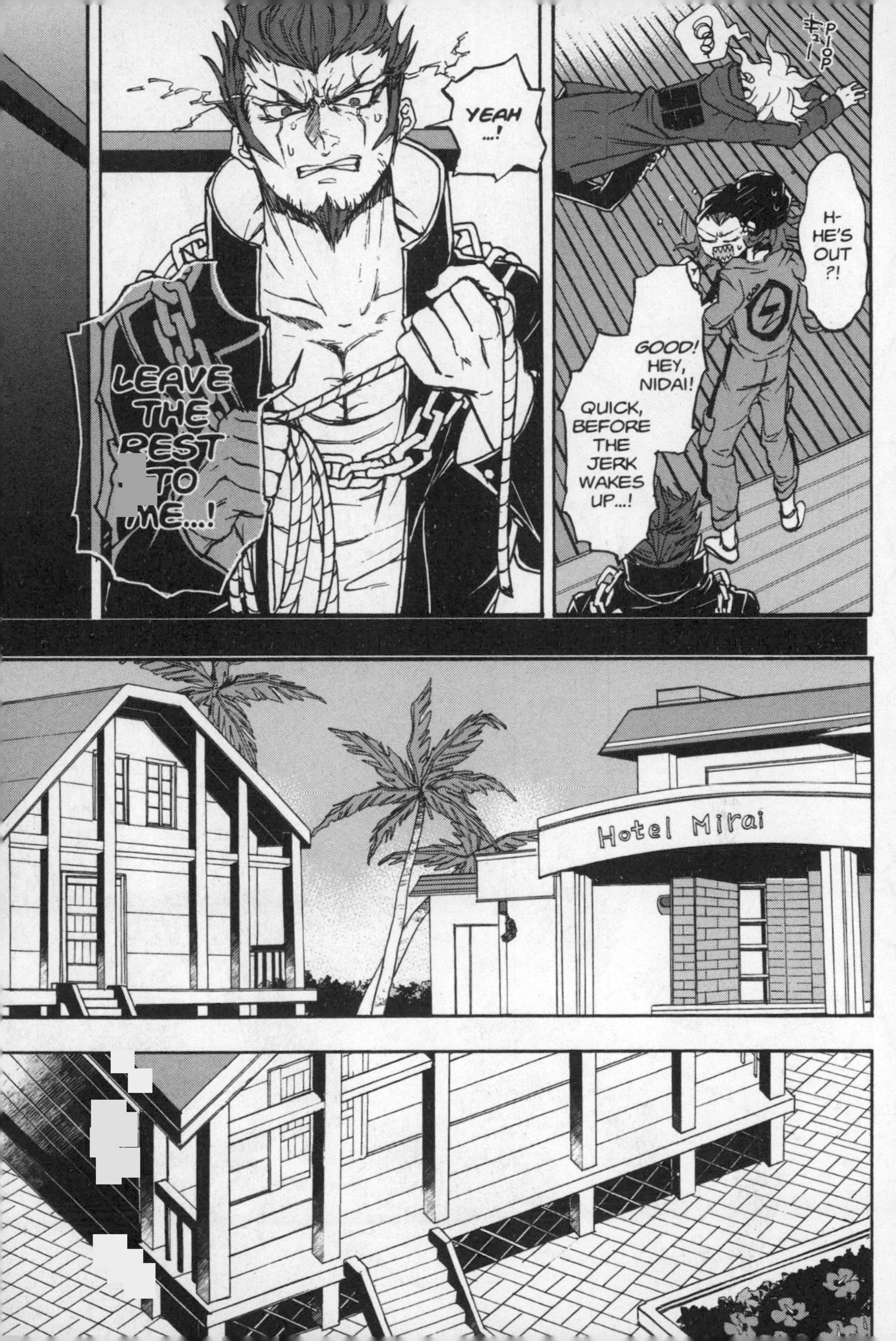
PIOP
H- HE'S OUT ?!
GOOD! HEY, NIDAI!
QUICK, BEFORE THE JERK WAKES UP...!
YEAH ...!
LEAVE THE REST TO ME...!
Hotel Mirai

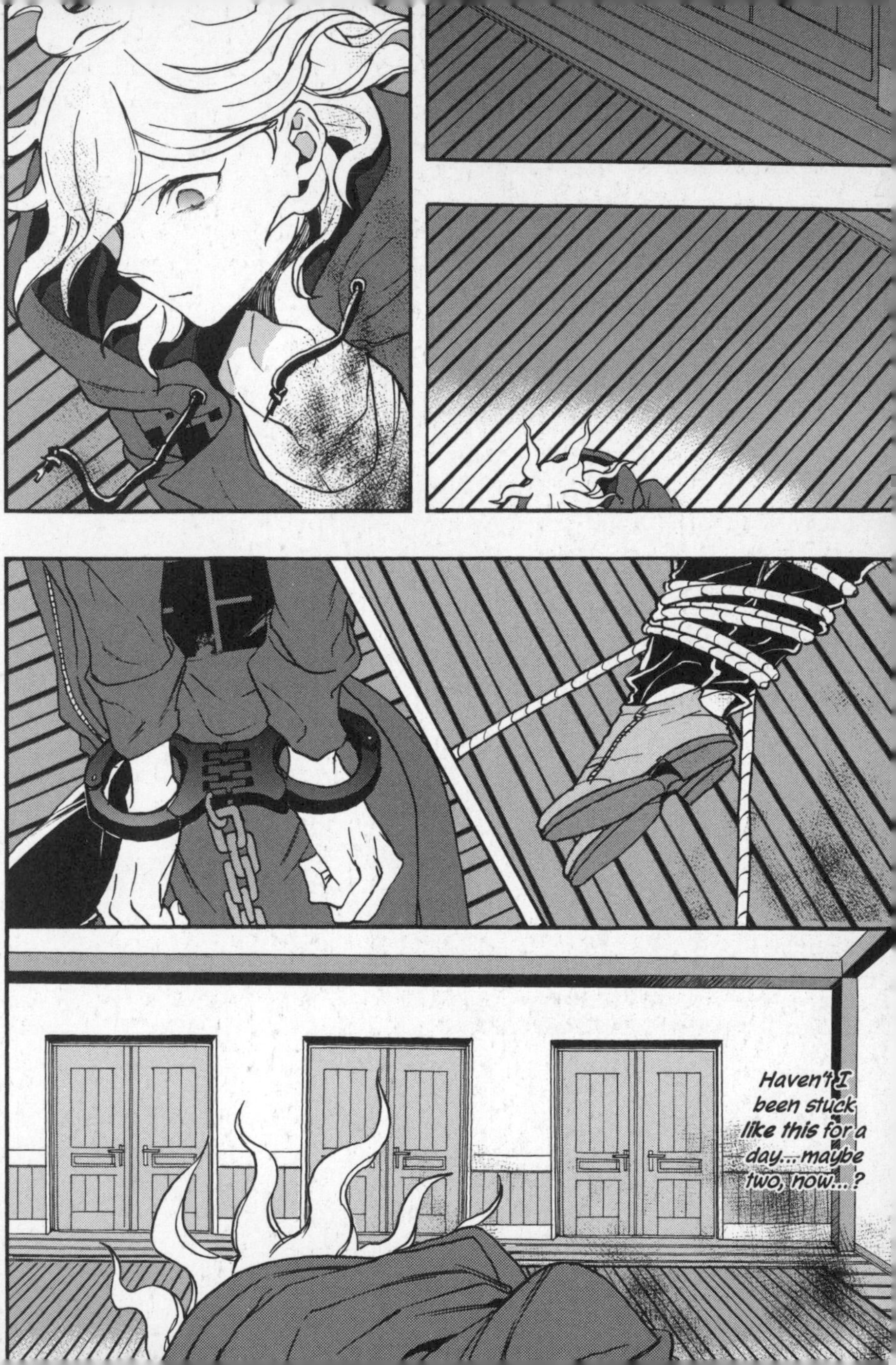
Haven't I been stuck like this for a day... maybe two, now...?

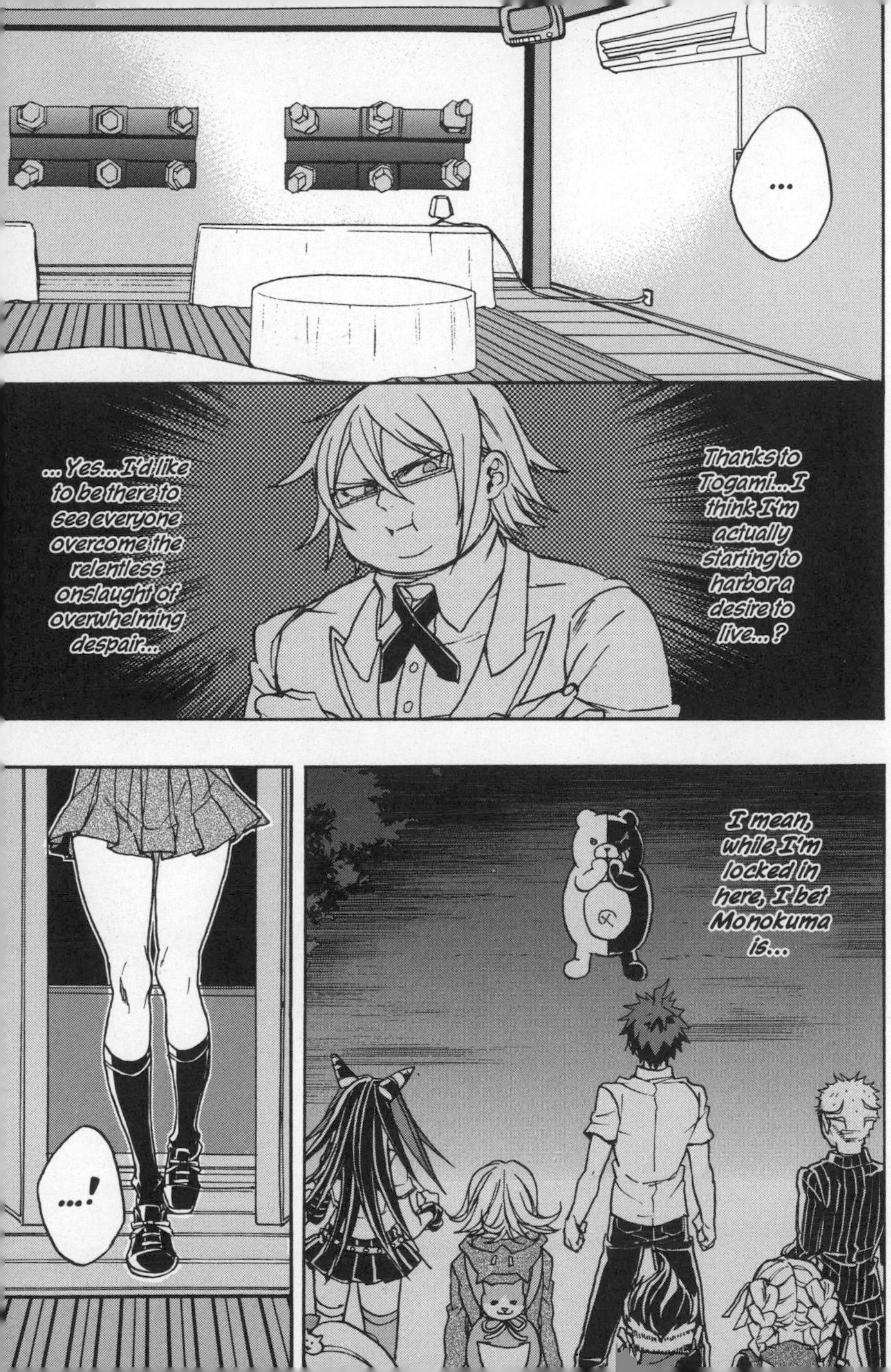
...
Thanks to Togami...I think I'm actually starting to harbor a desire to live...?
...Yes...I'd like to be there to see everyone overcome the relentless onslaught of overwhelming despair...
I mean, while I'm locked in here, I bet Monokuma is...
...!

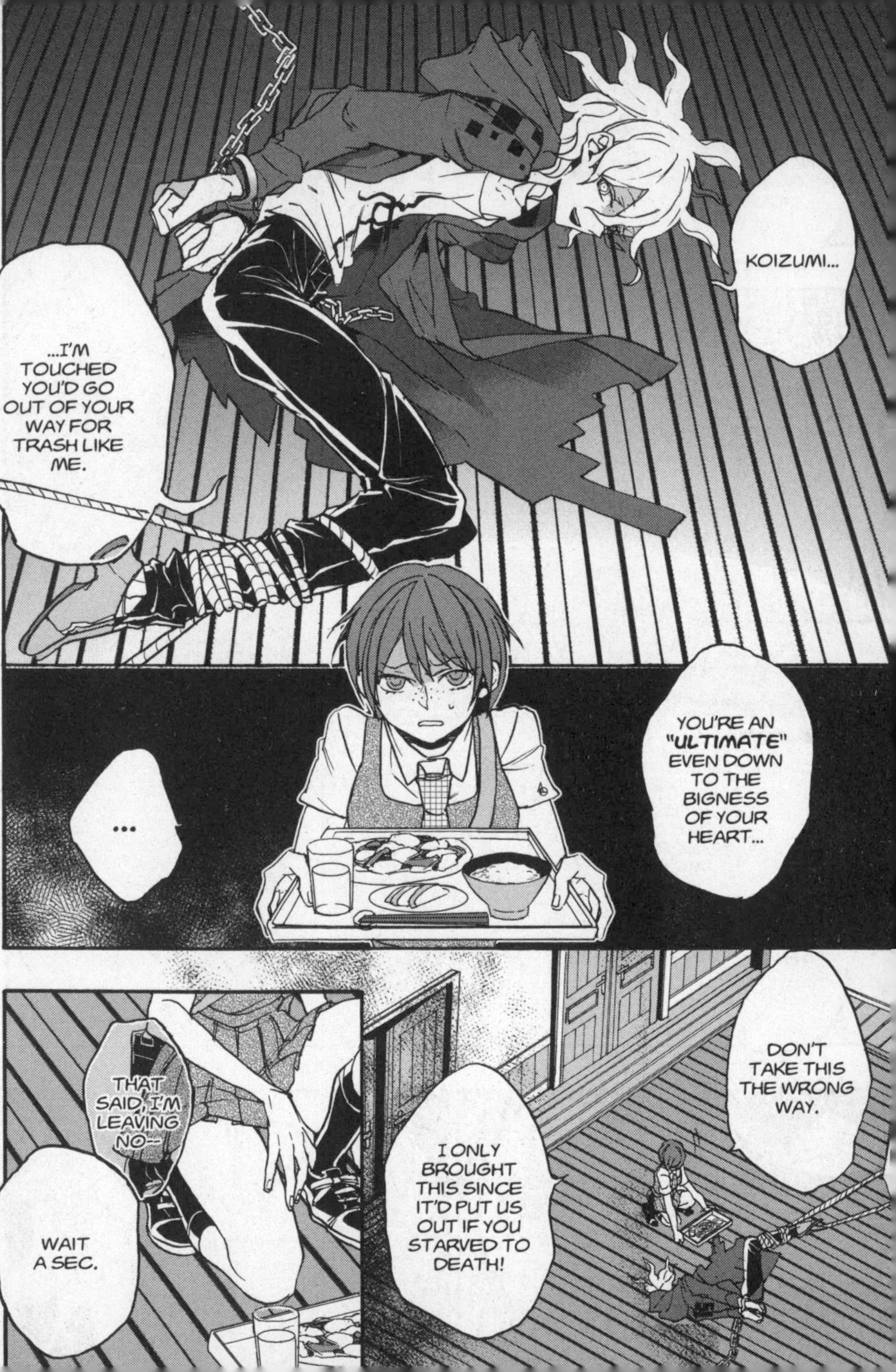
KOIZUMI...
...I'M TOUCHED YOU'D GO OUT OF YOUR WAY FOR TRASH LIKE ME.
YOU'RE AN "ULTIMATE" EVEN DOWN TO THE BIGNESS OF YOUR HEART...
...
DON'T TAKE THIS THE WRONG WAY.
I ONLY BROUGHT THIS SINCE IT'D PUT US OUT IF YOU STARVED TO DEATH!
THAT SAID, I'M LEAVING NO--
WAIT A SEC.

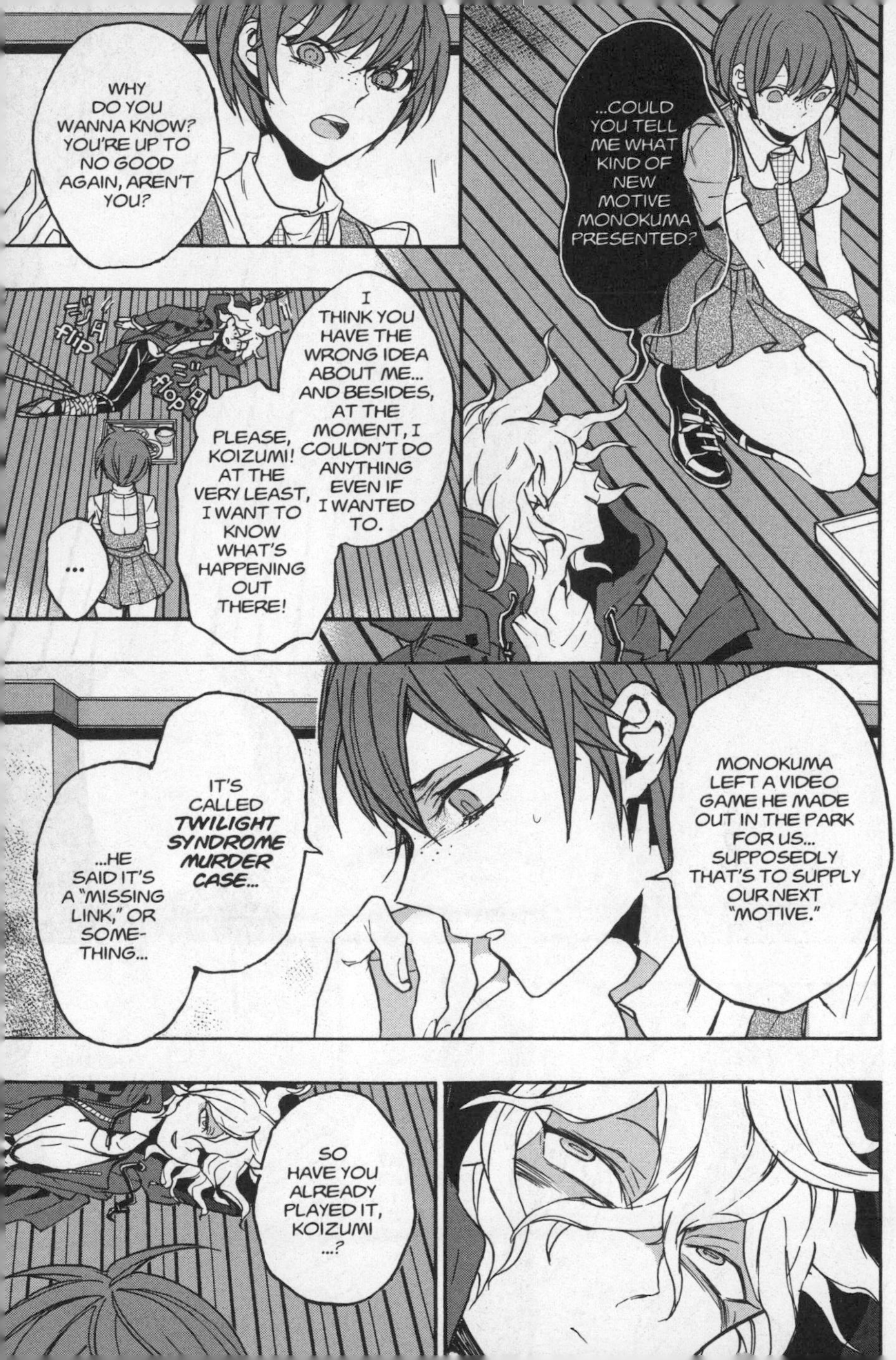
...COULD YOU TELL ME WHAT KIND OF NEW MOTIVE MONOKUMA PRESENTED?
WHY DO YOU WANNA KNOW? YOU'RE UP TO NO GOOD AGAIN, AREN'T YOU?
I THINK YOU HAVE THE WRONG IDEA ABOUT ME... AND BESIDES, AT THE MOMENT, I COULDN'T DO ANYTHING EVEN IF I WANTED TO.
flip
flop
PLEASE, KOIZUMI! AT THE VERY LEAST, I WANT TO KNOW WHAT'S HAPPENING OUT THERE!
...
MONOKUMA LEFT A VIDEO GAME HE MADE OUT IN THE PARK FOR US... SUPPOSEDLY THAT'S TO SUPPLY OUR NEXT "MOTIVE."
IT'S CALLED ***TWILIGHT SYNDROME MURDER CASE***...
...HE SAID IT'S A "MISSING LINK," OR SOME-THING...
SO HAVE YOU ALREADY PLAYED IT, KOIZUMI ...?

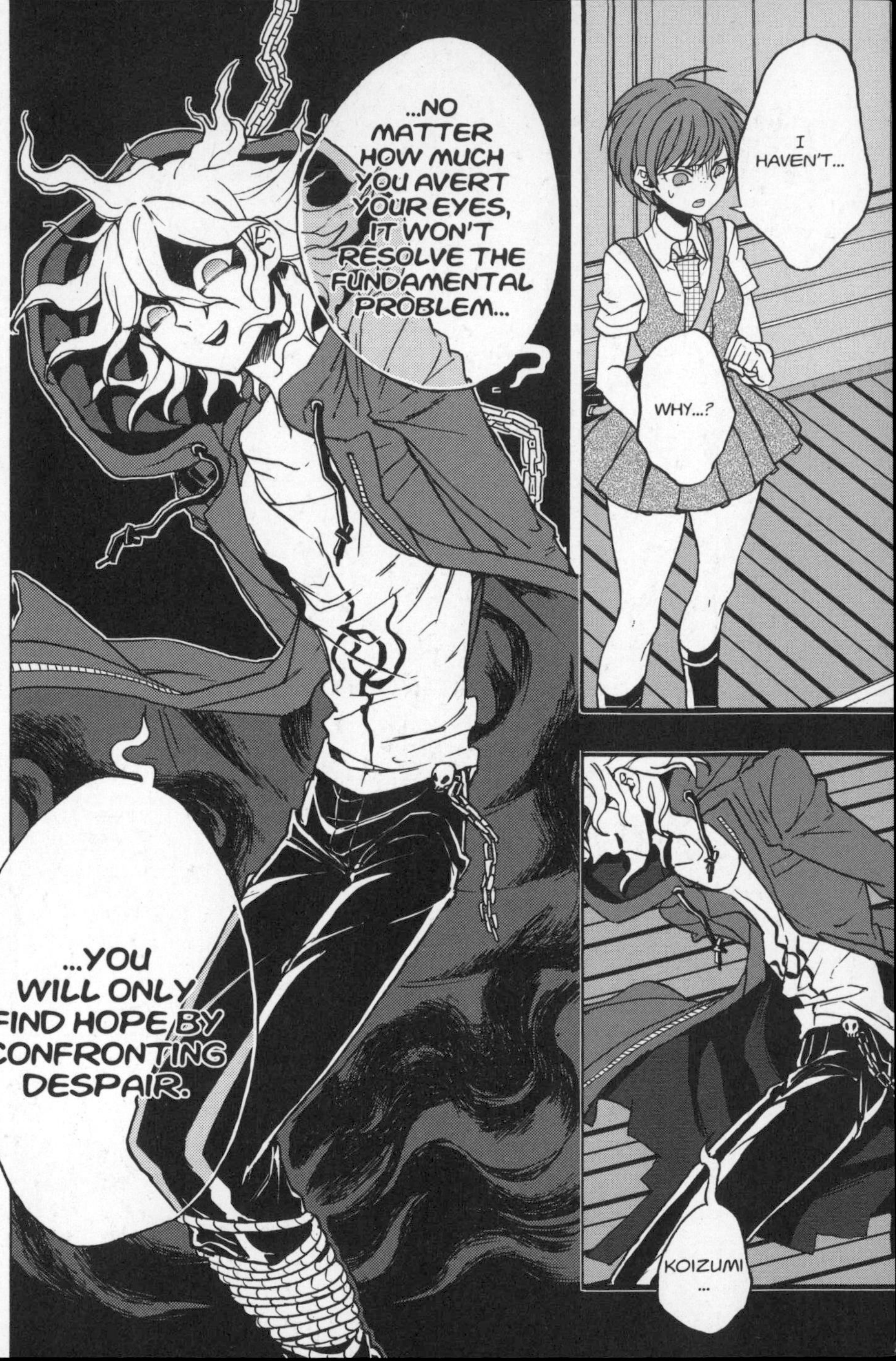
I HAVEN'T...
WHY...?
...NO MATTER HOW MUCH YOU AVERT YOUR EYES, IT WON'T RESOLVE THE FUNDAMENTAL PROBLEM...
KOIZUMI ...
...YOU WILL ONLY FIND HOPE BY CONFRONTING DESPAIR.

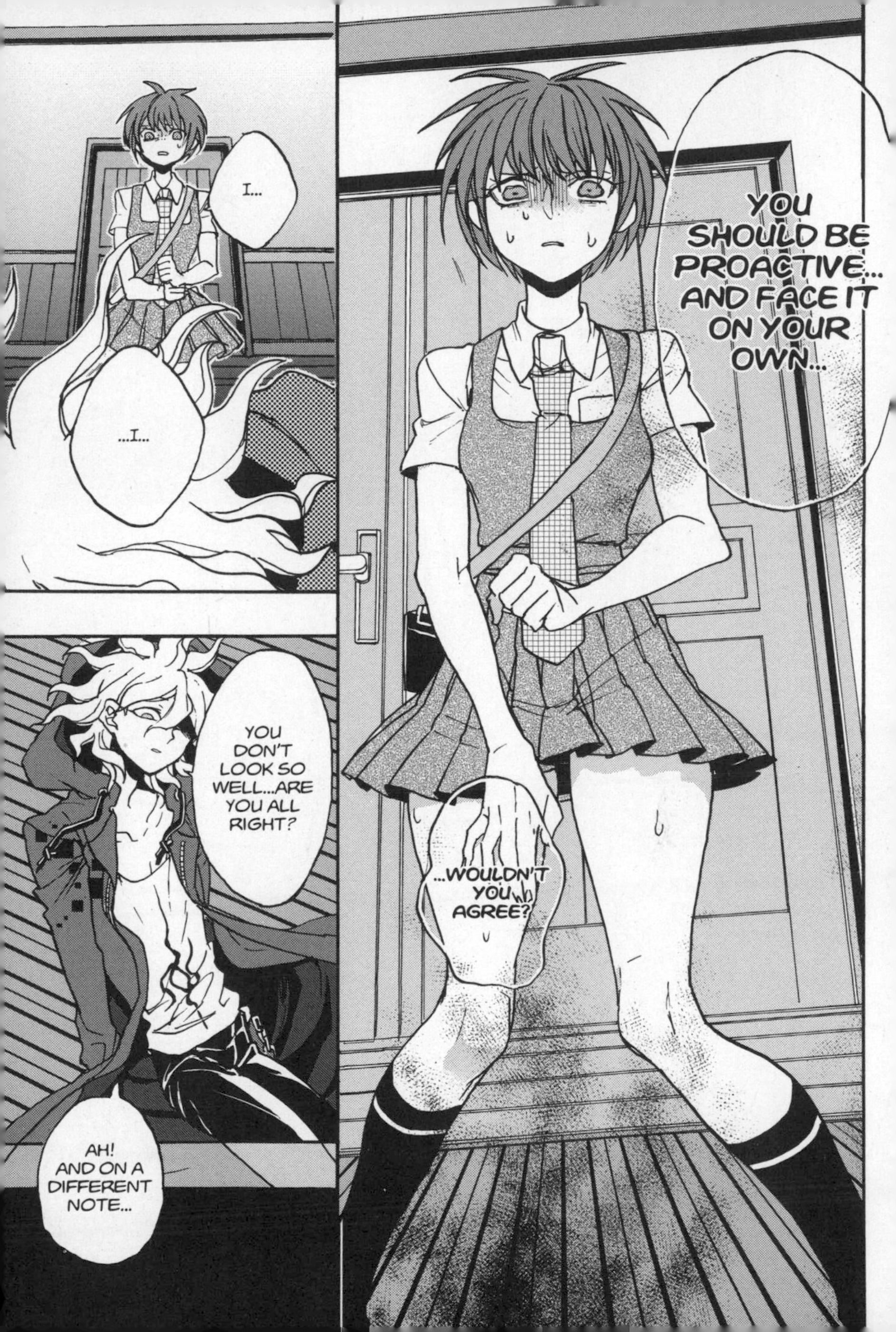
YOU SHOULD BE PROACTIVE... AND FACE IT ON YOUR OWN...
...WOULDN'T YOU AGREE?
I...
...I...
YOU DON'T LOOK SO WELL...ARE YOU ALL RIGHT?
AH! AND ON A DIFFERENT NOTE...

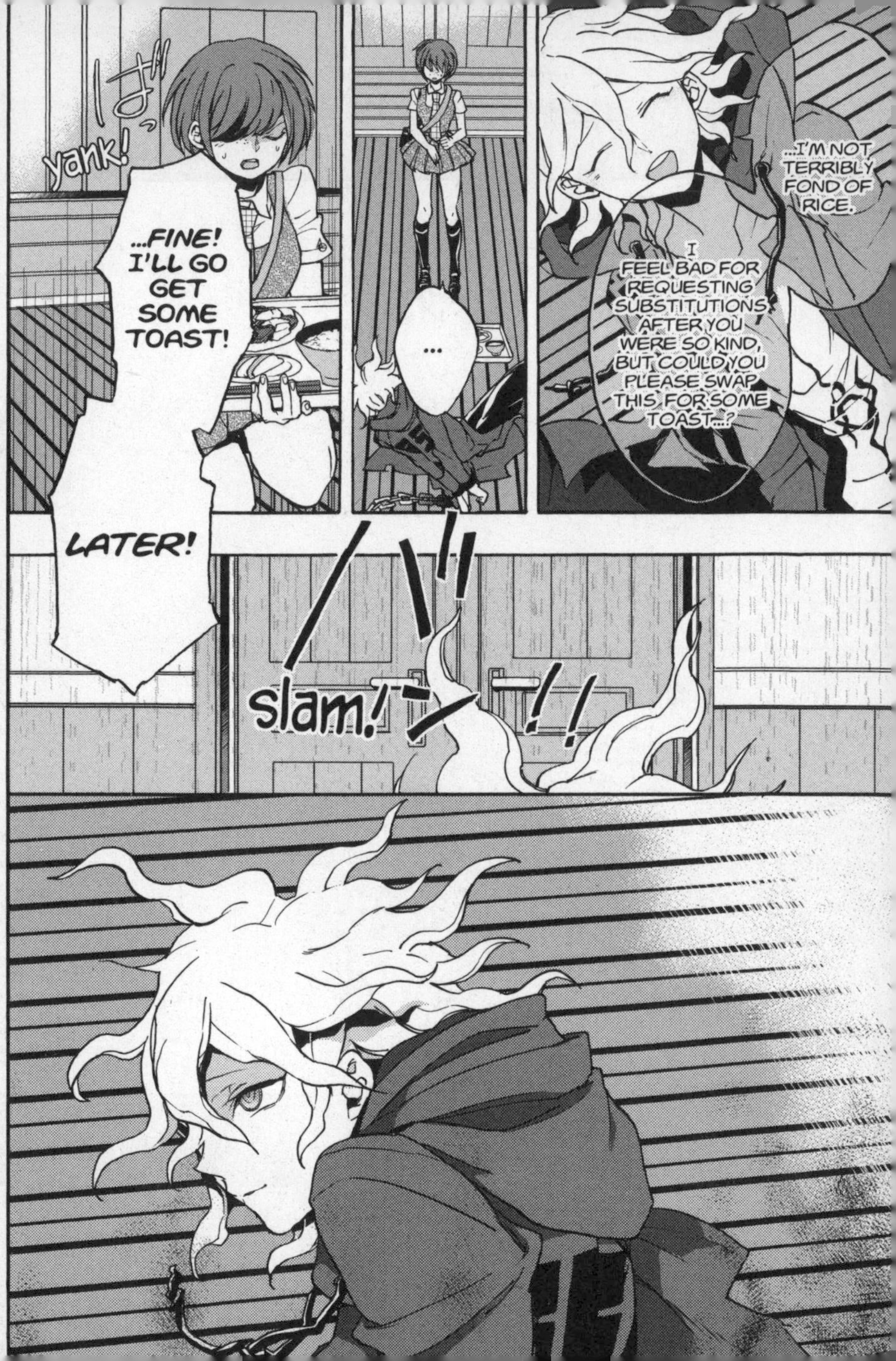
...I'M NOT TERRIBLY FOND OF RICE.
I FEEL BAD FOR REQUESTING SUBSTITUTIONS AFTER YOU WERE SO KIND, BUT COULD YOU PLEASE SWAP THIS FOR SOME TOAST...?
...
yank!
...FINE! I'LL GO GET SOME TOAST!
LATER!
slam!

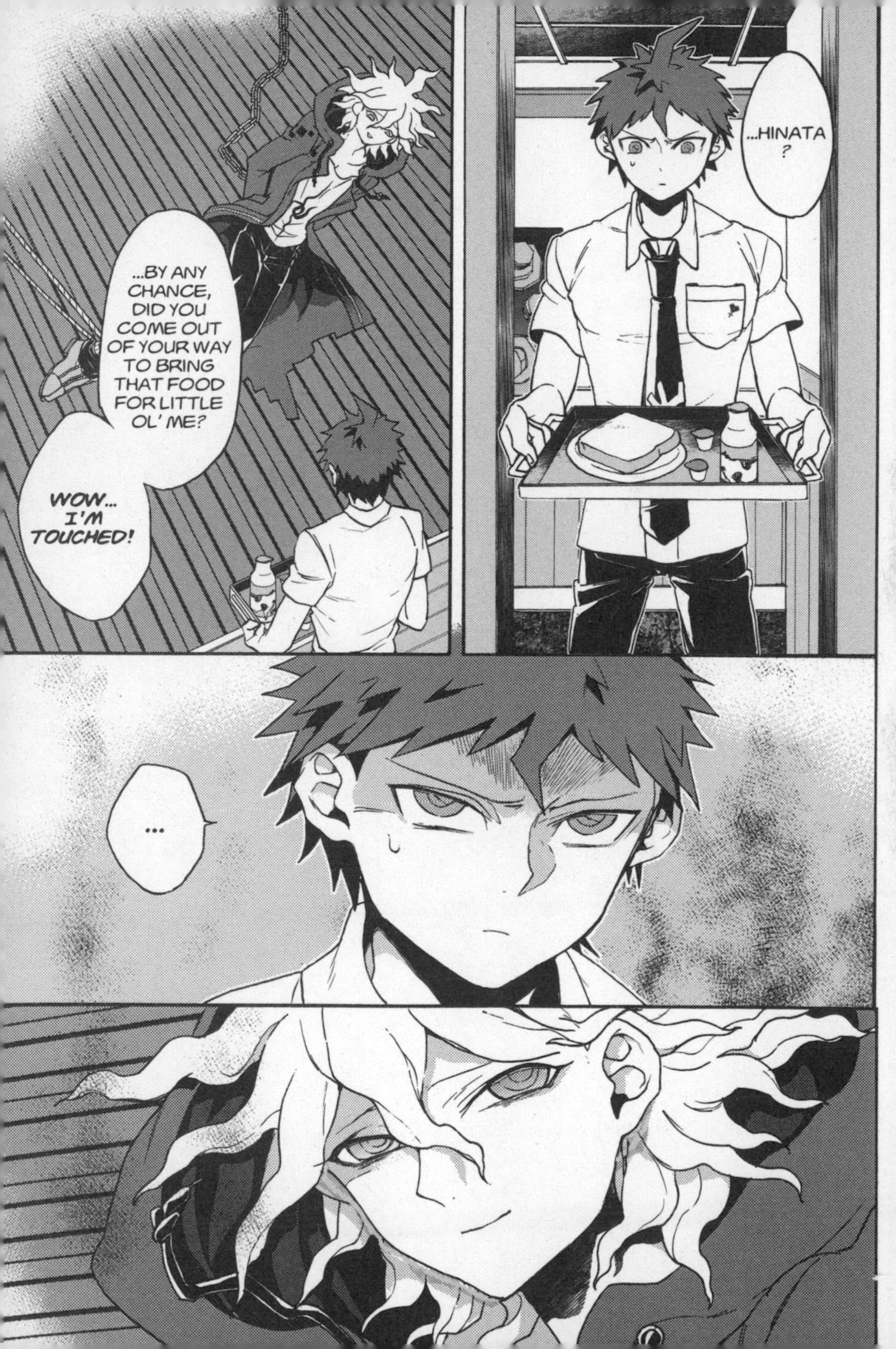
...HINATA?
...BY ANY CHANCE, DID YOU COME OUT OF YOUR WAY TO BRING THAT FOOD FOR LITTLE OL' ME?
WOW... I'M TOUCHED!
...

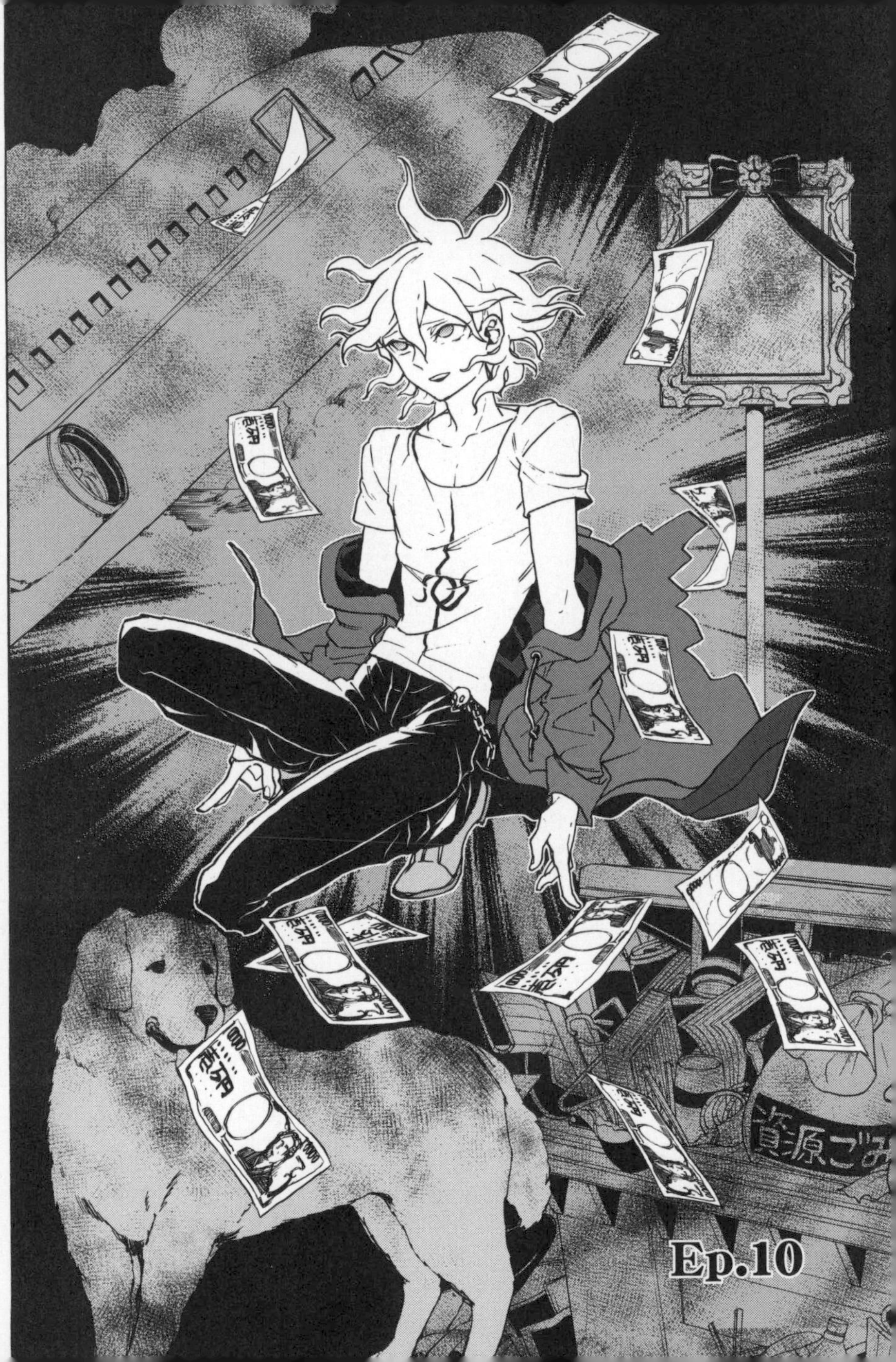
資源ご
Ep.10

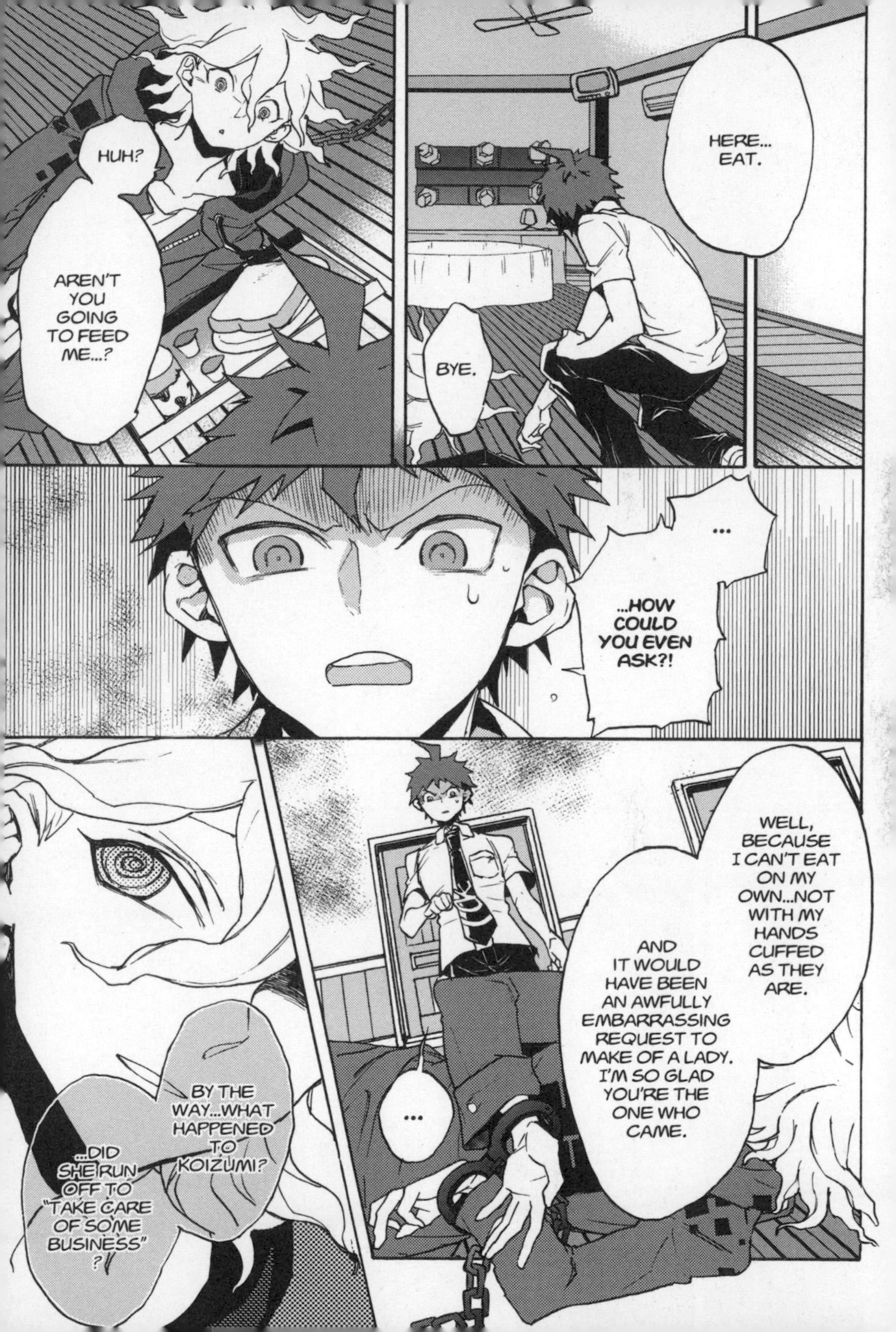
HERE... EAT.
BYE.
HUH?
AREN'T YOU GOING TO FEED ME...?
...
...HOW COULD YOU EVEN ASK?!
WELL, BECAUSE I CAN'T EAT ON MY OWN...NOT WITH MY HANDS CUFFED AS THEY ARE.
AND IT WOULD HAVE BEEN AN AWFULLY EMBARRASSING REQUEST TO MAKE OF A LADY. I'M SO GLAD YOU'RE THE ONE WHO CAME.
...
BY THE WAY...WHAT HAPPENED TO KOIZUMI?
...DID SHE RUN OFF TO "TAKE CARE OF SOME BUSINESS"?

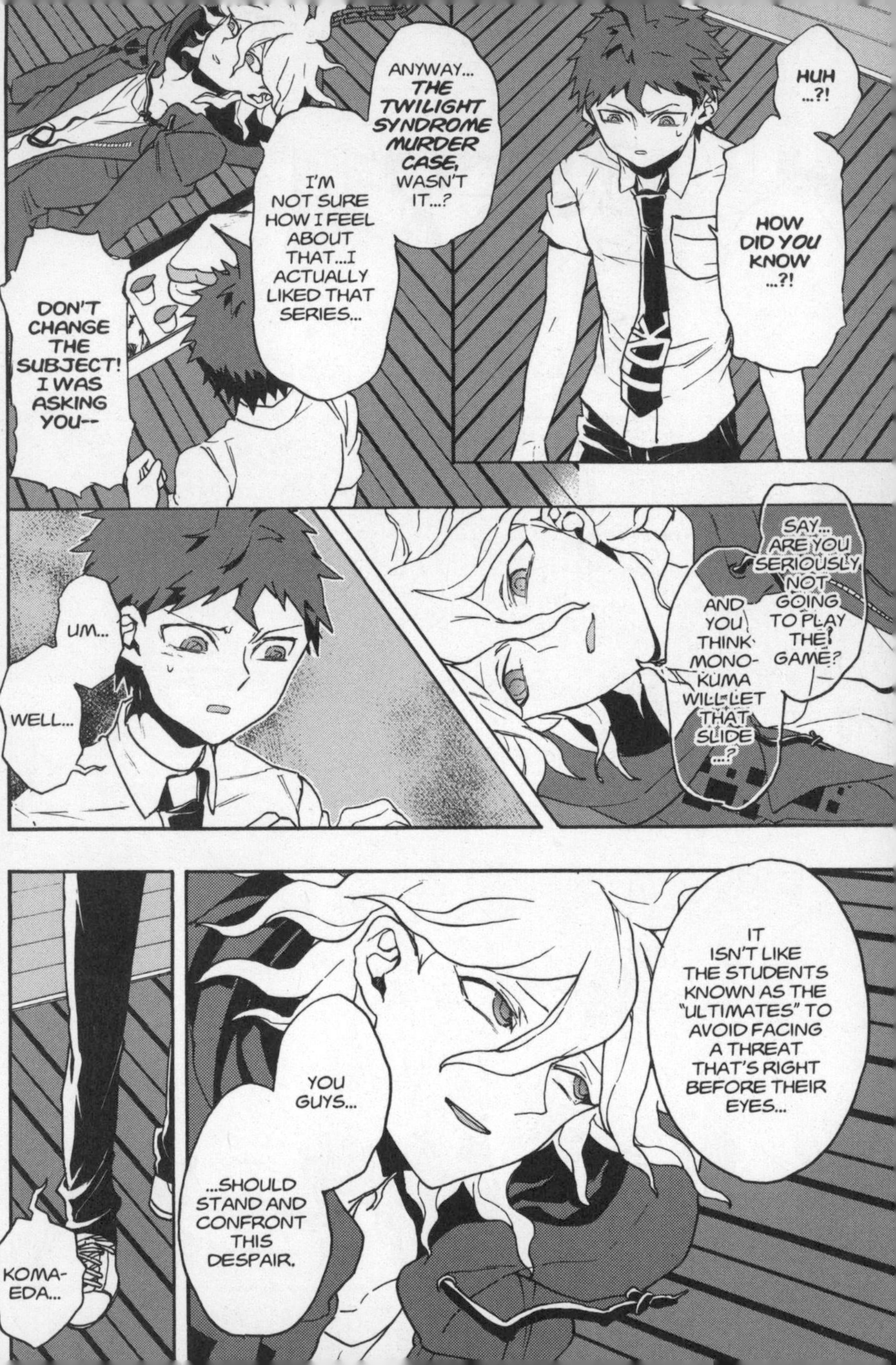
HUH ...?!
HOW DID YOU KNOW ...?!
ANYWAY... THE TWILIGHT SYNDROME MURDER CASE, WASN'T IT...?
I'M NOT SURE HOW I FEEL ABOUT THAT...I ACTUALLY LIKED THAT SERIES...
DON'T CHANGE THE SUBJECT! I WAS ASKING YOU--
SAY... ARE YOU SERIOUSLY NOT GOING TO PLAY THE GAME?
AND YOU THINK MONO-KUMA WILL LET THAT SLIDE ...?
UM...
WELL...
IT ISN'T LIKE THE STUDENTS KNOWN AS THE "ULTIMATES" TO AVOID FACING A THREAT THAT'S RIGHT BEFORE THEIR EYES...
YOU GUYS...
...SHOULD STAND AND CONFRONT THIS DESPAIR.
KOMA-EDA...

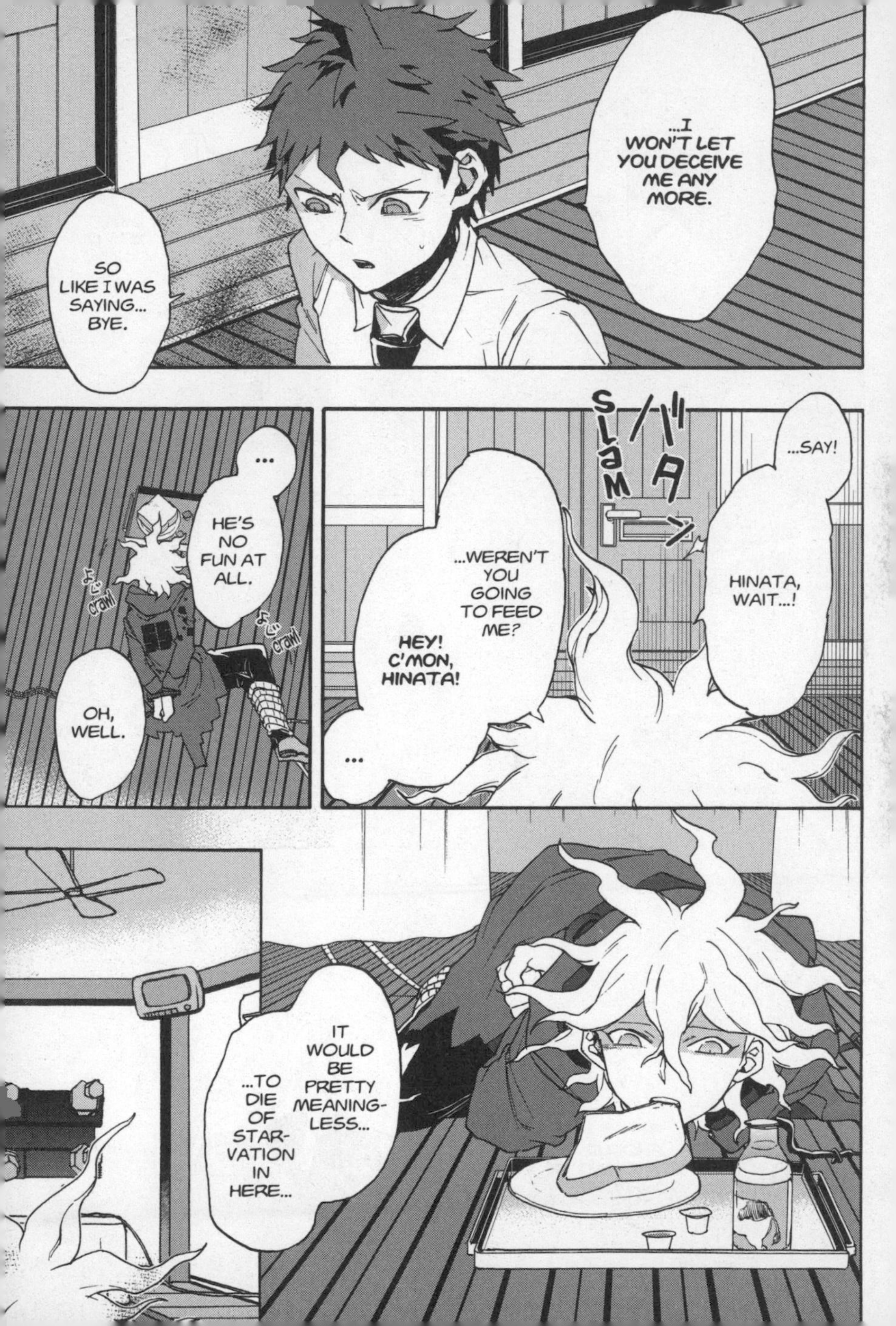
...I WON'T LET YOU DECEIVE ME ANY MORE.
SO LIKE I WAS SAYING... BYE.
SLAM
バタン
...SAY!
HINATA, WAIT...!
...WEREN'T YOU GOING TO FEED ME?
HEY! C'MON, HINATA!
...
...
HE'S NO FUN AT ALL.
crawl
crawl
OH, WELL.
IT WOULD BE PRETTY MEANINGLESS...
...TO DIE OF STARVATION IN HERE...

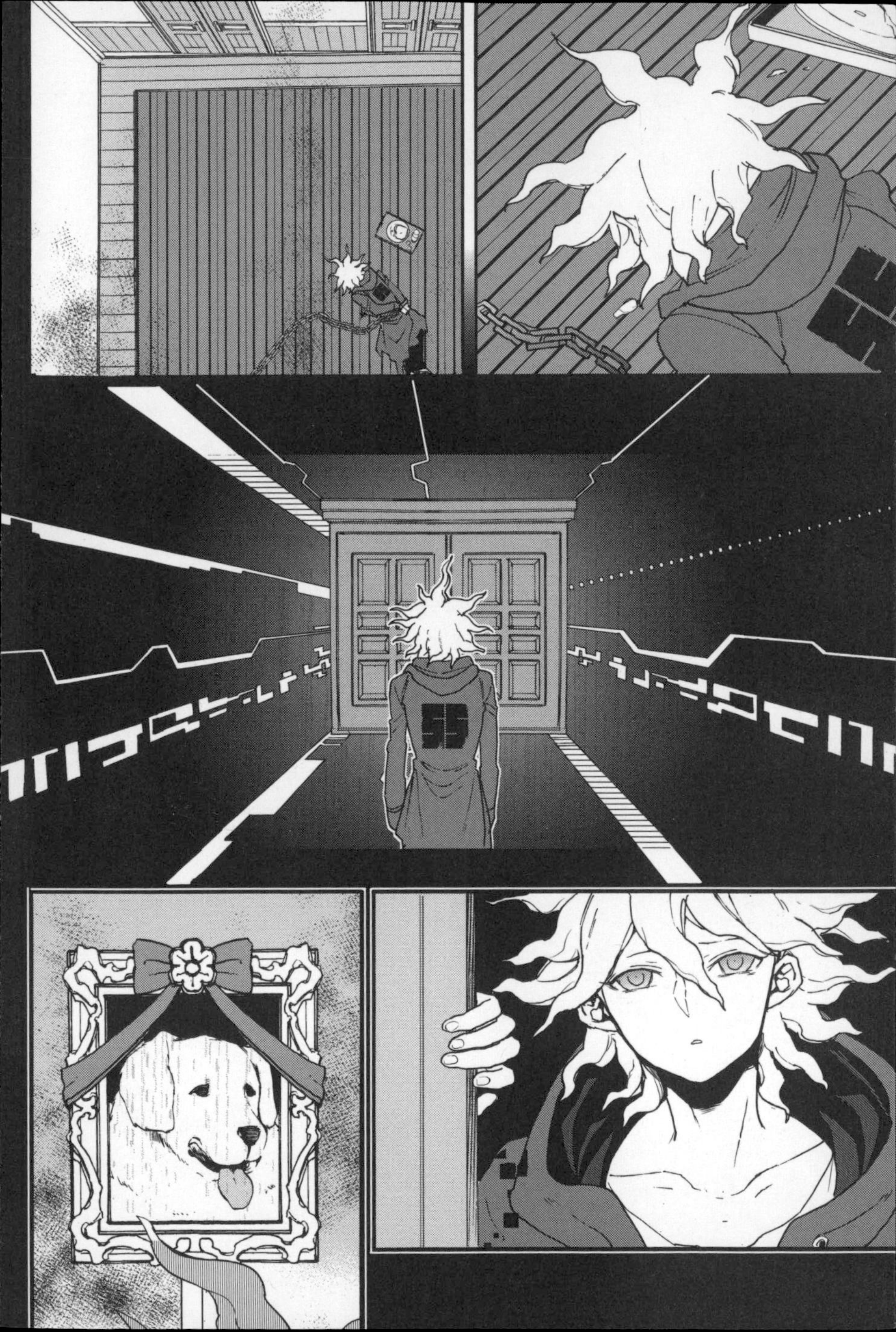

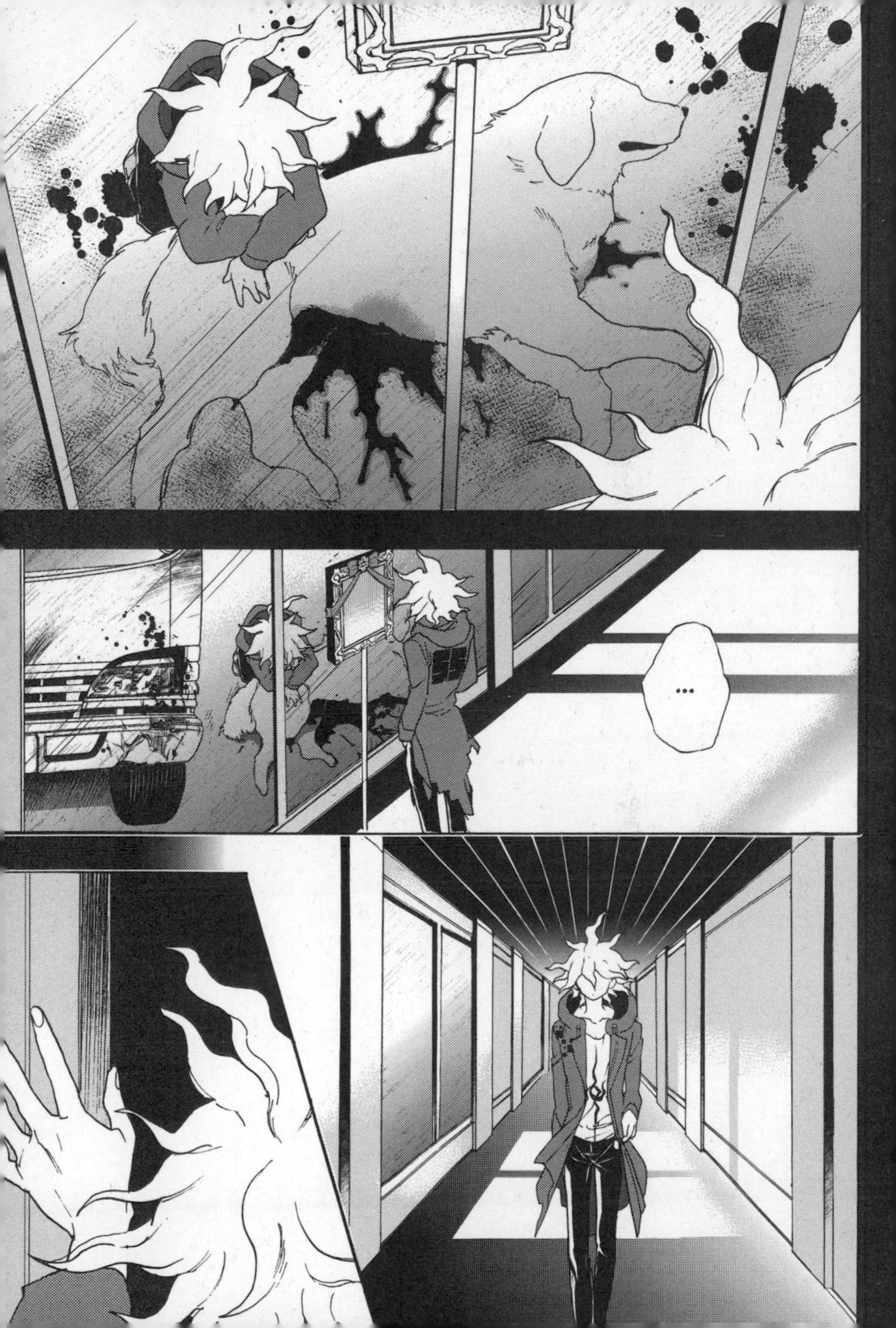
...

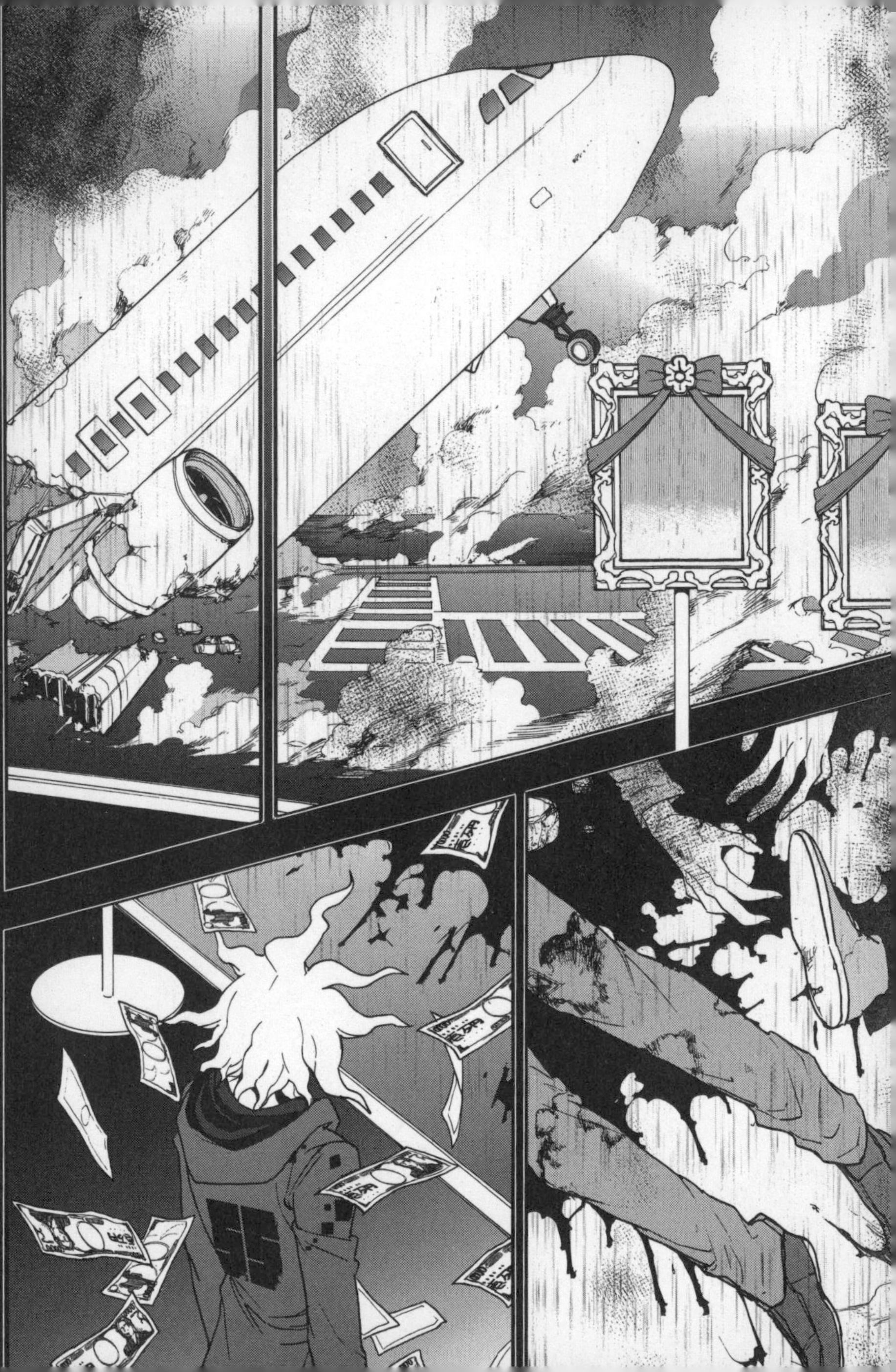

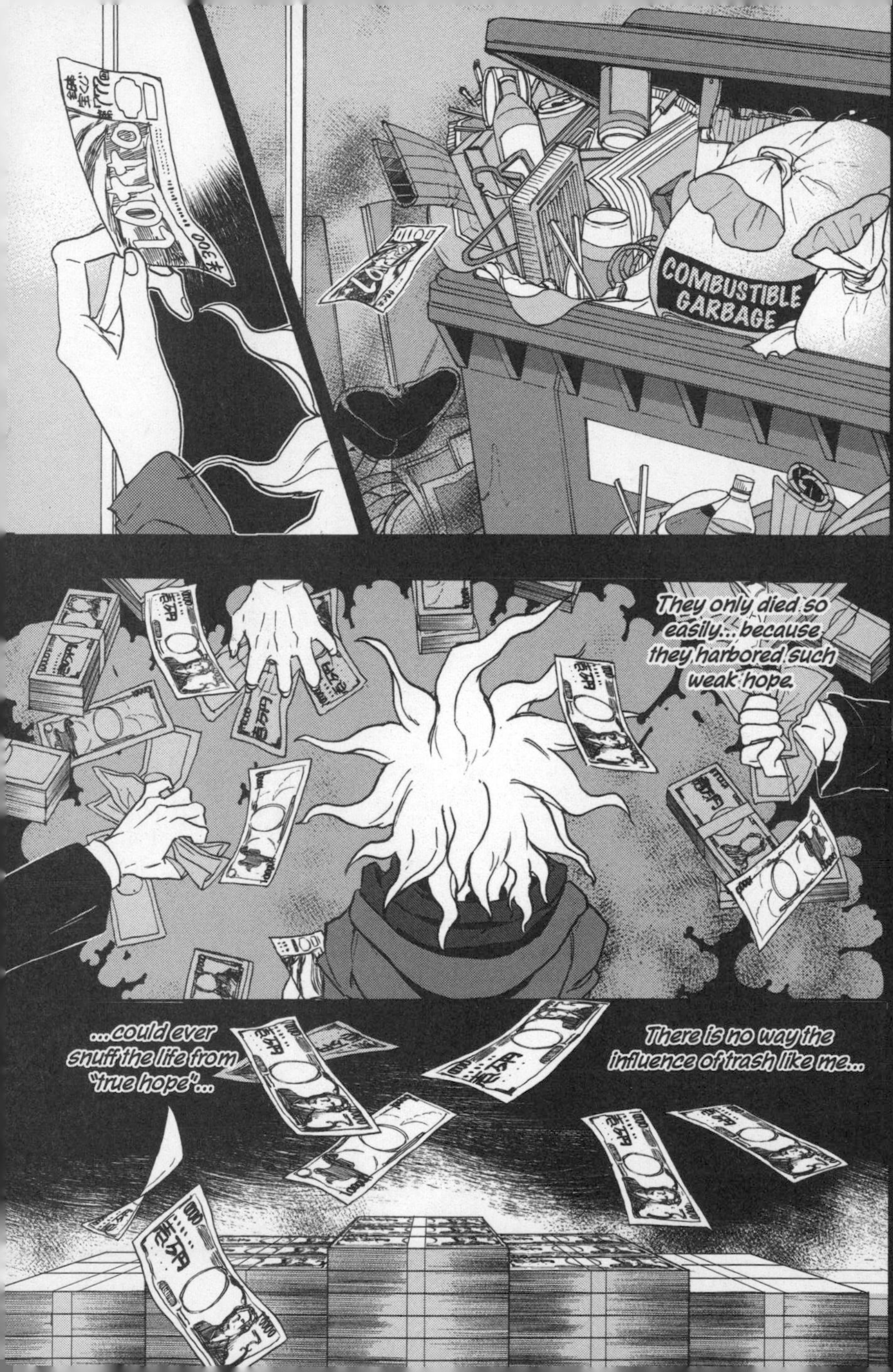
COMBUSTIBLE GARBAGE
They only died so easily... because they harbored such weak hope.
There is no way the influence of trash like me...
...could ever snuff the life from "true hope"...

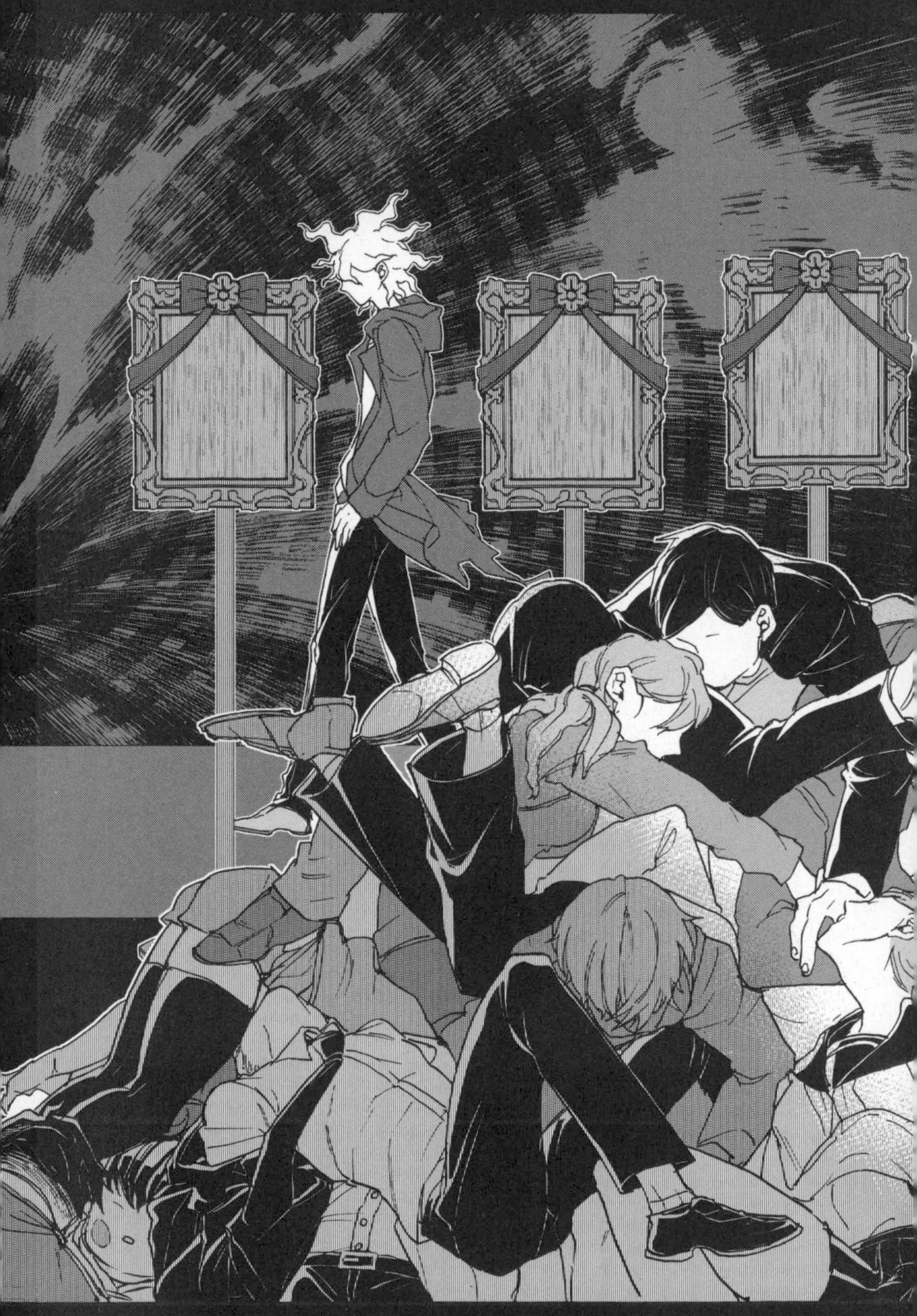

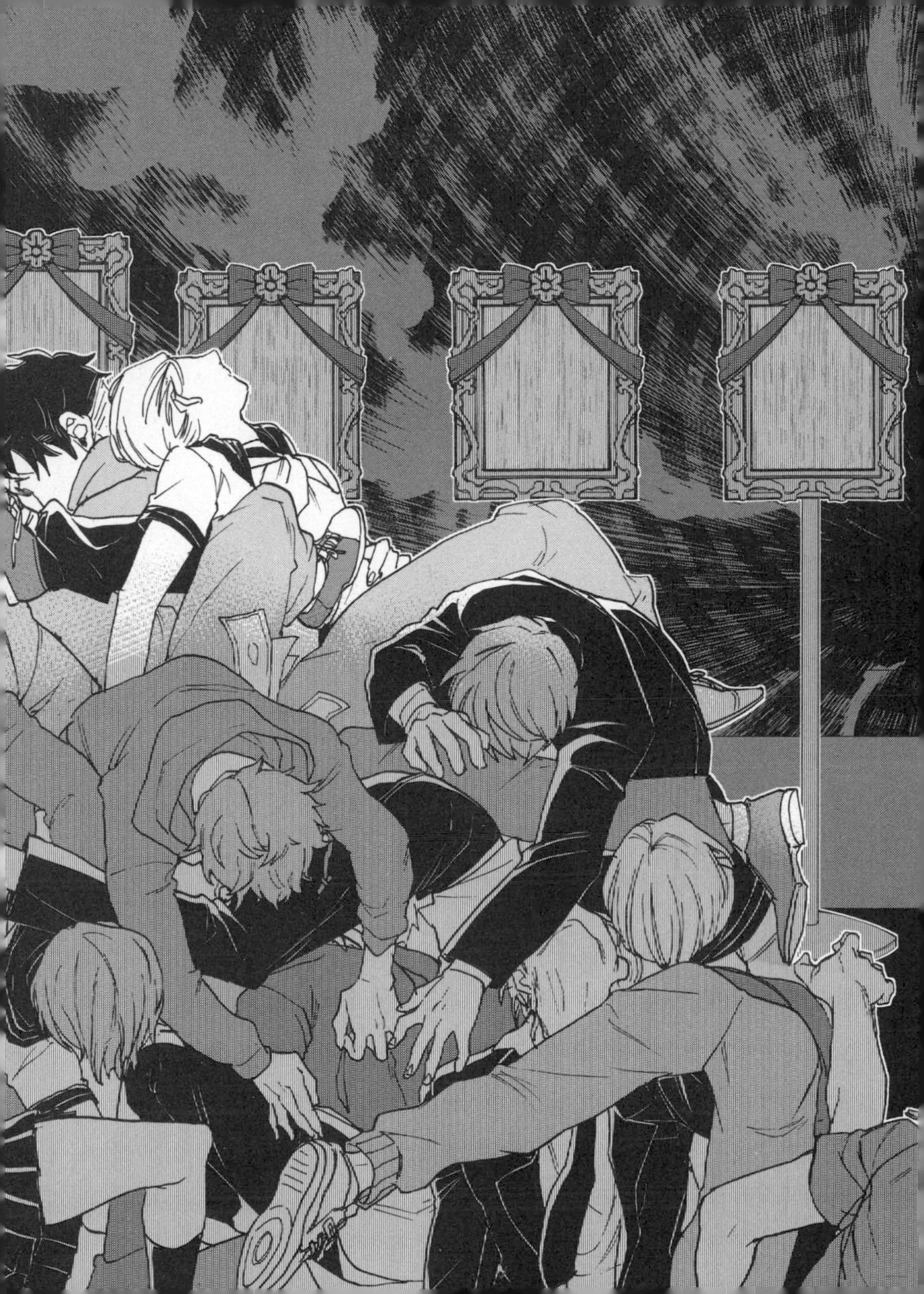

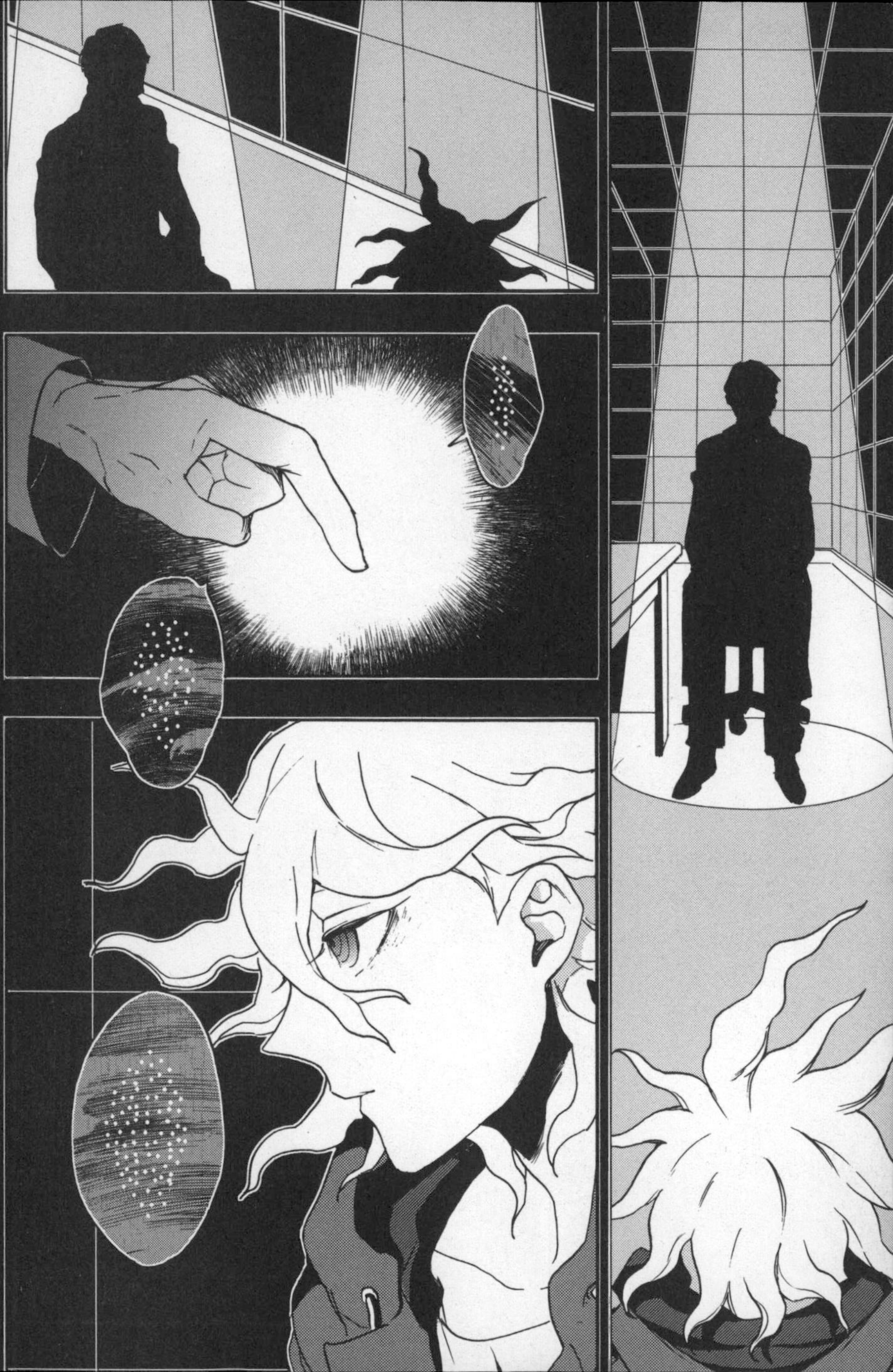

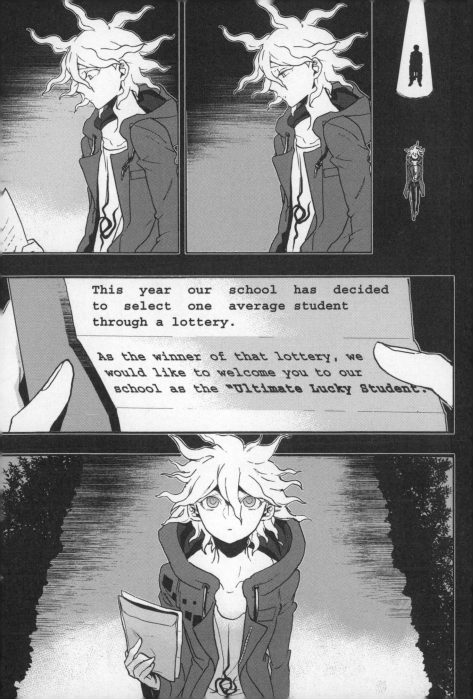

This year our school has decided to select one average student through a lottery.

As the winner of that lottery, we would like to welcome you to our school as the "Ultimate Lucky Student."

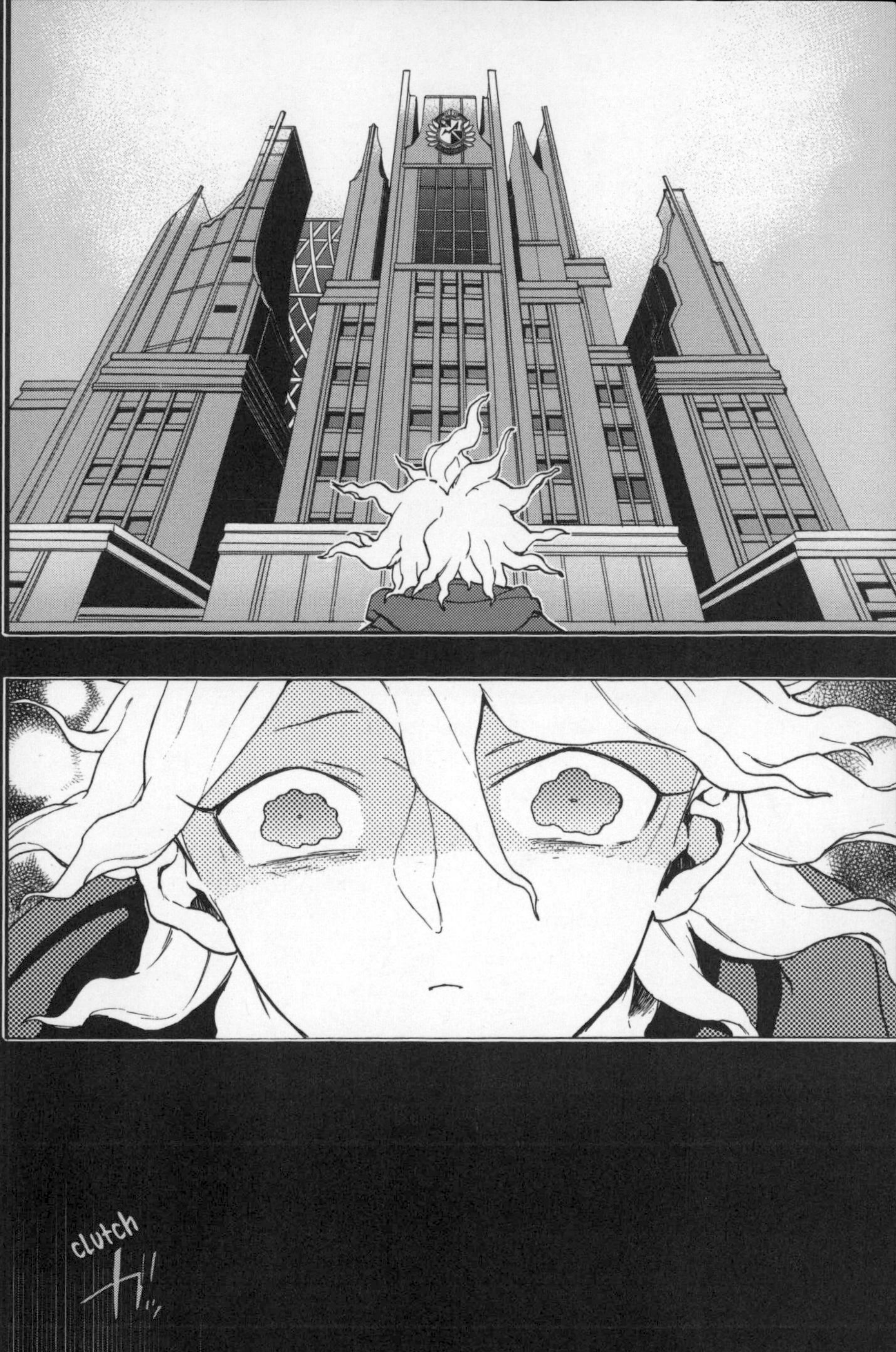
clutch

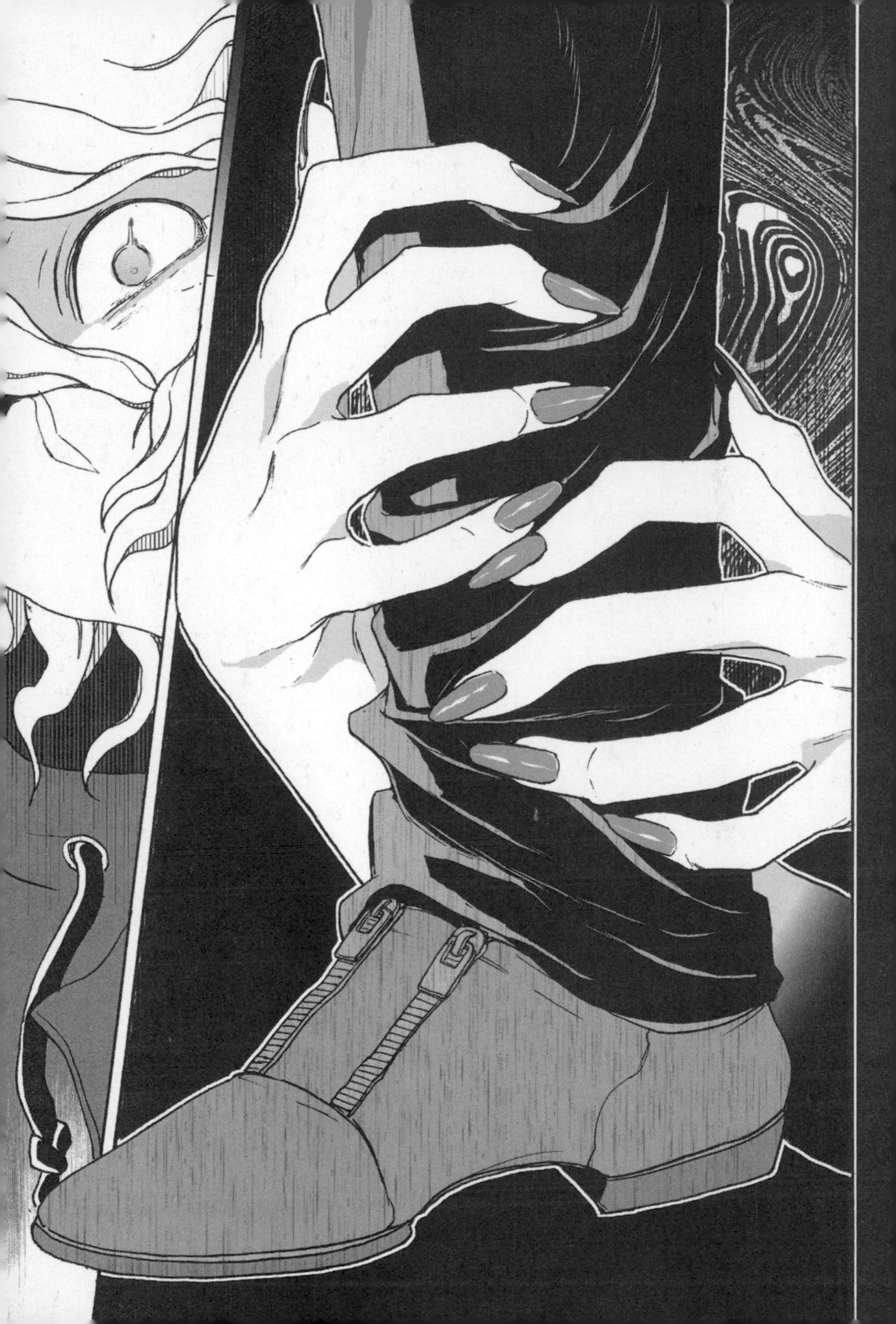

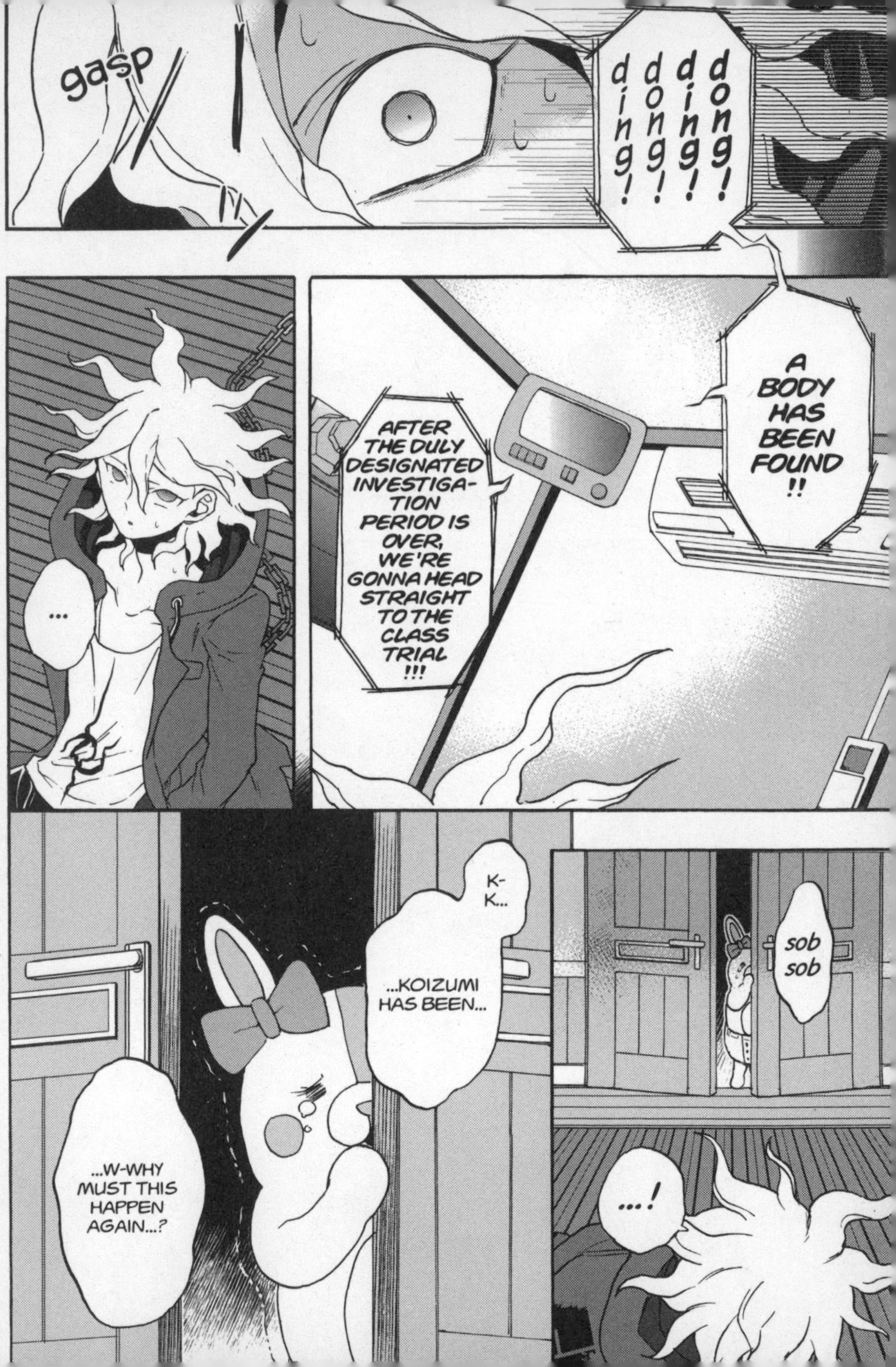
ding! dong! ding! dong!
gasp
A BODY HAS BEEN FOUND!!
AFTER THE DULY DESIGNATED INVESTIGATION PERIOD IS OVER, WE'RE GONNA HEAD STRAIGHT TO THE CLASS TRIAL!!!
...
sob sob
...!
K-K...
...KOIZUMI HAS BEEN...
...W-WHY MUST THIS HAPPEN AGAIN...?

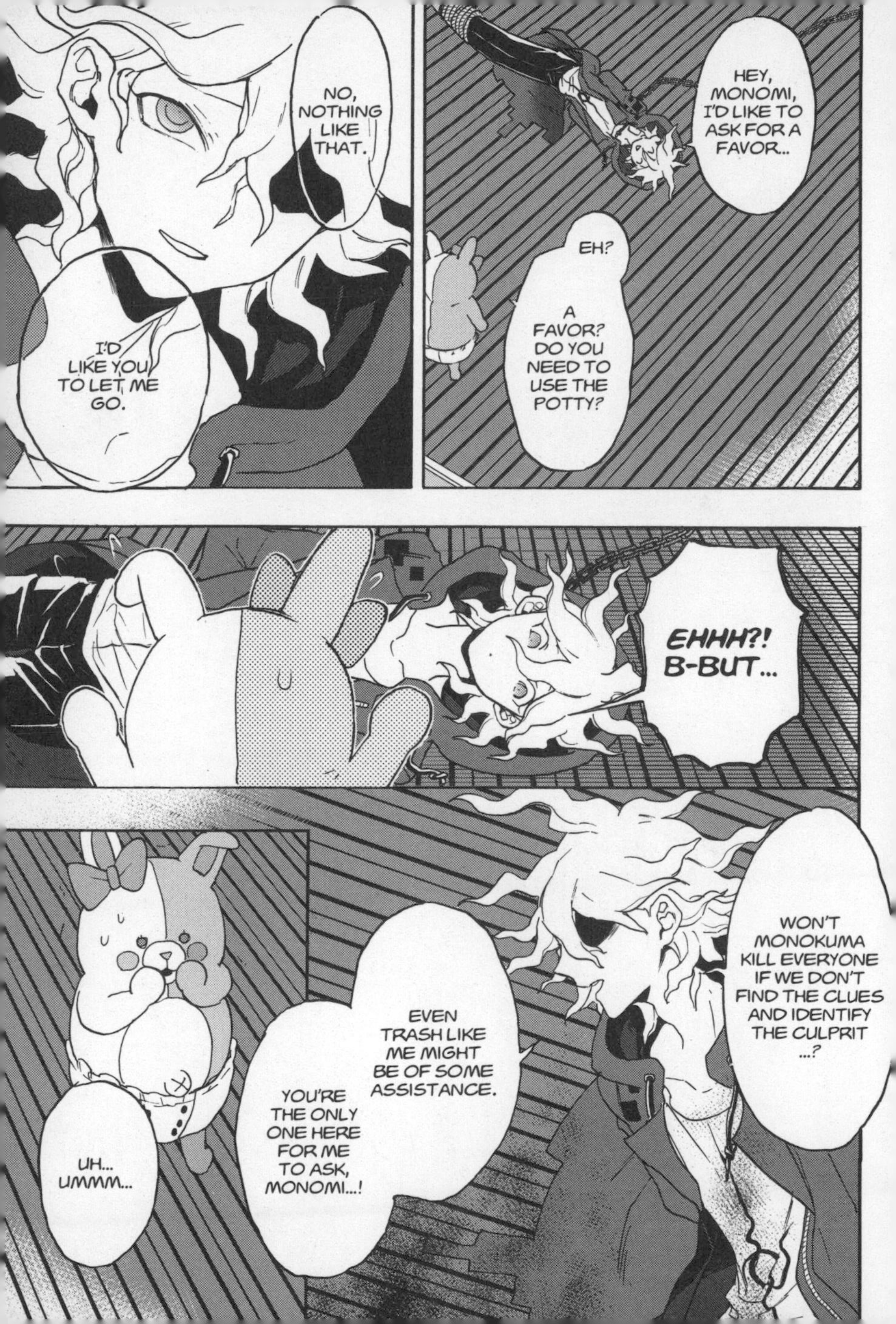
HEY, MONOMI, I'D LIKE TO ASK FOR A FAVOR...
EH?
A FAVOR? DO YOU NEED TO USE THE POTTY?
NO, NOTHING LIKE THAT.
I'D LIKE YOU TO LET ME GO.
EHHH?! B-BUT...
WON'T MONOKUMA KILL EVERYONE IF WE DON'T FIND THE CLUES AND IDENTIFY THE CULPRIT ...?
EVEN TRASH LIKE ME MIGHT BE OF SOME ASSISTANCE.
YOU'RE THE ONLY ONE HERE FOR ME TO ASK, MONOMI...!
UH... UMMM...

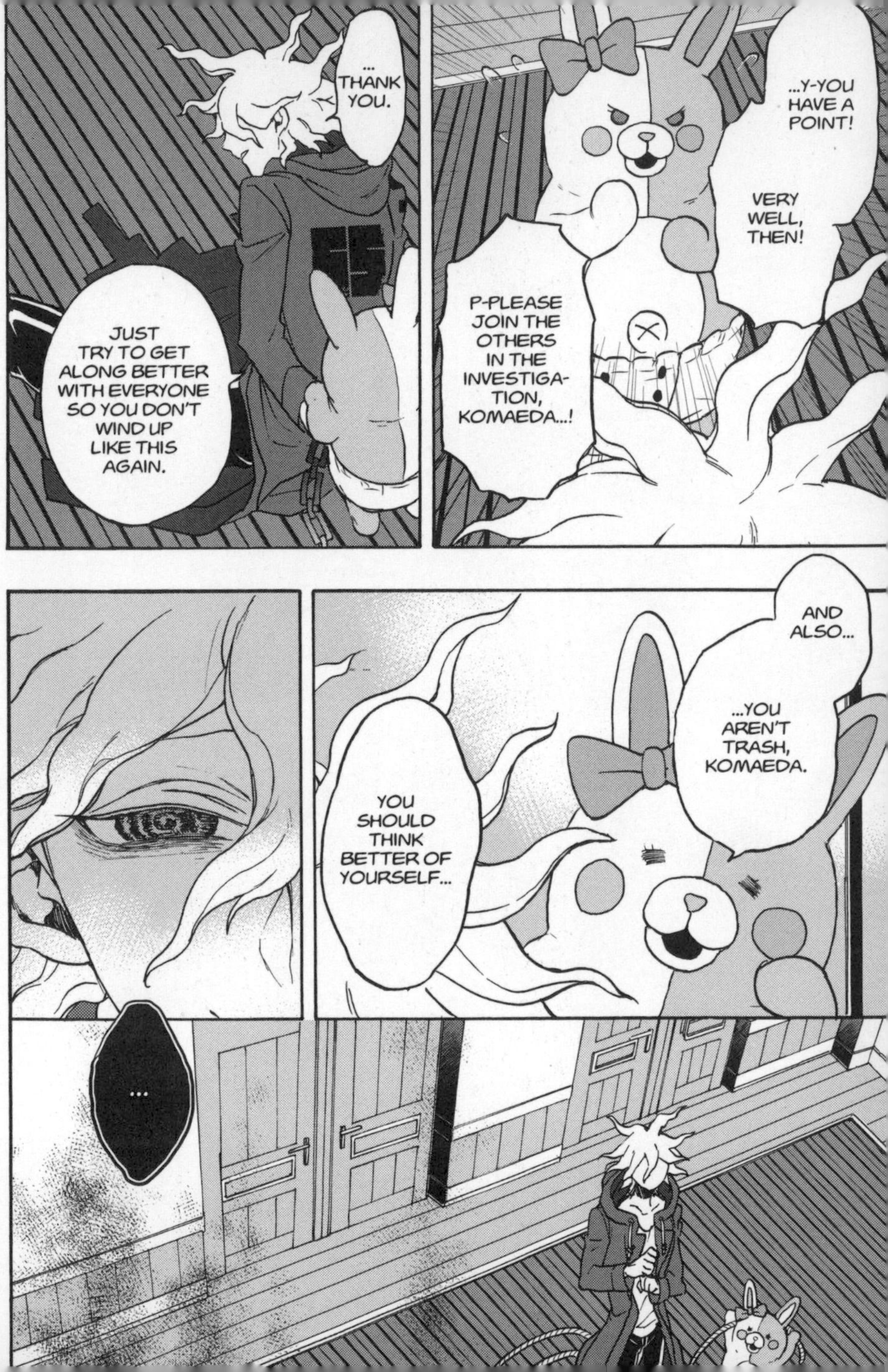
...Y-YOU HAVE A POINT!
VERY WELL, THEN!
P-PLEASE JOIN THE OTHERS IN THE INVESTIGA-TION, KOMAEDA...!
... THANK YOU.
JUST TRY TO GET ALONG BETTER WITH EVERYONE SO YOU DON'T WIND UP LIKE THIS AGAIN.
AND ALSO...
...YOU AREN'T TRASH, KOMAEDA.
YOU SHOULD THINK BETTER OF YOURSELF...
...

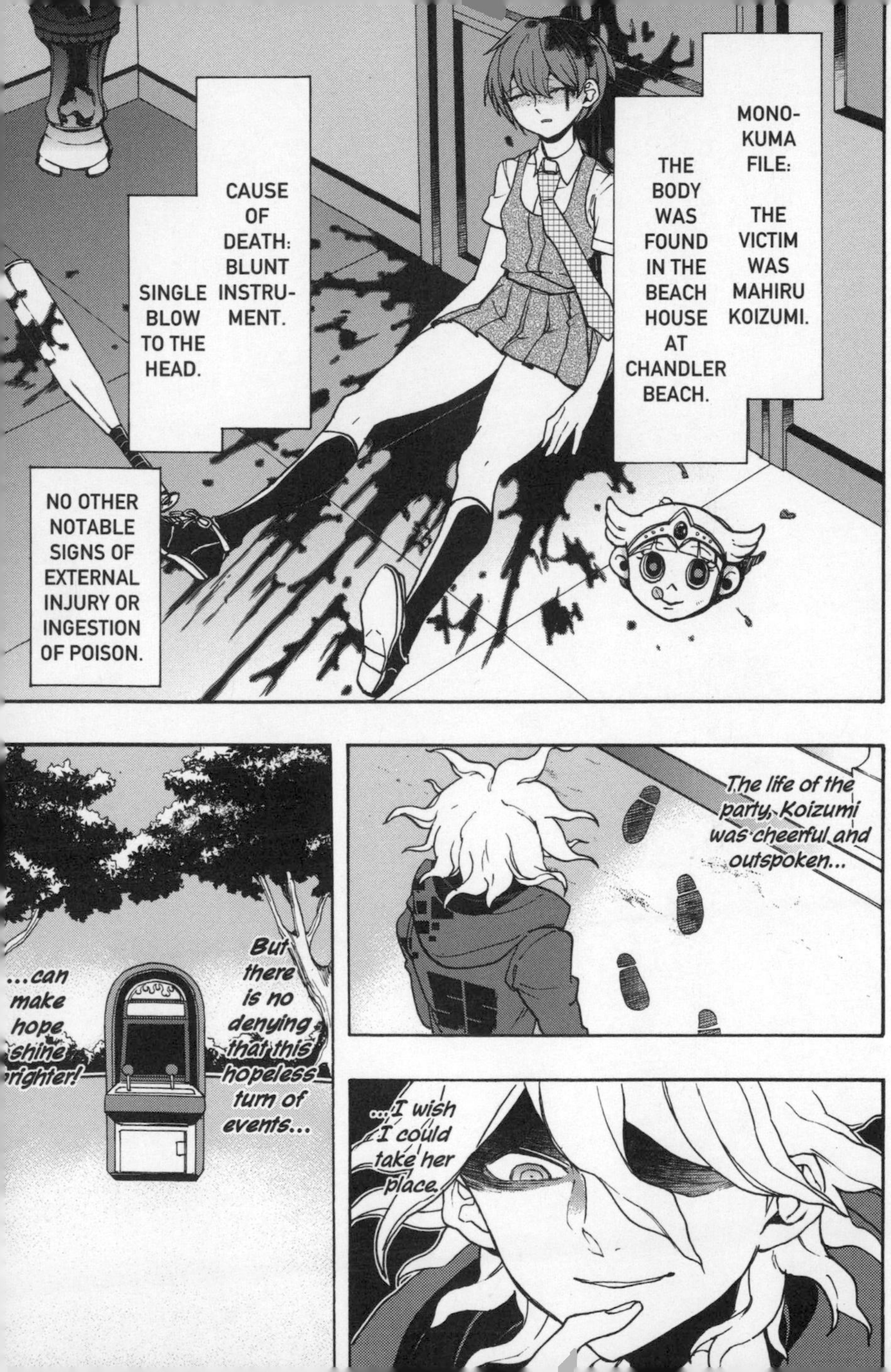
MONOKUMA FILE: THE VICTIM WAS MAHIRU KOIZUMI.
THE BODY WAS FOUND IN THE BEACH HOUSE AT CHANDLER BEACH.
CAUSE OF DEATH: BLUNT INSTRUMENT.
SINGLE BLOW TO THE HEAD.
NO OTHER NOTABLE SIGNS OF EXTERNAL INJURY OR INGESTION OF POISON.
The life of the party, Koizumi was cheerful and outspoken...
...I wish I could take her place.
But there is no denying that this hopeless turn of events...
...can make hope shine brighter!

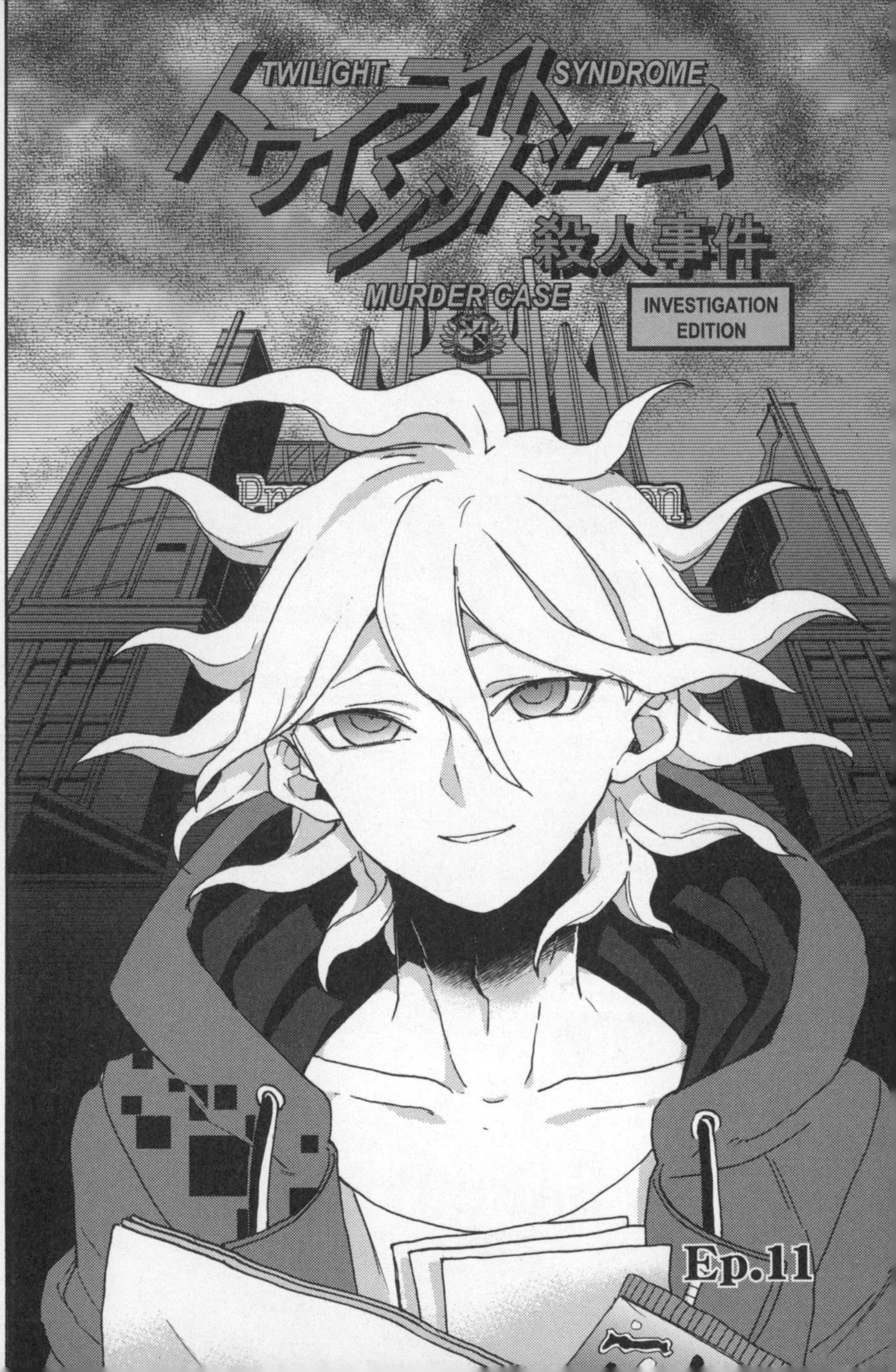
TWILIGHT SYNDROME
トワイライトシンドローム
殺人事件
MURDER CASE
INVESTIGATION EDITION
Ep.11

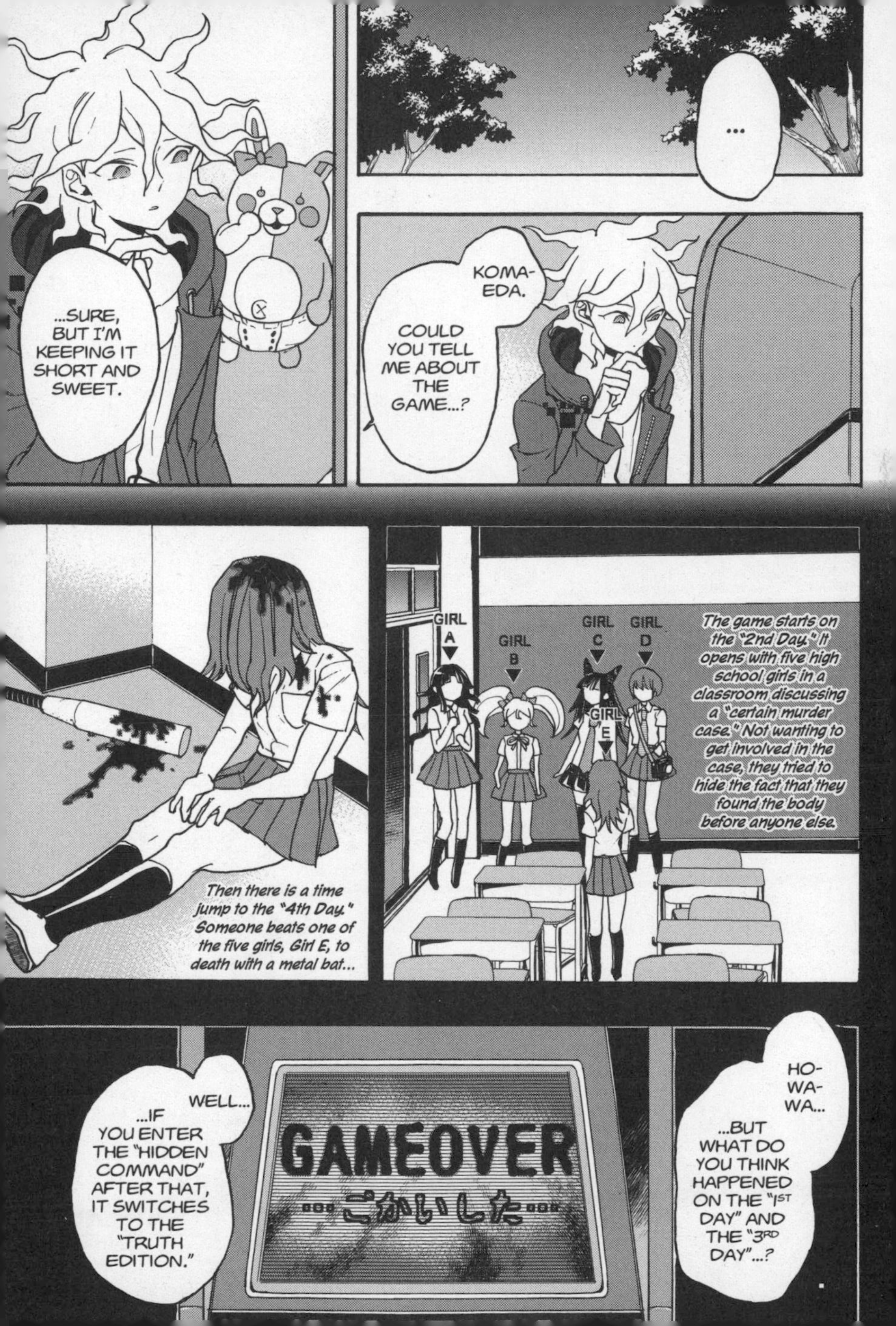
...
KOMA-EDA.
COULD YOU TELL ME ABOUT THE GAME...?
...SURE, BUT I'M KEEPING IT SHORT AND SWEET.
GIRL A
GIRL B
GIRL C
GIRL D
GIRL E
The game starts on the "2nd Day." It opens with five high school girls in a classroom discussing a "certain murder case." Not wanting to get involved in the case, they tried to hide the fact that they found the body before anyone else.
Then there is a time jump to the "4th Day." Someone beats one of the five girls, Girl E, to death with a metal bat...
HO-WA-WA...
...BUT WHAT DO YOU THINK HAPPENED ON THE "1ST DAY" AND THE "3RD DAY"...?
GAMEOVER
…こかいした…
WELL...
...IF YOU ENTER THE "HIDDEN COMMAND" AFTER THAT, IT SWITCHES TO THE "TRUTH EDITION."

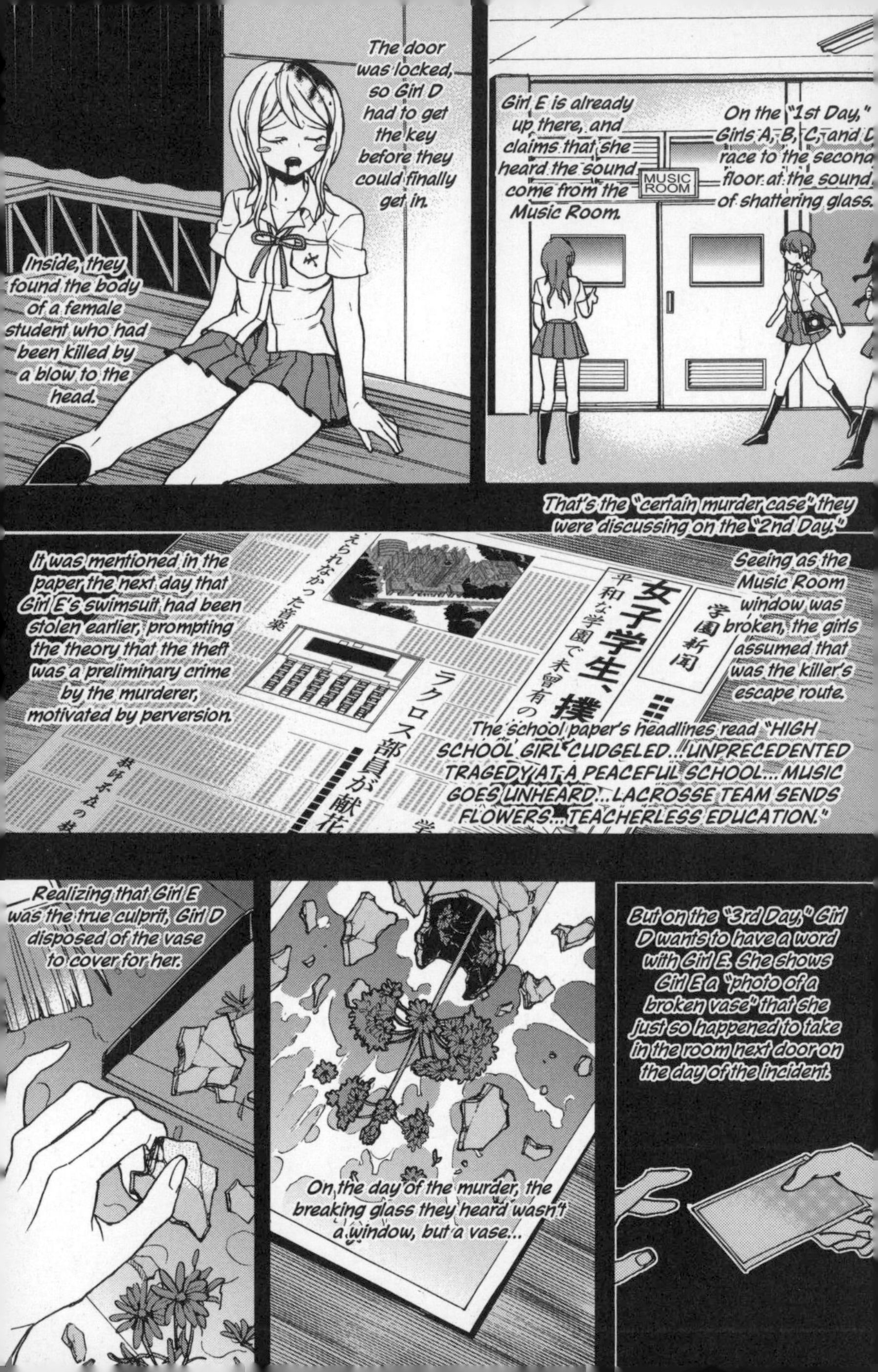
On the "1st Day," Girls A, B, C, and D race to the second floor at the sound of shattering glass.
Girl E is already up there, and claims that she heard the sound come from the Music Room.
MUSIC ROOM
The door was locked, so Girl D had to get the key before they could finally get in.
Inside, they found the body of a female student who had been killed by a blow to the head.
That's the "certain murder case" they were discussing on the "2nd Day."
Seeing as the Music Room window was broken, the girls assumed that was the killer's escape route.
学園新聞
女子学生、撲
平和な学園で未曾有の
ラクロス部員が献花
えられなかった音楽
It was mentioned in the paper the next day that Girl E's swimsuit had been stolen earlier, prompting the theory that the theft was a preliminary crime by the murderer, motivated by perversion.
The school paper's headlines read "HIGH SCHOOL GIRL CUDGELED... UNPRECEDENTED TRAGEDY AT A PEACEFUL SCHOOL... MUSIC GOES UNHEARD... LACROSSE TEAM SENDS FLOWERS... TEACHERLESS EDUCATION."
But on the "3rd Day," Girl D wants to have a word with Girl E. She shows Girl E a "photo of a broken vase" that she just so happened to take in the room next door on the day of the incident.
On the day of the murder, the breaking glass they heard wasn't a window, but a vase...
Realizing that Girl E was the true culprit, Girl D disposed of the vase to cover for her.

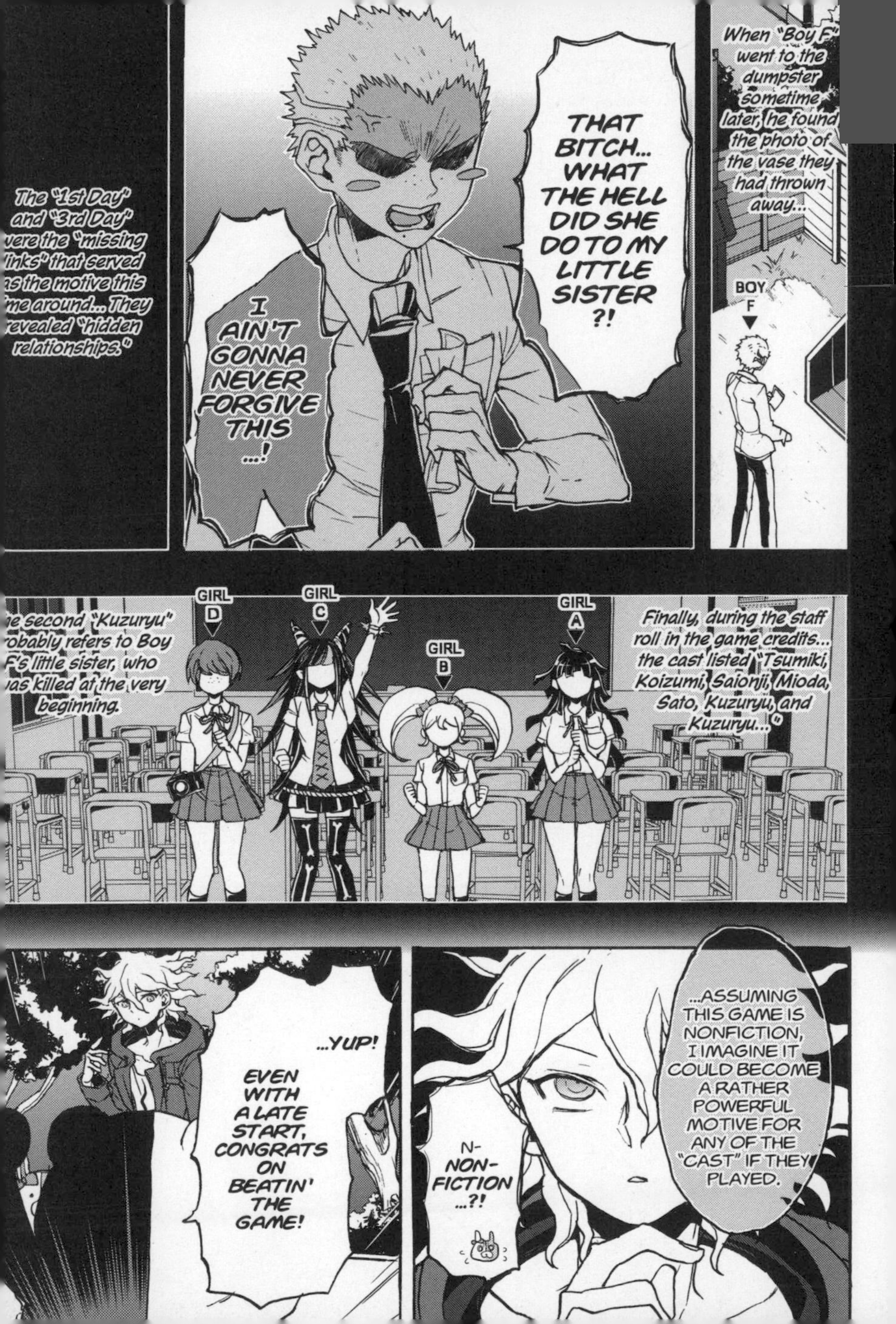
When "Boy F" went to the dumpster sometime later, he found the photo of the vase they had thrown away...
BOY F
THAT BITCH... WHAT THE HELL DID SHE DO TO MY LITTLE SISTER ?!
I AIN'T GONNA NEVER FORGIVE THIS ...!
The "1st Day" and "3rd Day" ere the "missing inks" that served as the motive this me around... They revealed "hidden relationships."
Finally, during the staff roll in the game credits... the cast listed "Tsumiki, Koizumi, Saionji, Mioda, Sato, Kuzuryu, and Kuzuryu..."
GIRL A
GIRL B
GIRL C
GIRL D
he second "Kuzuryu" robably refers to Boy F's little sister, who as killed at the very beginning.
...ASSUMING THIS GAME IS NONFICTION, I IMAGINE IT COULD BECOME A RATHER POWERFUL MOTIVE FOR ANY OF THE "CAST" IF THEY PLAYED.
N- NON- FICTION ...?!
...YUP!
EVEN WITH A LATE START, CONGRATS ON BEATIN' THE GAME!

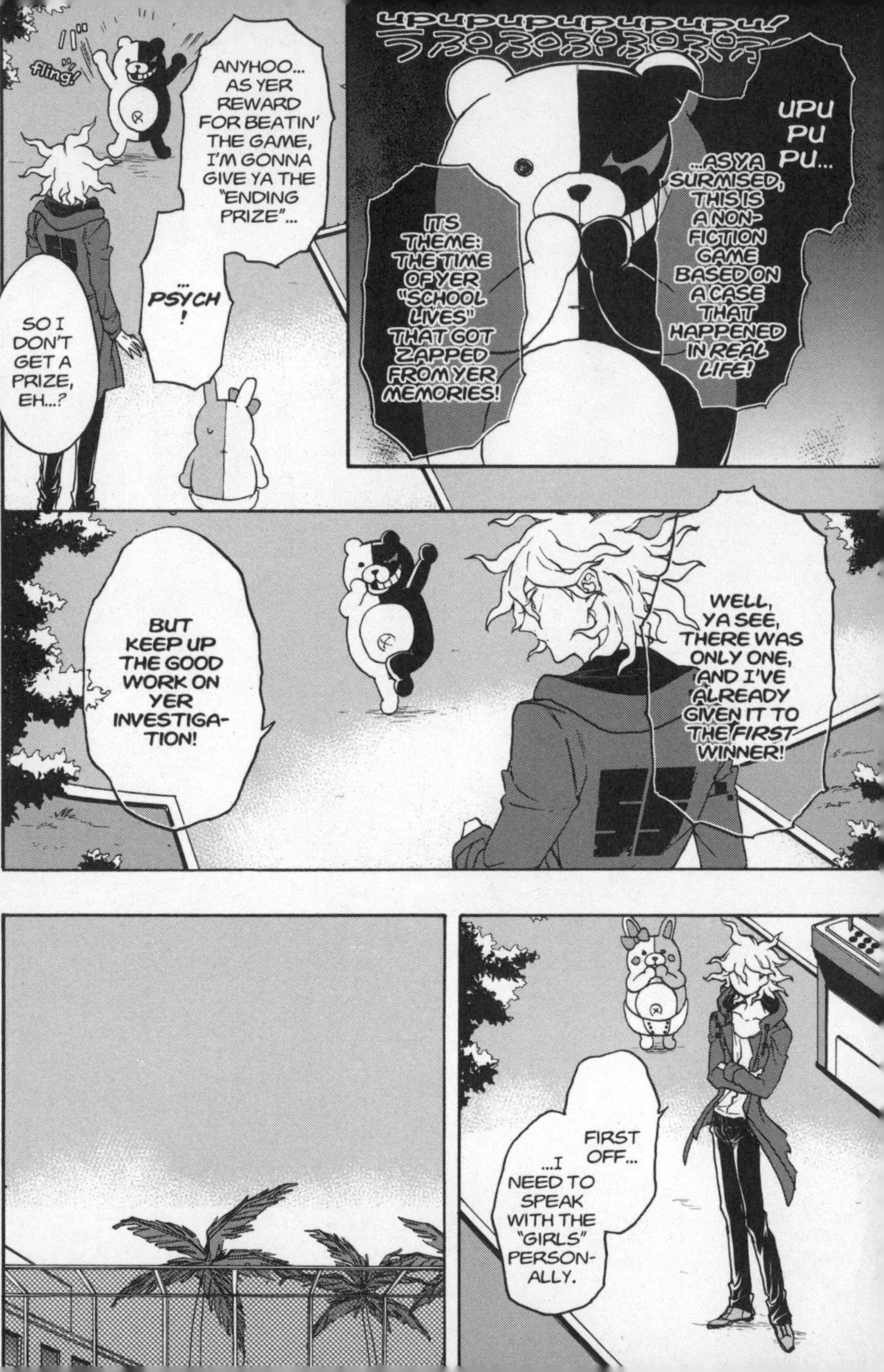
upupupupupupupu!
UPU PU PU...
...AS YA SURMISED, THIS IS A NON-FICTION GAME BASED ON A CASE THAT HAPPENED IN REAL LIFE!
ITS THEME: THE TIME OF YER "SCHOOL LIVES" THAT GOT ZAPPED FROM YER MEMORIES!
fling!
ANYHOO... AS YER REWARD FOR BEATIN' THE GAME, I'M GONNA GIVE YA THE "ENDING PRIZE"...
...PSYCH!
SO I DON'T GET A PRIZE, EH...?
WELL, YA SEE, THERE WAS ONLY ONE, AND I'VE ALREADY GIVEN IT TO THE FIRST WINNER!
BUT KEEP UP THE GOOD WORK ON YER INVESTIGATION!
FIRST OFF...
...I NEED TO SPEAK WITH THE "GIRLS" PERSONALLY.

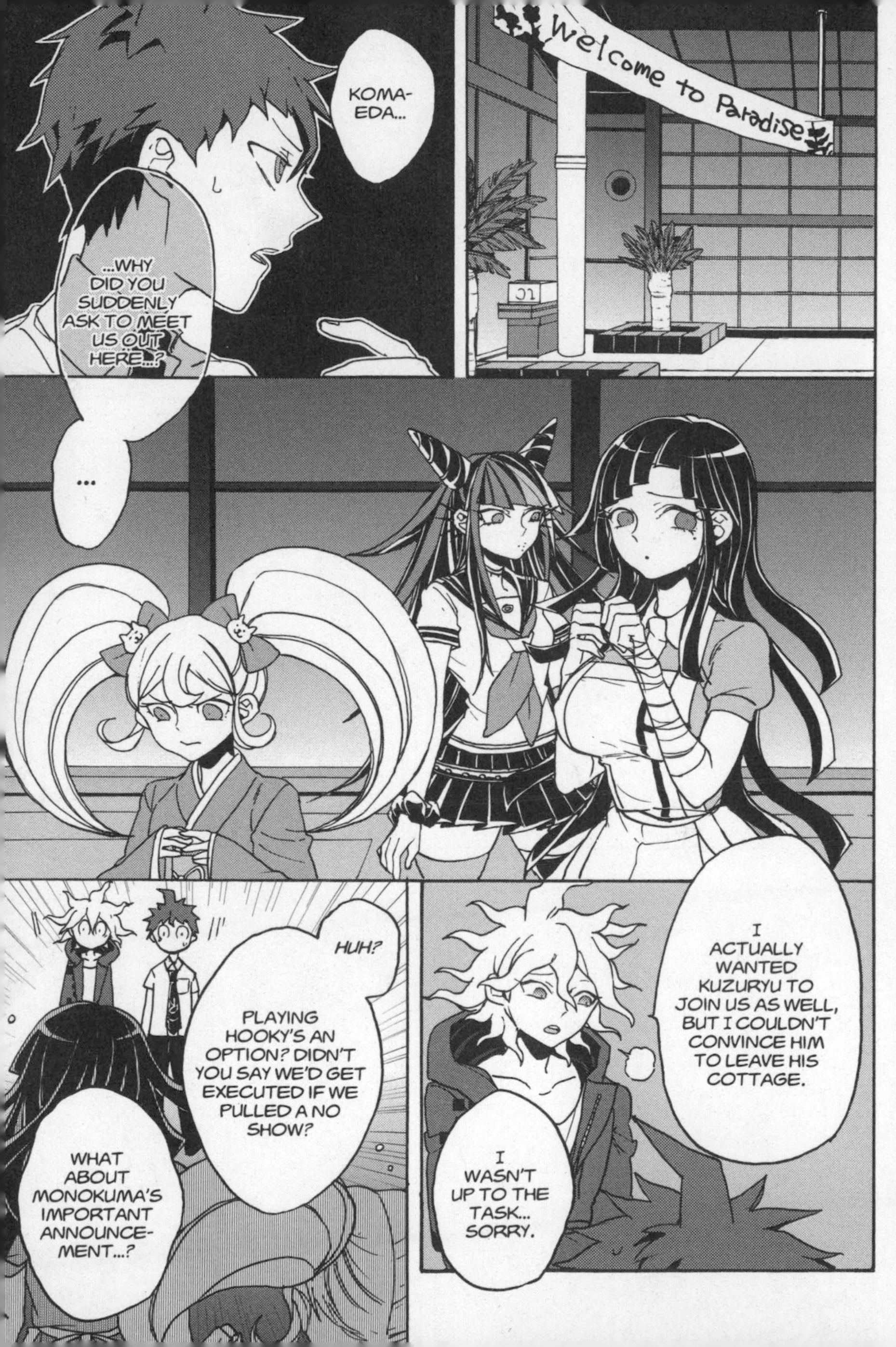
Welcome to Paradise
KOMA-EDA...
...WHY DID YOU SUDDENLY ASK TO MEET US OUT HERE...?
...
I ACTUALLY WANTED KUZURYU TO JOIN US AS WELL, BUT I COULDN'T CONVINCE HIM TO LEAVE HIS COTTAGE.
I WASN'T UP TO THE TASK... SORRY.
HUH?
PLAYING HOOKY'S AN OPTION? DIDN'T YOU SAY WE'D GET EXECUTED IF WE PULLED A NO SHOW?
WHAT ABOUT MONOKUMA'S IMPORTANT ANNOUNCE-MENT...?

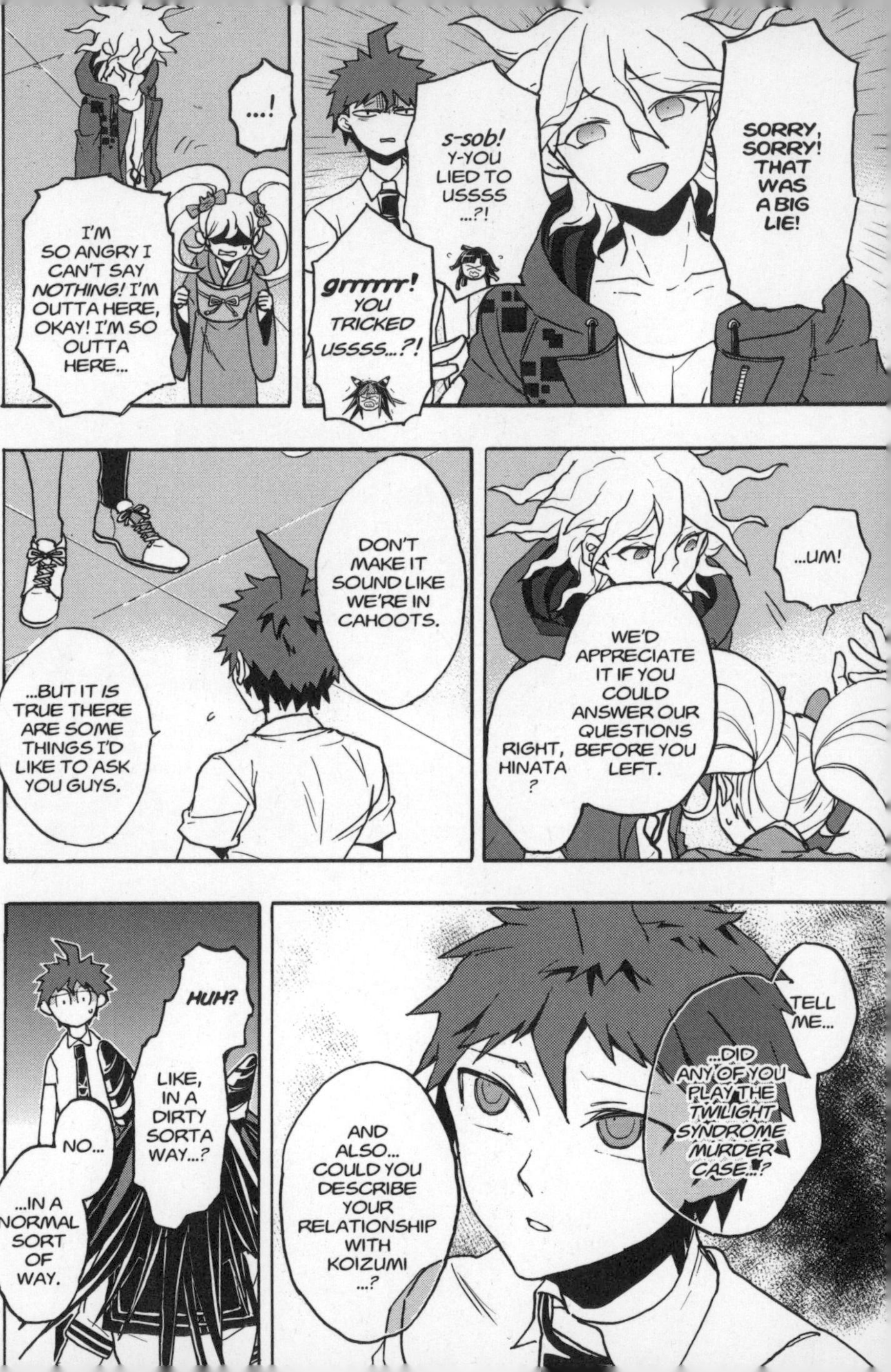
SORRY, SORRY! THAT WAS A BIG LIE!
s-sob! Y-YOU LIED TO USSSS ...?!
grrrrrr! YOU TRICKED USSSS...?!
...!
I'M SO ANGRY I CAN'T SAY NOTHING! I'M OUTTA HERE, OKAY! I'M SO OUTTA HERE...
...UM!
WE'D APPRECIATE IT IF YOU COULD ANSWER OUR QUESTIONS BEFORE YOU LEFT.
RIGHT, HINATA?
DON'T MAKE IT SOUND LIKE WE'RE IN CAHOOTS.
...BUT IT IS TRUE THERE ARE SOME THINGS I'D LIKE TO ASK YOU GUYS.
TELL ME...
...DID ANY OF YOU PLAY THE TWILIGHT SYNDROME MURDER CASE...?
AND ALSO... COULD YOU DESCRIBE YOUR RELATIONSHIP WITH KOIZUMI...?
HUH?
LIKE, IN A DIRTY SORTA WAY...?
NO...
...IN A NORMAL SORT OF WAY.

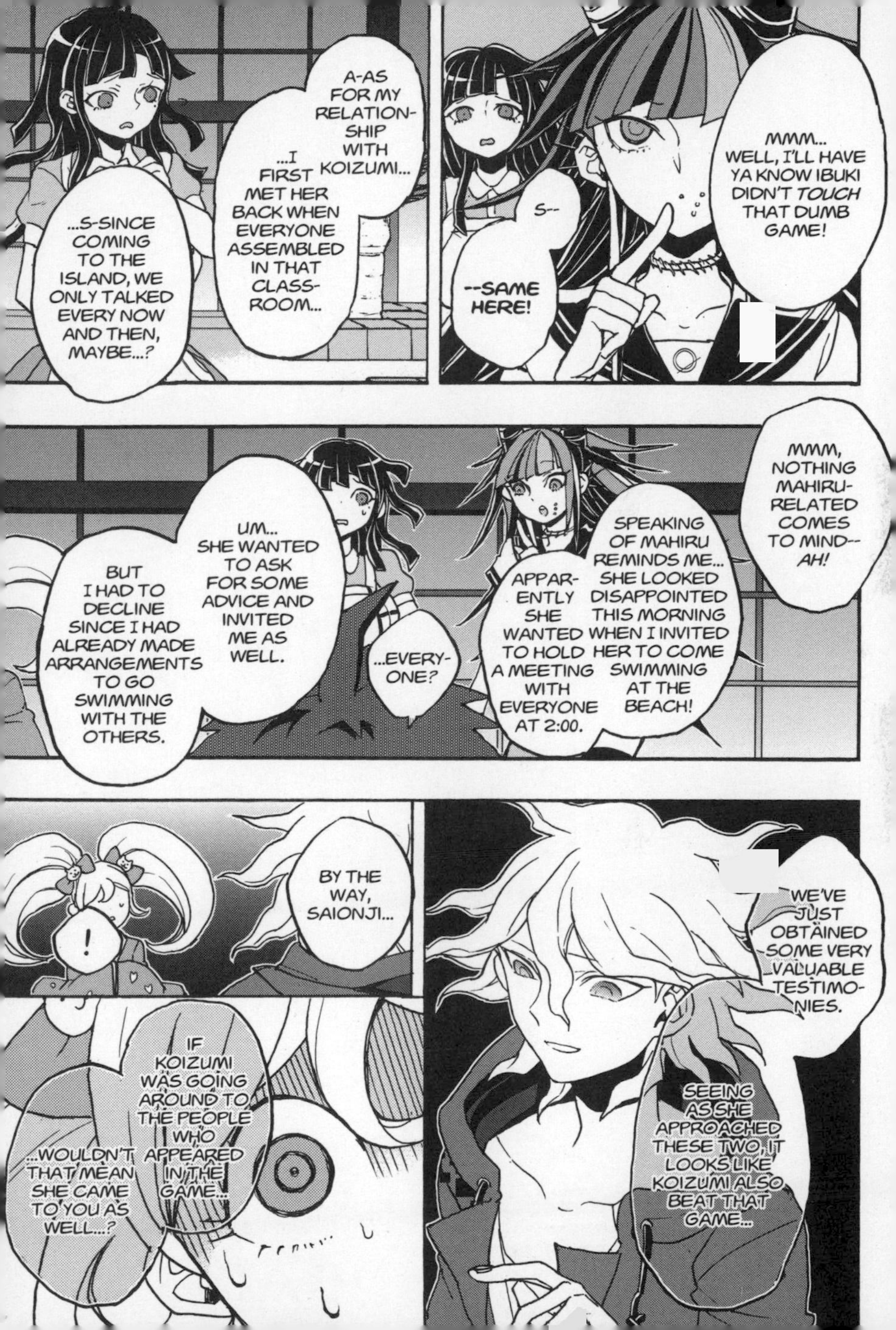
MMM... WELL, I'LL HAVE YA KNOW IBUKI DIDN'T *TOUCH* THAT DUMB GAME!
S--
--SAME HERE!
A-AS FOR MY RELATIONSHIP WITH KOIZUMI...
...I FIRST MET HER BACK WHEN EVERYONE ASSEMBLED IN THAT CLASSROOM...
...S-SINCE COMING TO THE ISLAND, WE ONLY TALKED EVERY NOW AND THEN, MAYBE...?
MMM, NOTHING MAHIRU-RELATED COMES TO MIND-- *AH!*
SPEAKING OF MAHIRU REMINDS ME... SHE LOOKED DISAPPOINTED THIS MORNING WHEN I INVITED HER TO COME SWIMMING AT THE BEACH!
APPARENTLY SHE WANTED TO HOLD A MEETING WITH EVERYONE AT 2:00.
...EVERYONE?
UM... SHE WANTED TO ASK FOR SOME ADVICE AND INVITED ME AS WELL.
BUT I HAD TO DECLINE SINCE I HAD ALREADY MADE ARRANGEMENTS TO GO SWIMMING WITH THE OTHERS.
WE'VE JUST OBTAINED SOME VERY VALUABLE TESTIMONIES.
SEEING AS SHE APPROACHED THESE TWO, IT LOOKS LIKE KOIZUMI ALSO BEAT THAT GAME...
BY THE WAY, SAIONJI...
!
IF KOIZUMI WAS GOING AROUND TO THE PEOPLE WHO APPEARED IN THE GAME...
...WOULDN'T THAT MEAN SHE CAME TO YOU AS WELL...?

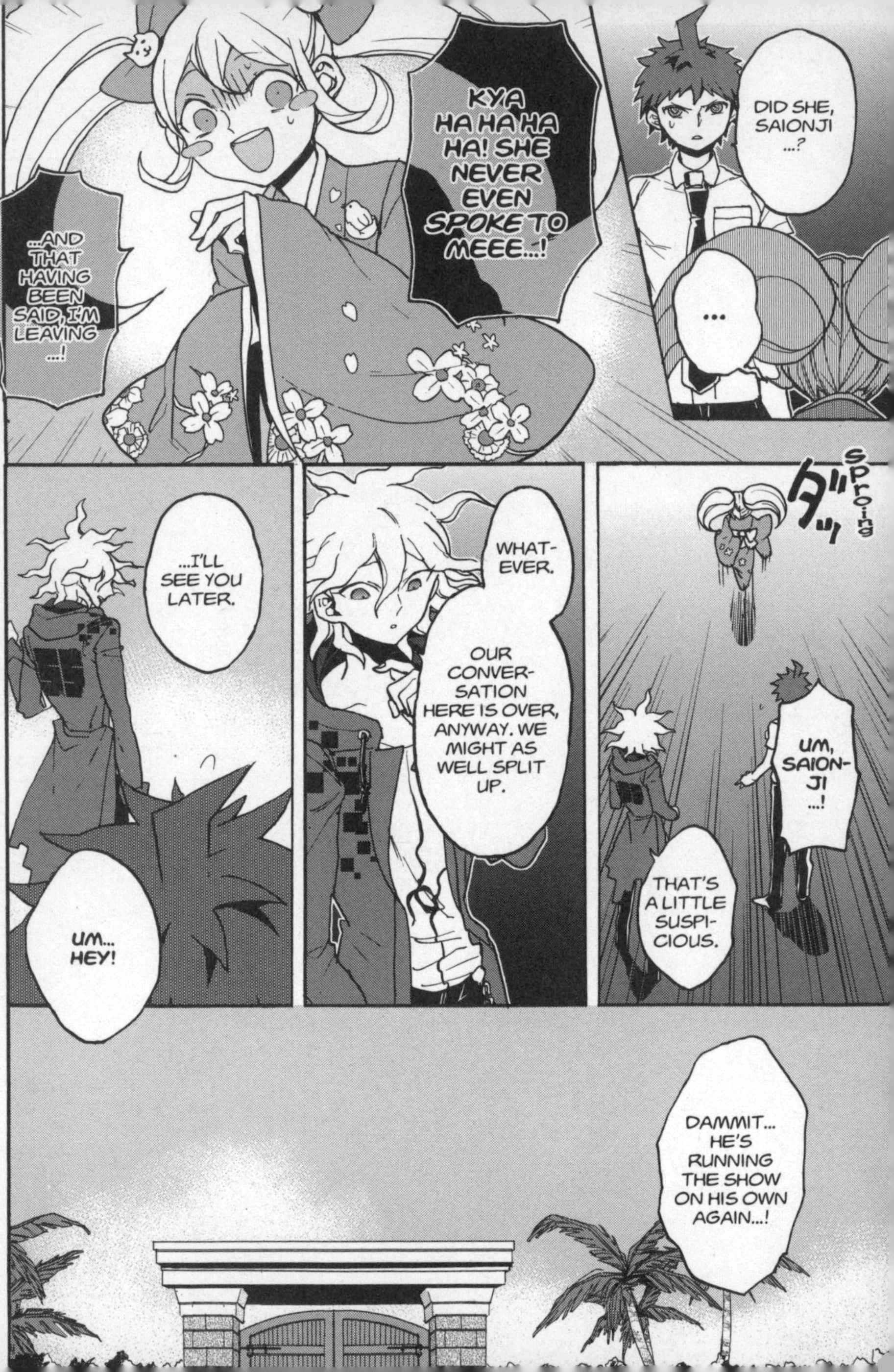
DID SHE, SAIONJI ...?
...
KYA HA HA HA HA! SHE NEVER EVEN SPOKE TO MEEE...!
...AND THAT HAVING BEEN SAID, I'M LEAVING ...!
タッ
Sproing
UM, SAION-JI ...!
THAT'S A LITTLE SUSPICIOUS.
WHAT-EVER.
OUR CONVER-SATION HERE IS OVER, ANYWAY. WE MIGHT AS WELL SPLIT UP.
...I'LL SEE YOU LATER.
UM... HEY!
DAMMIT... HE'S RUNNING THE SHOW ON HIS OWN AGAIN...!

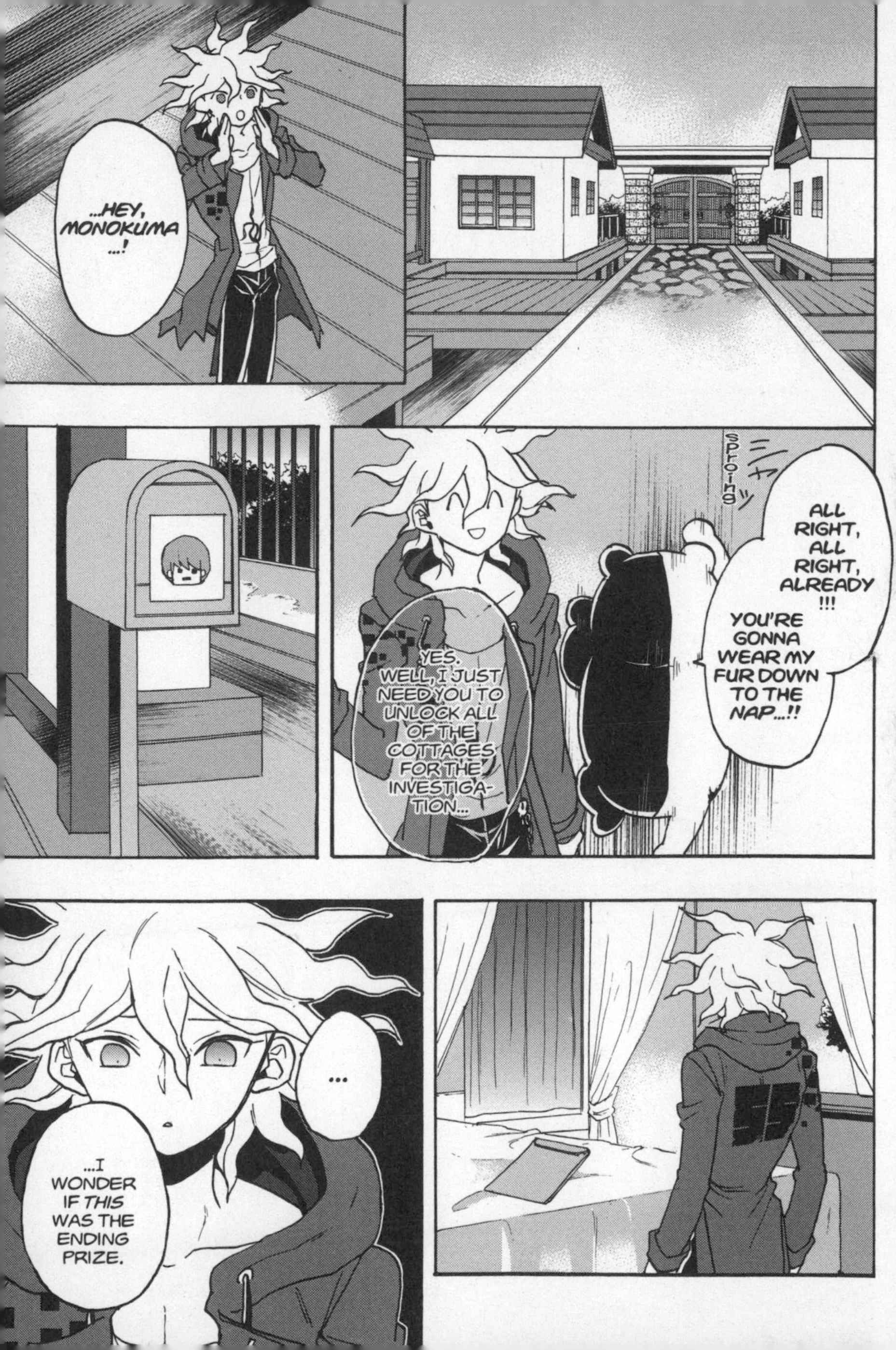
...HEY, MONOKUMA ...!
sproing
ALL RIGHT, ALL RIGHT, ALREADY!!! YOU'RE GONNA WEAR MY FUR DOWN TO THE NAP...!!
YES. WELL, I JUST NEED YOU TO UNLOCK ALL OF THE COTTAGES FOR THE INVESTIGATION...
...
...I WONDER IF *THIS* WAS THE ENDING PRIZE.

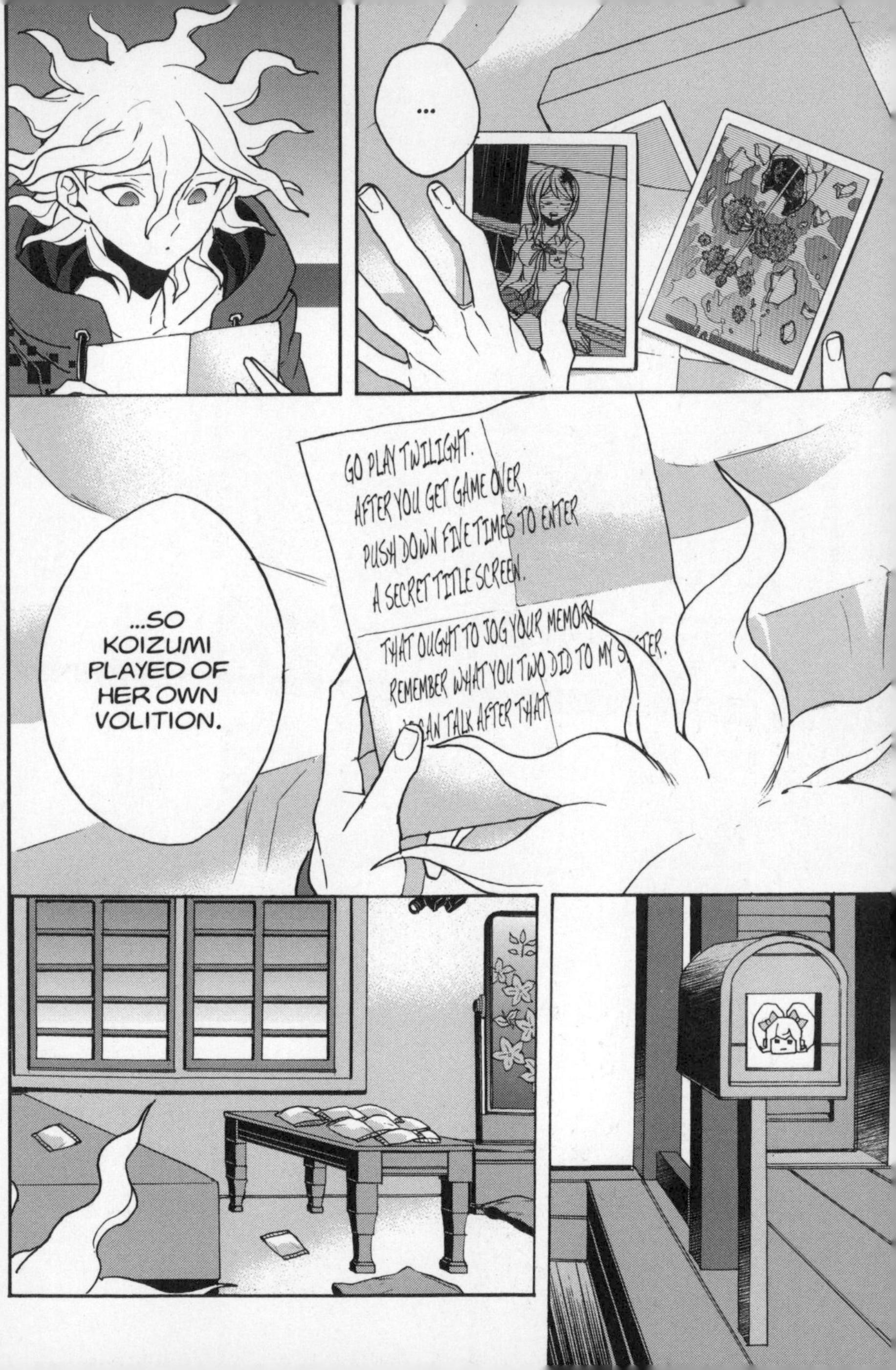
...
GO PLAY TWILIGHT.
AFTER YOU GET GAME OVER,
PUSH DOWN FIVE TIMES TO ENTER
A SECRET TITLE SCREEN.
THAT OUGHT TO JOG YOUR MEMORY
REMEMBER WHAT YOU TWO DID TO MY S
CAN TALK AFTER THAT
...SO KOIZUMI PLAYED OF HER OWN VOLITION.

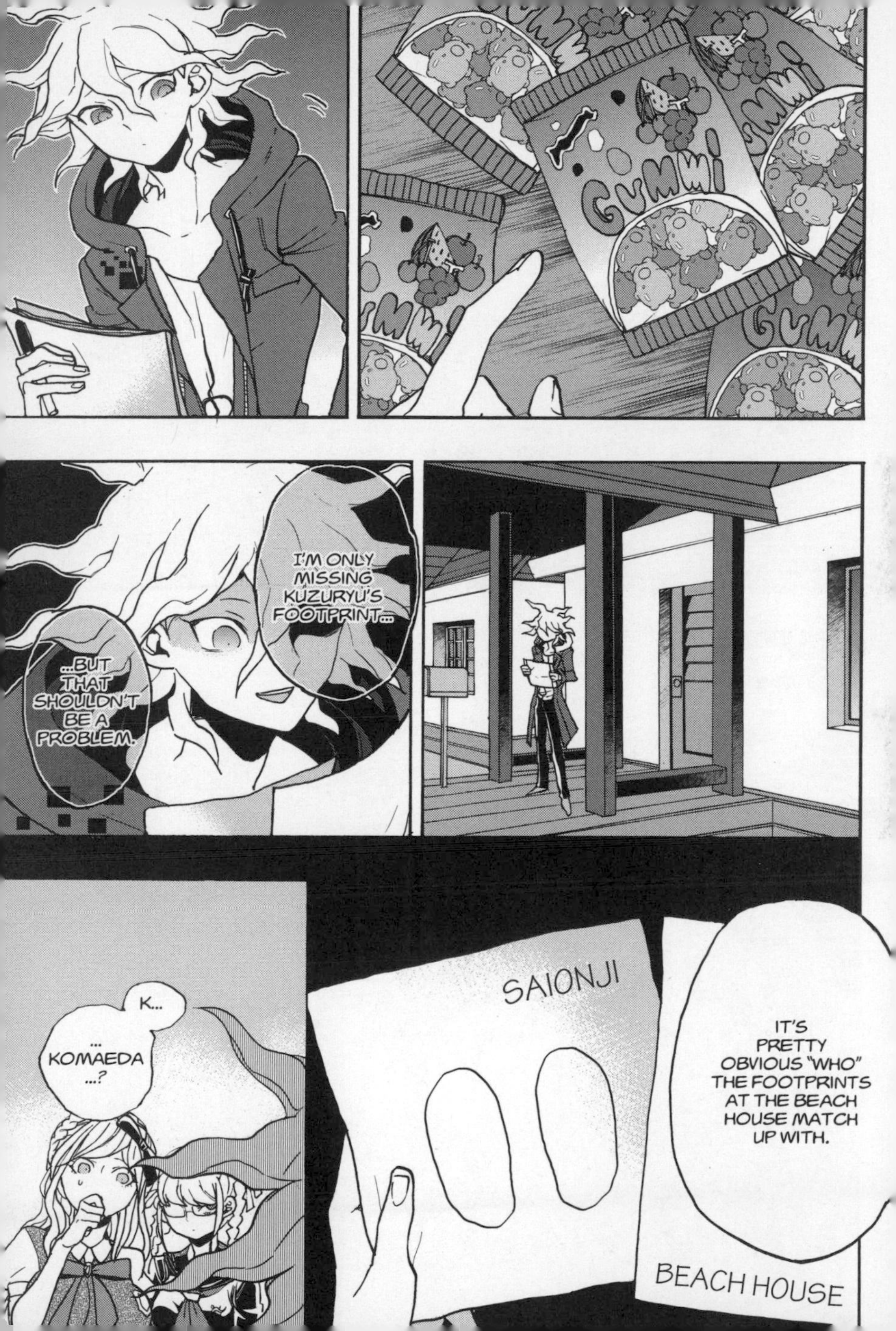
GUMMI
I'M ONLY MISSING KUZURYU'S FOOTPRINT...
...BUT THAT SHOULDN'T BE A PROBLEM.
IT'S PRETTY OBVIOUS "WHO" THE FOOTPRINTS AT THE BEACH HOUSE MATCH UP WITH.
SAIONJI
BEACH HOUSE
K...
...KOMAEDA...?

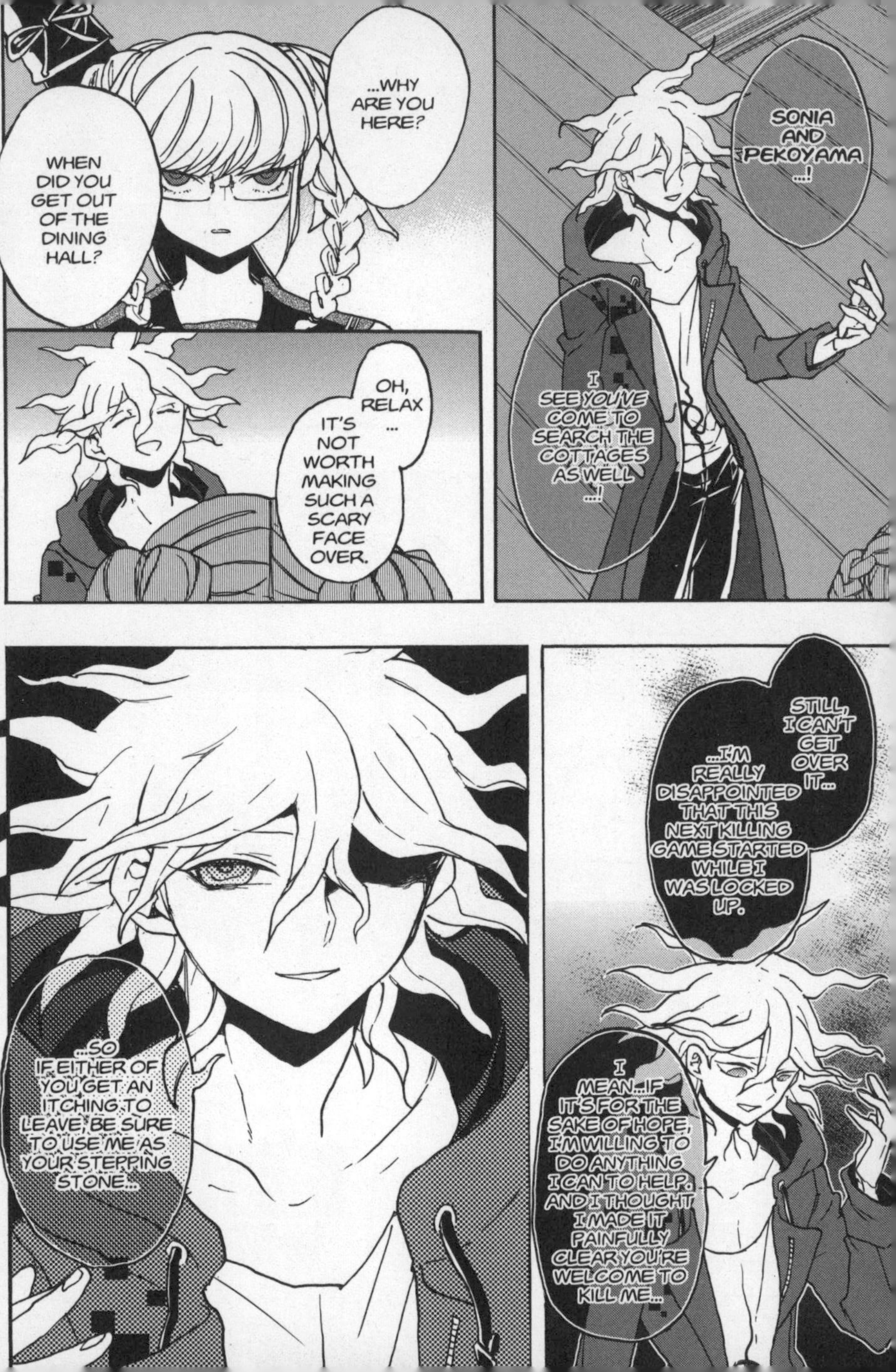
SONIA AND PEKOYAMA ...!
I SEE YOU'VE COME TO SEARCH THE COTTAGES AS WELL ...!
...WHY ARE YOU HERE?
WHEN DID YOU GET OUT OF THE DINING HALL?
OH, RELAX ...
IT'S NOT WORTH MAKING SUCH A SCARY FACE OVER.
STILL, I CAN'T GET OVER IT...
...I'M REALLY DISAPPOINTED THAT THIS NEXT KILLING GAME STARTED WHILE I WAS LOCKED UP.
I MEAN...IF IT'S FOR THE SAKE OF HOPE, I'M WILLING TO DO ANYTHING I CAN TO HELP. AND I THOUGHT I MADE IT PAINFULLY CLEAR YOU'RE WELCOME TO KILL ME...
...SO IF EITHER OF YOU GET AN ITCHING TO LEAVE, BE SURE TO USE ME AS YOUR STEPPING STONE...

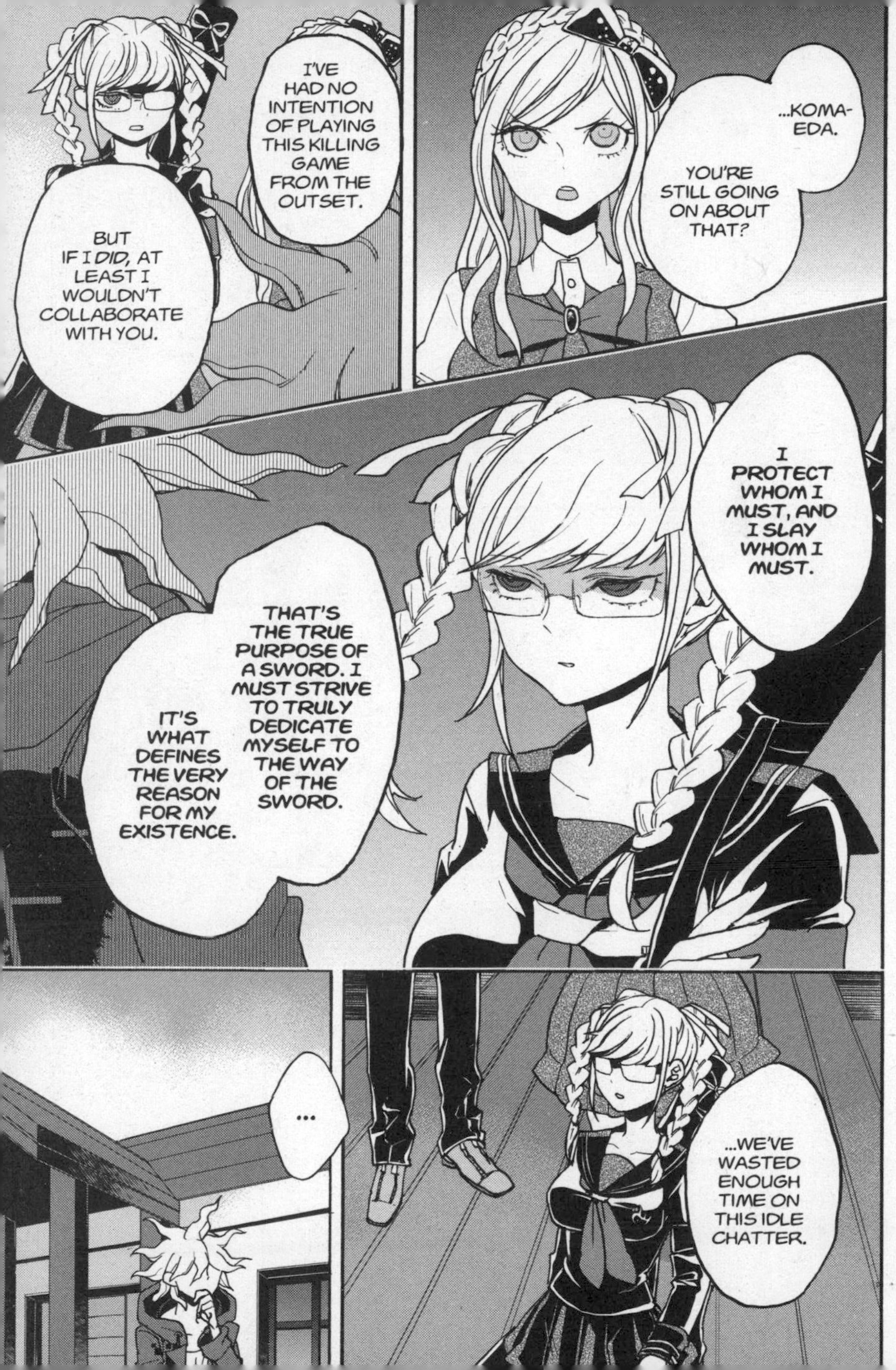
...KOMA-EDA.
YOU'RE STILL GOING ON ABOUT THAT?
I'VE HAD NO INTENTION OF PLAYING THIS KILLING GAME FROM THE OUTSET.
BUT IF I *DID*, AT LEAST I WOULDN'T COLLABORATE WITH YOU.
I PROTECT WHOM I MUST, AND I SLAY WHOM I MUST.
THAT'S THE TRUE PURPOSE OF A SWORD. I MUST STRIVE TO TRULY DEDICATE MYSELF TO THE WAY OF THE SWORD.
IT'S WHAT DEFINES THE VERY REASON FOR MY EXISTENCE.
...WE'VE WASTED ENOUGH TIME ON THIS IDLE CHATTER.
...

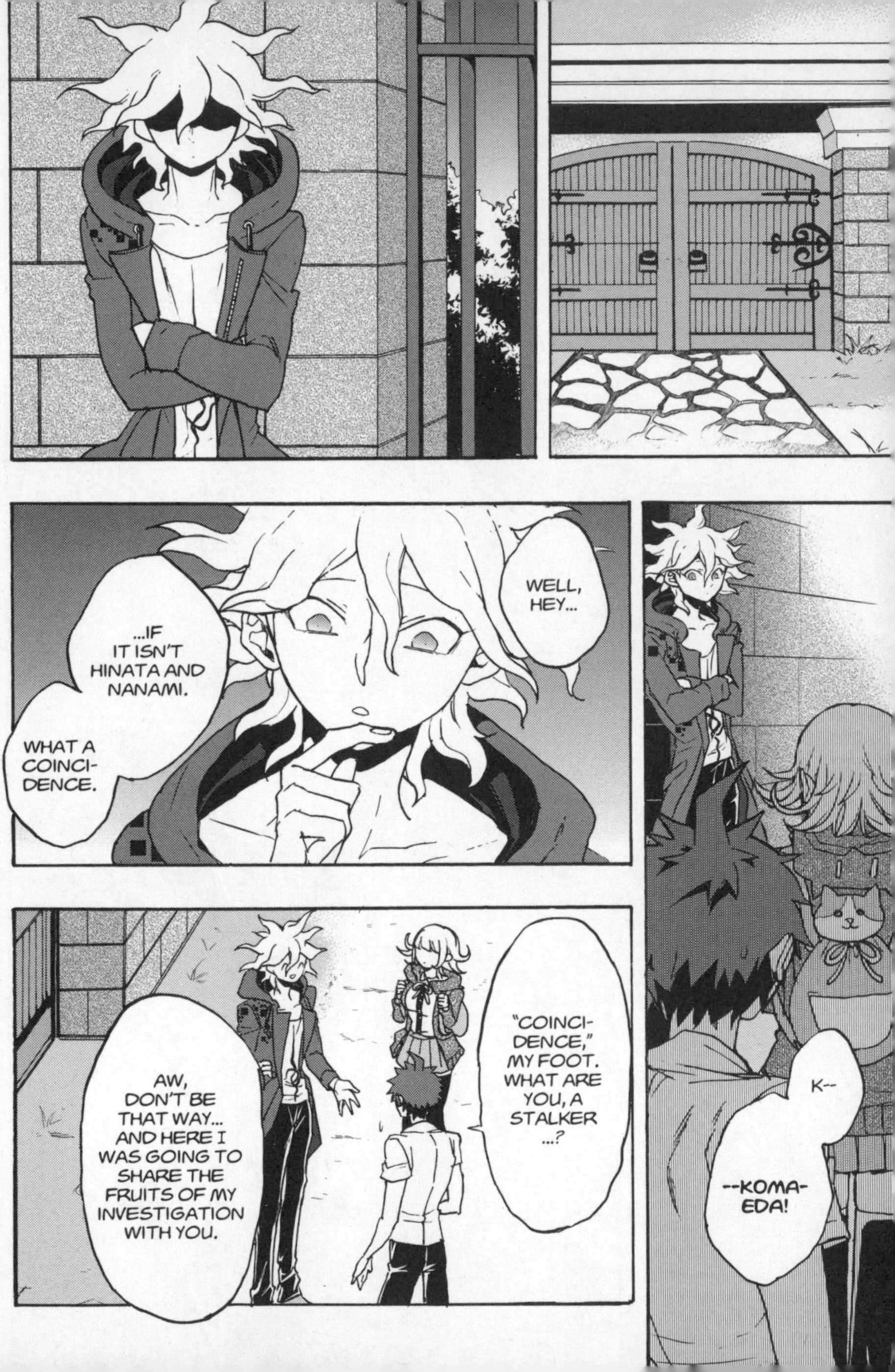
K--
--KOMA-EDA!
WELL, HEY...
...IF IT ISN'T HINATA AND NANAMI.
WHAT A COINCI-DENCE.
"COINCI-DENCE," MY FOOT. WHAT ARE YOU, A STALKER ...?
AW, DON'T BE THAT WAY... AND HERE I WAS GOING TO SHARE THE FRUITS OF MY INVESTIGATION WITH YOU.

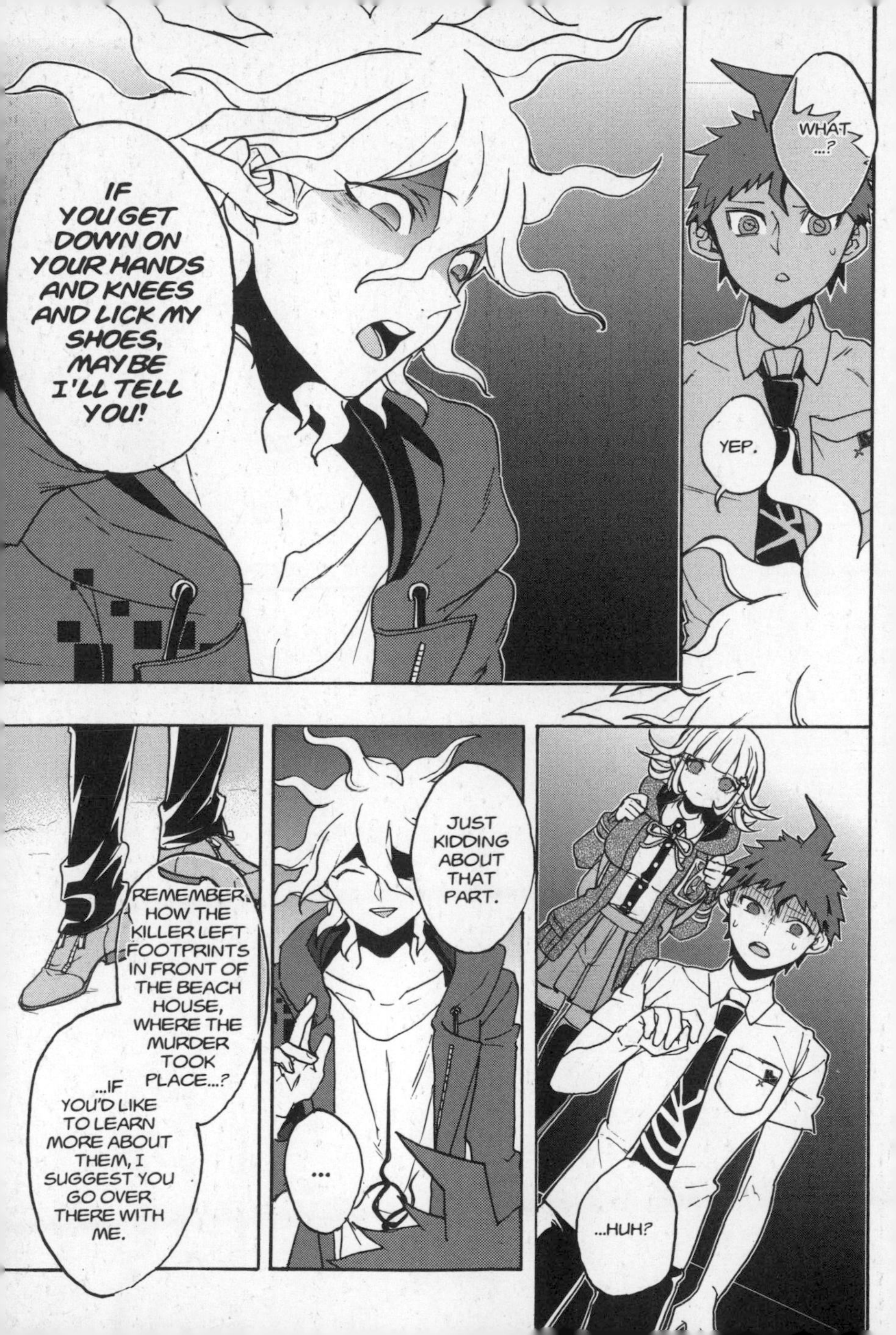
WHAT ...?
YEP.
IF YOU GET DOWN ON YOUR HANDS AND KNEES AND LICK MY SHOES, MAYBE I'LL TELL YOU!
...HUH?
JUST KIDDING ABOUT THAT PART.
...
REMEMBER HOW THE KILLER LEFT FOOTPRINTS IN FRONT OF THE BEACH HOUSE, WHERE THE MURDER TOOK PLACE...?
...IF YOU'D LIKE TO LEARN MORE ABOUT THEM, I SUGGEST YOU GO OVER THERE WITH ME.

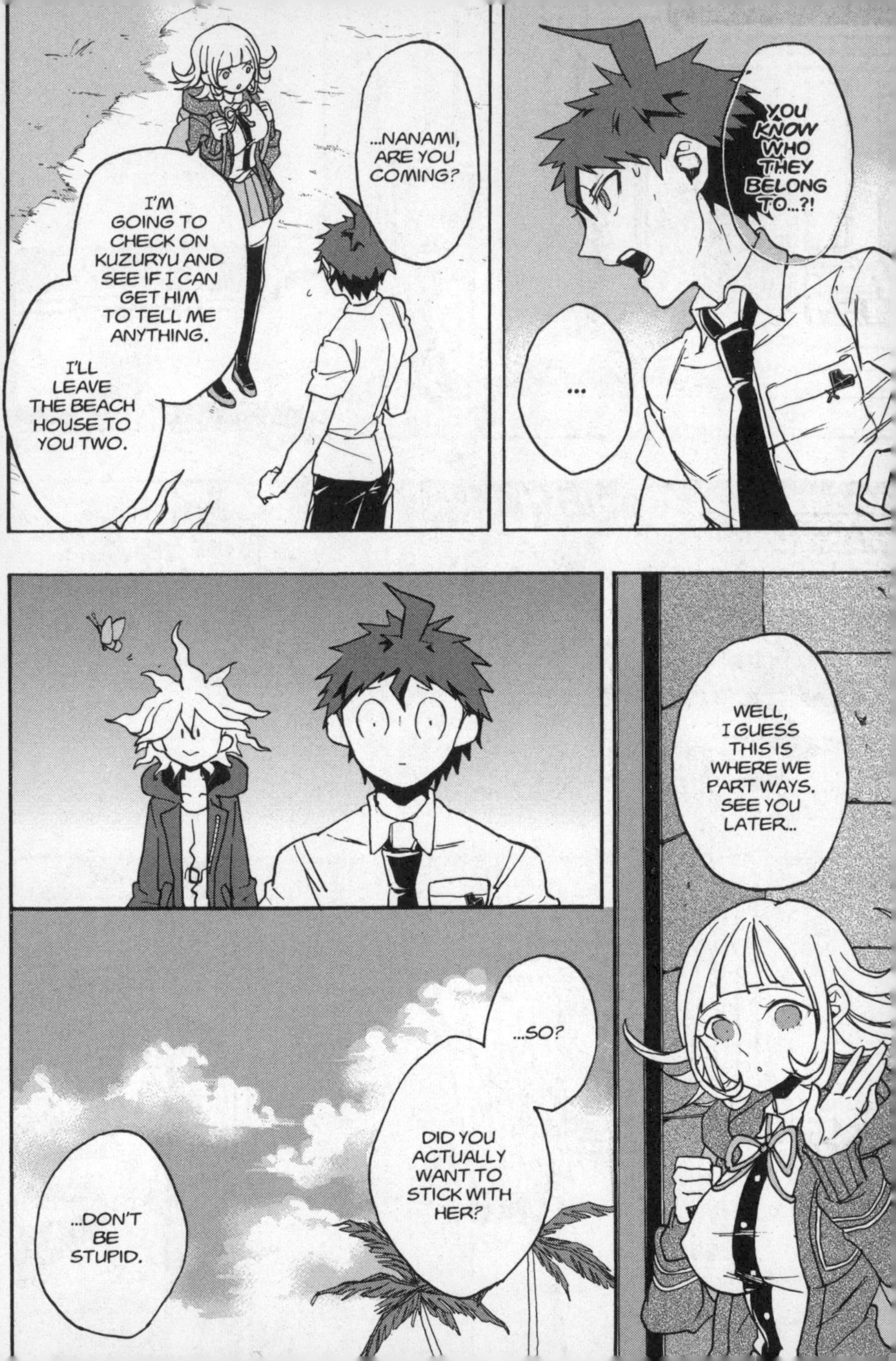
YOU KNOW WHO THEY BELONG TO...?!
...
...NANAMI, ARE YOU COMING?
I'M GOING TO CHECK ON KUZURYU AND SEE IF I CAN GET HIM TO TELL ME ANYTHING.
I'LL LEAVE THE BEACH HOUSE TO YOU TWO.
WELL, I GUESS THIS IS WHERE WE PART WAYS. SEE YOU LATER...
...SO?
DID YOU ACTUALLY WANT TO STICK WITH HER?
...DON'T BE STUPID.

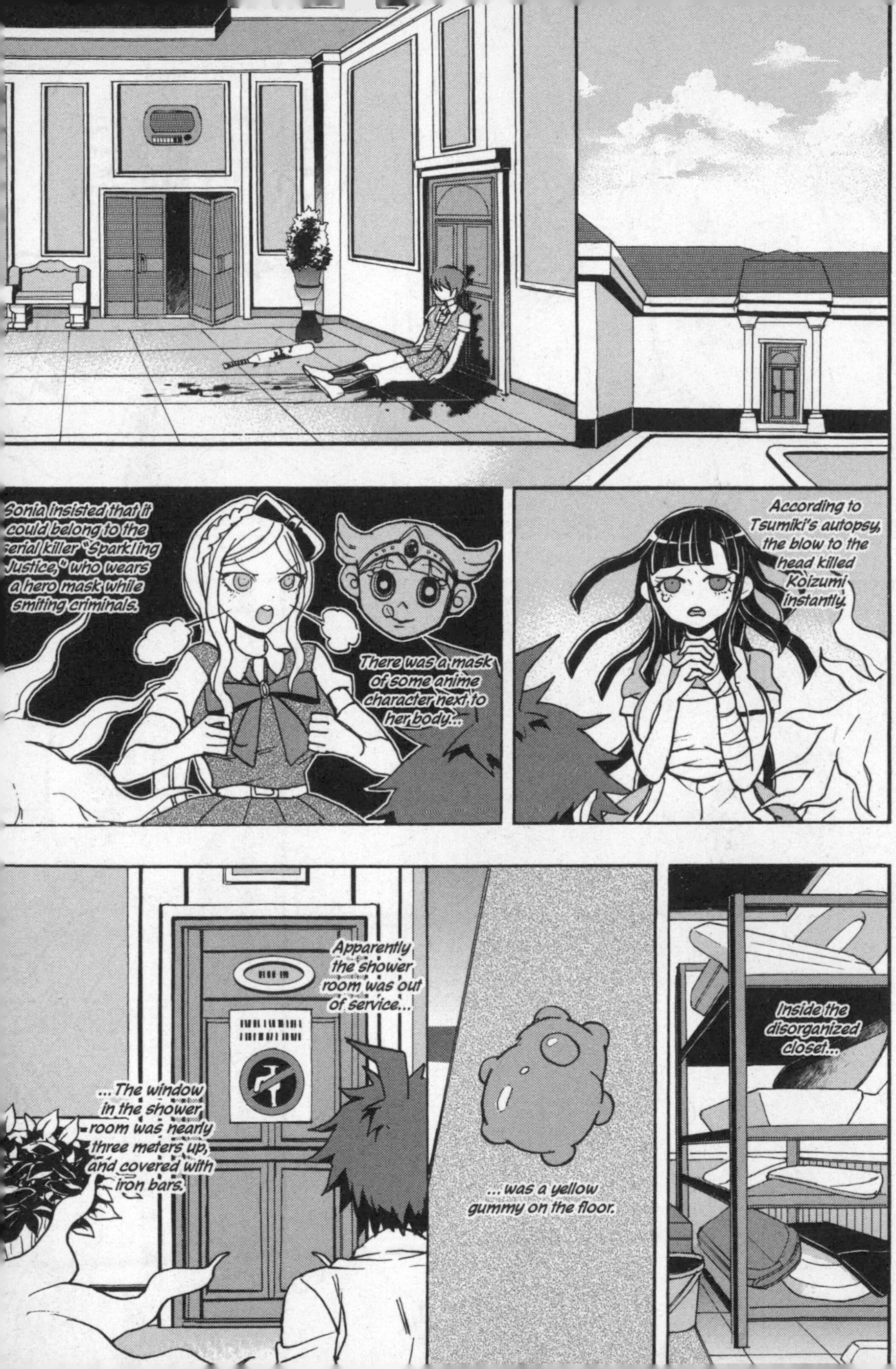
According to Tsumiki's autopsy, the blow to the head killed Koizumi instantly.
There was a mask of some anime character next to her body...
Sonia insisted that it could belong to the serial killer "Sparkling Justice," who wears a hero mask while smiting criminals.
Inside the disorganized closet...
... was a yellow gummy on the floor.
Apparently the shower room was out of service...
...The window in the shower room was nearly three meters up, and covered with iron bars.

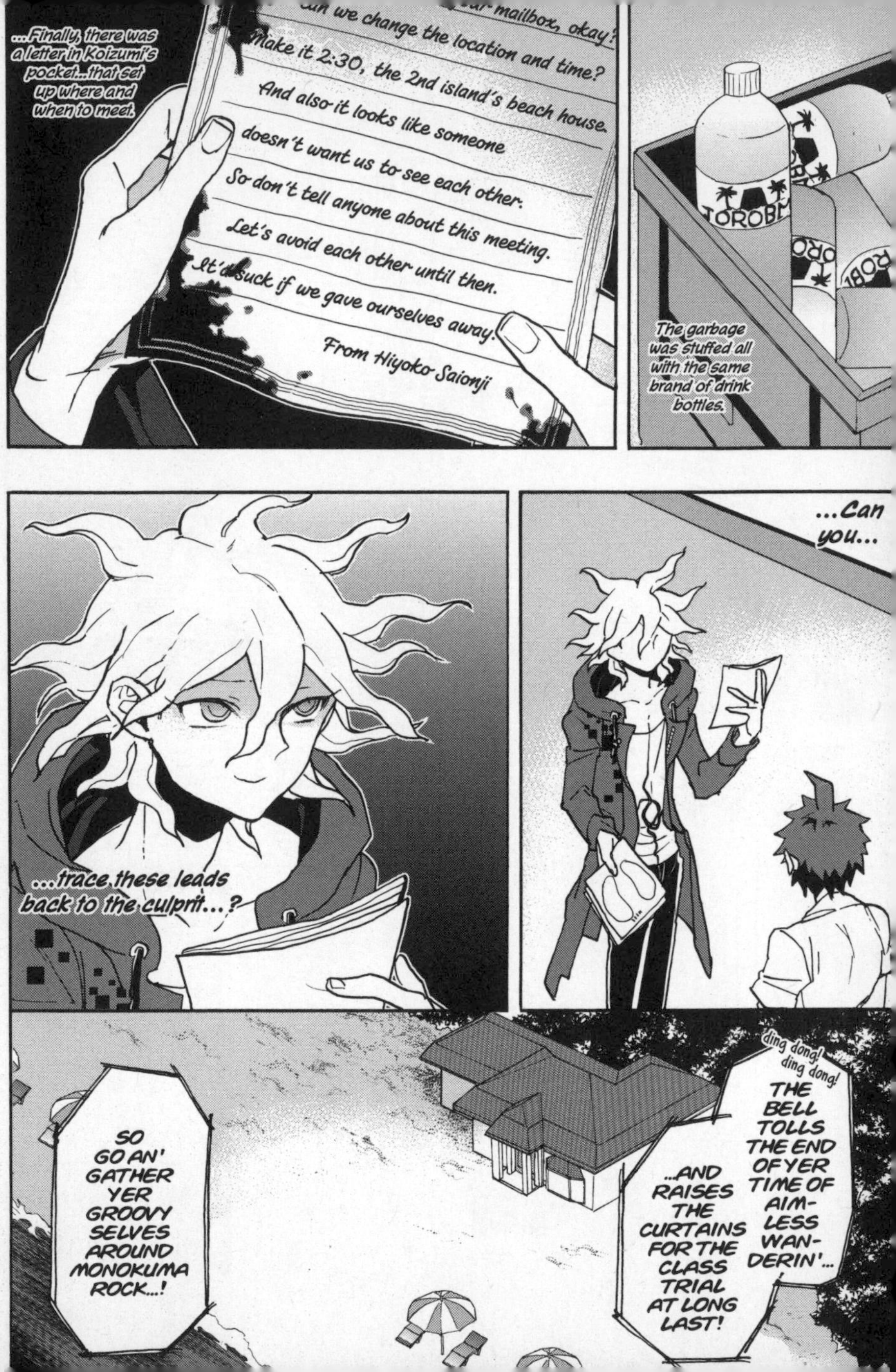
The garbage was stuffed all with the same brand of drink bottles.
...Finally, there was a letter in Koizumi's pocket...that set up where and when to meet.
mailbox, okay?
can we change the location and time?
Make it 2:30, the 2nd island's beach house.
And also it looks like someone
doesn't want us to see each other.
So don't tell anyone about this meeting.
Let's avoid each other until then.
It'd suck if we gave ourselves away.
From Hiyoko Saionji
...Can you...
...trace these leads back to the culprit...?
ding dong! ding dong!
THE BELL TOLLS THE END OF YER TIME OF AIMLESS WANDERIN'...
...AND RAISES THE CURTAINS FOR THE CLASS TRIAL AT LONG LAST!
SO GO AN' GATHER YER GROOVY SELVES AROUND MONOKUMA ROCK...!

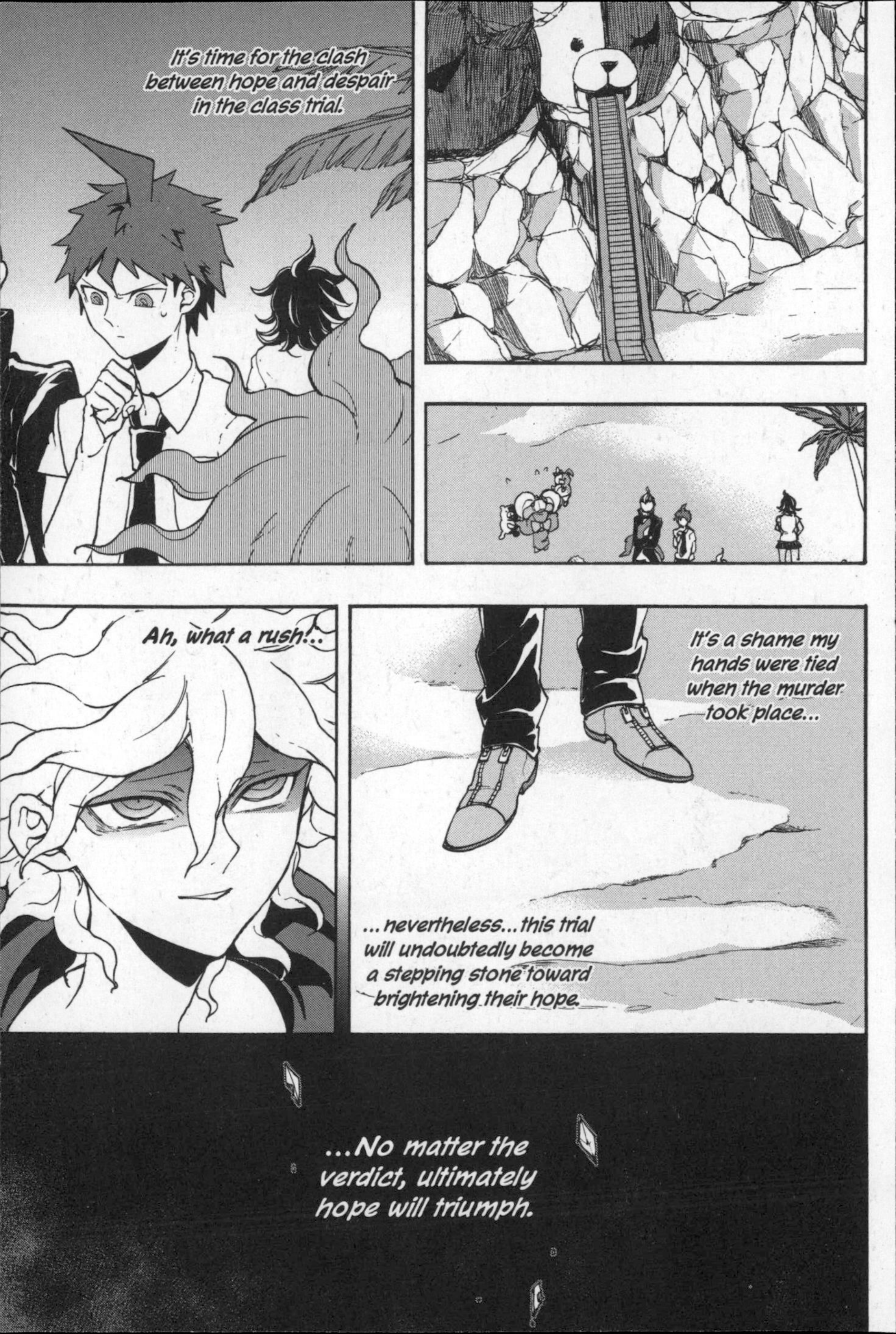
It's time for the clash between hope and despair in the class trial.
It's a shame my hands were tied when the murder took place...
...nevertheless...this trial will undoubtedly become a stepping stone toward brightening their hope.
Ah, what a rush!...
...No matter the verdict, ultimately hope will triumph.

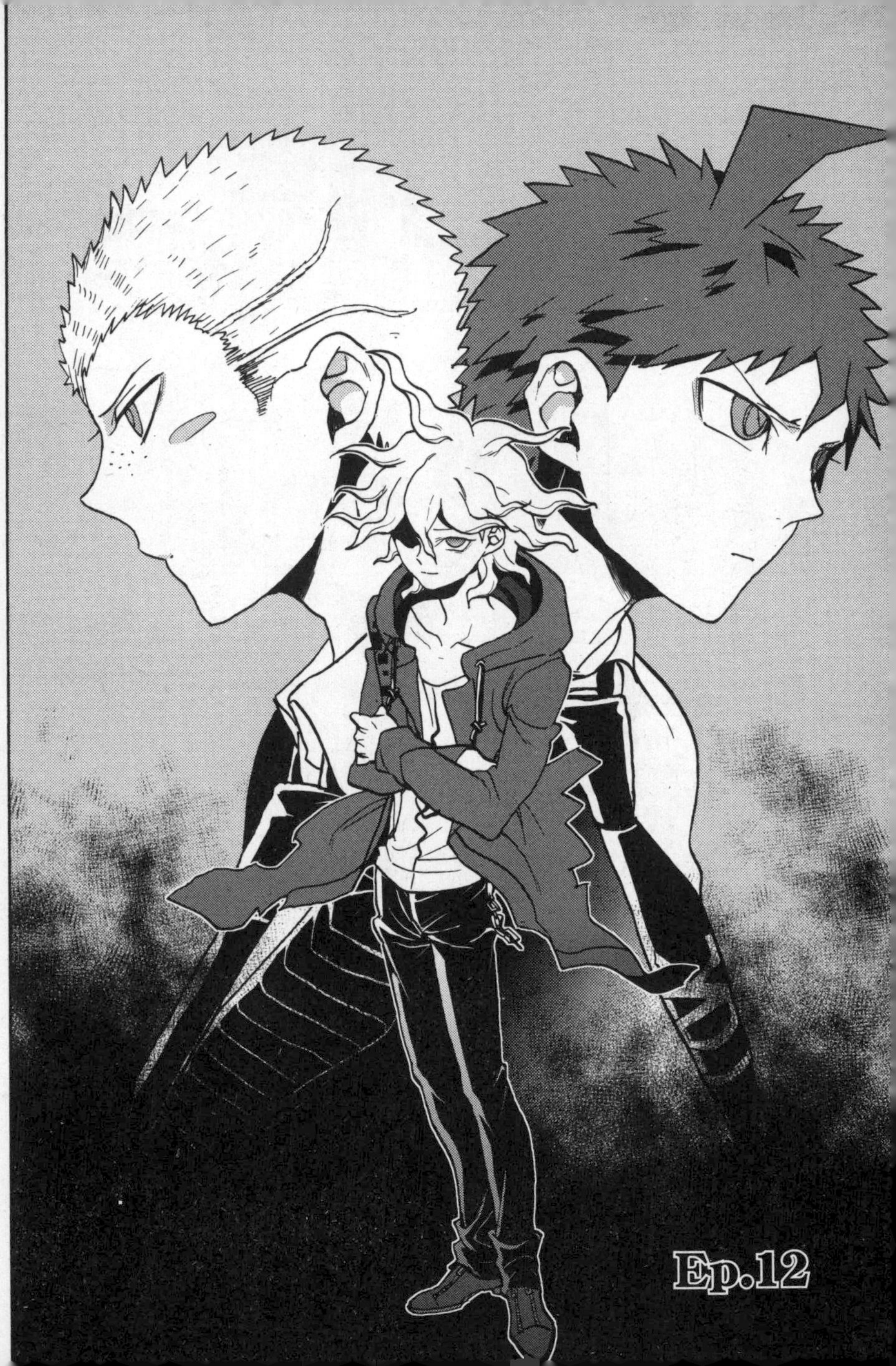
Ep.12

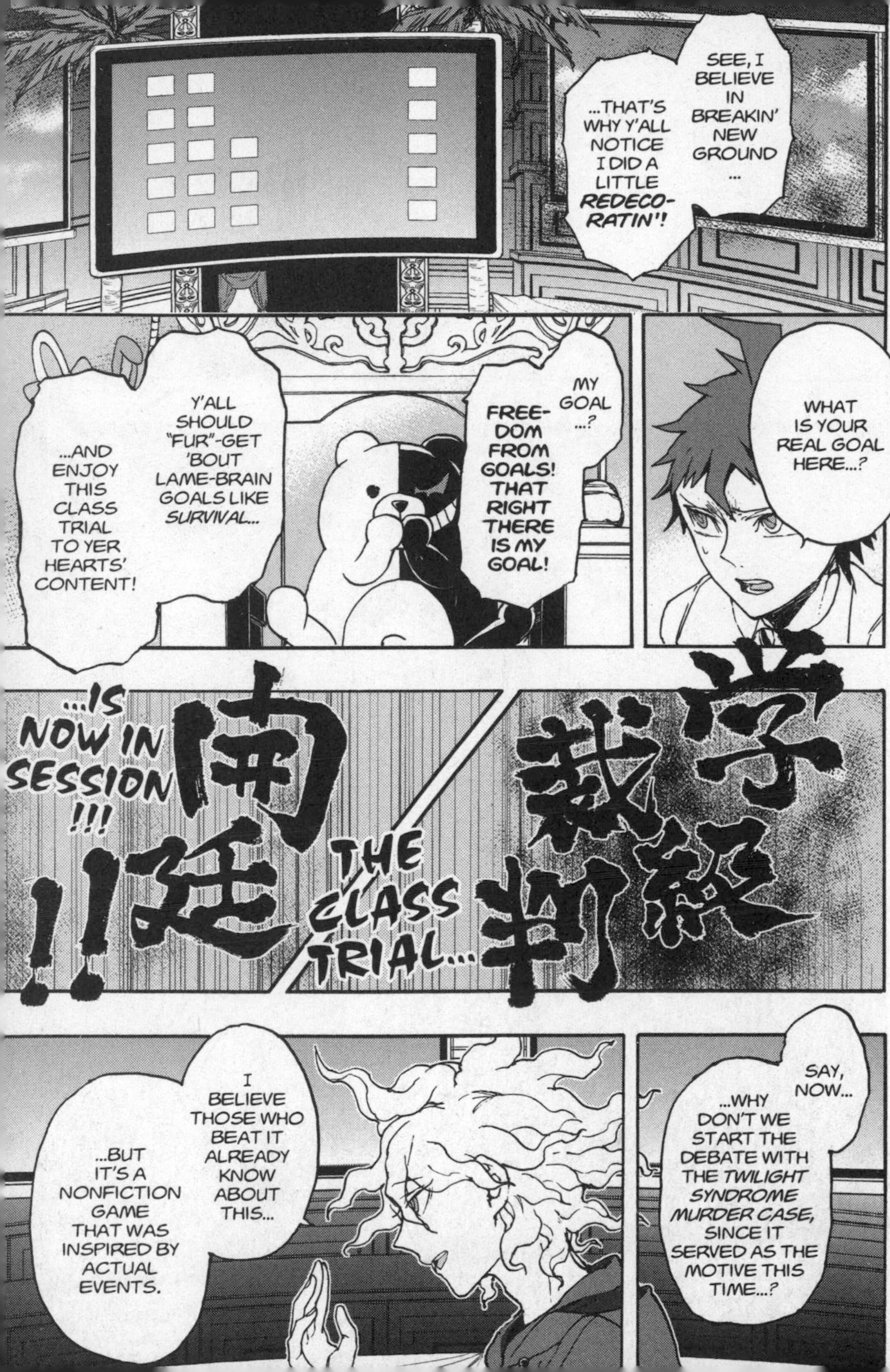
SEE, I BELIEVE IN BREAKIN' NEW GROUND ...
...THAT'S WHY Y'ALL NOTICE I DID A LITTLE *REDECO-RATIN'*!
WHAT IS YOUR REAL GOAL HERE...?
MY GOAL ...?
FREE-DOM FROM GOALS! THAT RIGHT THERE IS MY GOAL!
Y'ALL SHOULD "FUR"-GET 'BOUT LAME-BRAIN GOALS LIKE *SURVIVAL*...
...AND ENJOY THIS CLASS TRIAL TO YER HEARTS' CONTENT!
学級裁判
THE CLASS TRIAL...
開廷!!
...IS NOW IN SESSION!!!
SAY, NOW...
...WHY DON'T WE START THE DEBATE WITH THE *TWILIGHT SYNDROME MURDER CASE*, SINCE IT SERVED AS THE MOTIVE THIS TIME...?
I BELIEVE THOSE WHO BEAT IT ALREADY KNOW ABOUT THIS...
...BUT IT'S A NONFICTION GAME THAT WAS INSPIRED BY ACTUAL EVENTS.

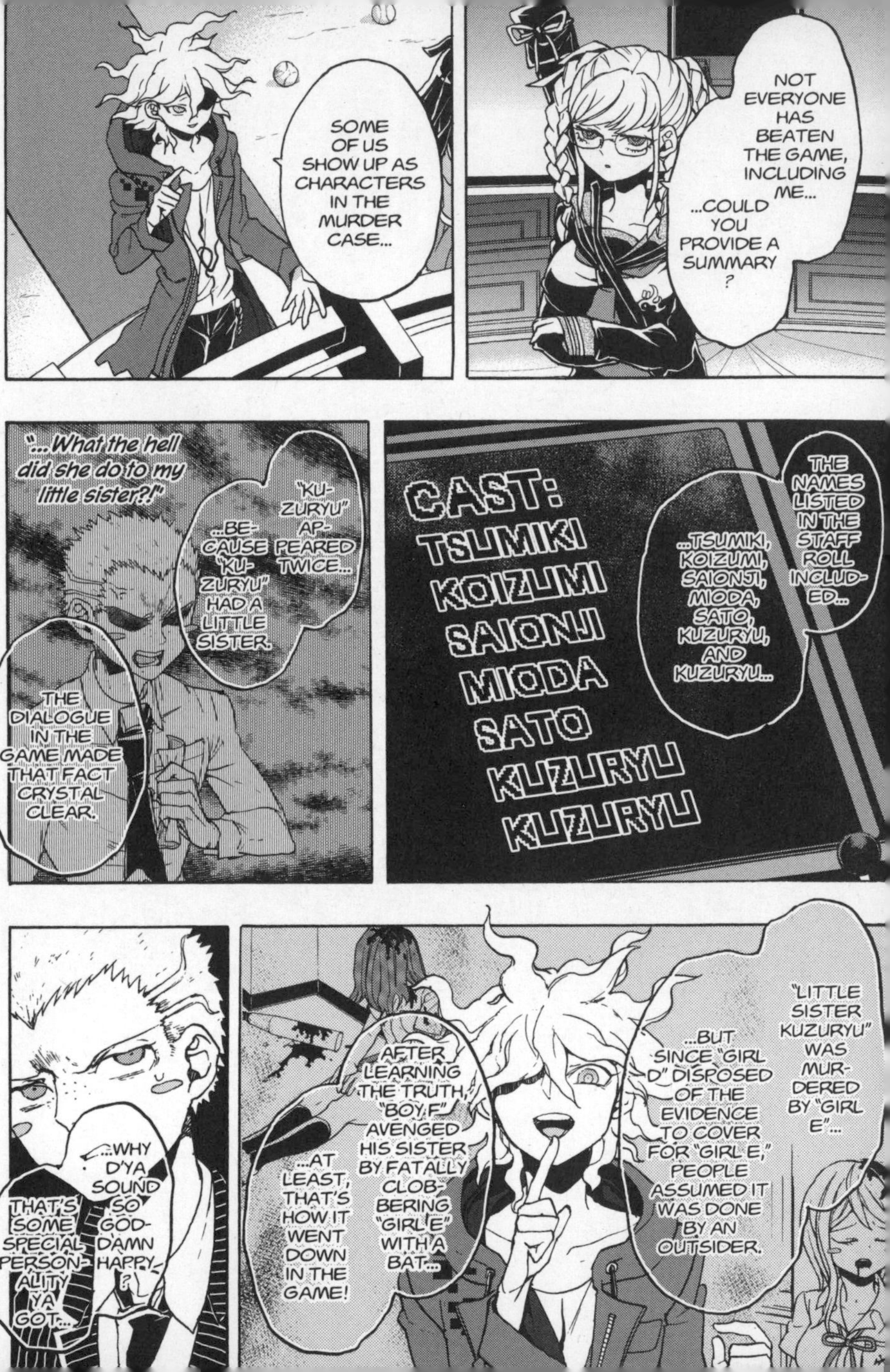
NOT EVERYONE HAS BEATEN THE GAME, INCLUDING ME...
...COULD YOU PROVIDE A SUMMARY?
SOME OF US SHOW UP AS CHARACTERS IN THE MURDER CASE...
THE NAMES LISTED IN THE STAFF ROLL INCLUDED...
...TSUMIKI, KOIZUMI, SAIONJI, MIODA, SATO, KUZURYU, AND KUZURYU...
CAST: TSUMIKI KOIZUMI SAIONJI MIODA SATO KUZURYU KUZURYU
"KUZURYU" APPEARED TWICE...
...BECAUSE "KUZURYU" HAD A LITTLE SISTER.
"...What the hell did she do to my little sister?!"
THE DIALOGUE IN THE GAME MADE THAT FACT CRYSTAL CLEAR.
"LITTLE SISTER KUZURYU" WAS MURDERED BY "GIRL E"...
...BUT SINCE "GIRL D" DISPOSED OF THE EVIDENCE TO COVER FOR "GIRL E," PEOPLE ASSUMED IT WAS DONE BY AN OUTSIDER.
AFTER LEARNING THE TRUTH, "BOY F" AVENGED HIS SISTER BY FATALLY CLOBBERING "GIRL E" WITH A BAT...
...AT LEAST, THAT'S HOW IT WENT DOWN IN THE GAME!
...WHY D'YA SOUND SO GODDAMN HAPPY?
THAT'S SOME SPECIAL PERSONALITY YA GOT...

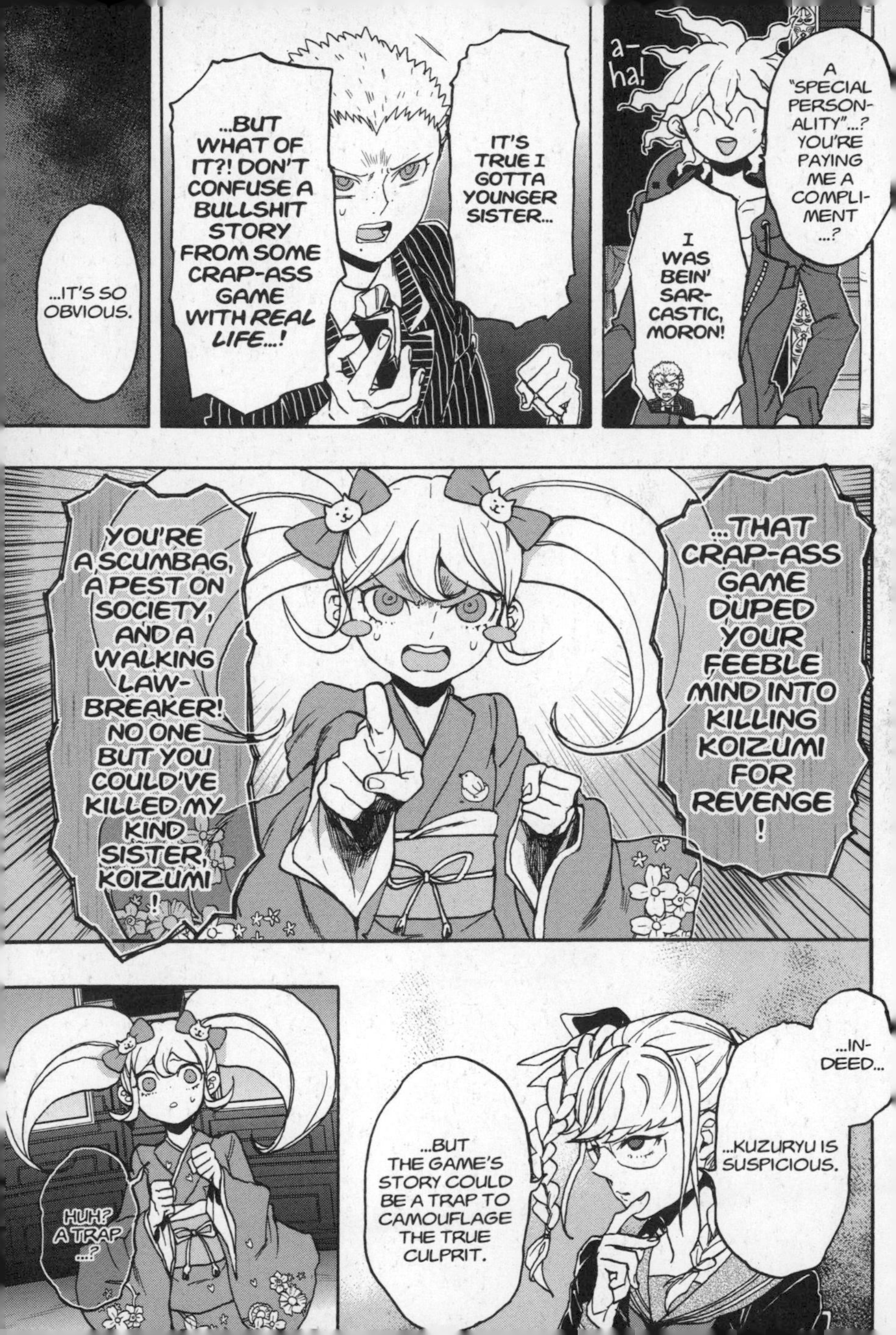
A "SPECIAL PERSONALITY"...? YOU'RE PAYING ME A COMPLIMENT...?
a-ha!
I WAS BEIN' SARCASTIC, MORON!
IT'S TRUE I GOTTA YOUNGER SISTER...
...BUT WHAT OF IT?! DON'T CONFUSE A BULLSHIT STORY FROM SOME CRAP-ASS GAME WITH *REAL LIFE*...!
...IT'S SO OBVIOUS.
...THAT CRAP-ASS GAME DUPED YOUR FEEBLE MIND INTO KILLING KOIZUMI FOR REVENGE!
YOU'RE A SCUMBAG, A PEST ON SOCIETY, AND A WALKING LAW-BREAKER! NO ONE BUT YOU COULD'VE KILLED MY KIND SISTER, KOIZUMI!
...INDEED...
...KUZURYU IS SUSPICIOUS.
...BUT THE GAME'S STORY COULD BE A TRAP TO CAMOUFLAGE THE TRUE CULPRIT.
HUH? A TRAP...?

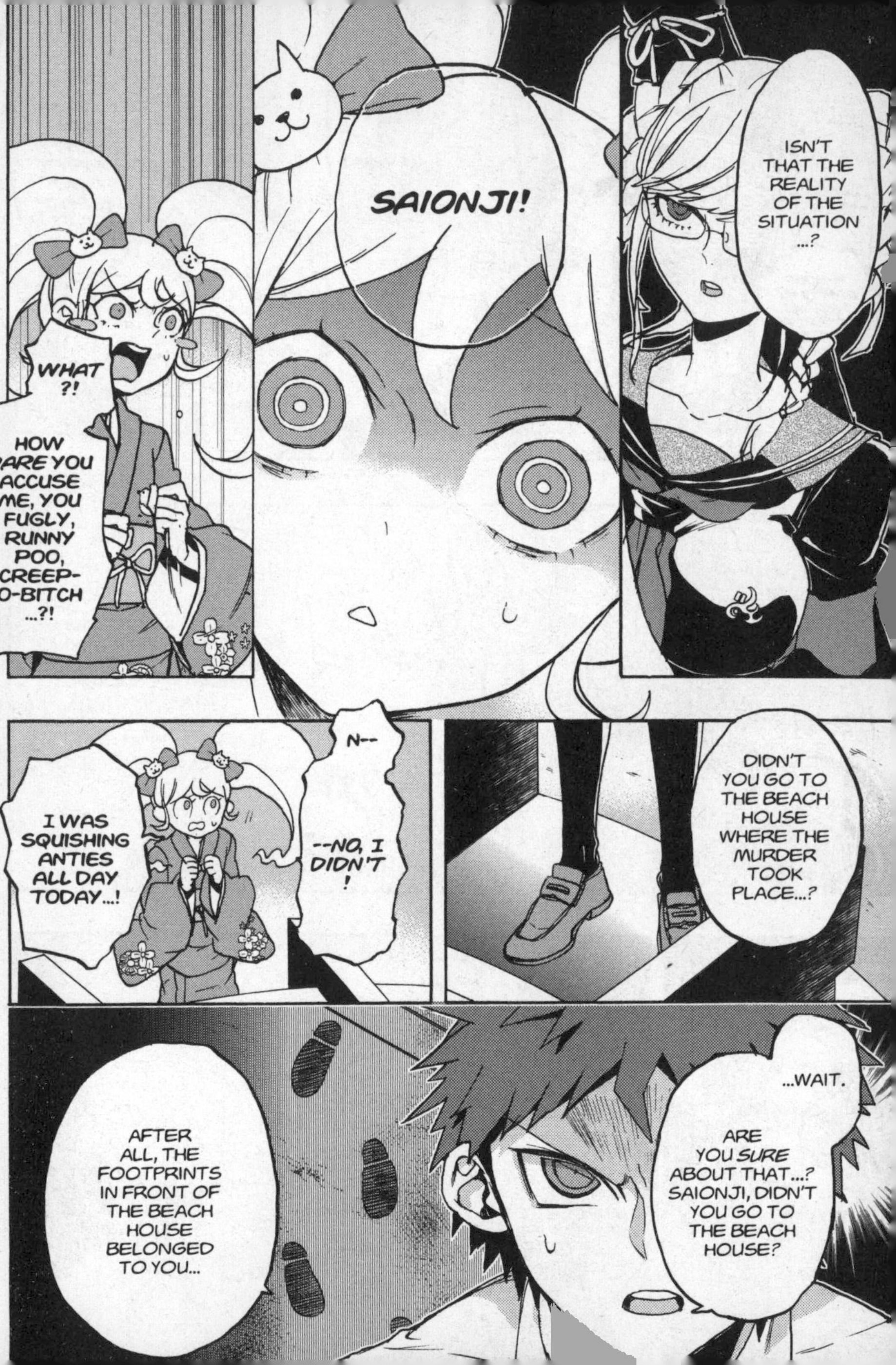
ISN'T THAT THE REALITY OF THE SITUATION ...?
SAIONJI!
WHAT ?!
HOW DARE YOU ACCUSE ME, YOU FUGLY, RUNNY POO, CREEP-O-BITCH ...?!
DIDN'T YOU GO TO THE BEACH HOUSE WHERE THE MURDER TOOK PLACE...?
N--
--NO, I DIDN'T !
I WAS SQUISHING ANTIES ALL DAY TODAY...!
...WAIT.
ARE YOU SURE ABOUT THAT...? SAIONJI, DIDN'T YOU GO TO THE BEACH HOUSE?
AFTER ALL, THE FOOTPRINTS IN FRONT OF THE BEACH HOUSE BELONGED TO YOU...

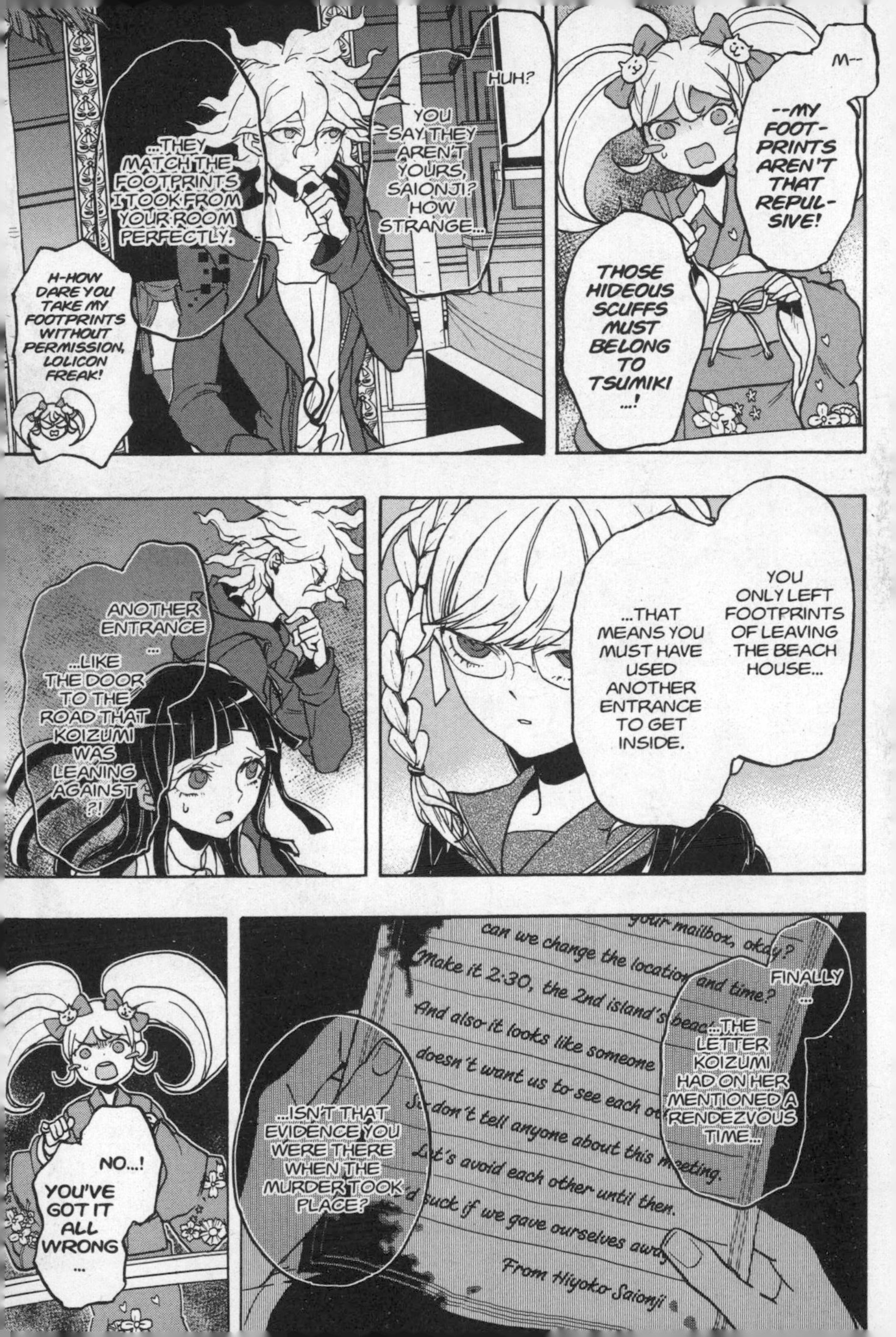
M--
--MY FOOT-PRINTS AREN'T THAT REPUL-SIVE!
THOSE HIDEOUS SCUFFS MUST BELONG TO TSUMIKI ...!
HUH?
YOU SAY THEY AREN'T YOURS, SAIONJI? HOW STRANGE...
...THEY MATCH THE FOOTPRINTS I TOOK FROM YOUR ROOM PERFECTLY.
H-HOW DARE YOU TAKE MY FOOTPRINTS WITHOUT PERMISSION, LOLICON FREAK!
YOU ONLY LEFT FOOTPRINTS OF LEAVING THE BEACH HOUSE...
...THAT MEANS YOU MUST HAVE USED ANOTHER ENTRANCE TO GET INSIDE.
ANOTHER ENTRANCE ...
...LIKE THE DOOR TO THE ROAD THAT KOIZUMI WAS LEANING AGAINST ?!
your mailbox, okay?
can we change the location and time?
Make it 2:30, the 2nd island's beac
And also it looks like someone
doesn't want us to see each o
S don't tell anyone about this meeting.
Let's avoid each other until then.
d suck if we gave ourselves aw
From Hiyoko Saionji
FINALLY ...
...THE LETTER KOIZUMI HAD ON HER MENTIONED A RENDEZVOUS TIME...
...ISN'T THAT EVIDENCE YOU WERE THERE WHEN THE MURDER TOOK PLACE?
NO...!
YOU'VE GOT IT ALL WRONG ...

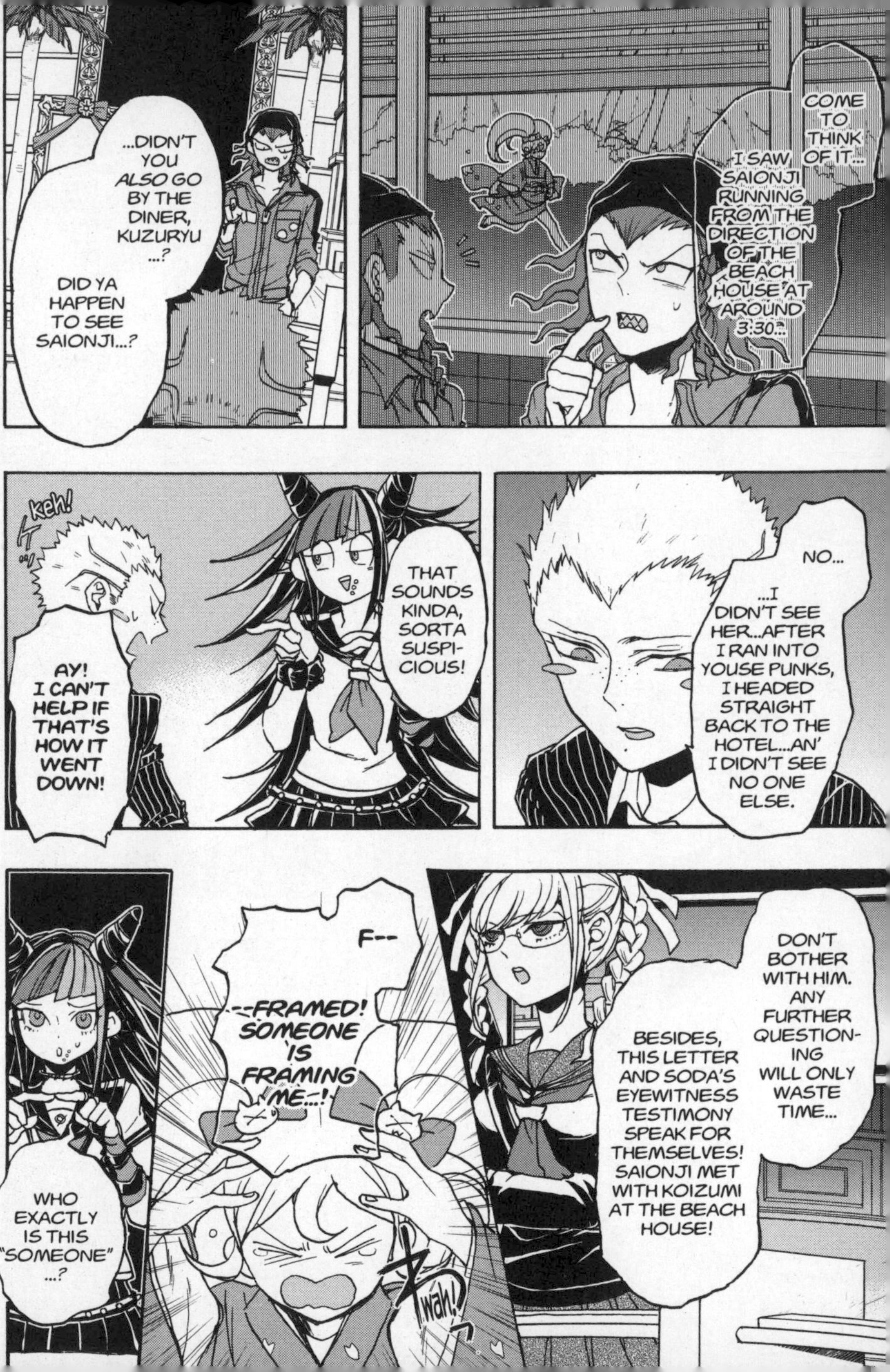
COME TO THINK OF IT...
I SAW SAIONJI RUNNING FROM THE DIRECTION OF THE BEACH HOUSE AT AROUND 3:30...
...DIDN'T YOU ALSO GO BY THE DINER, KUZURYU...?
DID YA HAPPEN TO SEE SAIONJI...?
NO...
...I DIDN'T SEE HER...AFTER I RAN INTO YOUSE PUNKS, I HEADED STRAIGHT BACK TO THE HOTEL...AN' I DIDN'T SEE NO ONE ELSE.
THAT SOUNDS KINDA, SORTA SUSPICIOUS!
keh!
AY! I CAN'T HELP IF THAT'S HOW IT WENT DOWN!
DON'T BOTHER WITH HIM. ANY FURTHER QUESTIONING WILL ONLY WASTE TIME...
BESIDES, THIS LETTER AND SODA'S EYEWITNESS TESTIMONY SPEAK FOR THEMSELVES! SAIONJI MET WITH KOIZUMI AT THE BEACH HOUSE!
F--
--FRAMED! SOMEONE IS FRAMING ME...!
wah!
WHO EXACTLY IS THIS "SOMEONE"...?

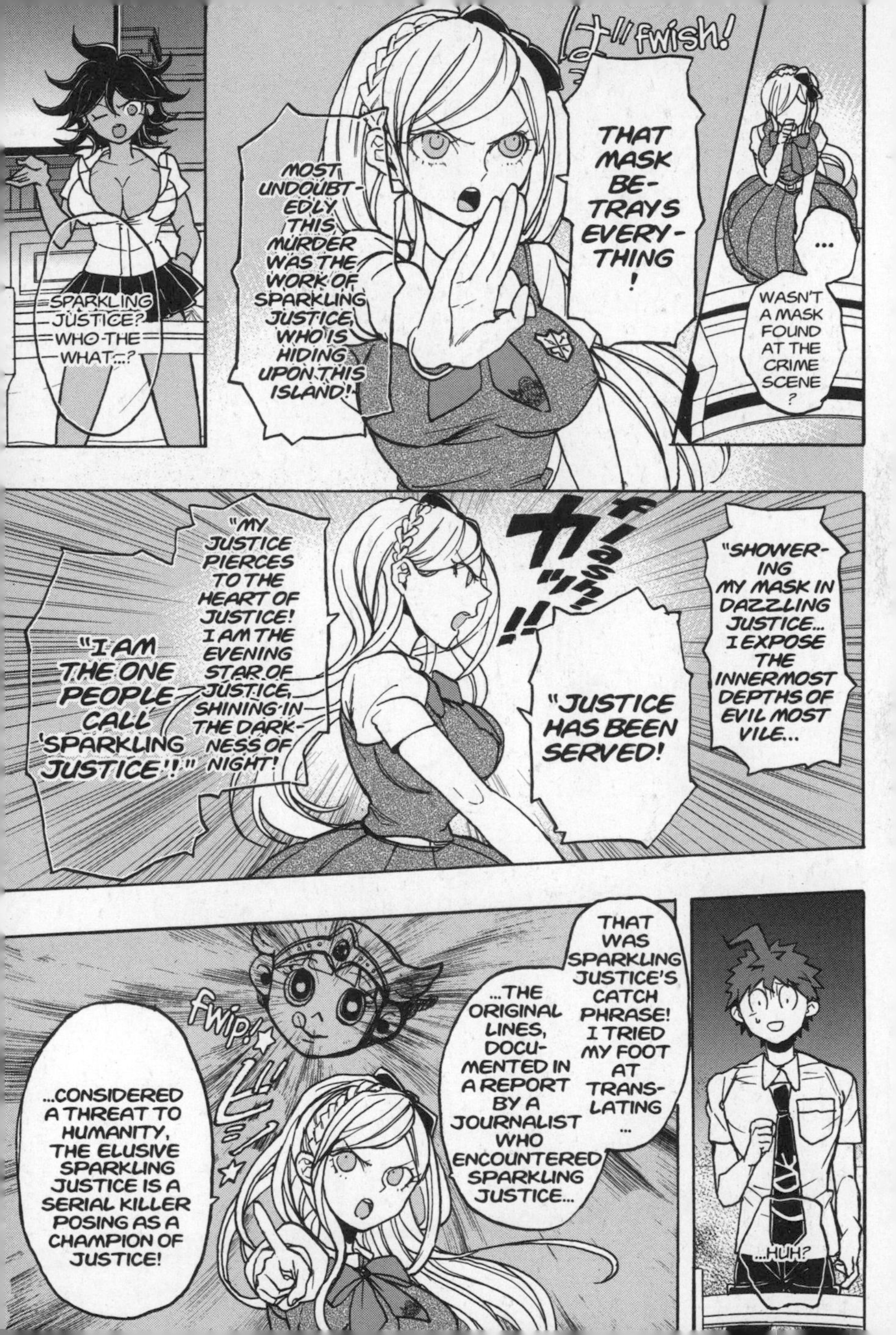
...
WASN'T A MASK FOUND AT THE CRIME SCENE?
fwish!
THAT MASK BETRAYS EVERYTHING!
MOST UNDOUBTEDLY THIS MURDER WAS THE WORK OF SPARKLING JUSTICE, WHO IS HIDING UPON THIS ISLAND!
SPARKLING JUSTICE? WHO THE WHAT...?
"SHOWERING MY MASK IN DAZZLING JUSTICE... I EXPOSE THE INNERMOST DEPTHS OF EVIL MOST VILE...
"JUSTICE HAS BEEN SERVED!
flash!!
"MY JUSTICE PIERCES TO THE HEART OF JUSTICE! I AM THE EVENING STAR OF JUSTICE, SHINING IN THE DARKNESS OF NIGHT!
"I AM THE ONE PEOPLE CALL 'SPARKLING JUSTICE'!"
THAT WAS SPARKLING JUSTICE'S CATCH PHRASE! I TRIED MY FOOT AT TRANSLATING...
...THE ORIGINAL LINES, DOCUMENTED IN A REPORT BY A JOURNALIST WHO ENCOUNTERED SPARKLING JUSTICE...
fwip!
...CONSIDERED A THREAT TO HUMANITY, THE ELUSIVE SPARKLING JUSTICE IS A SERIAL KILLER POSING AS A CHAMPION OF JUSTICE!
...HUH?

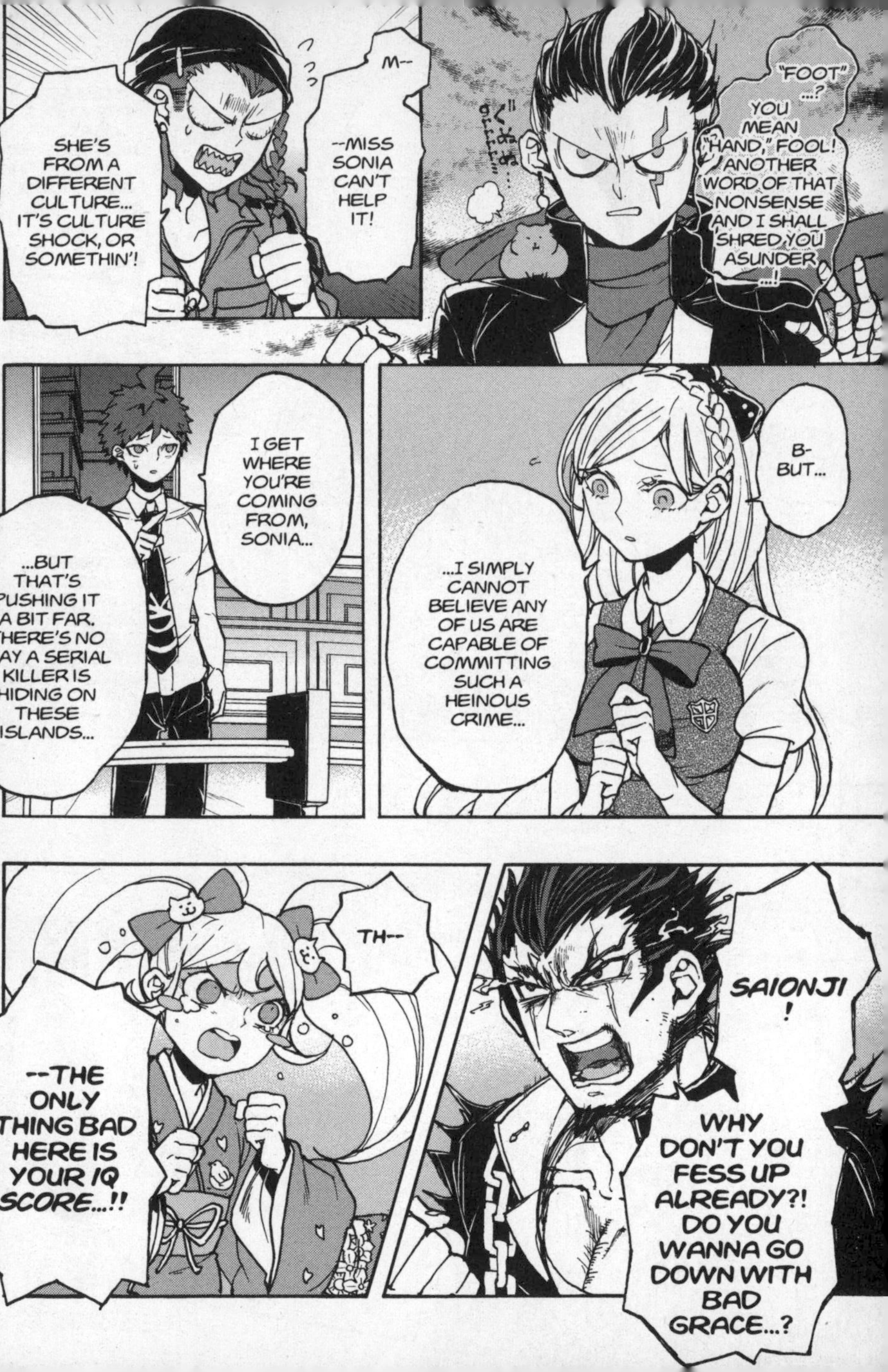
"FOOT" ...? YOU MEAN "HAND," FOOL! ANOTHER WORD OF THAT NONSENSE AND I SHALL SHRED YOU ASUNDER ...!
M--
--MISS SONIA CAN'T HELP IT!
SHE'S FROM A DIFFERENT CULTURE... IT'S CULTURE SHOCK, OR SOMETHIN'!
B-BUT...
...I SIMPLY CANNOT BELIEVE ANY OF US ARE CAPABLE OF COMMITTING SUCH A HEINOUS CRIME...
I GET WHERE YOU'RE COMING FROM, SONIA...
...BUT THAT'S PUSHING IT A BIT FAR. THERE'S NO WAY A SERIAL KILLER IS HIDING ON THESE ISLANDS...
SAIONJI!
WHY DON'T YOU FESS UP ALREADY?! DO YOU WANNA GO DOWN WITH BAD GRACE...?
TH--
--THE ONLY THING BAD HERE IS YOUR IQ SCORE...!!

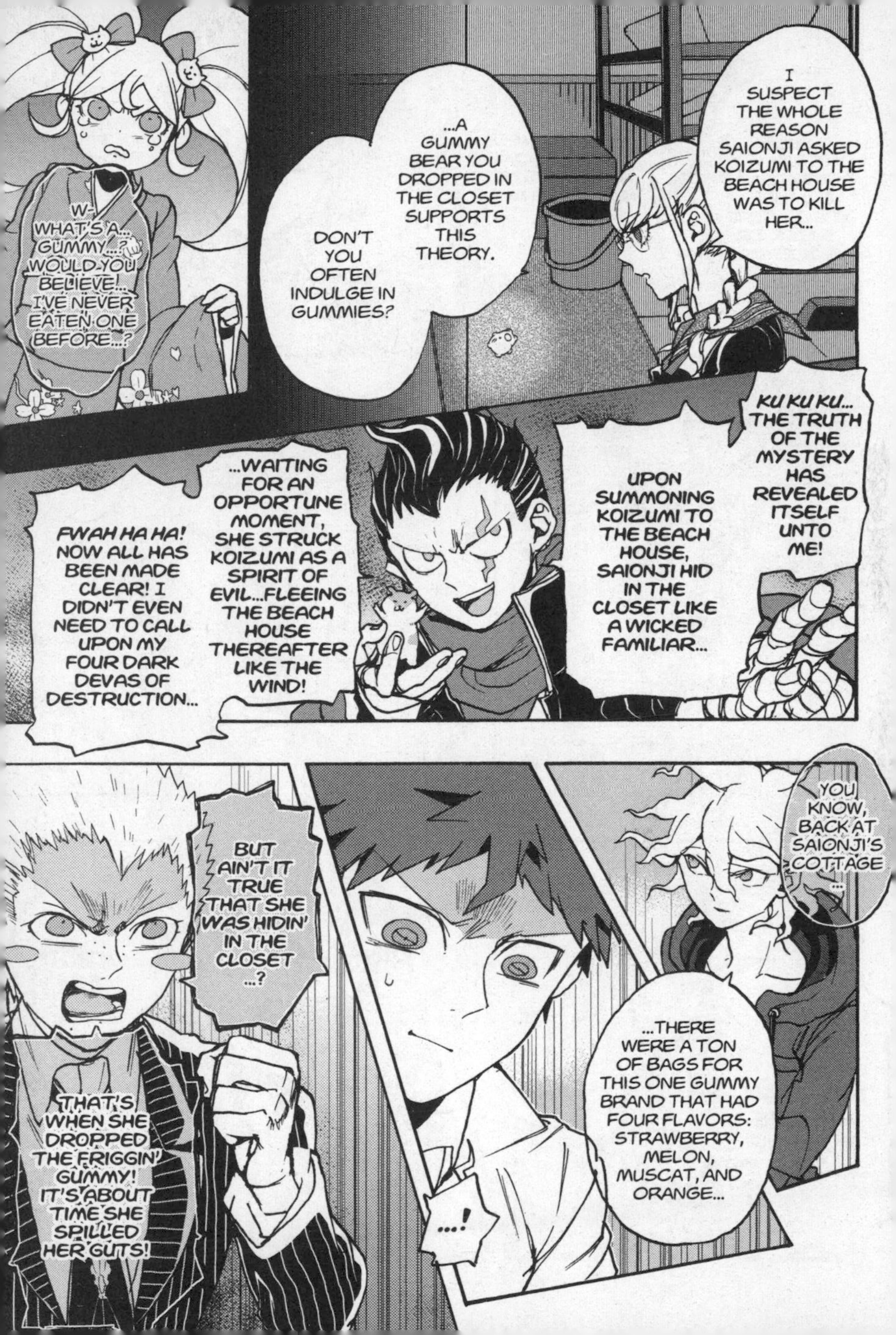
I SUSPECT THE WHOLE REASON SAIONJI ASKED KOIZUMI TO THE BEACH HOUSE WAS TO KILL HER...
...A GUMMY BEAR YOU DROPPED IN THE CLOSET SUPPORTS THIS THEORY.
DON'T YOU OFTEN INDULGE IN GUMMIES?
W-WHAT'S A... GUMMY...? WOULD YOU BELIEVE... I'VE NEVER EATEN ONE BEFORE...?
KU KU KU... THE TRUTH OF THE MYSTERY HAS REVEALED ITSELF UNTO ME!
UPON SUMMONING KOIZUMI TO THE BEACH HOUSE, SAIONJI HID IN THE CLOSET LIKE A WICKED FAMILIAR...
...WAITING FOR AN OPPORTUNE MOMENT, SHE STRUCK KOIZUMI AS A SPIRIT OF EVIL...FLEEING THE BEACH HOUSE THEREAFTER LIKE THE WIND!
FWAH HA HA! NOW ALL HAS BEEN MADE CLEAR! I DIDN'T EVEN NEED TO CALL UPON MY FOUR DARK DEVAS OF DESTRUCTION...
YOU KNOW, BACK AT SAIONJI'S COTTAGE...
...THERE WERE A TON OF BAGS FOR THIS ONE GUMMY BRAND THAT HAD FOUR FLAVORS: STRAWBERRY, MELON, MUSCAT, AND ORANGE...
...!
BUT AIN'T IT TRUE THAT SHE WAS HIDIN' IN THE CLOSET ...?
THAT'S WHEN SHE DROPPED THE FRIGGIN' GUMMY! IT'S ABOUT TIME SHE SPILLED HER GUTS!

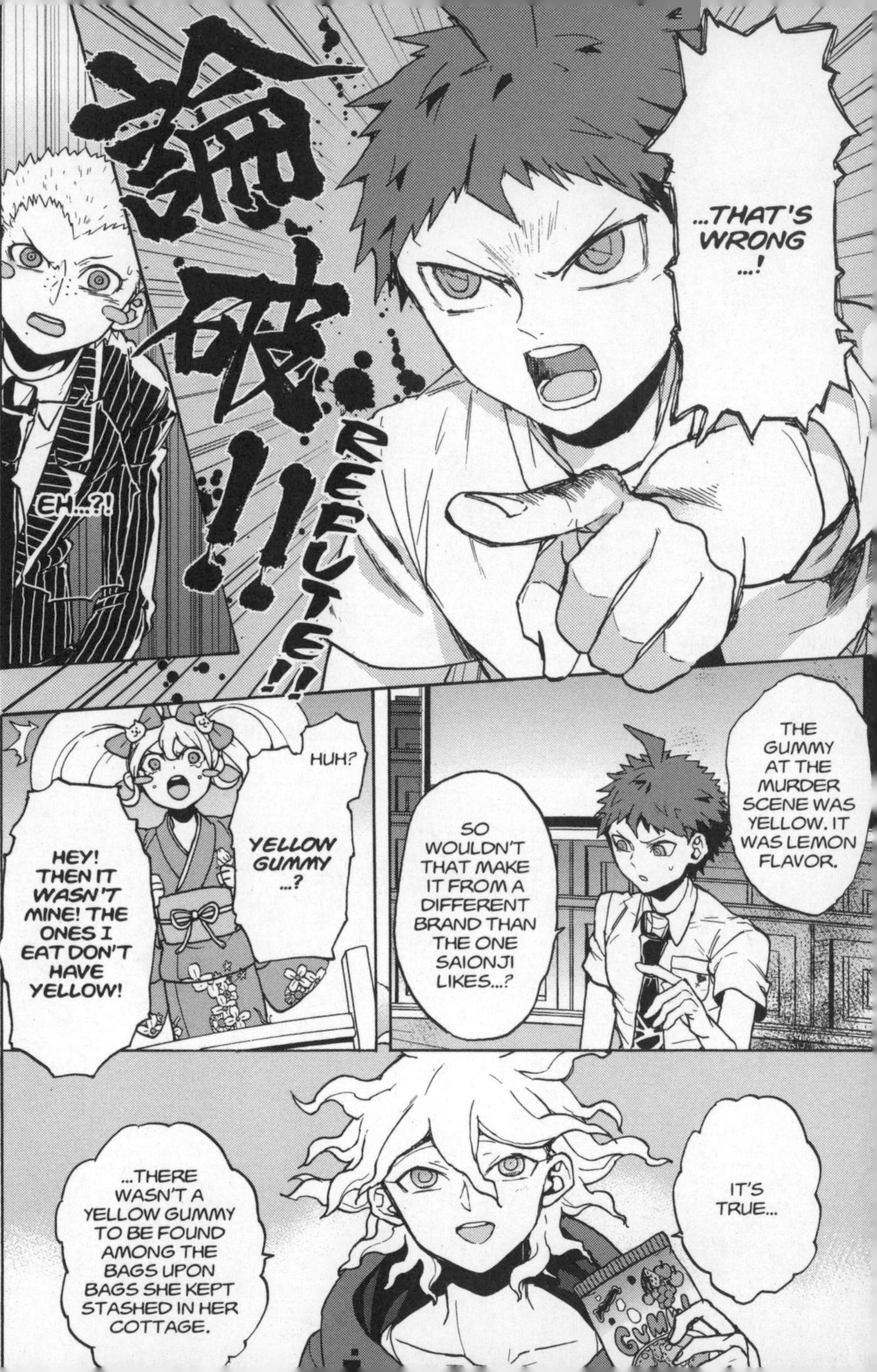
...THAT'S WRONG ...!
論破!!
REFUTE!!
EH...?!
THE GUMMY AT THE MURDER SCENE WAS YELLOW. IT WAS LEMON FLAVOR.
SO WOULDN'T THAT MAKE IT FROM A DIFFERENT BRAND THAN THE ONE SAIONJI LIKES...?
HUH?
YELLOW GUMMY ...?
HEY! THEN IT WASN'T MINE! THE ONES I EAT DON'T HAVE YELLOW!
IT'S TRUE...
...THERE WASN'T A YELLOW GUMMY TO BE FOUND AMONG THE BAGS UPON BAGS SHE KEPT STASHED IN HER COTTAGE.

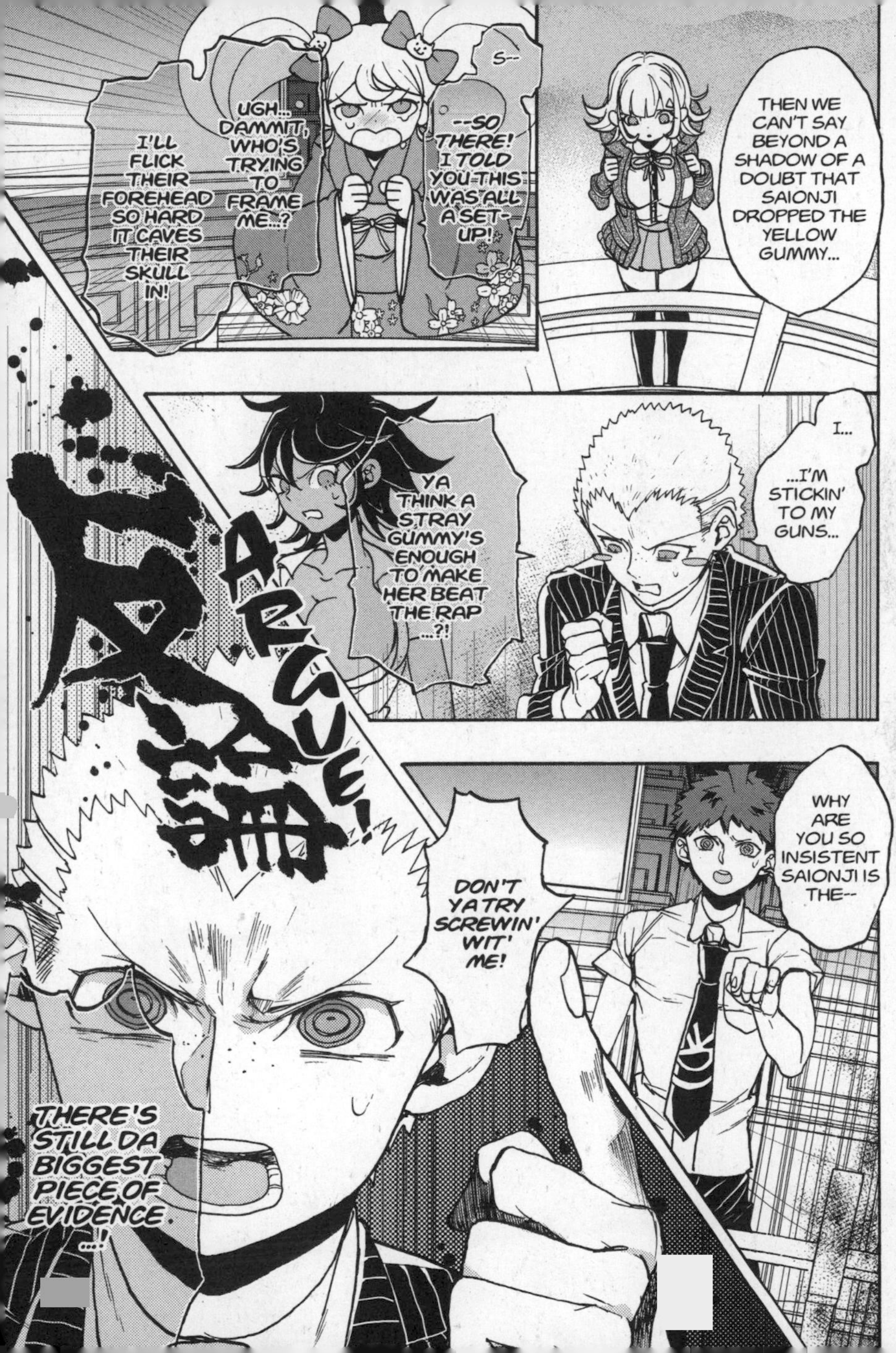
THEN WE CAN'T SAY BEYOND A SHADOW OF A DOUBT THAT SAIONJI DROPPED THE YELLOW GUMMY...
S--
--SO THERE! I TOLD YOU THIS WAS ALL A SET-UP!
UGH... DAMMIT, WHO'S TRYING TO FRAME ME...?
I'LL FLICK THEIR FOREHEAD SO HARD IT CAVES THEIR SKULL IN!
I...
...I'M STICKIN' TO MY GUNS...
YA THINK A STRAY GUMMY'S ENOUGH TO MAKE HER BEAT THE RAP ...?!
ARGUE!
WHY ARE YOU SO INSISTENT SAIONJI IS THE--
DON'T YA TRY SCREWIN' WIT' ME!
THERE'S STILL DA BIGGEST PIECE OF EVIDENCE. ...!

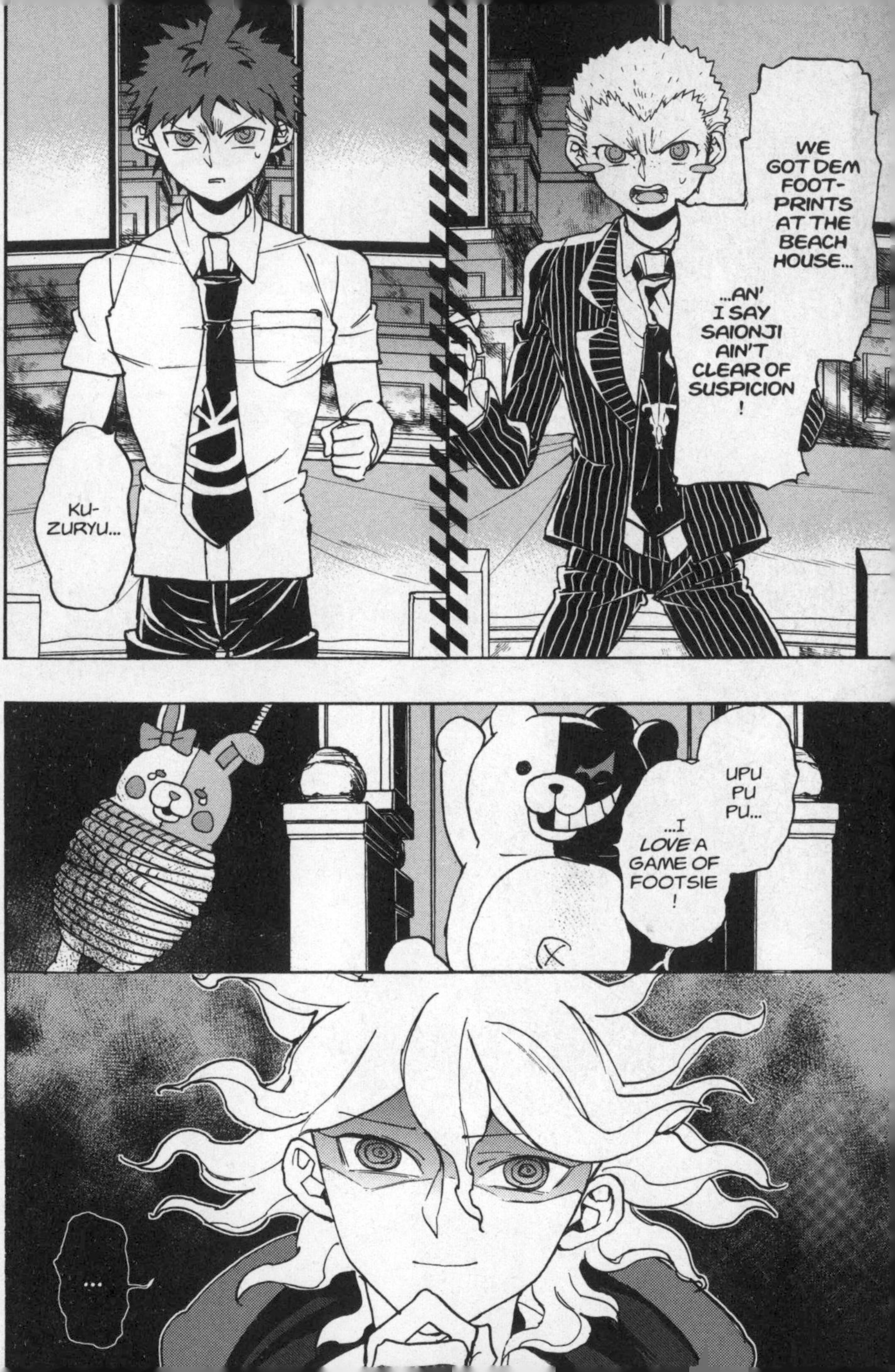
WE GOT DEM FOOT-PRINTS AT THE BEACH HOUSE...
...AN' I SAY SAIONJI AIN'T CLEAR OF SUSPICION!
KU-ZURYU...
UPU PU PU...
...I LOVE A GAME OF FOOTSIE!
...

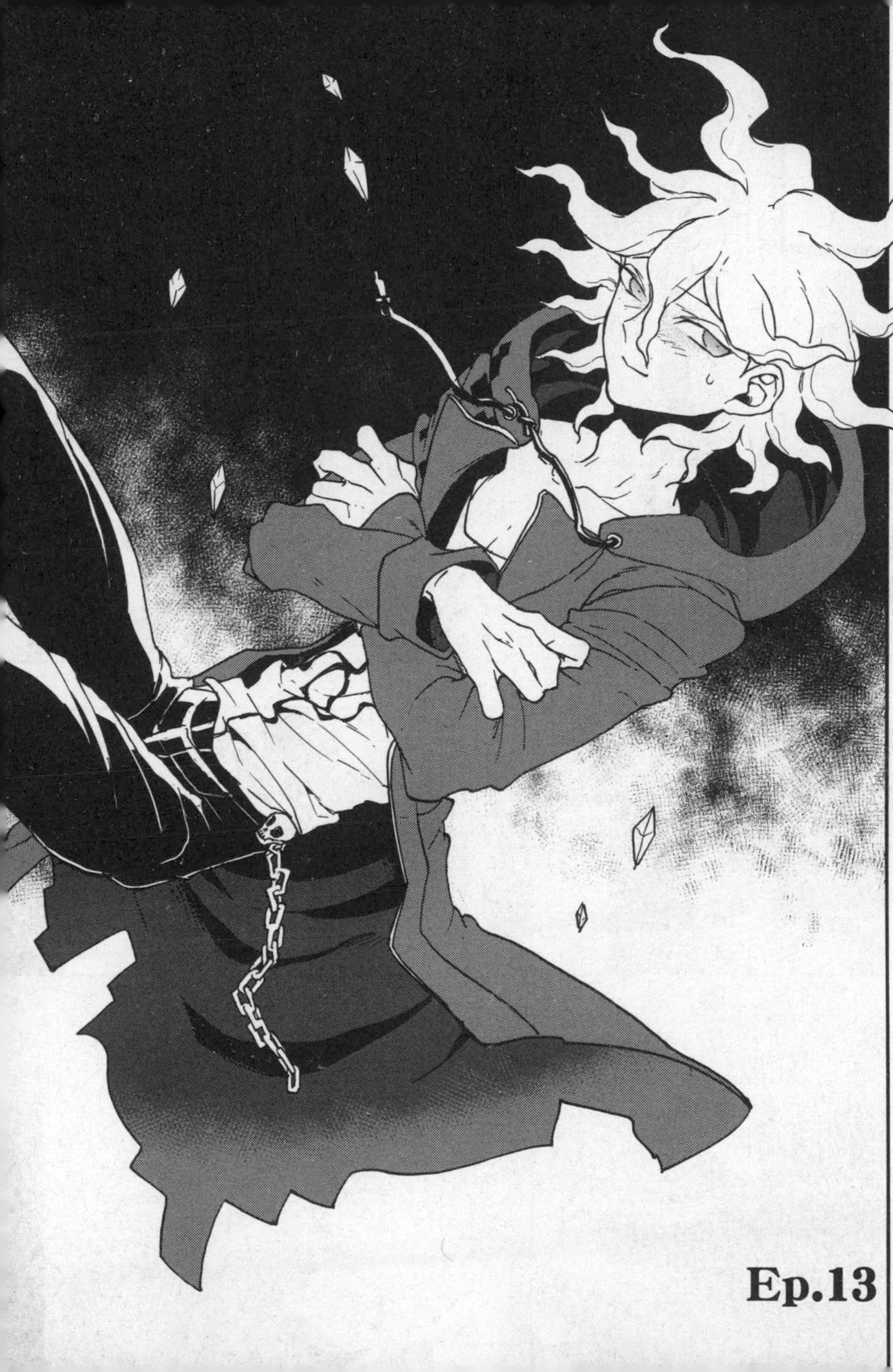

Ep.13

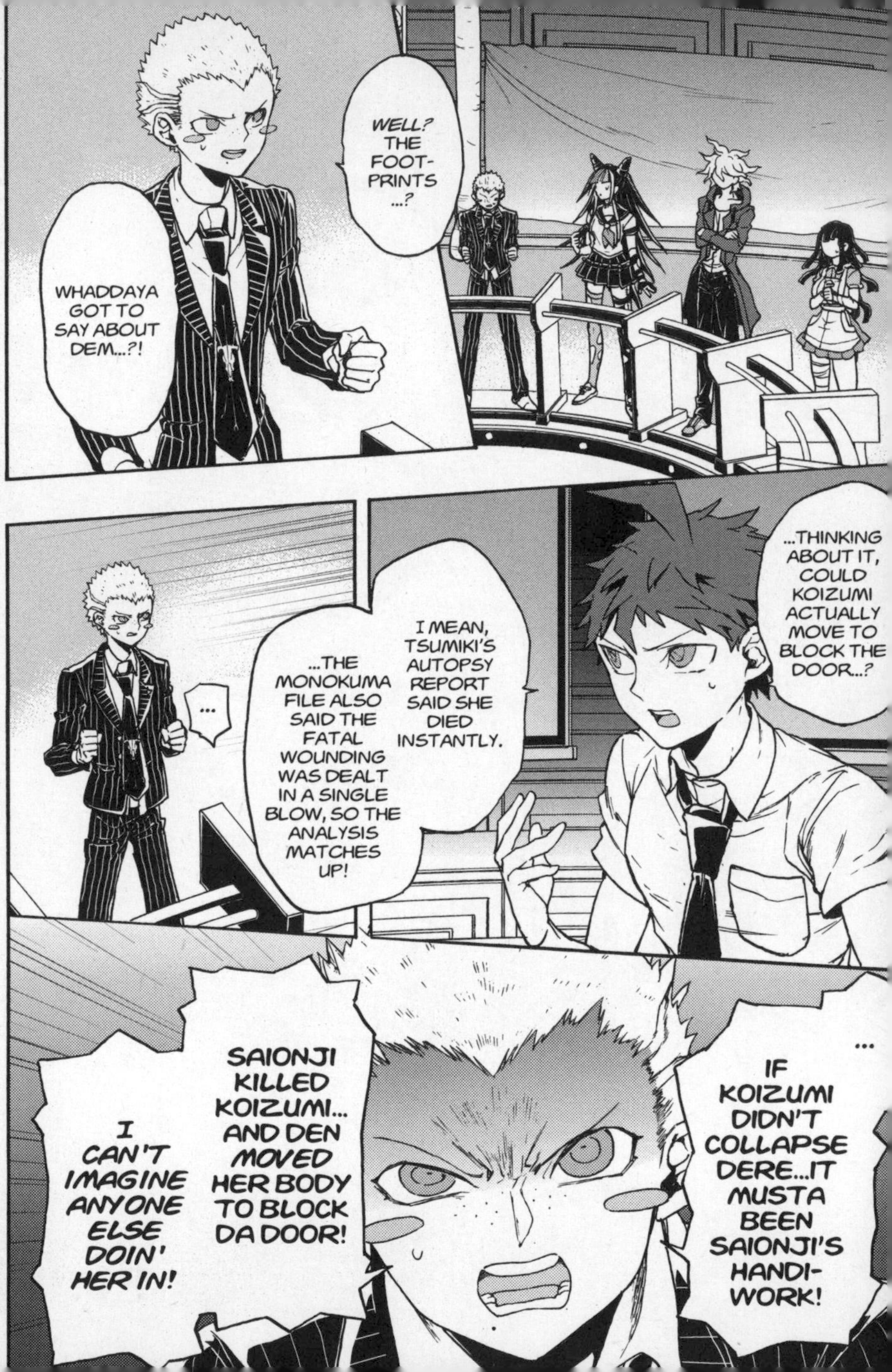
WELL? THE FOOT-PRINTS ...?
WHADDAYA GOT TO SAY ABOUT DEM...?!
...THINKING ABOUT IT, COULD KOIZUMI ACTUALLY MOVE TO BLOCK THE DOOR...?
I MEAN, TSUMIKI'S AUTOPSY REPORT SAID SHE DIED INSTANTLY.
...THE MONOKUMA FILE ALSO SAID THE FATAL WOUNDING WAS DEALT IN A SINGLE BLOW, SO THE ANALYSIS MATCHES UP!
...
...
IF KOIZUMI DIDN'T COLLAPSE DERE...IT MUSTA BEEN SAIONJI'S HANDI-WORK!
SAIONJI KILLED KOIZUMI... AND DEN MOVED HER BODY TO BLOCK DA DOOR!
I CAN'T IMAGINE ANYONE ELSE DOIN' HER IN!

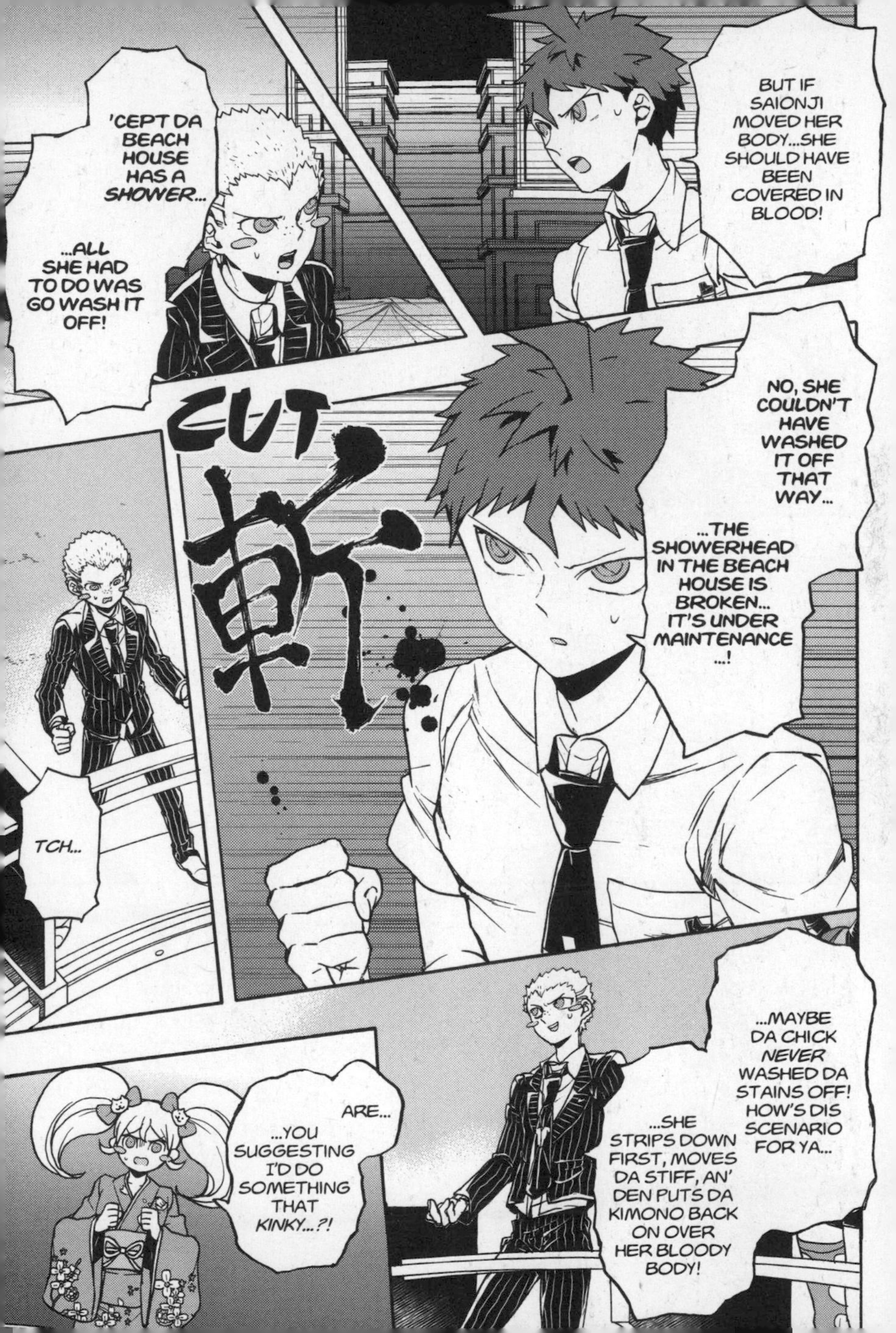
BUT IF SAIONJI MOVED HER BODY...SHE SHOULD HAVE BEEN COVERED IN BLOOD!
'CEPT DA BEACH HOUSE HAS A SHOWER...
...ALL SHE HAD TO DO WAS GO WASH IT OFF!
NO, SHE COULDN'T HAVE WASHED IT OFF THAT WAY...
...THE SHOWERHEAD IN THE BEACH HOUSE IS BROKEN... IT'S UNDER MAINTENANCE ...!
CUT
斬
TCH...
...MAYBE DA CHICK *NEVER* WASHED DA STAINS OFF! HOW'S DIS SCENARIO FOR YA...
...SHE STRIPS DOWN FIRST, MOVES DA STIFF, AN' DEN PUTS DA KIMONO BACK ON OVER HER BLOODY BODY!
ARE...
...YOU SUGGESTING I'D DO SOMETHING THAT KINKY...?!

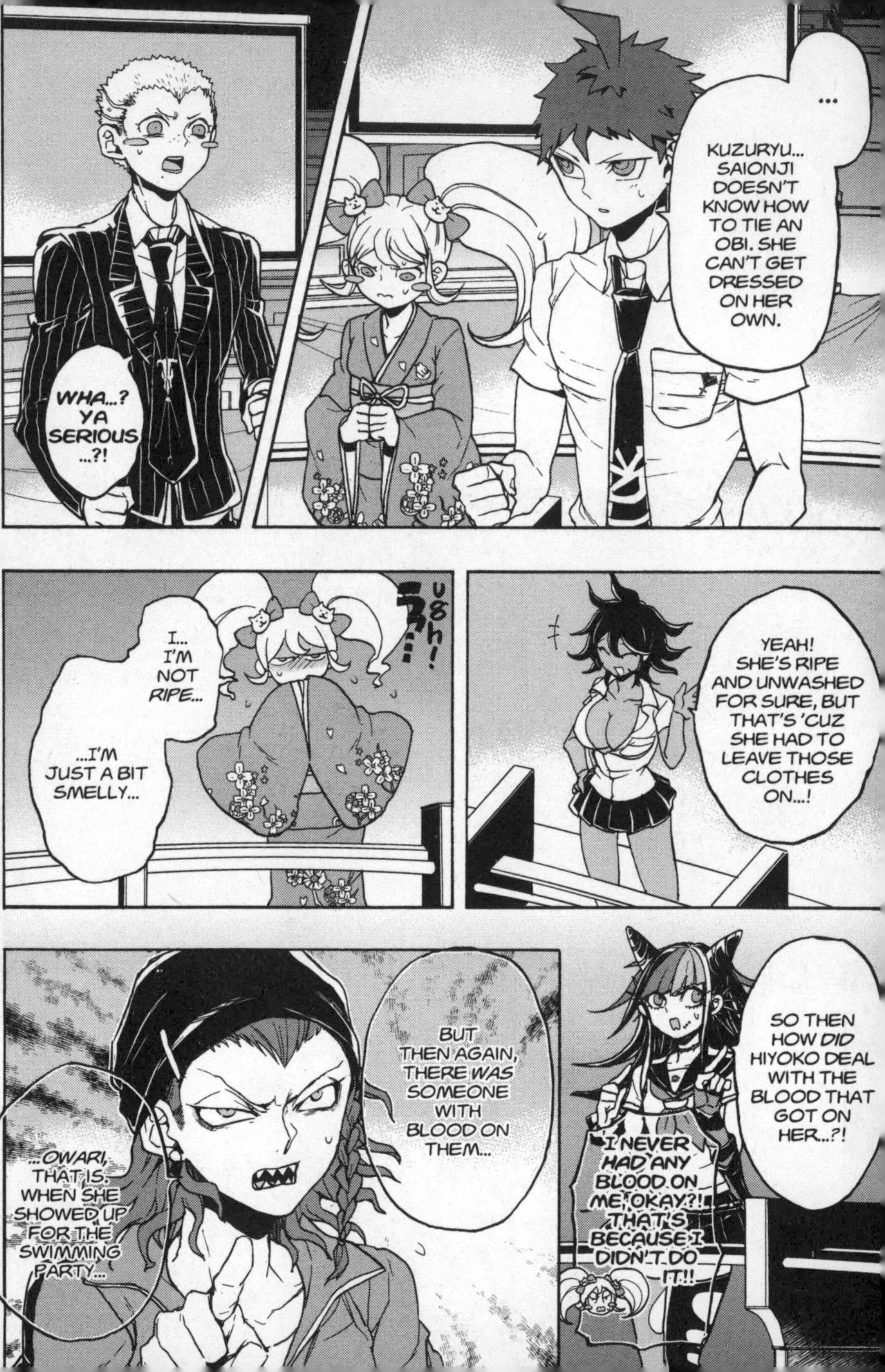
...
KUZURYU... SAIONJI DOESN'T KNOW HOW TO TIE AN OBI. SHE CAN'T GET DRESSED ON HER OWN.
WHA...? YA SERIOUS ...?!
YEAH! SHE'S RIPE AND UNWASHED FOR SURE, BUT THAT'S 'CUZ SHE HAD TO LEAVE THOSE CLOTHES ON...!
I... I'M NOT RIPE...
...I'M JUST A BIT SMELLY...
SO THEN HOW DID HIYOKO DEAL WITH THE BLOOD THAT GOT ON HER...?!
I NEVER HAD ANY BLOOD ON ME, OKAY?! THAT'S BECAUSE I DIDN'T DO IT!!
BUT THEN AGAIN, THERE WAS SOMEONE WITH BLOOD ON THEM...
...OWARI, THAT IS. WHEN SHE SHOWED UP FOR THE SWIMMING PARTY...

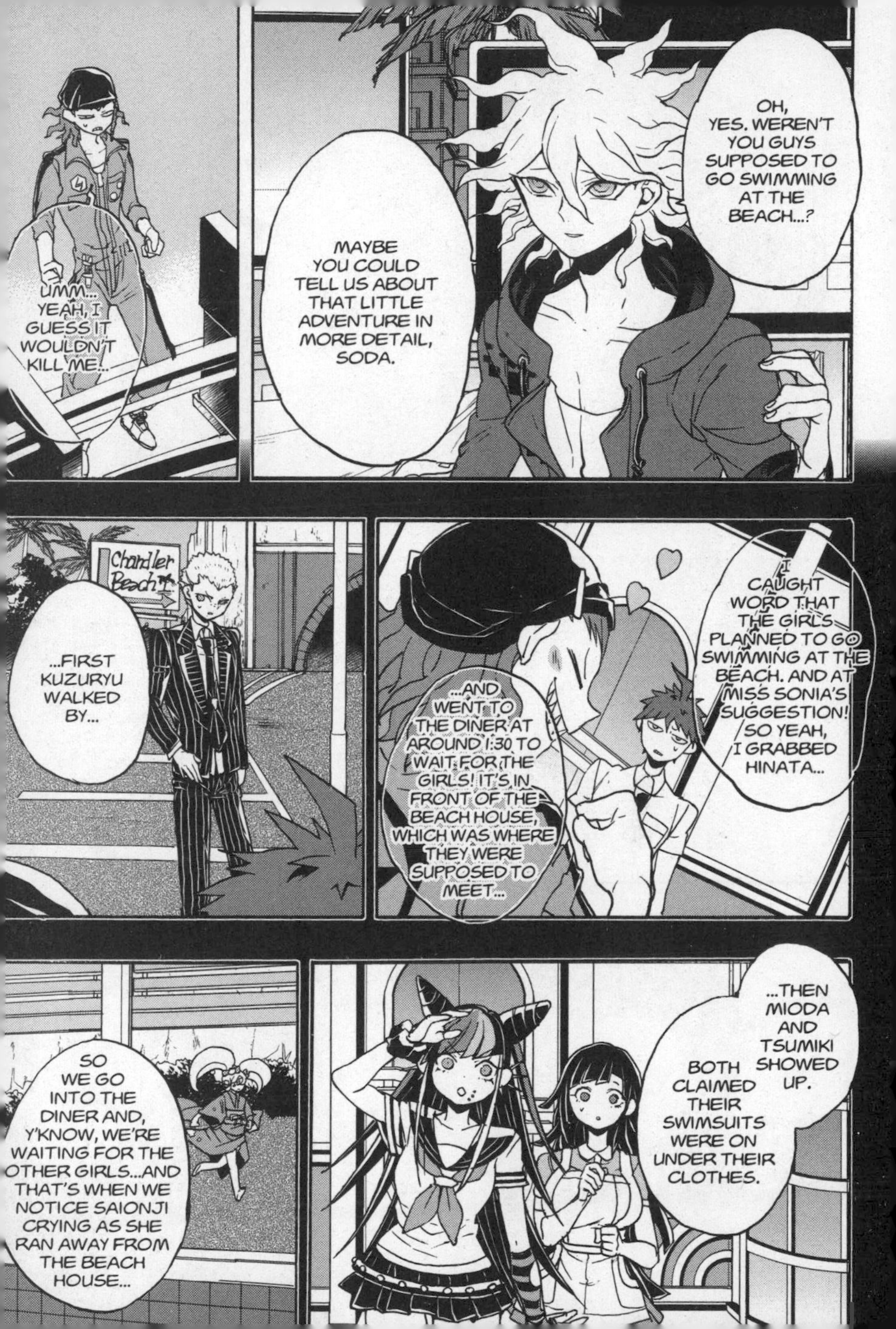
OH, YES. WEREN'T YOU GUYS SUPPOSED TO GO SWIMMING AT THE BEACH...?
MAYBE YOU COULD TELL US ABOUT THAT LITTLE ADVENTURE IN MORE DETAIL, SODA.
UMM... YEAH, I GUESS IT WOULDN'T KILL ME...
I CAUGHT WORD THAT THE GIRLS PLANNED TO GO SWIMMING AT THE BEACH. AND AT MISS SONIA'S SUGGESTION! SO YEAH, I GRABBED HINATA...
...AND WENT TO THE DINER AT AROUND 1:30 TO WAIT FOR THE GIRLS! IT'S IN FRONT OF THE BEACH HOUSE, WHICH WAS WHERE THEY WERE SUPPOSED TO MEET...
Chandler Beach
...FIRST KUZURYU WALKED BY...
...THEN MIODA AND TSUMIKI SHOWED UP.
BOTH CLAIMED THEIR SWIMSUITS WERE ON UNDER THEIR CLOTHES.
SO WE GO INTO THE DINER AND, Y'KNOW, WE'RE WAITING FOR THE OTHER GIRLS...AND THAT'S WHEN WE NOTICE SAIONJI CRYING AS SHE RAN AWAY FROM THE BEACH HOUSE...

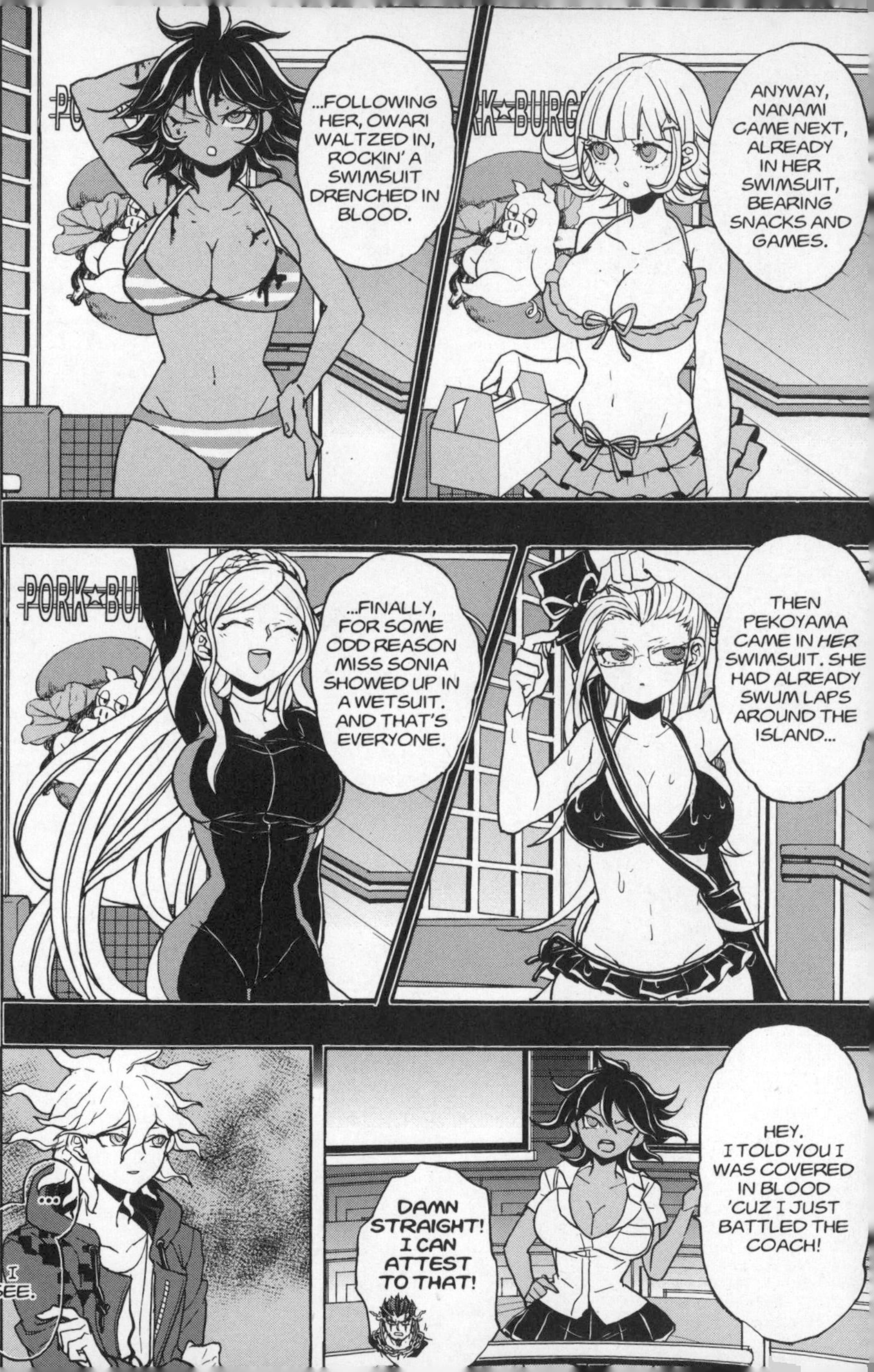
ANYWAY, NANAMI CAME NEXT, ALREADY IN HER SWIMSUIT, BEARING SNACKS AND GAMES.
...FOLLOWING HER, OWARI WALTZED IN, ROCKIN' A SWIMSUIT DRENCHED IN BLOOD.
THEN PEKOYAMA CAME IN *HER* SWIMSUIT. SHE HAD ALREADY SWUM LAPS AROUND THE ISLAND...
...FINALLY, FOR SOME ODD REASON MISS SONIA SHOWED UP IN A WETSUIT. AND THAT'S EVERYONE.
HEY. I TOLD YOU I WAS COVERED IN BLOOD 'CUZ I JUST BATTLED THE COACH!
DAMN STRAIGHT! I CAN ATTEST TO THAT!
...
I SEE.

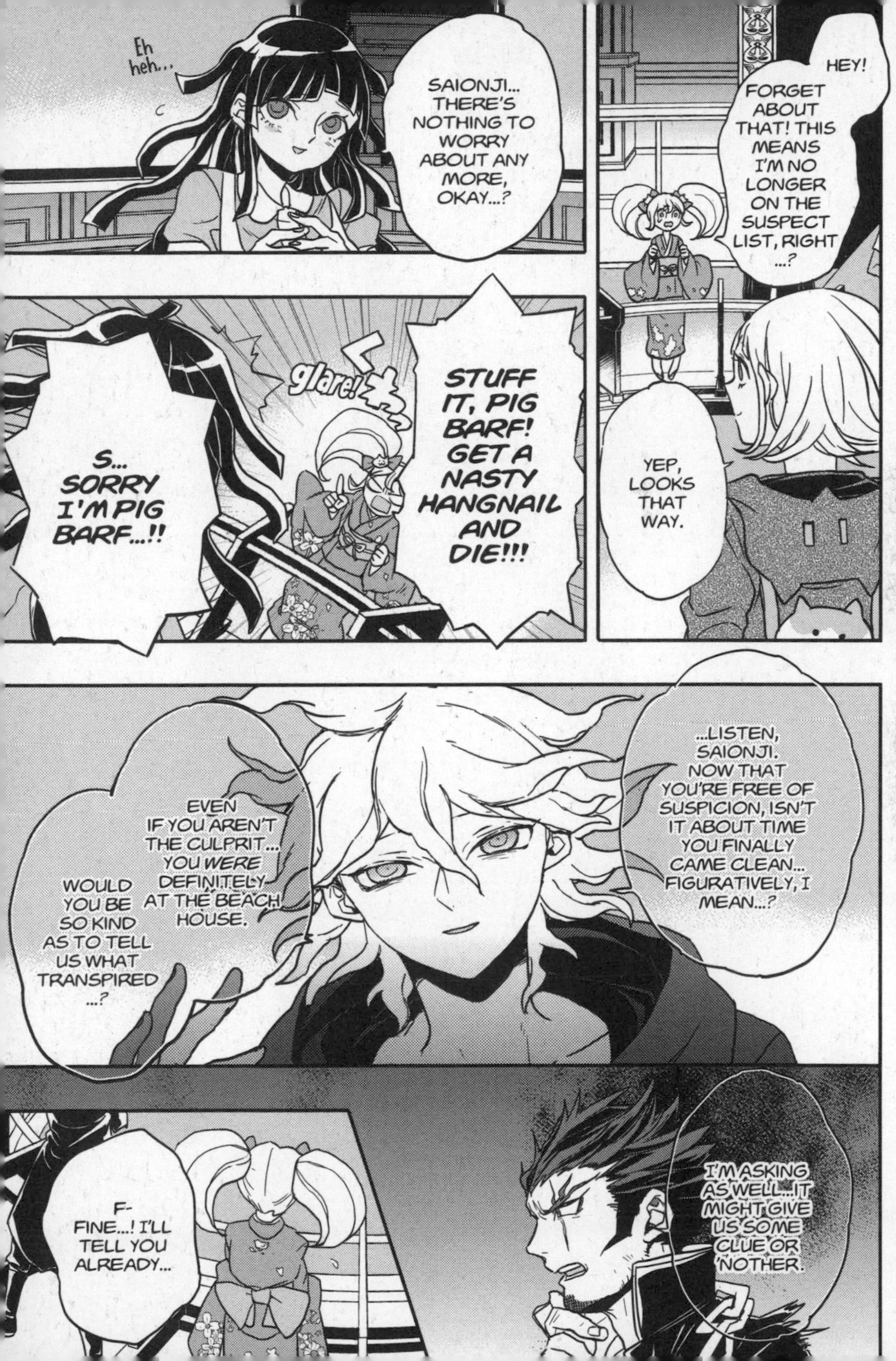
HEY!
FORGET ABOUT THAT! THIS MEANS I'M NO LONGER ON THE SUSPECT LIST, RIGHT ...?
YEP, LOOKS THAT WAY.
SAIONJI... THERE'S NOTHING TO WORRY ABOUT ANY MORE, OKAY...?
Eh heh...
STUFF IT, PIG BARF! GET A NASTY HANGNAIL AND DIE!!!
glare!
S... SORRY I'M PIG BARF...!!
...LISTEN, SAIONJI. NOW THAT YOU'RE FREE OF SUSPICION, ISN'T IT ABOUT TIME YOU FINALLY CAME CLEAN... FIGURATIVELY, I MEAN...?
EVEN IF YOU AREN'T THE CULPRIT... YOU WERE DEFINITELY AT THE BEACH HOUSE.
WOULD YOU BE SO KIND AS TO TELL US WHAT TRANSPIRED ...?
I'M ASKING AS WELL... IT MIGHT GIVE US SOME CLUE OR 'NOTHER.
F- FINE...! I'LL TELL YOU ALREADY...

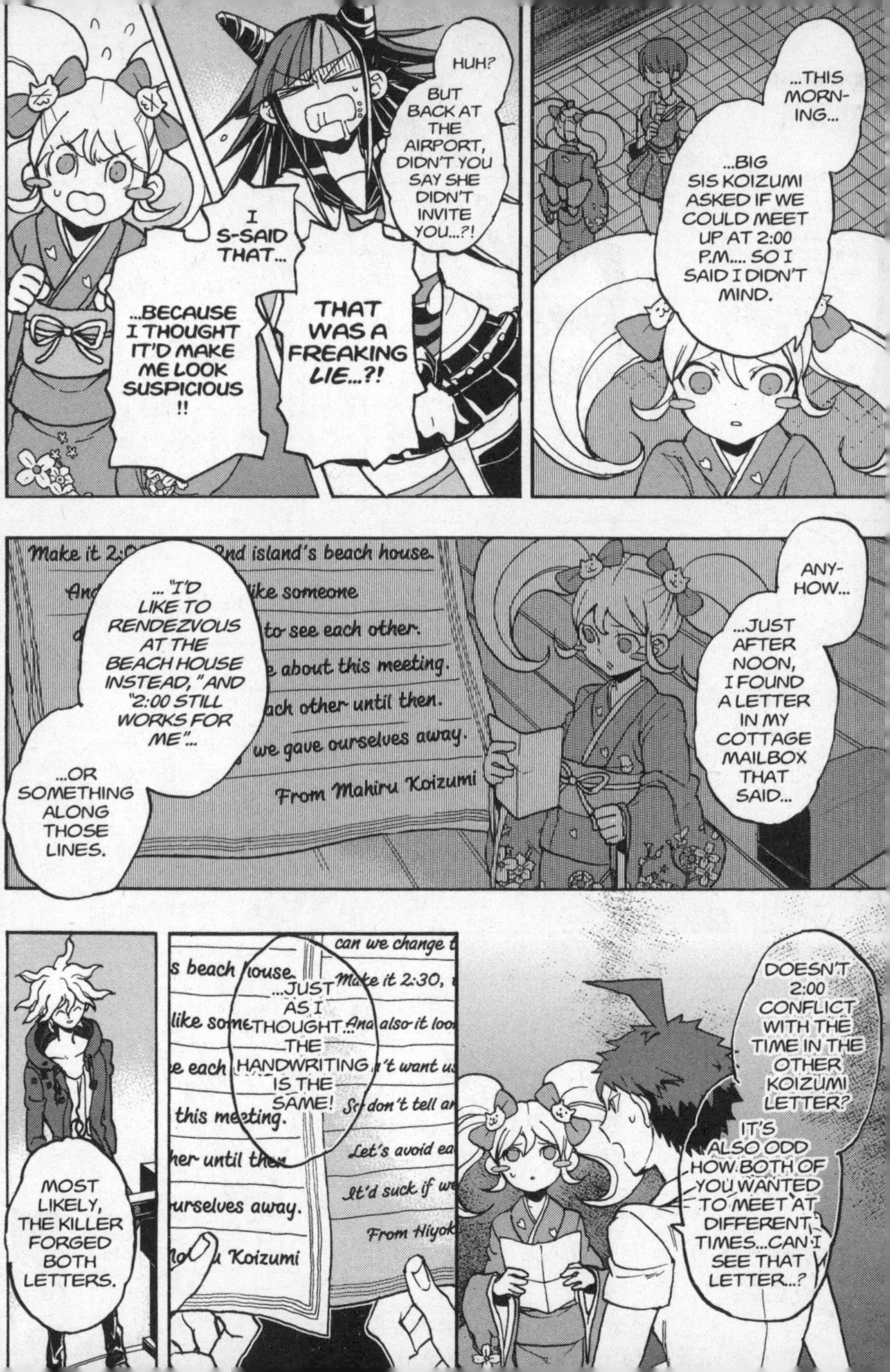

...THIS MORNING...
...BIG SIS KOIZUMI ASKED IF WE COULD MEET UP AT 2:00 P.M.... SO I SAID I DIDN'T MIND.
HUH? BUT BACK AT THE AIRPORT, DIDN'T YOU SAY SHE DIDN'T INVITE YOU...?!
THAT WAS A FREAKING LIE...?!
I S-SAID THAT...
...BECAUSE I THOUGHT IT'D MAKE ME LOOK SUSPICIOUS!!
ANYHOW...
...JUST AFTER NOON, I FOUND A LETTER IN MY COTTAGE MAILBOX THAT SAID...
..."I'D LIKE TO RENDEZVOUS AT THE BEACH HOUSE INSTEAD," AND "2:00 STILL WORKS FOR ME"...
...OR SOMETHING ALONG THOSE LINES.
From Mahiru Koizumi
DOESN'T 2:00 CONFLICT WITH THE TIME IN THE OTHER KOIZUMI LETTER?
IT'S ALSO ODD HOW BOTH OF YOU WANTED TO MEET AT DIFFERENT TIMES...CAN I SEE THAT LETTER...?
...JUST AS I THOUGHT... THE HANDWRITING IS THE SAME!
MOST LIKELY, THE KILLER FORGED BOTH LETTERS.

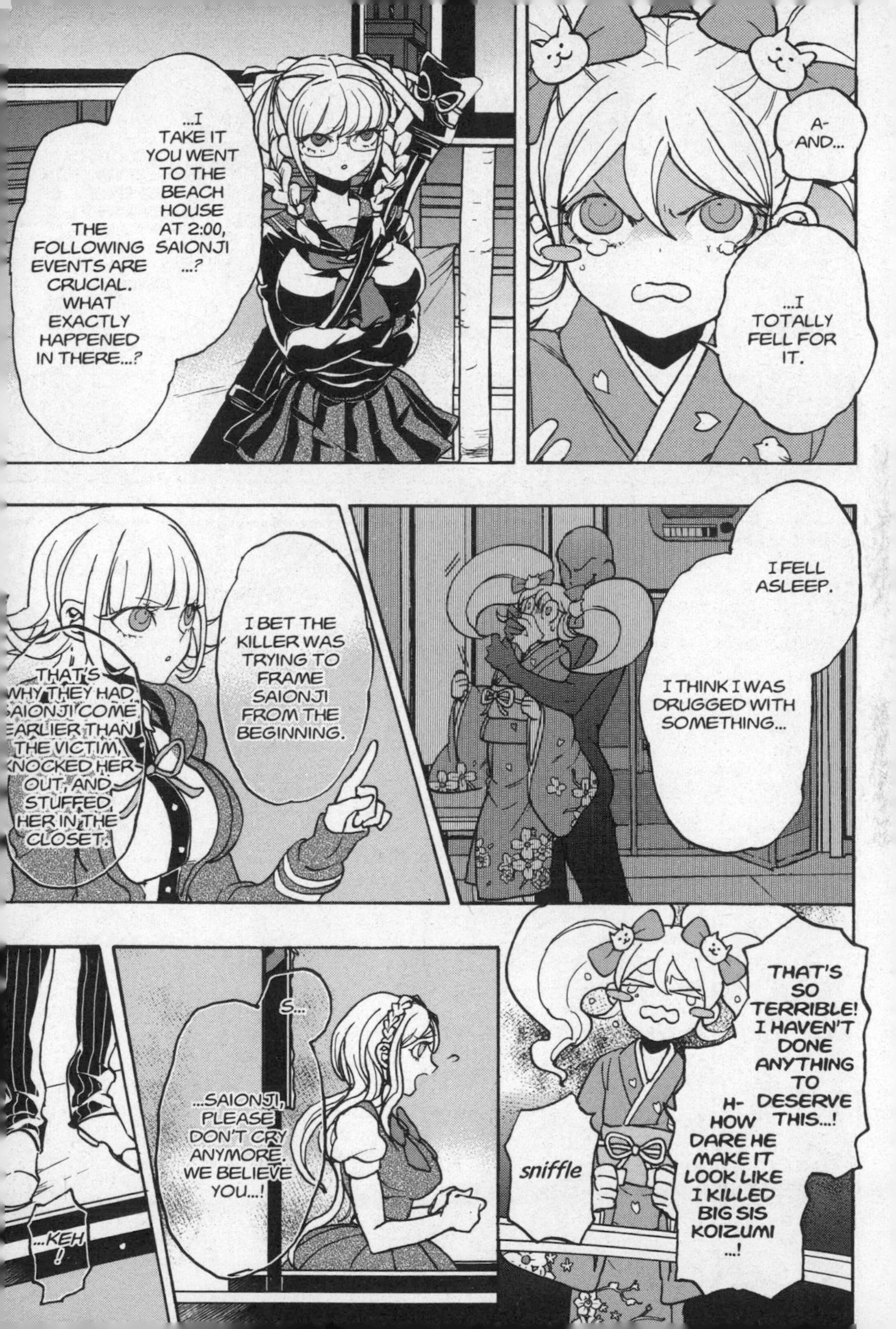
A- AND...
...I TOTALLY FELL FOR IT.
...I TAKE IT YOU WENT TO THE BEACH HOUSE AT 2:00, SAIONJI ...?
THE FOLLOWING EVENTS ARE CRUCIAL. WHAT EXACTLY HAPPENED IN THERE...?
I FELL ASLEEP.
I THINK I WAS DRUGGED WITH SOMETHING...
I BET THE KILLER WAS TRYING TO FRAME SAIONJI FROM THE BEGINNING.
THAT'S WHY THEY HAD SAIONJI COME EARLIER THAN THE VICTIM, KNOCKED HER OUT, AND STUFFED HER IN THE CLOSET.
THAT'S SO TERRIBLE! I HAVEN'T DONE ANYTHING TO DESERVE THIS...!
H- HOW DARE HE MAKE IT LOOK LIKE I KILLED BIG SIS KOIZUMI ...!
sniffle
S...
...SAIONJI, PLEASE DON'T CRY ANYMORE. WE BELIEVE YOU...!
...KEH!

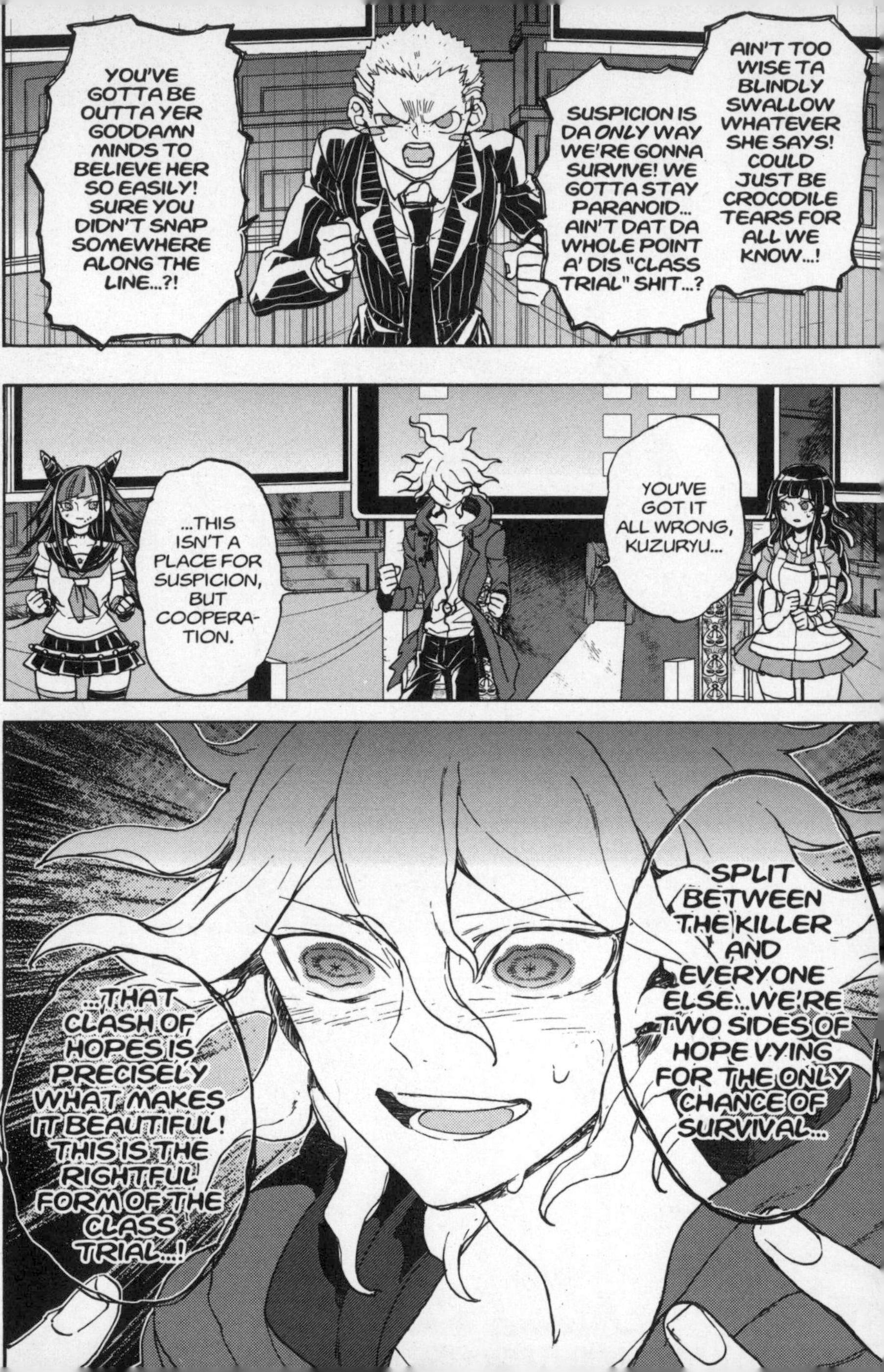
AIN'T TOO WISE TA BLINDLY SWALLOW WHATEVER SHE SAYS! COULD JUST BE CROCODILE TEARS FOR ALL WE KNOW...!
SUSPICION IS DA *ONLY* WAY WE'RE GONNA SURVIVE! WE GOTTA STAY PARANOID... AIN'T DAT DA WHOLE POINT A' DIS "CLASS TRIAL" SHIT...?
YOU'VE GOTTA BE OUTTA YER GODDAMN MINDS TO BELIEVE HER SO EASILY! SURE YOU DIDN'T SNAP SOMEWHERE ALONG THE LINE...?!
YOU'VE GOT IT ALL WRONG, KUZURYU...
...THIS ISN'T A PLACE FOR SUSPICION, BUT COOPERA-TION.
SPLIT BETWEEN THE KILLER AND EVERYONE ELSE...WE'RE TWO SIDES OF HOPE VYING FOR THE ONLY CHANCE OF SURVIVAL...
...THAT CLASH OF HOPES IS PRECISELY WHAT MAKES IT BEAUTIFUL! THIS IS THE RIGHTFUL FORM OF THE CLASS TRIAL...!

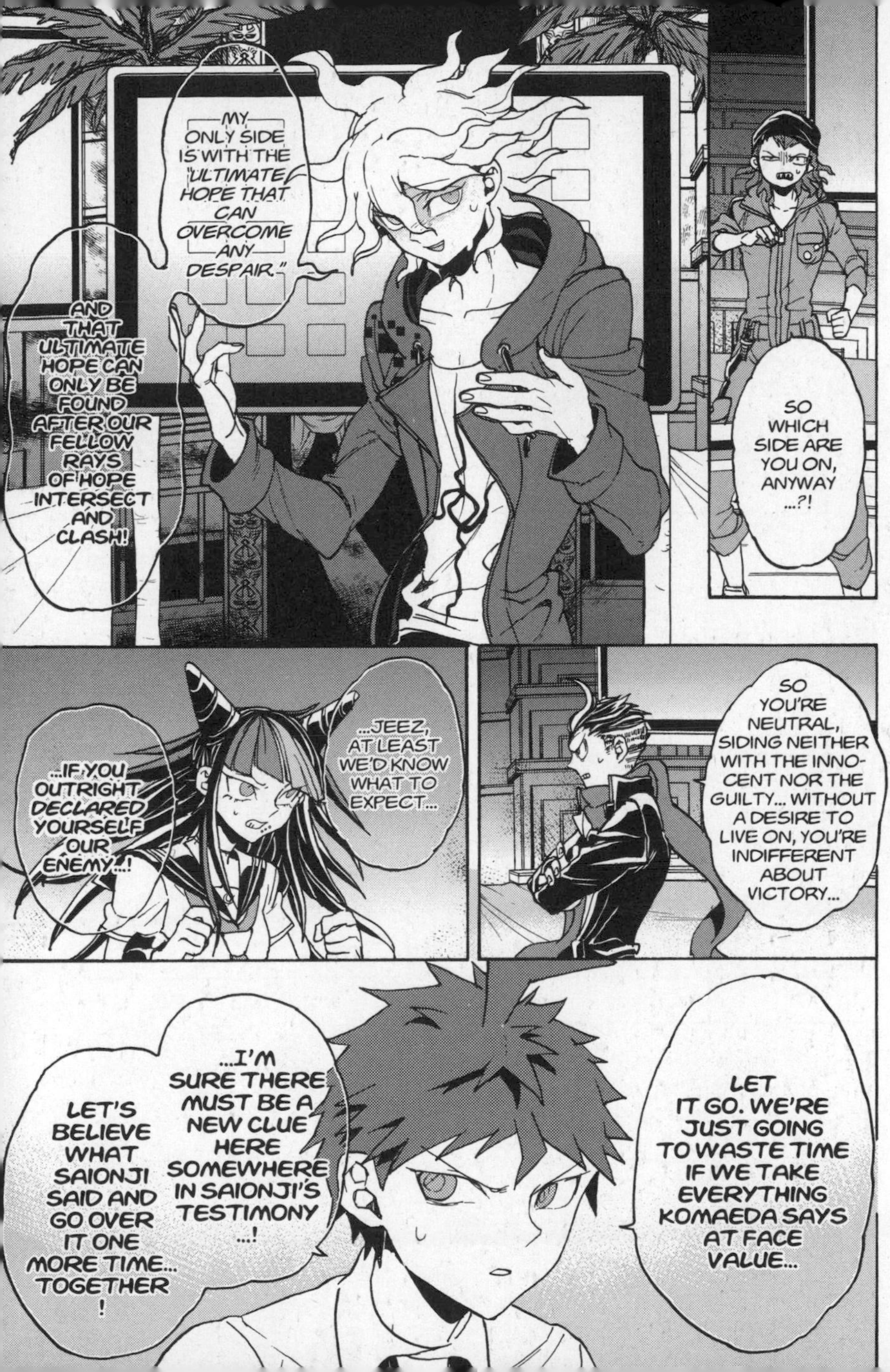
SO WHICH SIDE ARE YOU ON, ANYWAY ...?!
MY ONLY SIDE IS WITH THE "ULTIMATE HOPE THAT CAN OVERCOME ANY DESPAIR."
AND THAT ULTIMATE HOPE CAN ONLY BE FOUND AFTER OUR FELLOW RAYS OF HOPE INTERSECT AND CLASH!
SO YOU'RE NEUTRAL, SIDING NEITHER WITH THE INNO-CENT NOR THE GUILTY... WITHOUT A DESIRE TO LIVE ON, YOU'RE INDIFFERENT ABOUT VICTORY...
...JEEZ, AT LEAST WE'D KNOW WHAT TO EXPECT...
...IF YOU OUTRIGHT DECLARED YOURSELF OUR ENEMY...!
LET IT GO. WE'RE JUST GOING TO WASTE TIME IF WE TAKE EVERYTHING KOMAEDA SAYS AT FACE VALUE...
...I'M SURE THERE MUST BE A NEW CLUE HERE SOMEWHERE IN SAIONJI'S TESTIMONY ...!
LET'S BELIEVE WHAT SAIONJI SAID AND GO OVER IT ONE MORE TIME... TOGETHER !

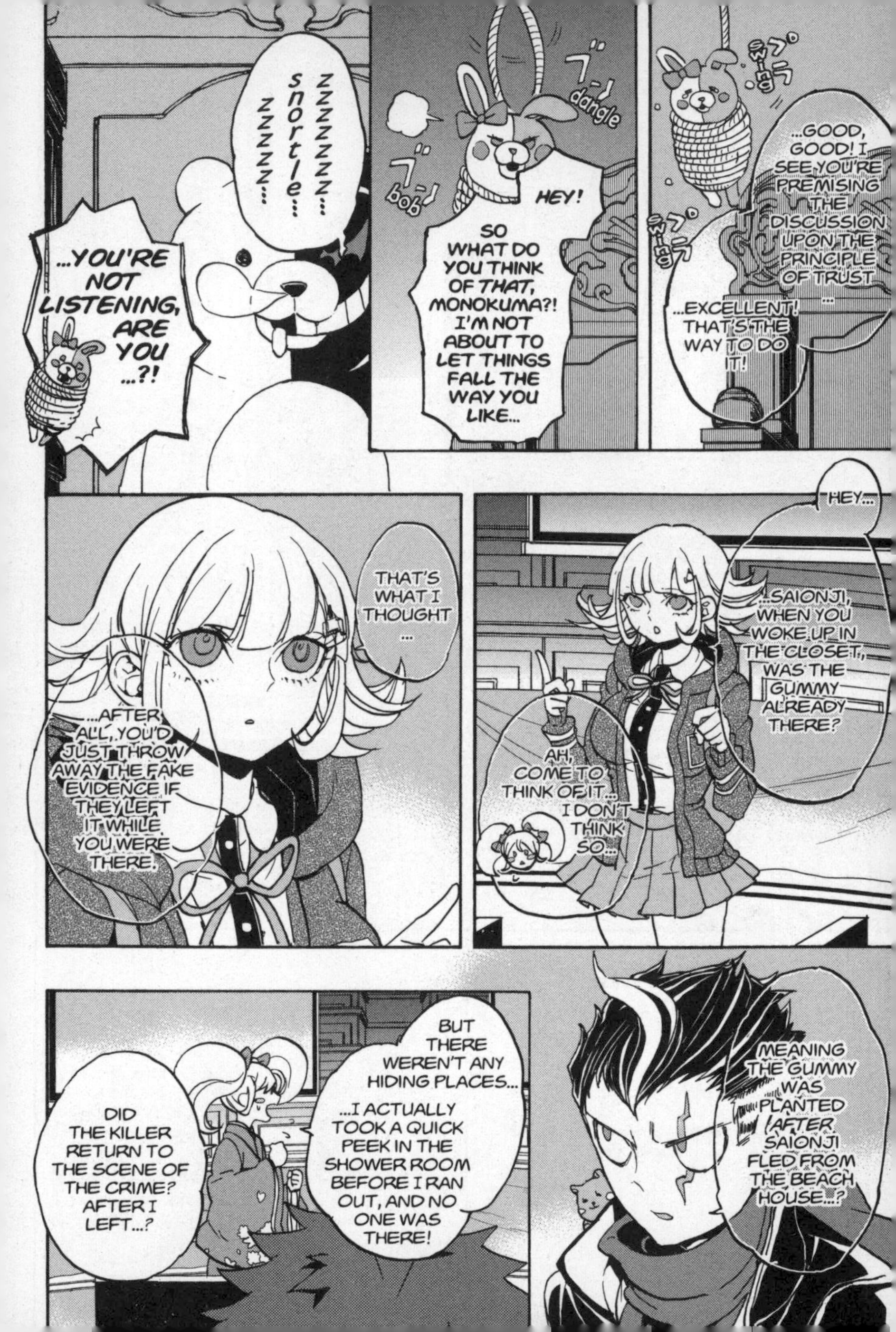
swing
...GOOD, GOOD! I SEE YOU'RE PREMISING THE DISCUSSION UPON THE PRINCIPLE OF TRUST...
swing
...EXCELLENT! THAT'S THE WAY TO DO IT!
dangle
HEY!
bob
SO WHAT DO YOU THINK OF THAT, MONOKUMA?! I'M NOT ABOUT TO LET THINGS FALL THE WAY YOU LIKE...
ZZZZZZ... snortle... ZZZZZ...
...YOU'RE NOT LISTENING, ARE YOU...?!
HEY...
...SAIONJI, WHEN YOU WOKE UP IN THE CLOSET, WAS THE GUMMY ALREADY THERE?
AH, COME TO THINK OF IT... I DON'T THINK SO...
THAT'S WHAT I THOUGHT...
...AFTER ALL, YOU'D JUST THROW AWAY THE FAKE EVIDENCE IF THEY LEFT IT WHILE YOU WERE THERE.
MEANING THE GUMMY WAS PLANTED AFTER SAIONJI FLED FROM THE BEACH HOUSE...?
BUT THERE WEREN'T ANY HIDING PLACES...
...I ACTUALLY TOOK A QUICK PEEK IN THE SHOWER ROOM BEFORE I RAN OUT, AND NO ONE WAS THERE!
DID THE KILLER RETURN TO THE SCENE OF THE CRIME? AFTER I LEFT...?

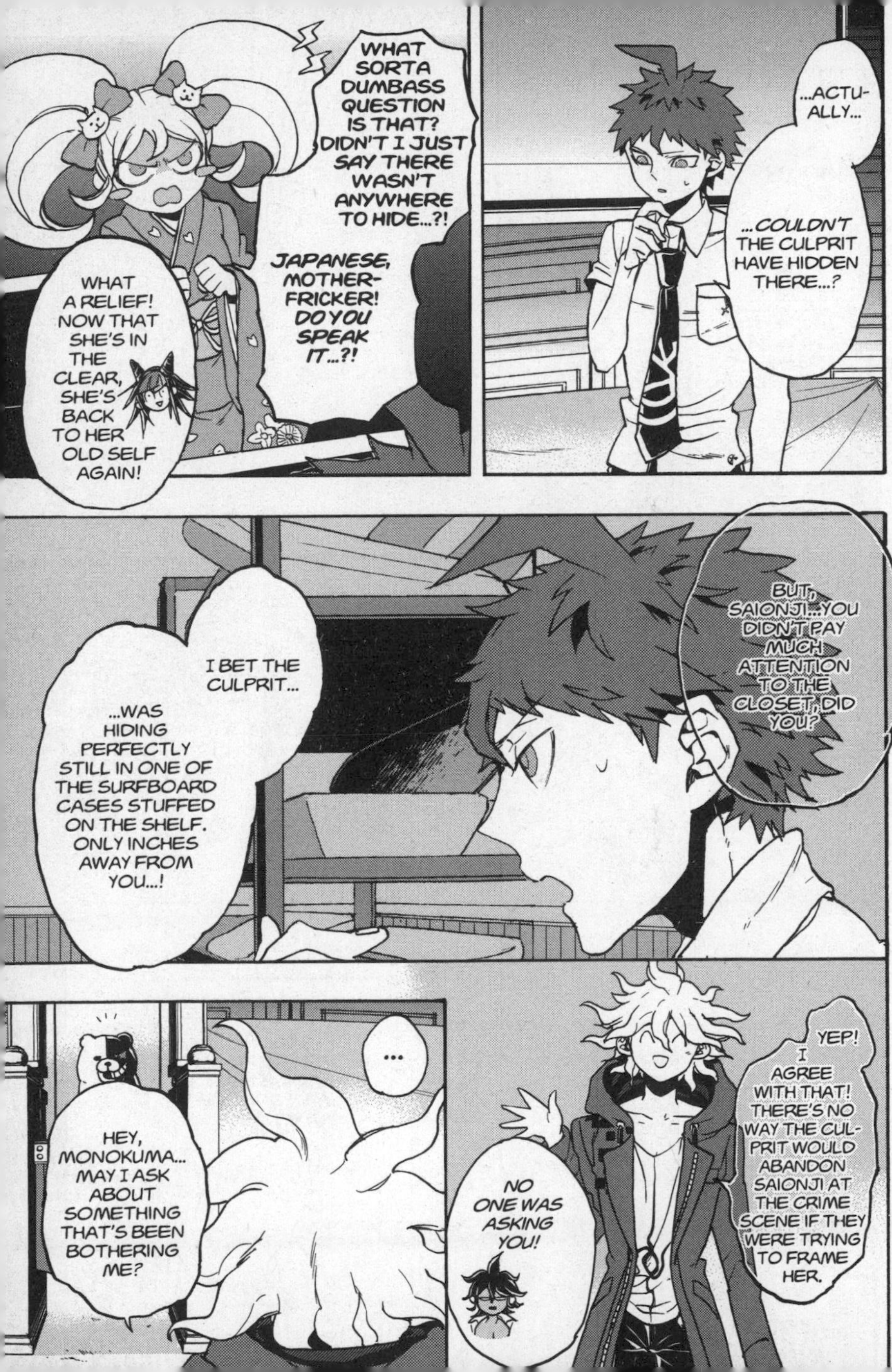
...ACTU-ALLY...
...COULDN'T THE CULPRIT HAVE HIDDEN THERE...?
WHAT SORTA DUMBASS QUESTION IS THAT? DIDN'T I JUST SAY THERE WASN'T ANYWHERE TO HIDE...?!
JAPANESE, MOTHER-FRICKER! DO YOU SPEAK IT...?!
WHAT A RELIEF! NOW THAT SHE'S IN THE CLEAR, SHE'S BACK TO HER OLD SELF AGAIN!
BUT, SAIONJI...YOU DIDN'T PAY MUCH ATTENTION TO THE CLOSET, DID YOU?
I BET THE CULPRIT...
...WAS HIDING PERFECTLY STILL IN ONE OF THE SURFBOARD CASES STUFFED ON THE SHELF. ONLY INCHES AWAY FROM YOU...!
YEP! I AGREE WITH THAT! THERE'S NO WAY THE CUL-PRIT WOULD ABANDON SAIONJI AT THE CRIME SCENE IF THEY WERE TRYING TO FRAME HER.
NO ONE WAS ASKING YOU!
...
HEY, MONOKUMA... MAY I ASK ABOUT SOMETHING THAT'S BEEN BOTHERING ME?

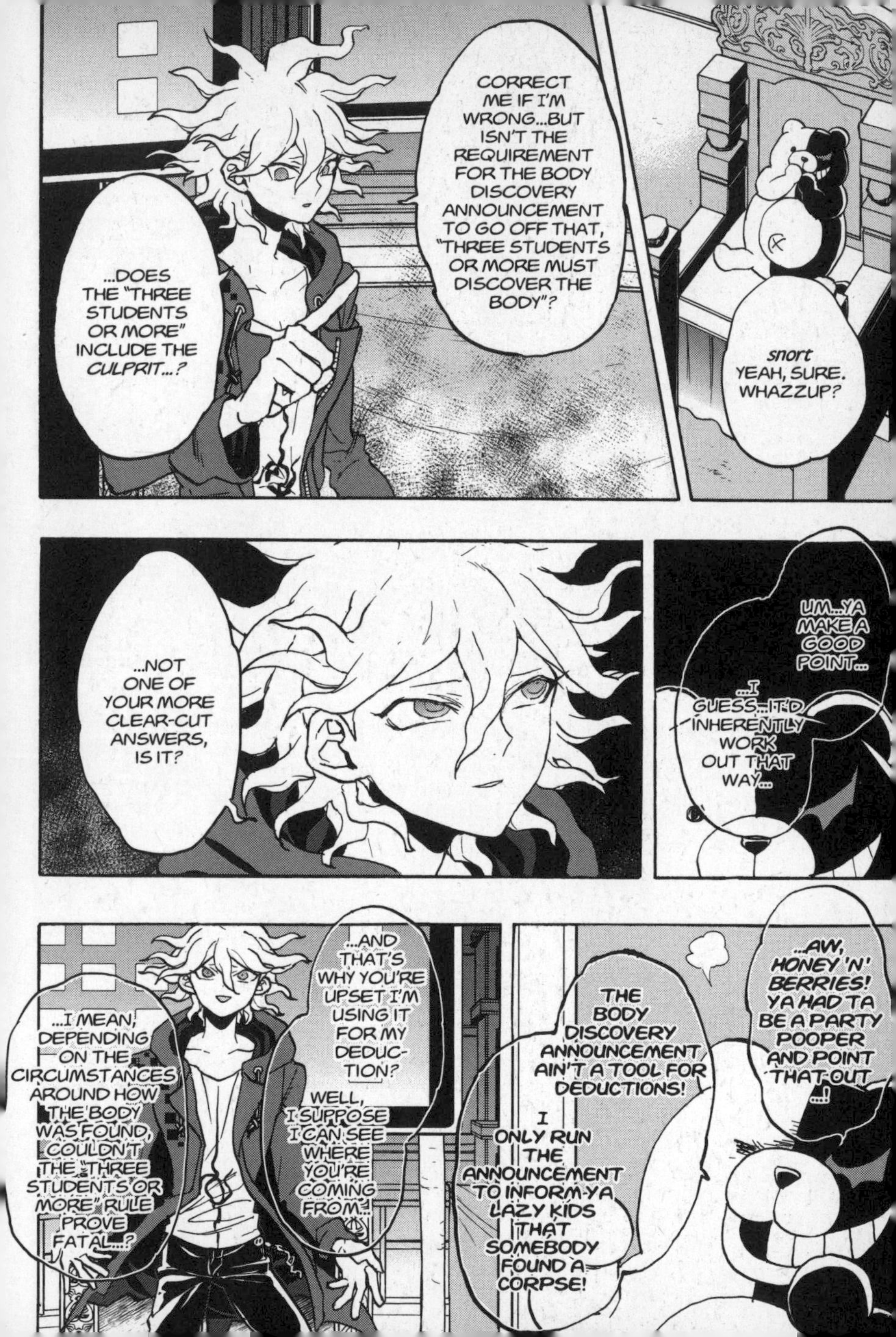

snort YEAH, SURE. WHAZZUP?
CORRECT ME IF I'M WRONG...BUT ISN'T THE REQUIREMENT FOR THE BODY DISCOVERY ANNOUNCEMENT TO GO OFF THAT, "THREE STUDENTS OR MORE MUST DISCOVER THE BODY"?
...DOES THE "THREE STUDENTS OR MORE" INCLUDE THE CULPRIT...?
UM...YA MAKE A GOOD POINT...
...I GUESS...IT'D INHERENTLY WORK OUT THAT WAY...
...NOT ONE OF YOUR MORE CLEAR-CUT ANSWERS, IS IT?
...AW, HONEY 'N' BERRIES! YA HAD TA BE A PARTY POOPER AND POINT THAT OUT...!
THE BODY DISCOVERY ANNOUNCEMENT AIN'T A TOOL FOR DEDUCTIONS!
I ONLY RUN THE ANNOUNCEMENT TO INFORM YA LAZY KIDS THAT SOMEBODY FOUND A CORPSE!
...AND THAT'S WHY YOU'RE UPSET I'M USING IT FOR MY DEDUCTION?
WELL, I SUPPOSE I CAN SEE WHERE YOU'RE COMING FROM...
...I MEAN, DEPENDING ON THE CIRCUMSTANCES AROUND HOW THE BODY WAS FOUND, COULDN'T THE "THREE STUDENTS OR MORE" RULE PROVE FATAL...?

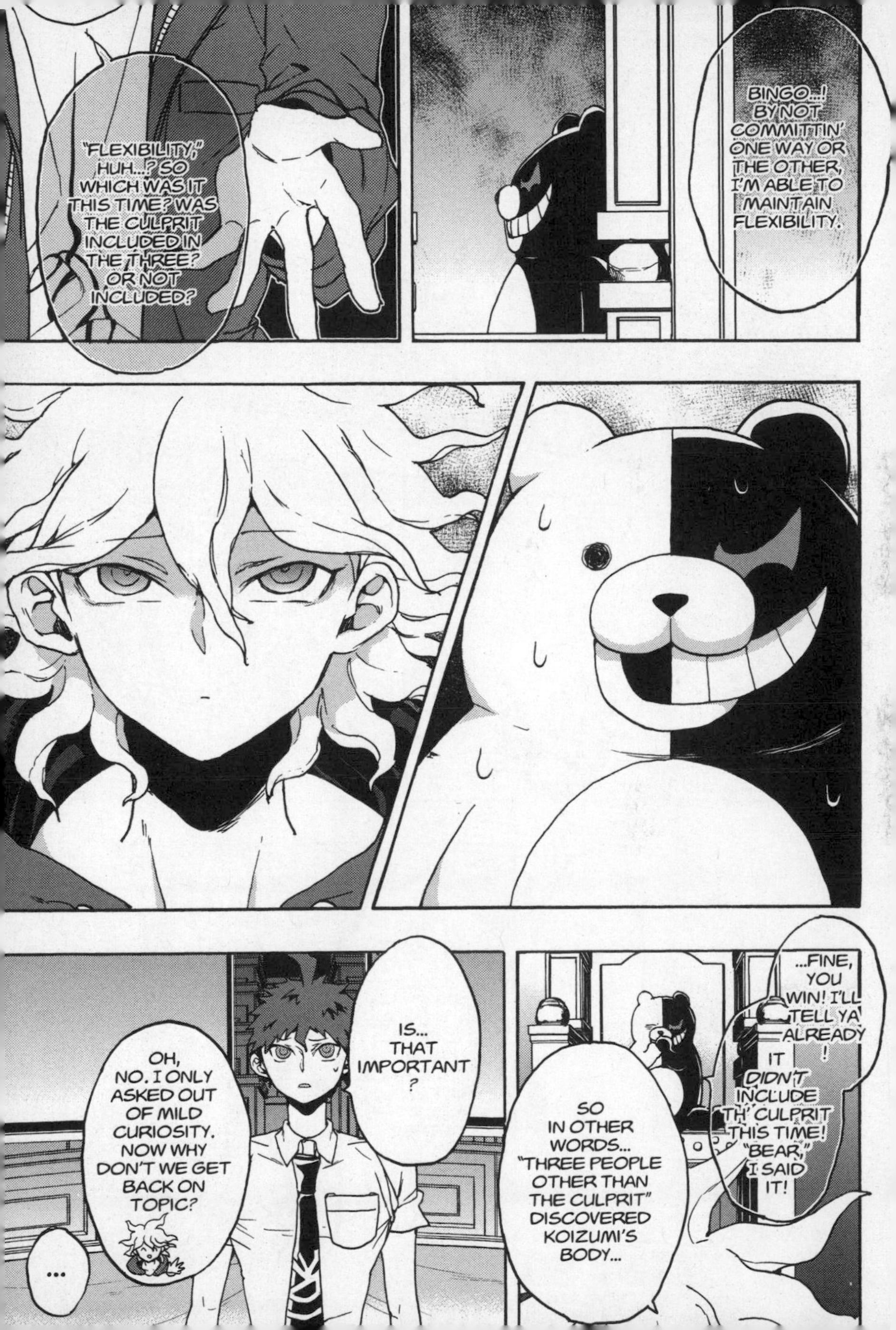
BINGO...! BY NOT COMMITTIN' ONE WAY OR THE OTHER, I'M ABLE TO MAINTAIN FLEXIBILITY.
"FLEXIBILITY," HUH...? SO WHICH WAS IT THIS TIME? WAS THE CULPRIT INCLUDED IN THE THREE? OR NOT INCLUDED?
...FINE, YOU WIN! I'LL TELL YA ALREADY!
IT DIDN'T INCLUDE TH' CULPRIT THIS TIME! "BEAR," I SAID IT!
SO IN OTHER WORDS... "THREE PEOPLE OTHER THAN THE CULPRIT" DISCOVERED KOIZUMI'S BODY...
IS... THAT IMPORTANT?
OH, NO. I ONLY ASKED OUT OF MILD CURIOSITY. NOW WHY DON'T WE GET BACK ON TOPIC?
...

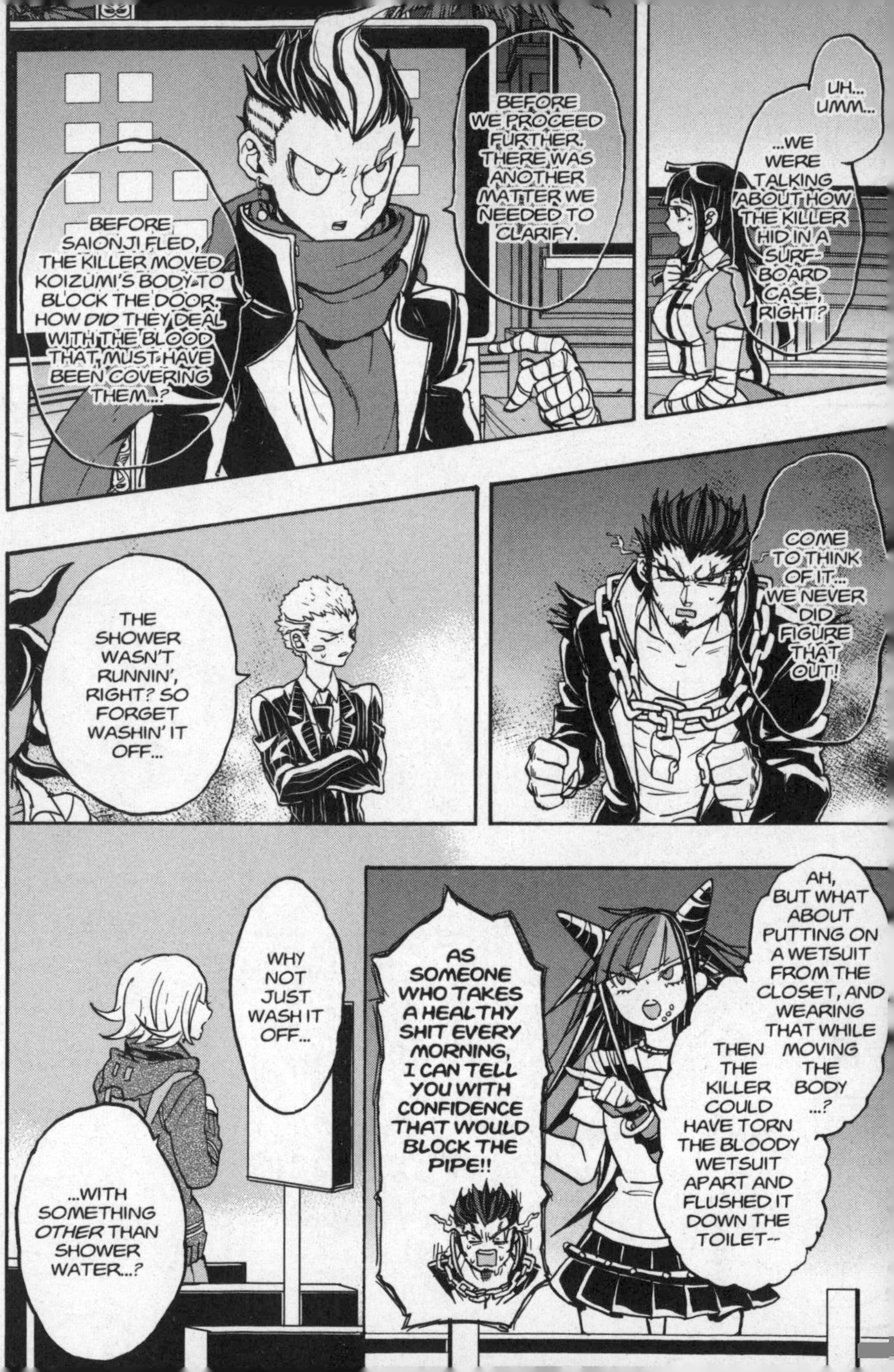
UH... UMM...
...WE WERE TALKING ABOUT HOW THE KILLER HID IN A SURF-BOARD CASE, RIGHT?
BEFORE WE PROCEED FURTHER. THERE WAS ANOTHER MATTER WE NEEDED TO CLARIFY.
BEFORE SAIONJI FLED, THE KILLER MOVED KOIZUMI'S BODY TO BLOCK THE DOOR. HOW *DID* THEY DEAL WITH THE BLOOD THAT MUST HAVE BEEN COVERING THEM...?
COME TO THINK OF IT... WE NEVER DID FIGURE THAT OUT!
THE SHOWER WASN'T RUNNIN', RIGHT? SO FORGET WASHIN' IT OFF...
AH, BUT WHAT ABOUT PUTTING ON A WETSUIT FROM THE CLOSET, AND WEARING THAT WHILE MOVING THE BODY...?
THEN THE KILLER COULD HAVE TORN THE BLOODY WETSUIT APART AND FLUSHED IT DOWN THE TOILET--
AS SOMEONE WHO TAKES A HEALTHY SHIT EVERY MORNING, I CAN TELL YOU WITH CONFIDENCE THAT WOULD BLOCK THE PIPE!!
WHY NOT JUST WASH IT OFF...
...WITH SOMETHING *OTHER* THAN SHOWER WATER...?

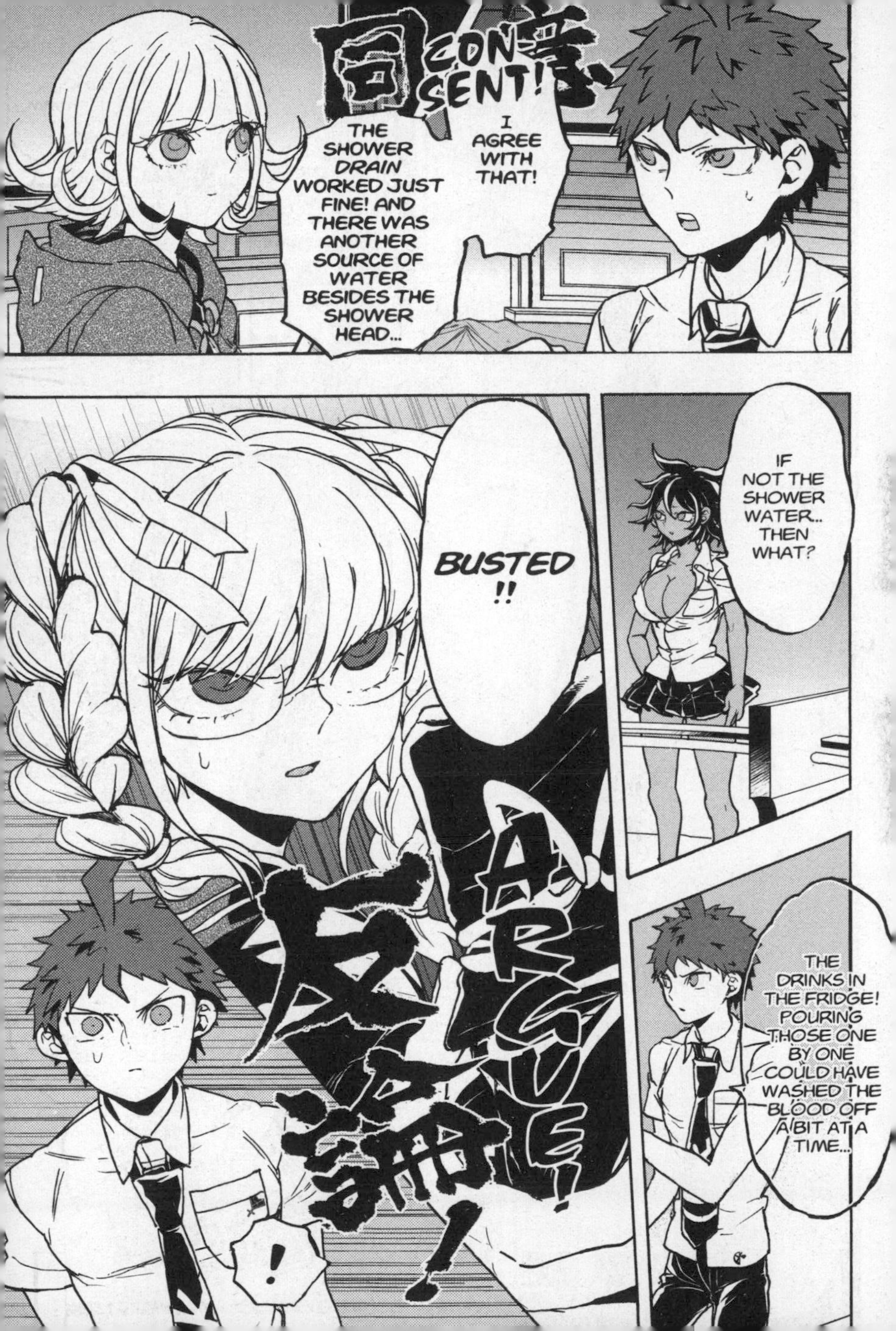
CON-SENT!
I AGREE WITH THAT!
THE SHOWER DRAIN WORKED JUST FINE! AND THERE WAS ANOTHER SOURCE OF WATER BESIDES THE SHOWER HEAD...
IF NOT THE SHOWER WATER.. THEN WHAT?
THE DRINKS IN THE FRIDGE! POURING THOSE ONE BY ONE COULD HAVE WASHED THE BLOOD OFF A BIT AT A TIME...
BUSTED !!
ARGUE!
!

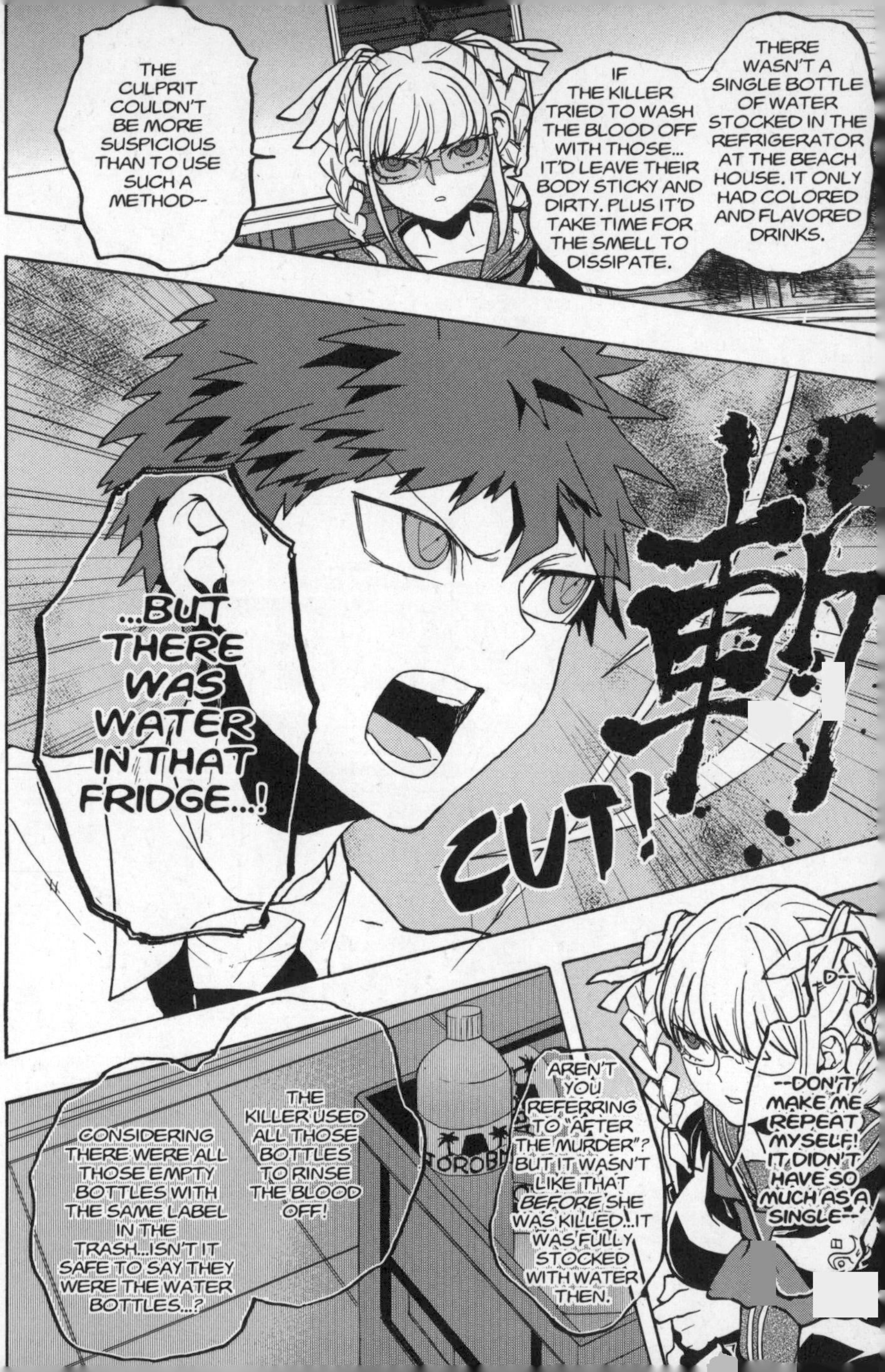
THERE WASN'T A SINGLE BOTTLE OF WATER STOCKED IN THE REFRIGERATOR AT THE BEACH HOUSE. IT ONLY HAD COLORED AND FLAVORED DRINKS.
IF THE KILLER TRIED TO WASH THE BLOOD OFF WITH THOSE... IT'D LEAVE THEIR BODY STICKY AND DIRTY. PLUS IT'D TAKE TIME FOR THE SMELL TO DISSIPATE.
THE CULPRIT COULDN'T BE MORE SUSPICIOUS THAN TO USE SUCH A METHOD--
斬
CUT!
...BUT THERE WAS WATER IN THAT FRIDGE...!
D--
--DON'T MAKE ME REPEAT MYSELF! IT DIDN'T HAVE SO MUCH AS A SINGLE--
AREN'T YOU REFERRING TO "AFTER THE MURDER"? BUT IT WASN'T LIKE THAT BEFORE SHE WAS KILLED...IT WAS FULLY STOCKED WITH WATER THEN.
THE KILLER USED ALL THOSE BOTTLES TO RINSE THE BLOOD OFF!
CONSIDERING THERE WERE ALL THOSE EMPTY BOTTLES WITH THE SAME LABEL IN THE TRASH...ISN'T IT SAFE TO SAY THEY WERE THE WATER BOTTLES...?

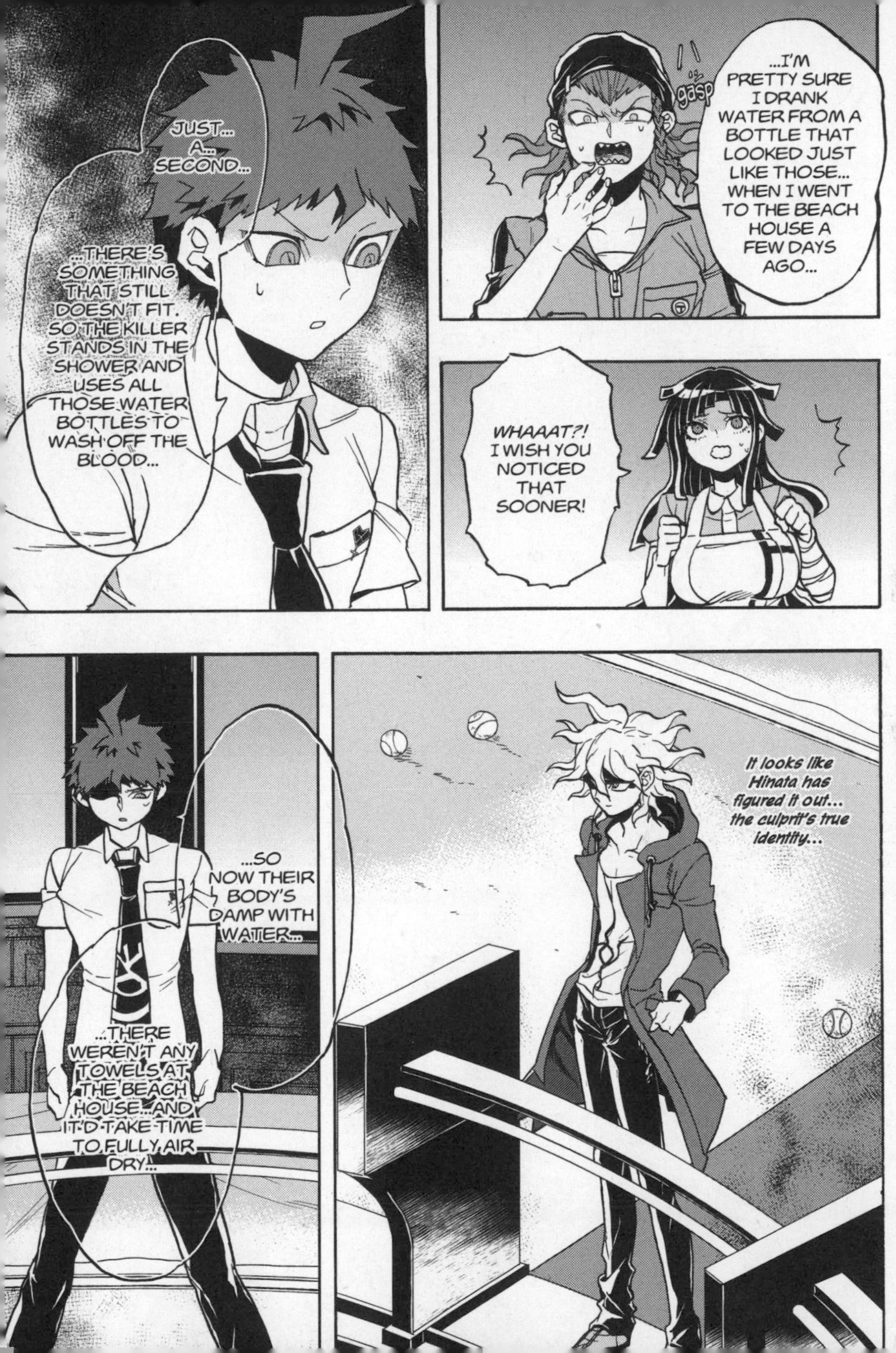
gasp
...I'M PRETTY SURE I DRANK WATER FROM A BOTTLE THAT LOOKED JUST LIKE THOSE... WHEN I WENT TO THE BEACH HOUSE A FEW DAYS AGO...
WHAAAT?! I WISH YOU NOTICED THAT SOONER!
JUST... A... SECOND...
...THERE'S SOMETHING THAT STILL DOESN'T FIT. SO THE KILLER STANDS IN THE SHOWER AND USES ALL THOSE WATER BOTTLES TO WASH OFF THE BLOOD...
It looks like Hinata has figured it out... the culprit's true identity...
...SO NOW THEIR BODY'S DAMP WITH WATER...
...THERE WEREN'T ANY TOWELS AT THE BEACH HOUSE... AND IT'D TAKE TIME TO FULLY AIR DRY...

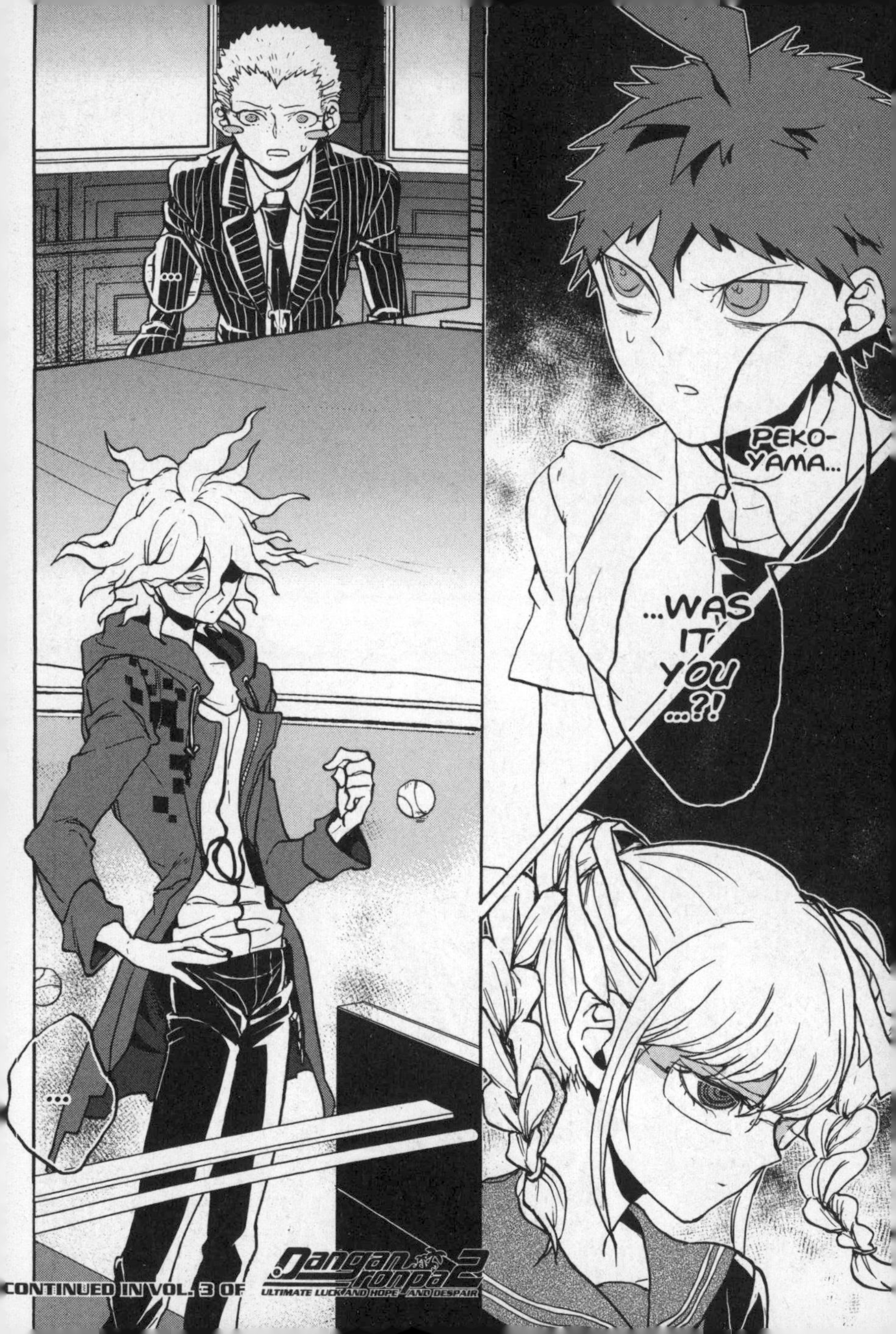
PEKO-YAMA...
...WAS IT YOU ...?!
...
...
CONTINUED IN VOL. 3 OF
Danganronpa 2
ULTIMATE LUCK AND HOPE AND DESPAIR

ILLUSTRATION

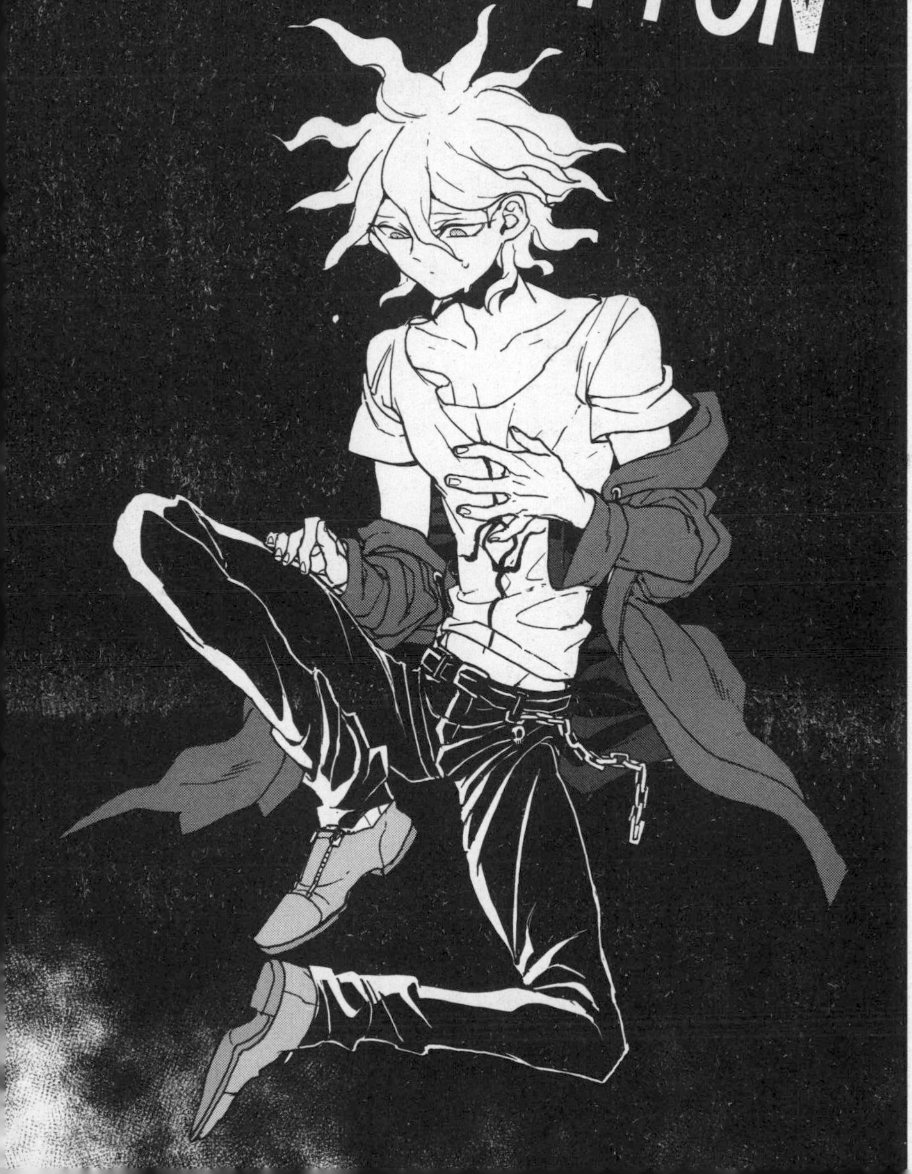

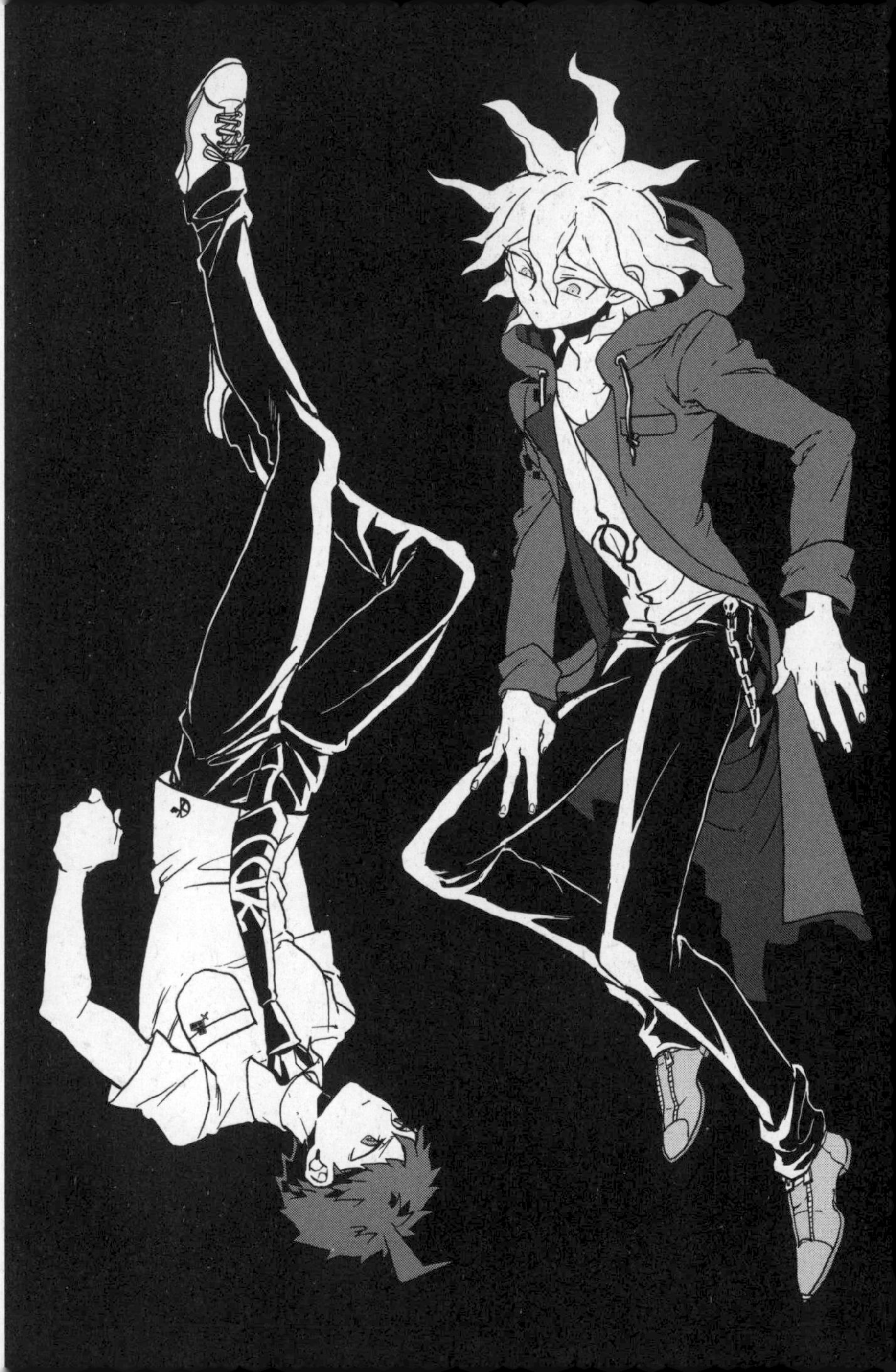

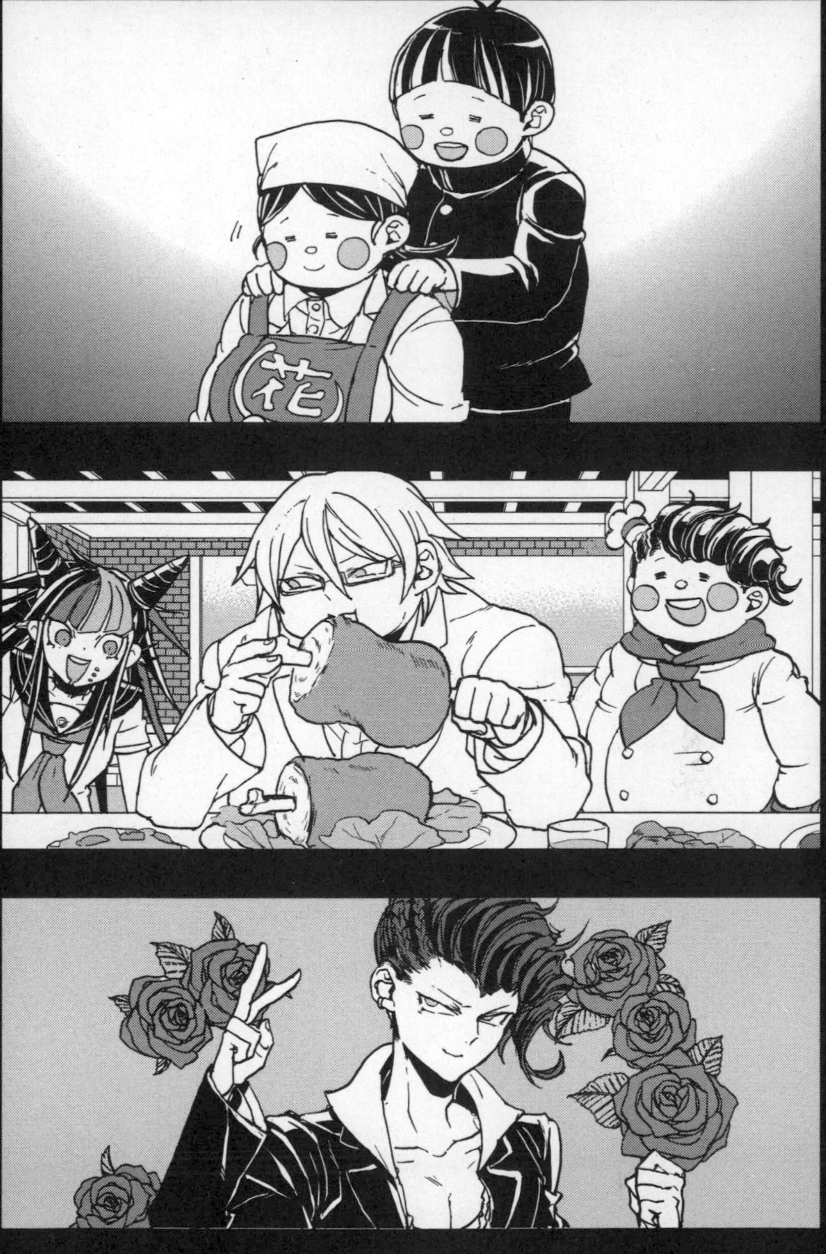
花

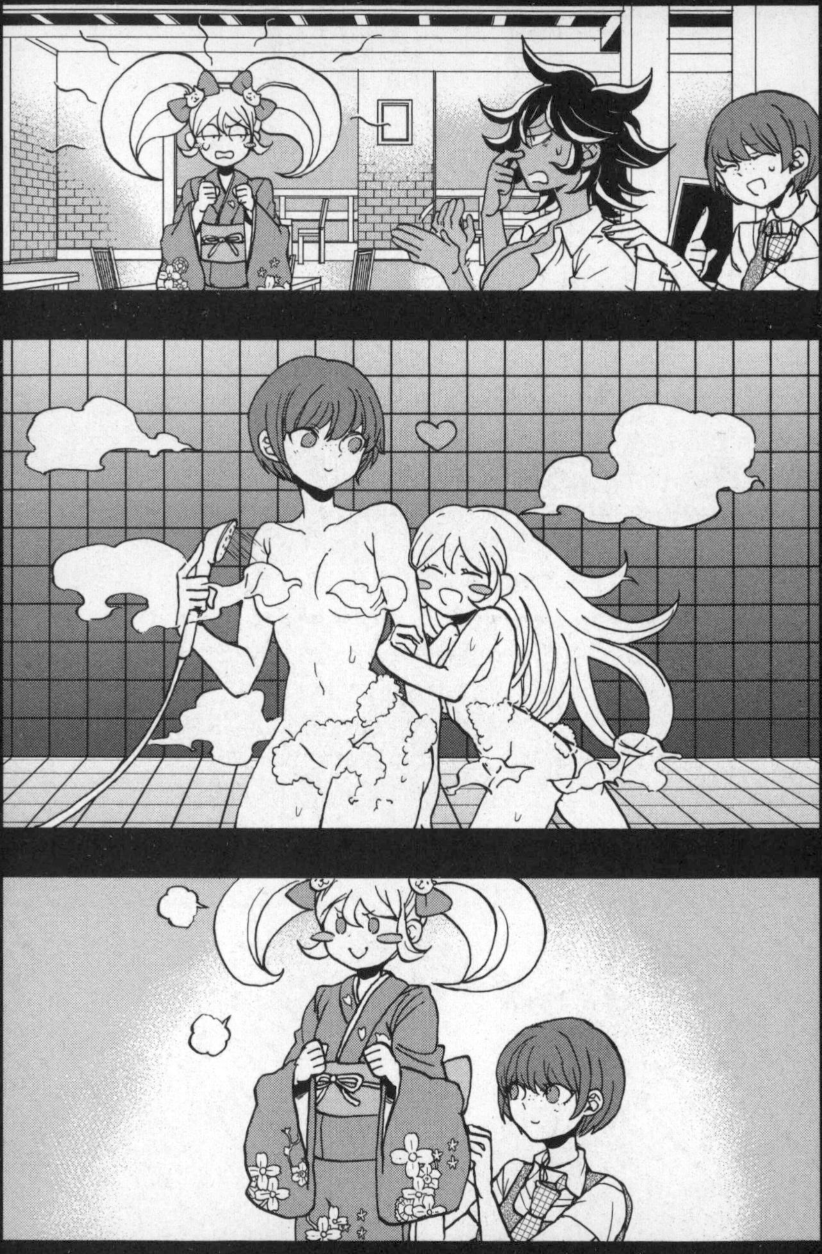

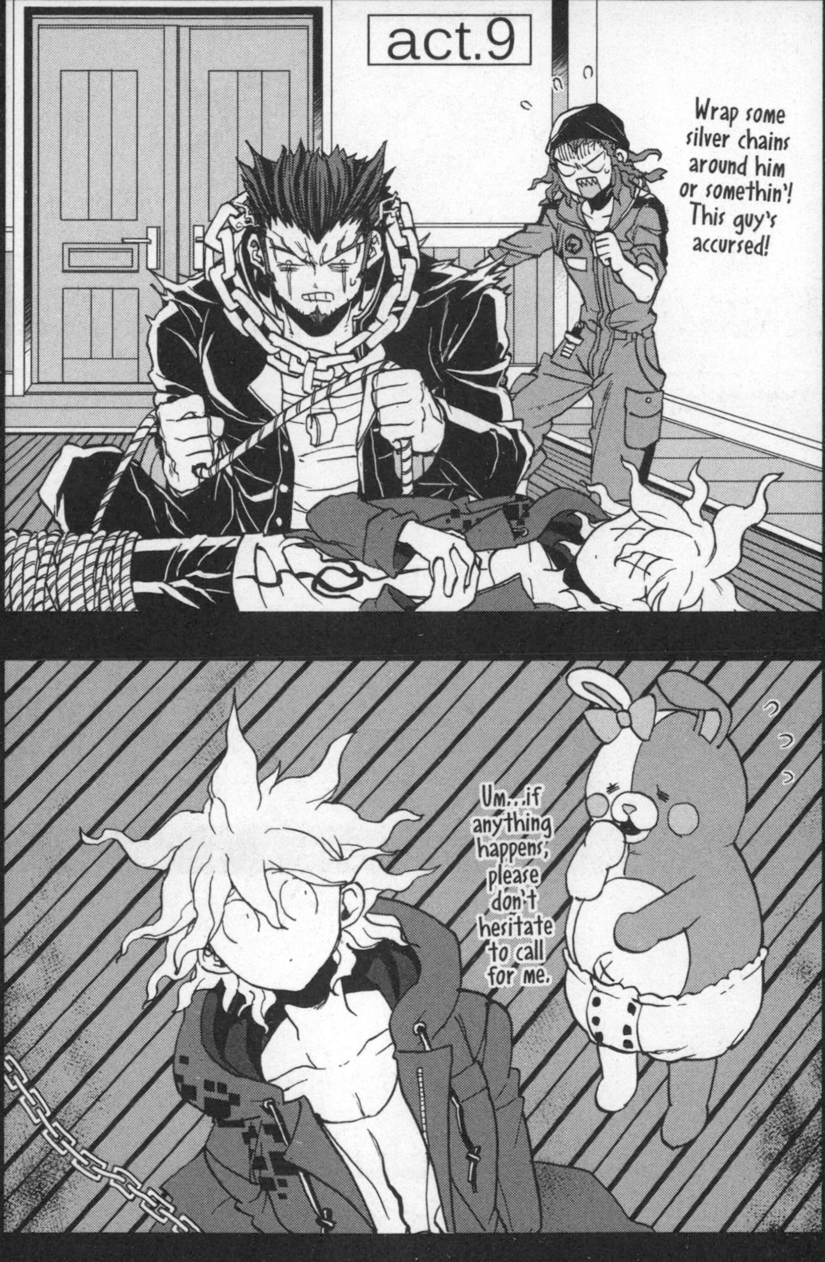
act.9
Wrap some silver chains around him or somethin'! This guy's accursed!
Um...if anything happens, please don't hesitate to call for me.

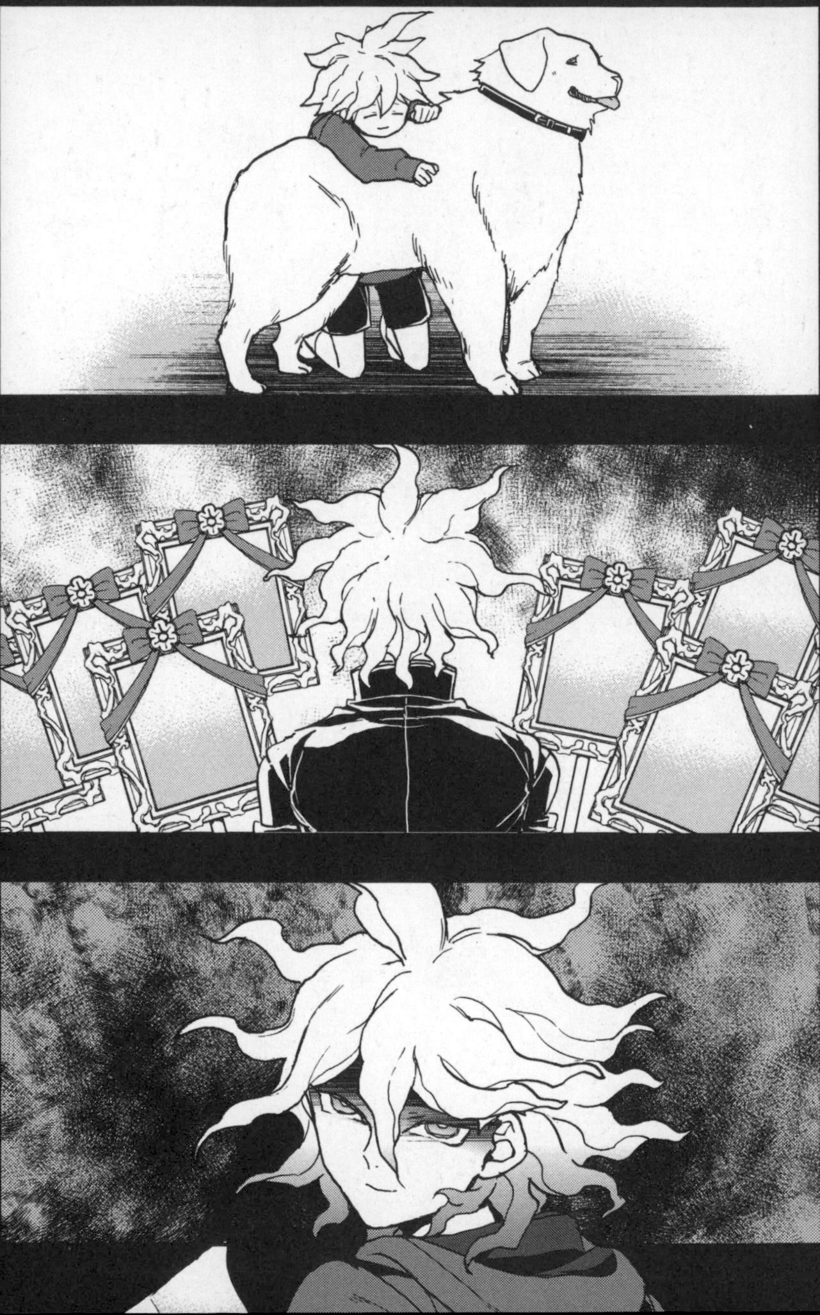

Hello, I'm Kyousuke Suga. Thanks once again for getting this edition of Danganronpa 2: Ultimate Luck and Hope and Despair, Volume 2!

Thanks to everyone at Spike Chunsoft, my editor, everyone involved with the book, and above all, the fans of the original game who are reading this manga rendition, I was able to release Volume 2 without a hitch...! I am bursting with gratitude! On another note, the editor "W," whom I mentioned in the previous volume, resigned around August of 2013. I am currently with the editor who replaced him. I have the utmost gratitude for both people...!

As a major Danganronpa fan, I am really, really excited to see where the series is headed next with the upcoming Ultra Despair Girls release...! While I may not be worthy, I shall continue to pour love into drawing this manga, so please stick with me! I hope to see you again in the next volume!*

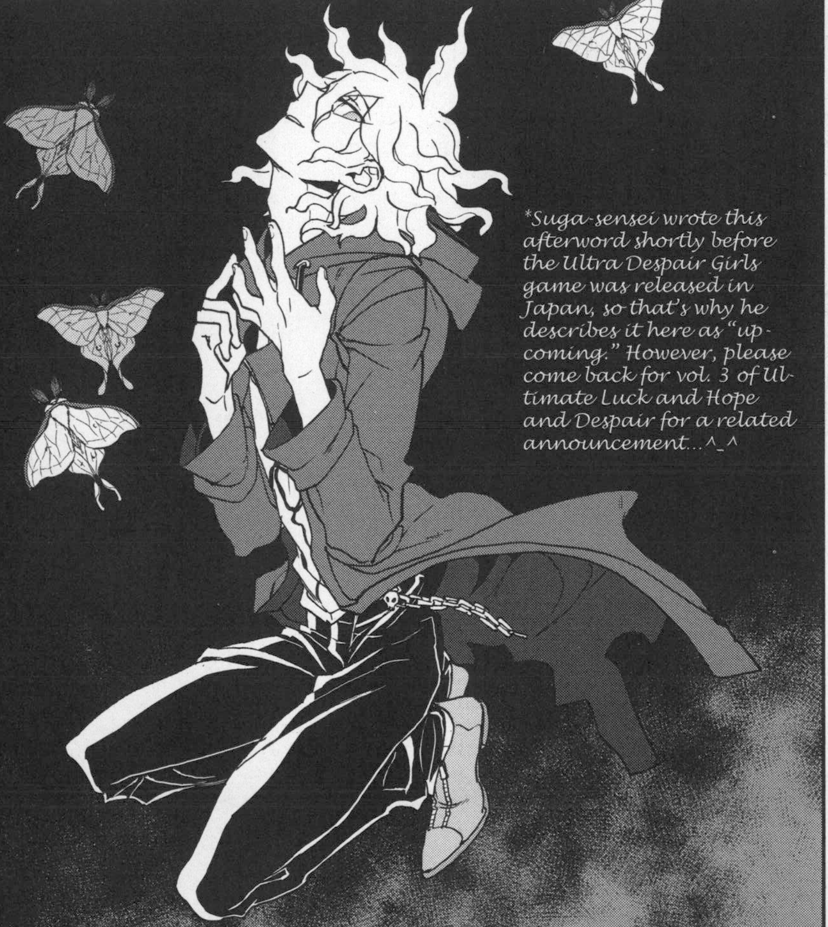

**Suga-sensei wrote this afterword shortly before the Ultra Despair Girls game was released in Japan, so that's why he describes it here as "upcoming." However, please come back for vol. 3 of Ultimate Luck and Hope and Despair for a related announcement...^_^*

president and publisher
MIKE RICHARDSON

designer
SARAH TERRY

ultimate digital art technician
SAMANTHA HUMMER

English-language version produced by Dark Horse Comics

DANGANRONPA 2: ULTIMATE LUCK AND HOPE AND DESPAIR VOLUME 2

Published by
Dark Horse Manga
A division of Dark Horse Comics LLC
10956 SE Main Street I Milwaukie, OR 97222

DarkHorse.com

To find a comics shop in your area, visit comicshoplocator.com.

First edition: January 2019
ISBN 978-1-50670-734-1
Digital ISBN 978-1-50670-737-2

8 9 10

Printed in the United States of America

DESPAIR MAIL

c/o Dark Horse Comics | 10956 SE Main St. | Milwaukie, OR 97222 | danganronpa@darkhorse.com

AHEM! The first thing to do is to say we're sorry for vol. 1 being late, although I like to think that, just like Kei and Yuri, it wasn't our fault. Nevertheless, I would like to apologize sincerely the way the politicians do in Japan, if you've ever seen it on NHK-TV. You know, that bow made while sitting down at a news conference, or, for especially grave situations, standing up from your chair at a news conference and then bowing.

But you and I know there's only one proper way to make atonement . . . U PU PUU . . . that's with more DESPAIR MAIL, the place for Ultimate Danganronpa Fans! If you'd like to share your thoughts or comments on Danganronpa . . . pictures of your Danganronpa cosplay . . . or your Danganronpa fan art—this is the place for you! Send it to the address/e-mail at the top of the page, and remember to use high resolution (300 dpi or better) for your photos or images, so it'll look good in print! We're okay with you sending us images even if they happen to be fairly large, say, 3 or 4 MB.

In fact, we're still catching up with all the contributions readers sent in for our first Danganronpa manga series (Danganronpa: The Animation), so thank you, everyone, for your patience. Do you remember how I mentioned last time that volume 1 of our Danganronpa: The Animation manga had just gone into its fifth printing? Well, since then, both volume 2 and volume 4 have gone into a fourth printing . . . meaning that new readers are continuing to get into the manga! If you're one of those new readers, thank you especially, and we'll hope to see your contributions in DESPAIR MAIL as well.

It seems that people would like even more Danganronpa . . . so we would like you reading this to be the first to know that we're going to release another Danganronpa manga series after Ultimate Luck and Hope and Despair concludes in the next volume. Actually, maybe it won't just be another series . . . maybe it'll be two other manga series . . . ?

I'm okay with telling you this stuff, because if there's one thing Danganronpa is all about, it's being able to keep a secret. And then, of course, spilling that secret under ruthless cross-examination at the class trial, followed by brutal and ironic punishment. Which brings us, of course, to . . .

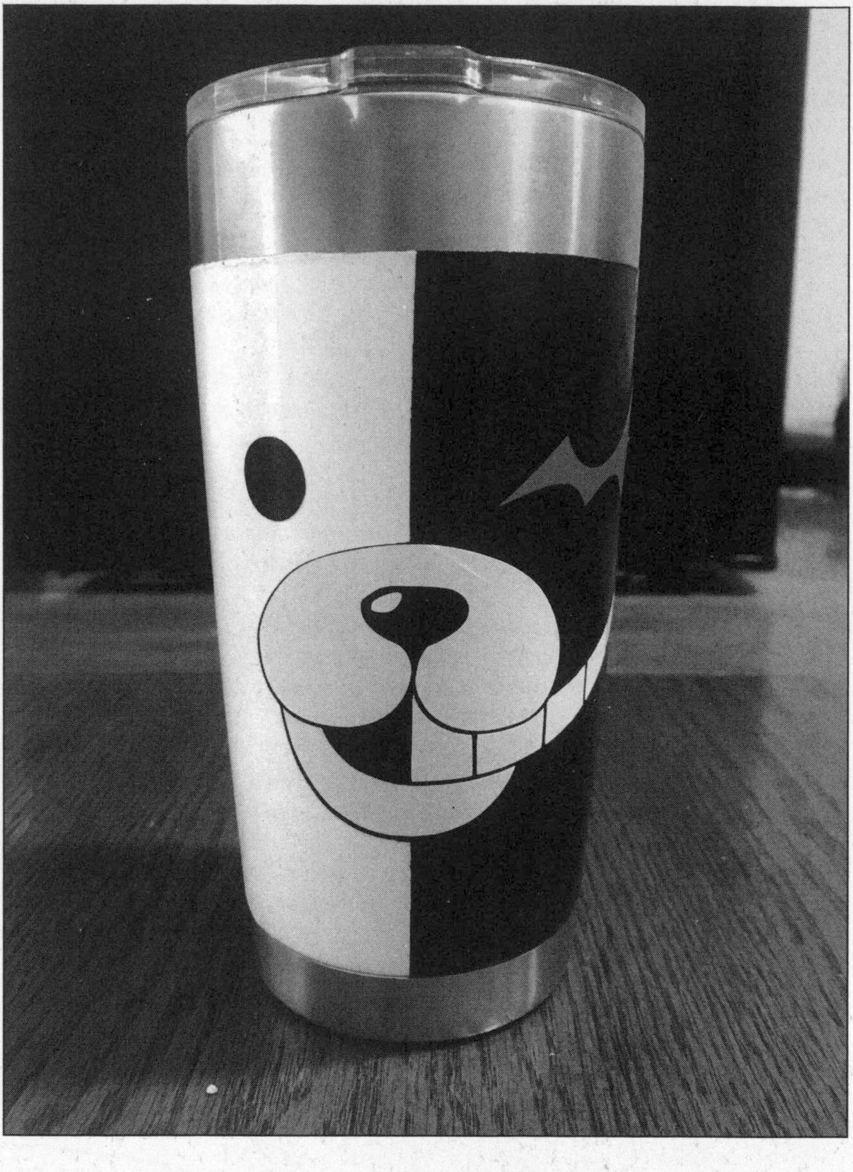

. . . the bear who brings the scare, Monokuma. This photo is from Tyler Burkett, who says: “My mother has created the Monocup. It was made by taking a YETI cup, spray paint, and village.” Village? I’m guessing an autocorrect with no sense of craft has cruelly struck down “decoupage.” Or could it be that it “takes a village” . . . ?

And then there's this full-body Monokuma from reader Carlos Alvarez Cabera, which remains intimidating even in its minimalism. Si te dan papel rayado, escribe de través.

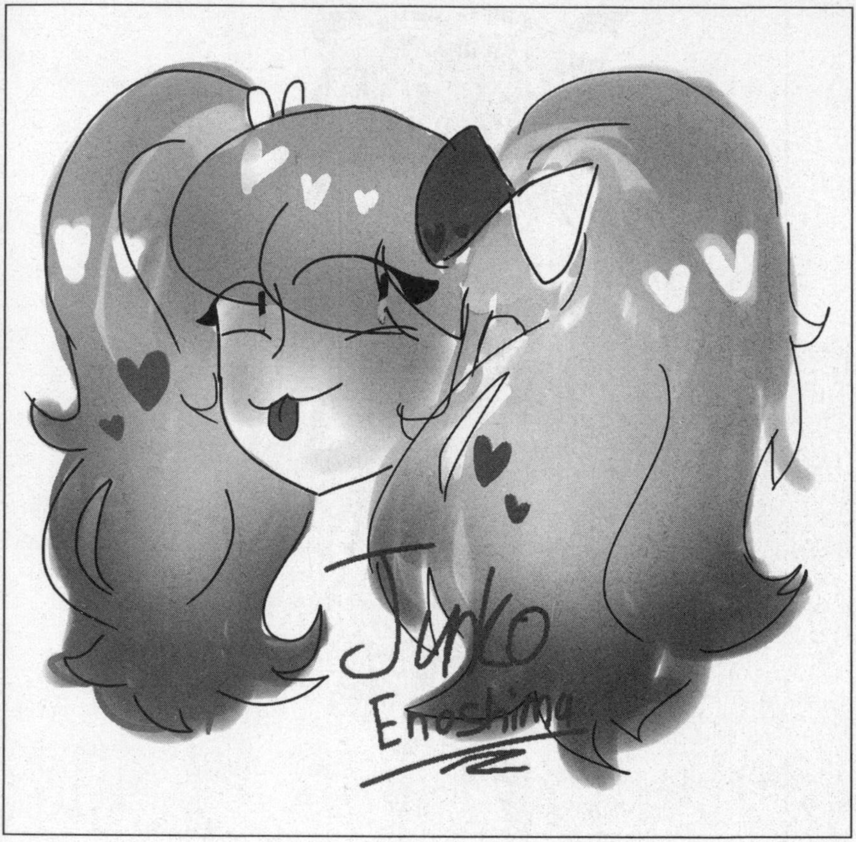
Junko
Enoshima

It is said that behind every great bear, there stands a brilliant but ruthless woman with multiple personalities and a superb sense of fashion. That woman, of course, is Junko Enoshima, depicted here by nya-tta, and I only regret that DESPAIR MAIL is not in color, so you could appreciate the rose quartz luster with which nya-tta imbued the mastermind of menace.

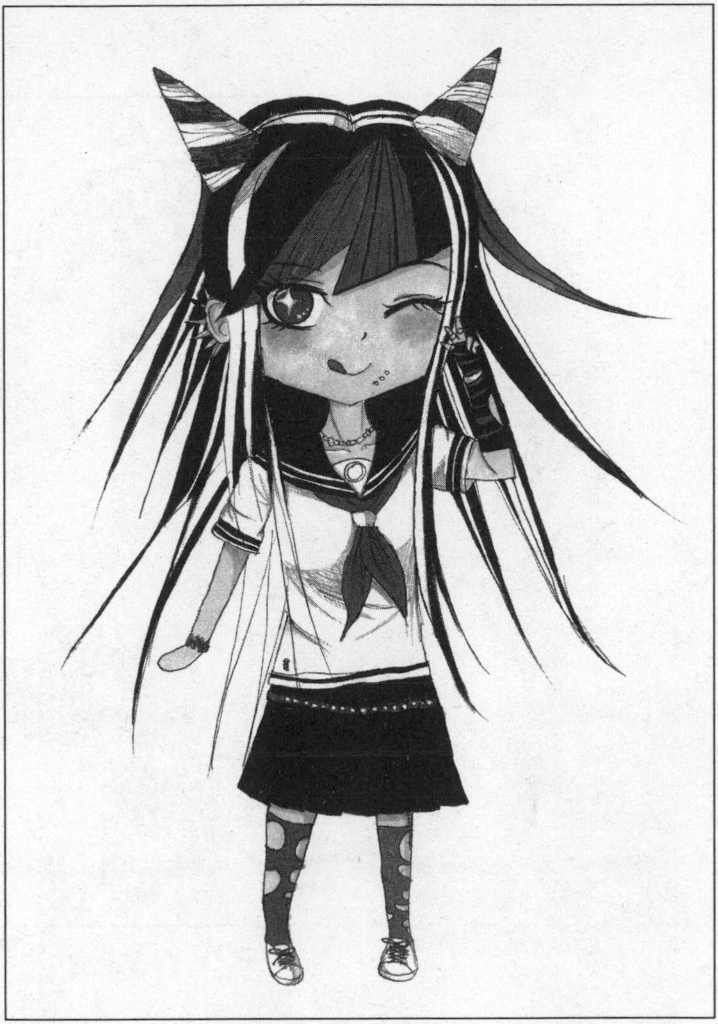

Mirjam Rajamets writes to say: "I'd like to thank Dark Horse so much for serializing *Danganronpa: The Animation*! I'm a big fan of *Danganronpa* (especially the games) and I'm very glad to also have the manga now! What I really like is that you include the DESPAIR MAIL section in every volume. It's interesting to see the other fans' pictures and comments. Here's a little contribution from me: a drawing of Ibuki Mioda, one of my favourite characters from the second game. I hope you can include this in vol. 4 of the manga!" Well, you see what I meant about patience—we couldn't include it in volume 4 of *Danganronpa: The Animation* . . . it had to wait for volume 2 of *Danganronpa 2: Ultimate Luck and Hope and Despair*! On the other hand, as Mirjam points out, Ibuki, the Ultimate Musician, is from the second game and not the first...so maybe she's right on time . . . ? I think she might have my favorite hairstyle out of all the characters, by the way. And that's saying something!

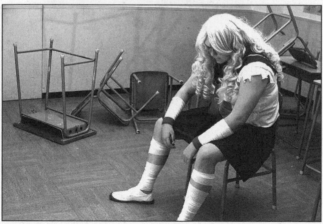

Stephanie Miller (chibbycookie) writes in to say: "I've been a huge huge huge fan of *Danganronpa* (or dangle rumps as me and my friends have called it) and I've always had a deep love for the character of Sakura Ogami. She's the character I relate to most, due to her dedication to her friends and self-sacrificial attitude! (I also have a collection of pins and merch dedicated to her but that's beside the point). I love her so much that I decided to cosplay her! I feel like she is the picture of what a true friend should be! I'm so happy that the manga version is being released! Thank you guys!" I'm sure many readers already know this, but Sakura's stoic repose in death—as Stephanie so well reenacts here—was itself a tribute to one of the most famous shots in all of manga (and later anime), from *Ashita no Joe* by Tetsuya Chiba.

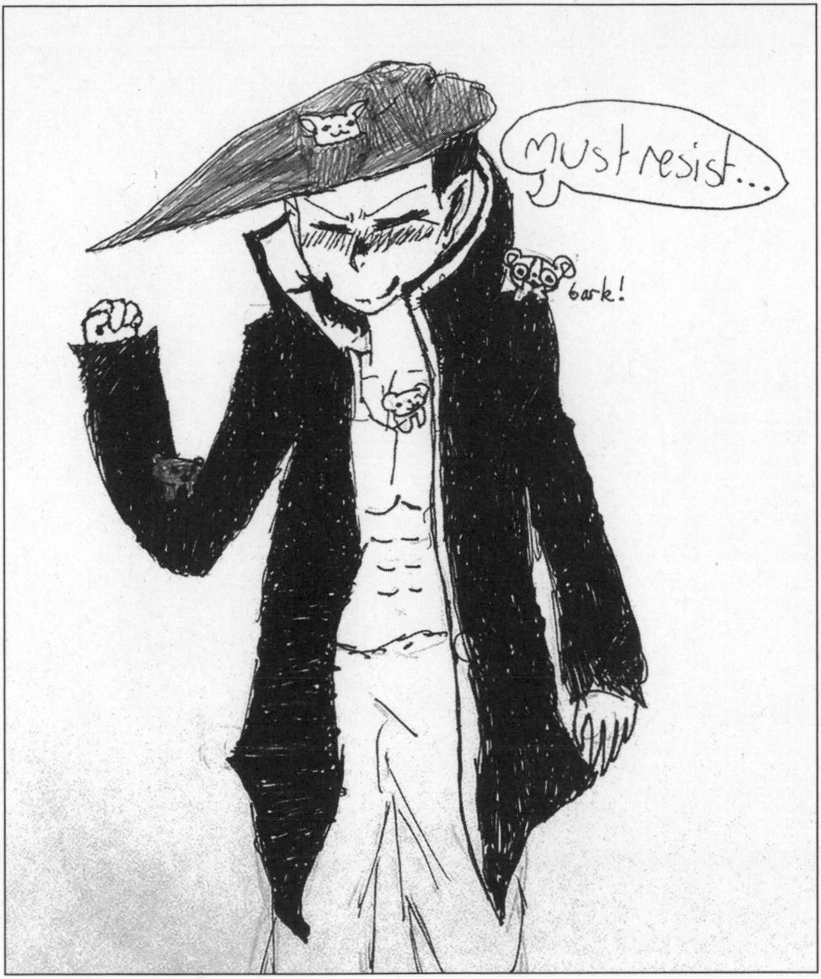
must resist...
bark!

Maheen Syed sends this contribution with these remarks: “Hiya, so as I was reading your splendid manga, I decided I would draw Mondo (with some puppies!) since he is my favourite character out of all the games. I only got into *Danganronpa* a few months ago and I'm already a super fan. I'm so glad that Dark Horse gave us the opportunity to see a manga of *Trigger Happy Havoc* and HOPEfully future games! (Hide from Nagito.) I'm so glad that *Danganronpa* is becoming more popular but I don't wish for it to become that big of a fandom that it dies out quickly. Yet again, thank you so much for bringing *Danganronpa* to England!” Thanks, Maheen! British fans have had a lot of influence on me, ever since that moment at Anime Expo '92 when I saw someone walking down the hall with a copy of an amazing magazine from that era, *Anime UK*. It was edited by Helen McCarthy, a journalist and author who became one of my sempai, and someone that I still very much look up to.

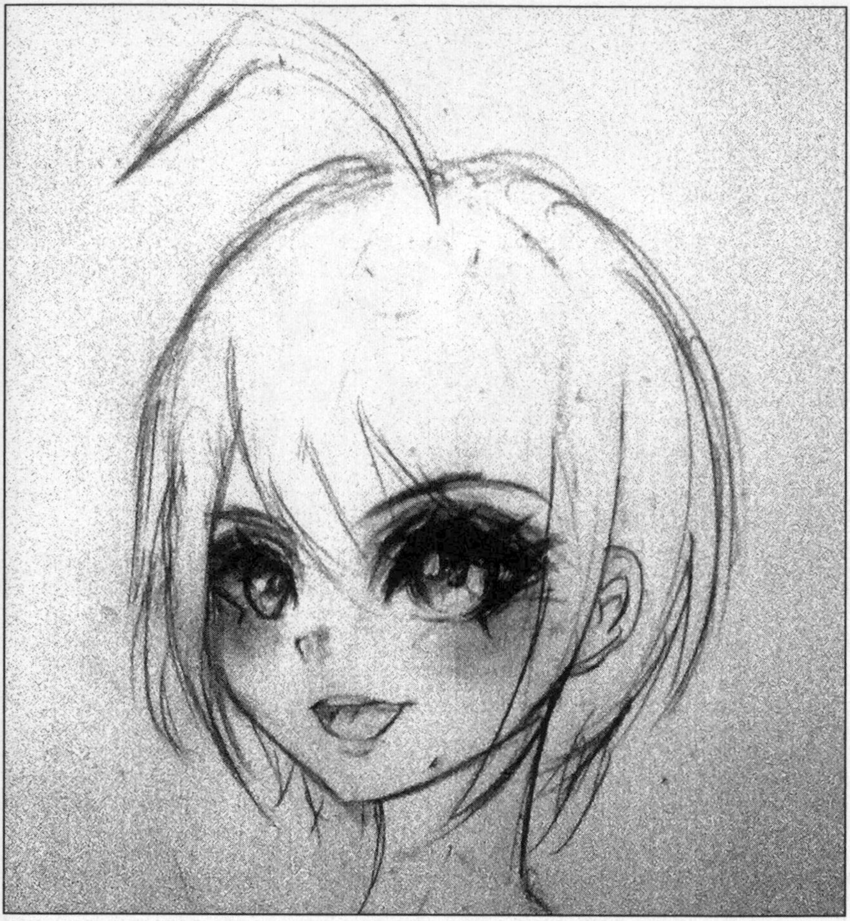

Ashley Lizotte writes in to say, "I'm a huge fan of the whole *Danganronpa* series and recently got finished with Another Episode, so I drew a portrait of Komaru!" Say, it would be a good idea if in the future, we published a manga based on Another Episode. Don't you think so . . . ? Maybe we should do that . . . ? ^_~

Sarah Haddad, a contributor to our previous series *Danganronpa: The Animation*, returns with this *Danganronpa 2* piece and says, "Hey there! I just wanted to say thank you for featuring me in the fan art section of the *Danganronpa* manga volumes 3 and 4. It means a whole lot to me! If the *Danganronpa* series continues please consider me again! :) Also if there are any fan art pages in any other manga let me know, I would love to do more! Thanks again!"

We (that is, Dark Horse) don't have any other regular fan art sections in our other manga at the moment, although in the past we had long-running ones for previous series such as *Blade of the Immortal*, *Evangelion*, *Oh My Goddess!*, and *Oreimo*, among others. As you may know, Dark Horse is also one of the oldest independent comic book companies in the United States, and fan letter columns are an important part of the comics tradition, so naturally we brought it into our manga.

It's hard to predict, however, what kind of response we'll get. For example, we published several *Vocaloid* manga, *Fate/Zero*, and *Psycho-Pass*, all of which certainly have a lot of fans, but I don't remember anyone ever sending in any fan art, cosplay photos, or letters for those titles. To be fair, readers may not have realized they could do so, because we didn't have a formal fan section in those books (although we would have probably printed contributions if we'd received them).

So you might be in a situation where you have a fan section, but no one shows up ^_^ Sometimes I even did some fan art myself, just to get things going. By contrast, as you know, *Danganronpa* fans are very active about sending in contributions!

AnekiCosplay (on Instagram) says: "I've done a lot of *Danganronpa* cosplay ~ My most fav thing is the Despair Sisters duo :) Upupupupuu. Here's Mukuro from when she sang 'Tsubasa o kudasai' in *Danganronpa 3: The End of Hope's Peak High School* (Despair Arc, Episode 7)."

And here's Junko: "Junko is one of my most favorite villains and characters of all time. I love everything from her first entrance in the anime to the fact that you simply cannot kill this villain—hero, in my case. I can never get enough of these two XD TEAM DESPAIR ALL THE WAY UPUPUPU . . ."

"My cosplay name is Miss.Mioda and I have both a Facebook page and an Instagram account! *Danganronpa* as a series means a lot to me! All the characters are relatable and have helped me and improved my life so much. The show has helped me get through bereavement and boosted my body confidence. The community is also amazing and all the people I hold dear and close to my heart I have met through the fandom xxx"

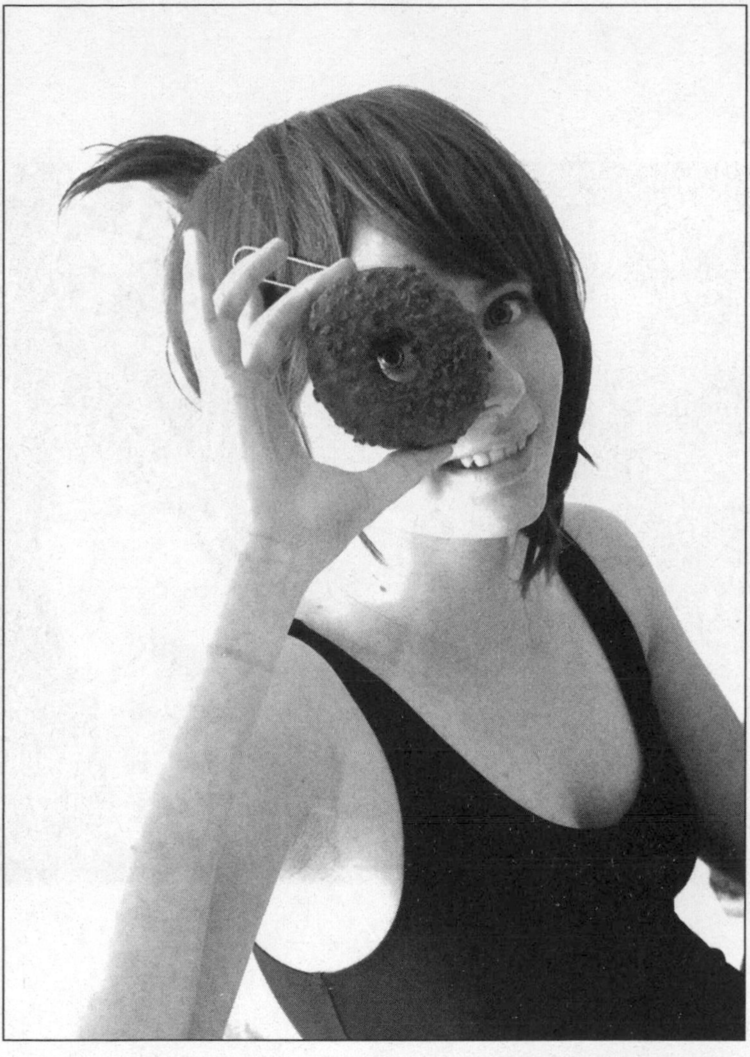

And here's also Miss.Mioda as Aoi Asahina—as if to say, here's looking at you (you've heard of Portland's Voodoo Doughnuts, but if you visit here, also try Blue Star—there's one in the airport!) . . . and see you all in vol. 3, the conclusion of *Danganronpa 2: Ultimate Luck and Hope and Despair*!

—CGH

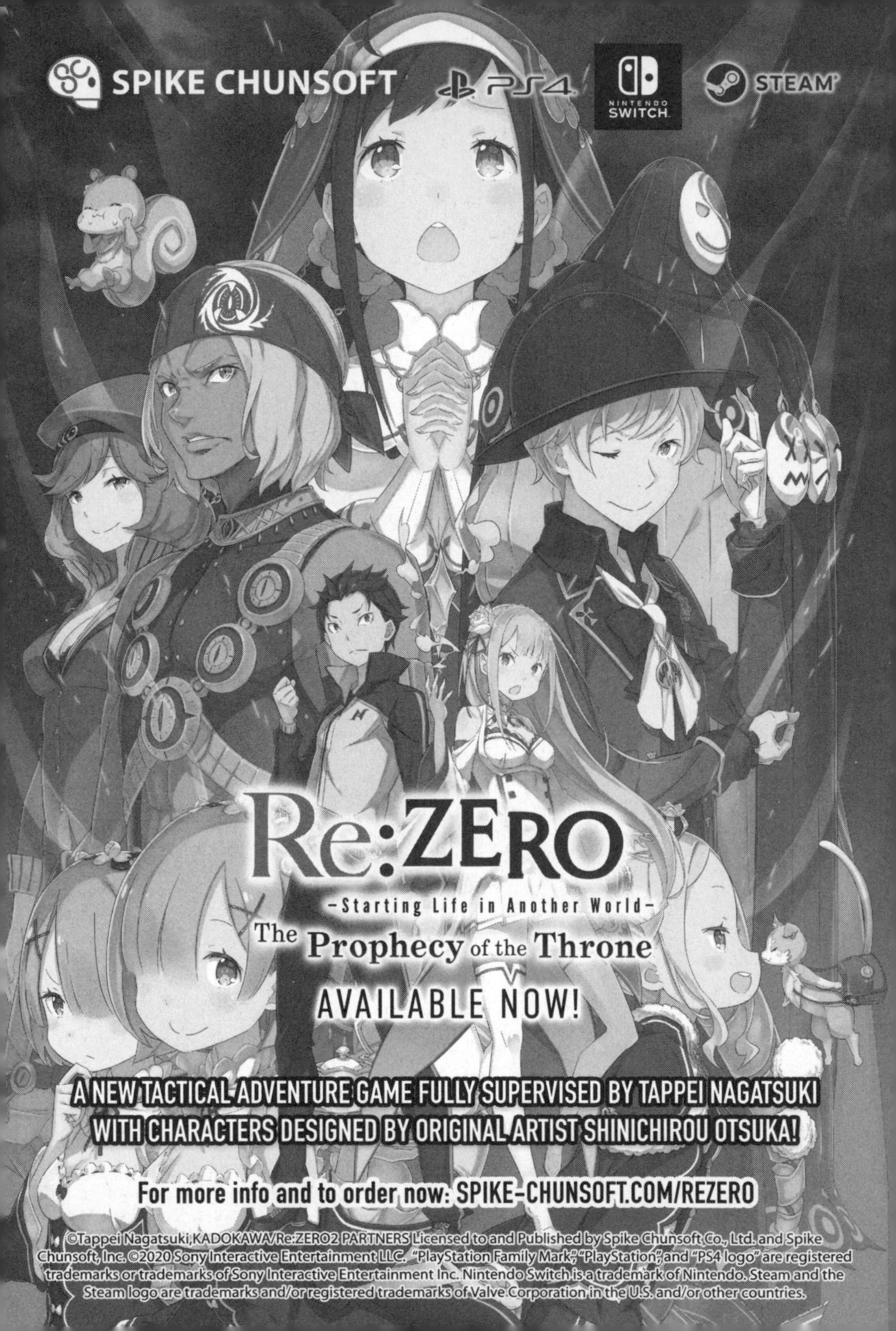
SPIKE CHUNSOFT
PS4
NINTENDO SWITCH
STEAM
Re:ZERO
-Starting Life in Another World-
The Prophecy of the Throne
AVAILABLE NOW!
A NEW TACTICAL ADVENTURE GAME FULLY SUPERVISED BY TAPPEI NAGATSUKI
WITH CHARACTERS DESIGNED BY ORIGINAL ARTIST SHINICHIROU OTSUKA!
For more info and to order now: SPIKE-CHUNSOFT.COM/REZERO
©Tappei Nagatsuki,KADOKAWA/Re:ZERO2 PARTNERS Licensed to and Published by Spike Chunsoft Co., Ltd. and Spike Chunsoft, Inc. ©2020 Sony Interactive Entertainment LLC. "PlayStation Family Mark," "PlayStation," and "PS4 logo" are registered trademarks or trademarks of Sony Interactive Entertainment Inc. Nintendo Switch is a trademark of Nintendo. Steam and the Steam logo are trademarks and/or registered trademarks of Valve Corporation in the U.S. and/or other countries.

NOW, PLEASE PAY CLOSE ATTENTION . . .

Nagito Komaeda, the Ultimate Lucky Student, would like to remind you that this is a manga, and like most manga, it reads right-to-left. Don't read it left-to-right, or you might miss some important clues. Also, reading it that way would be COMPLETELY INSANE.

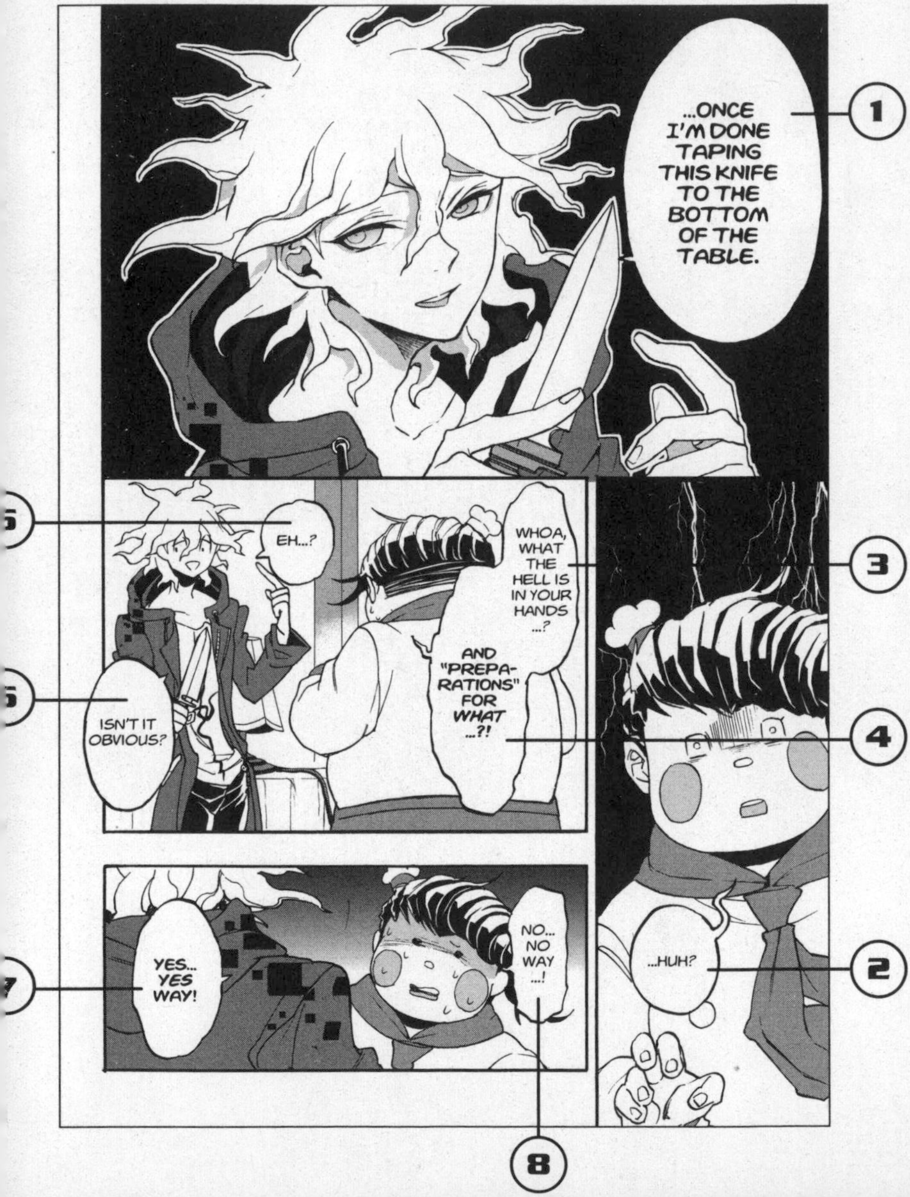
...ONCE I'M DONE TAPING THIS KNIFE TO THE BOTTOM OF THE TABLE.
...HUH?
WHOA, WHAT THE HELL IS IN YOUR HANDS ...?
AND "PREPARATIONS" FOR WHAT ...?!
EH...?
ISN'T IT OBVIOUS?
YES... YES WAY!
NO... NO WAY ...!